Neapolitan music is a hybrid form, combining both classical and popular culture. It is deeply rooted in everyday life, and draws its richness from the transformation of ancient melodies into a contemporary music that is celebrated today not only in Italy but also around the world. A seemingly infinite repertoire of instruments (*sonagli, zufoli, triccaballacchi, putipù*) combine to produce the dizzying cadences of its songs and dances.

Photograph: Musicians in Piedigrotta

Travelers to Vesuvius in the previous century
were obliged to make the journey on foot or
in sedan chairs, along paths paved with slabs
of lava. In 1870 the financier Ernesto
Emanuele Obljeght conceived the idea of
building a funicular that would ride right up
to the lip of the crater. Ten years later, for the
June 6 opening, Peppino Turco and Luigi
Densa composed the song *Funiculì-funiculà*,
which was to render the funicular famous
throughout the world. Destroyed on three
occasions by lava flows, the funicular was
finally closed after the 1944 eruption ▲ *240*.

Photograph: Vesuvius funicular, 1895

THIS GUIDE WAS ORIGINATED BY ADEFRI AND ITS PRESIDENT ALAIN SIMON, AND CONCEIVED WITH THE INSTITUT CULTUREL ITALIEN DE PARIS AND THE ASSOCIATION FRANÇAISE DE L'ACTION ARTISTIQUE. WE WISH TO THANK THE FOLLOWING ITALIAN CULTURAL INSTITUTIONS: SOPRAINTENDENZA AI BENI AMBIENTALI E ARCHITETTONICI, SOPRAINTENDENZA ARCHEOLOGICA, SOPRAINTENDENZA AI BENI ARTISTICI E CULTURALI DI NAPOLI, SOPRAINTENDENZA AI BENI ARTISTICI E CULTURALI DI SALERNO SOPRAINTENDENZA ARCHEOLOGICA DI POMPEI, GIANCARLO RICCIO (UNESCO). FINALLY, WE GIVE SPECIAL THANKS TO JEAN-NOËL SCHIFANO (WRITER AND HONORABLE CITIZEN OF NAPLES AND DIRECTOR OF THE INSTITUT FRANÇAIS DE NAPLES).

NAPLES AND POMPEII:
COORDINATION: Laure Raffaëlli-Fournel
EDITORS: Cécile Gall *assisted by* Michel Vajou and
Nicolas Christitch (Practical information). Updates
by Gwenhaelle Le Roy.
GRAPHICS: Élisabeth Cohat
ARCHITECTURE: Bruno Lenormand *with* Antonio Viola
PICTURE RESEARCH: William Fischer
TRANSLATION: Sabine Bosio and Corinne Paul *assisted by*
Giusi Dupont-Furno, François Haynard, Gabrièle
Kerleroux, Anouchka Lazarev, Christophe Musitelli,
Emanela Pace, Anne Savi, Cécile and Laurent Scotto,
Jean-Claude Zancarini
LAYOUT: Riccardo Tremori, François Chentrier
(Practical information)

SCIENTIFIC ADVISOR: Antonio Viola

NATURE: Philippe J. Dubois, Frédéric Bony *with*
Jean-Claude Bousquet, Lello Capaldo, Annamaria Ciarallo
and Tullio Secondo Pescatore
HISTORY: Jean-Michel Sallman, Antonella Tufano
(The scourges of Naples)
NEAPOLITAN LANGUAGE AND CULTURE: Corinne Paul,
Antonio Viola
ARTS AND TRADITIONS: Maria Grazia Carbone,
Antonio Viola ("White" art: pasta and pizza),
Elena Matacena (Neapolitan theater)
ARCHITECTURE: Ludovica Bucci de Santis,
Antonio Viola
NAPLES AS SEEN BY PAINTERS: Nicola Spinosa and
Umberto Bile
NAPLES AS SEEN IN THE MOVIES: Elena Matacena
NAPLES AS SEEN BY WRITERS: Raffaele La Capria

ITINERARIES:
NAPLES: *places of interest:* Mario De Cunzo,
Nicoletta Ricciardelli and Stefano De Caro (archeology)
nature: Lello Capaldo, Annamaria Ciarallo and Tullio
Secondo Pescatore
features: Stefano De Caro (Museo Archeologico Nazionale),
Gaetano Viscardi (San Gennaro), Nicola Spinosa and
Umberto Bile (Museo di Capodimonte)
CASERTA: Antonella Tufano
PHLEGRAEAN FIELDS:
places of interest: Stefano De Caro (archeology) and
Nicoletta Ricciardelli

nature: Lello Capaldo, Annamaria Ciarallo
and Tullio Secondo Pescatore
insert: Stefano De Caro
ISCHIA, PROCIDA:
places of interest: Nicoletta Ricciardelli and Stefano De Caro
(archeology)
nature: Lello Capaldo, Annamaria Ciarallo
and Tullio Secondo Pescatore
CAPRI:
places of interest: Nicoletta Ricciardelli and Stefano
De Caro (archeology)
nature: Lello Capaldo, Annamaria Ciarallo
and Tullio Secondo Pescatore
NAPLES TO SORRENTO:
places of interest: Nicoletta Ricciardelli and Stefano
De Caro (archeology)
nature: Lello Capaldo, Annamaria Ciarallo
and Tullio Secondo Pescatore
VESUVIUS: Lello Capaldo, Annamaria Ciarallo
and Tullio Secondo Pescatore
POMPEII AND HERCULANEUM:
sites: Ernesto De Carolis, Baldassare Conticello
(history of the excavations)
features: Annamaria Ciarallo (The gardens of Pompeii) and
Ernesto De Carolis (Thermae, Villa dei Misteri)
THE AMALFI COAST:
places of interest: Mariella Pasca
nature: Lello Capaldo, Annamaria Ciarallo and
Tullio Secondo Pescatore
PAESTUM: Emanuele Greco

PRACTICAL INFORMATION: Jean-Pierre Girard *with* Angela
Catello and Patrizia Antignani (ed. by Servizi per l'Editoria,
Napoli), Benedetta Rebecchi and Gilles Soigneux. Updates
by Claudia Casali, Angela Catello and Eugenia Romanelli

REGIONAL MAPS OF NAPLES: Adriana Baculo, titular professor
of Relief architecture, University Federico II, Naples

ILLUSTRATIONS:
NATURE: Denis Clavreul, Jean Chevallier, François
Desbordes, Pierre Felloni, Franck Stephan, Dominique
Mansion; Jean-Claude Bousquet (Computer graphics)
ARCHITECTURE: Jean-Benoît Héron, Donald Grant,
Jean-Marie Guillou, Jean-Michel Kacédan, Jean-François
Péneau, Claude Quiec, Jean-Sylvain Roveri
ITINERARIES: Jean-Philippe Chabot, Stéphane Girel,
Marc Lacaze
PRACTICAL INFORMATION: Maurice Pommier
MAPS: Vincent Brunot *with* Stéphane Girel,
Isabelle-Anne Chatellard ; Christine Adam,
Caroline Picard, Catherine Totems
COMPUTER GRAPHICS: Paul Coulbois

PHOTOGRAPHY: Fabio Donato, Philippe Francastel, Sylvain
Grandadam, Benoît Juge, Nicolas Pascarel, Luciano
Pedicini, Ghigo Roli

WE WOULD ALSO LIKE TO THANK: Lucio Taddeo,
Mario Monaco, Mario Lettieri, Mario De Camillis, Antonio
Fiorentino, Viviana Viola, Laura del Verme

TRANSLATED BY LAURA WARD AND WENDY ALLATSON.
EDITED AND TYPESET BY BOOK CREATION SERVICES, LONDON.
PRINTED IN ITALY BY EDITORIALE LIBRARIA.

NAPLES AND POMPEII

KNOPF GUIDES

CONTENTS

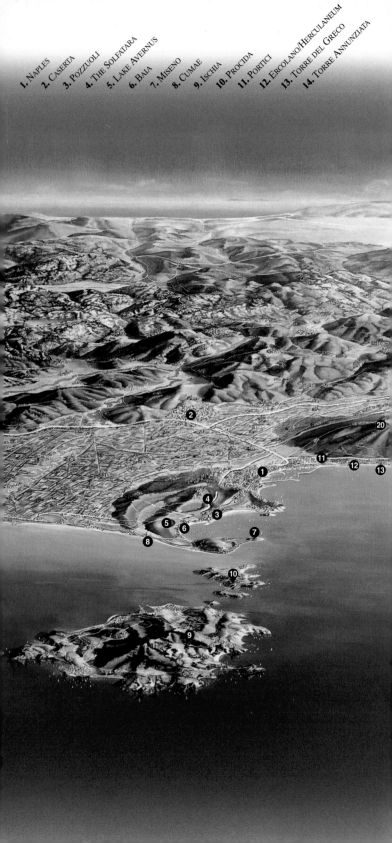

1. NAPLES   2. CASERTA   3. POZZUOLI   4. THE SOLFATARA   5. LAKE AVERNUS   6. BAIA   7. MISENO   8. CUMAE   9. ISCHIA   10. PROCIDA   11. PORTICI   12. ERCOLANO/HERCULANEUM   13. TORRE DEL GRECO   14. TORRE ANNUNZIATA

HOW TO USE THIS GUIDE
(Sample page shown from the guide to Venice)

The symbols at the top of each page refer to the different parts of the guide.

■ NATURAL ENVIRONMENT

● KEYS TO UNDERSTANDING

▲ ITINERARIES

◆ PRACTICAL INFORMATION

The itinerary map shows the main points of interest along the way and is intended to help you find your bearings.

The mini-map locates the particular itinerary within the wider area covered by the guide.

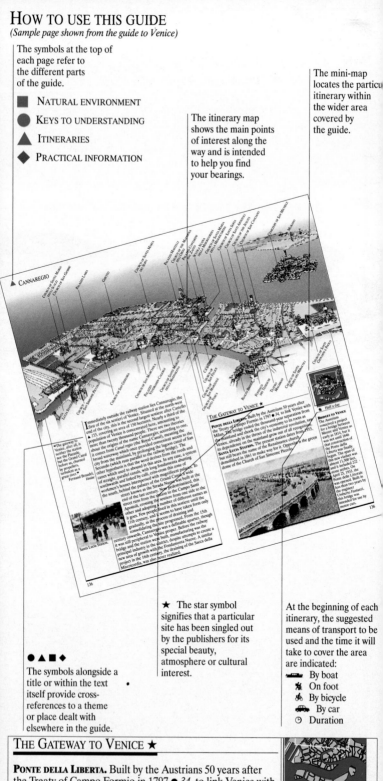

◄ The gateway to Venice, after all, is neither the station but the Grand Canal where we, churned by propellers, turbulent as a great river.
Fernand Braudel, Venice

Santa Lucia Station.

★ The star symbol signifies that a particular site has been singled out by the publishers for its special beauty, atmosphere or cultural interest.

● ▲ ■ ◆
The symbols alongside a title or within the text itself provide cross-references to a theme or place dealt with elsewhere in the guide.

At the beginning of each itinerary, the suggested means of transport to be used and the time it will take to cover the area are indicated:

🚤 By boat
🚶 On foot
🚲 By bicycle
🚗 By car
🕐 Duration

THE GATEWAY TO VENICE ★

PONTE DELLA LIBERTA. Built by the Austrians 50 years after the Treaty of Campo Formio in 1797 ● 34, to link Venice with Milan. The bridge ended the thousand-year separation from the mainland and shook the city's economy to its roots as Venice, already in the throes of the industrial revolution, saw

🚶 Half a day

BRIDGES TO VENICE

NATURE

PHYSICAL GEOGRAPHY

AN IDYLLIC CLIMATE. The region of Naples enjoys a particularly pleasant climate, owing to its proximity both to the sea and to the Apennines, which protect it from cold winds blowing across from the Balkans.

From Tuscany to Campania, volcanos occupy a large part of the terrain between the Tyrrhenian coast and the Apennine chain. While to the north they are ancient and long-extinct, to the south they are generally younger, and are frequently still active. Although Vesuvius is the most famous of them, volcanos characterize the length of the maritime flank of Campania, with the great Roccamonfina volcano to the north and, encircling the Bay of Naples to the west, the Phlegraean Fields and the islands of Procida and Ischia. All the Campanian volcanos were formed along a zone of geological weakness in the Apennine chain, whose limestone rocks surround the great plains of Caserta and Naples to the east and the south.

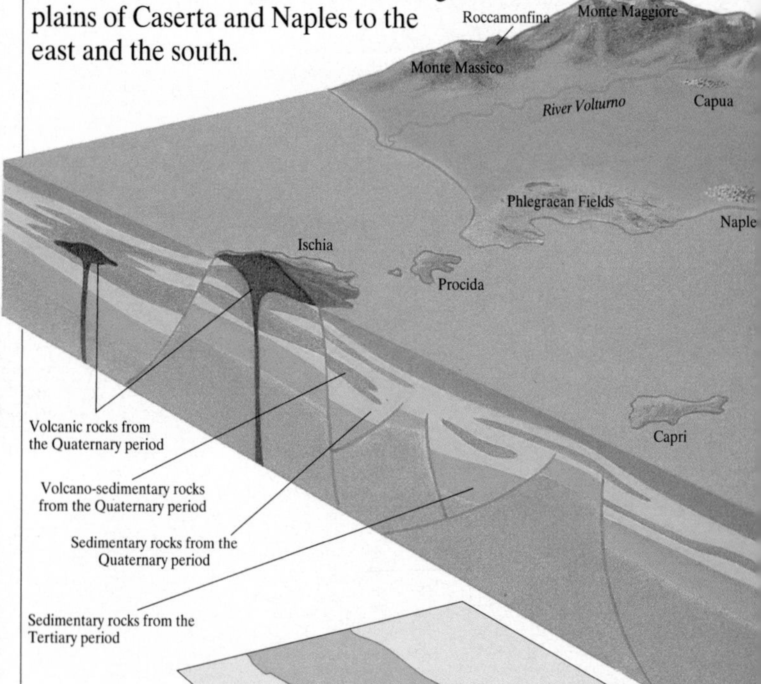

Roccamonfina   Monte Maggiore

Monte Massico

River Volturno   Capua

Monte Massico

Phlegraean Fields

Naple

Ischia

Procida

Capri

Volcanic rocks from the Quaternary period

Volcano-sedimentary rocks from the Quaternary period

Sedimentary rocks from the Quaternary period

Sedimentary rocks from the Tertiary period

VULSINI
SABATINI
ALBANI
ERNICI
VOLTURA
ROCCAMONFINA
VESUVIUS

FERTILE PLAINS
Thanks to volcanic activity fertile soils and soft rocks that are easy to shape have contributed to the richness of the Neapolitan region throughout much of its history.

STROMBOLI
USTICA   LIPARI
VULCANO
ETNA
PANTELLERIA

THE VOLCANOS OF ITALY
The volcanos of Italy and Sicily occur around the Tyrrhenian Sea. A number of theories relating to the formation of this oceanic area and the Apennine chain help to explain their presence. **VOLCANOS OF ITALY**

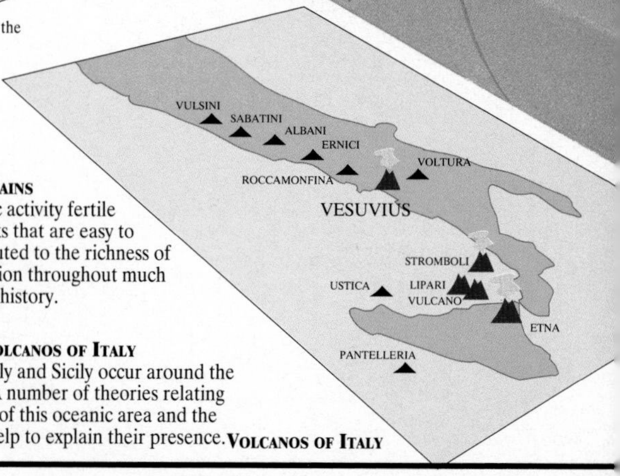

Some Italian volcanos are still active, either grumbling incessantly but presenting little danger, as with Stromboli and Etna (above, right) or less regularly and, occasionally, with devastating consequences, as in the case of Lipari, Vulcano and Vesuvius (above, left).

EARTHQUAKES

Toward the east, a further and not inconsiderable threat exists. The Apennines are crossed by fault lines, the most active of which run parallel to the mountain chain. The last earthquake (1980) ● *40* destroyed numerous villages in Irpinia (left, Senerchia).

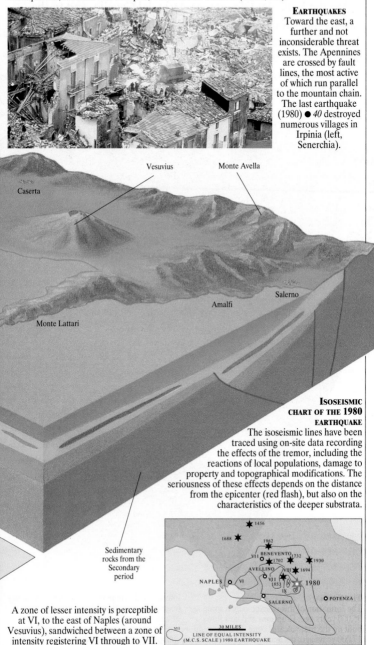

Vesuvius

Monte Avella

Caserta

Salerno

Amalfi

Monte Lattari

ISOSEISMIC CHART OF THE 1980 EARTHQUAKE

The isoseismic lines have been traced using on-site data recording the effects of the tremor, including the reactions of local populations, damage to property and topographical modifications. The seriousness of these effects depends on the distance from the epicenter (red flash), but also on the characteristics of the deeper substrata.

Sedimentary rocks from the Secondary period

A zone of lesser intensity is perceptible at VI, to the east of Naples (around Vesuvius), sandwiched between a zone of intensity registering VI through to VII.

VESUVIUS

Vesuvius rises above a highly populated region and constitutes a serious threat to the 700,000 people within a four-mile radius.

Vesuvius is in reality, comprised of two volcanos, with Vesuvius proper tucked inside an older volcano, called Monte Somma. The two structures are separated to the north by a depression, called the Valle del Gigante, or Atrio del Cavallo, and to the east by the Valle dell'Inferno. They are the result of an accumulation of volcanic emissions corresponding to different types of activity: lava flows have alternated with eruptions of rocks, ashes and lapilli, thereby gradually building up a "strato-volcano".

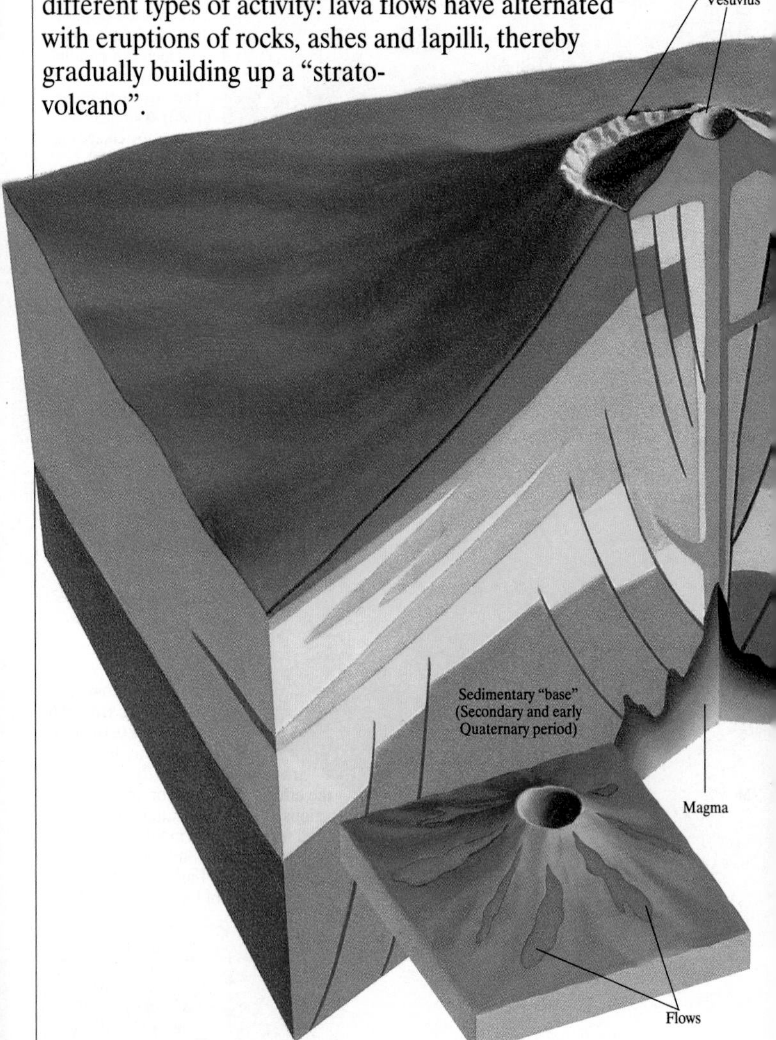

Monte Somma

Vesuvius

Sedimentary "base"
(Secondary and early
Quaternary period)

Magma

Flows

THE SOMMA
The formation of this volcano began some 35,000 years ago. Eruptions and lava flows built up the first volcanic cone. From around 17,000 years ago, dormant periods were interspersed with periods of activity, including five particularly disastrous eruptions, the last of which took place in AD 79. It was at this time that the structure gradually began to collapse, producing a caldera.

A CHANGE IN ACTIVITY
With the emergence of Vesuvius, the volcano's activity became more frequent and less explosive: numerous lava flows partially covered the slopes of Somma, the preserved lip of the caldera preventing flows "overflowing" northward (above, left and right).

THE 1944 ERUPTION ▲ *240* (above)
The last eruption of Vesuvius occurred in 1944. Lava flowed into the Atrio del Cavallo and then headed westward, the lip of the caldera having blocked its path northward.

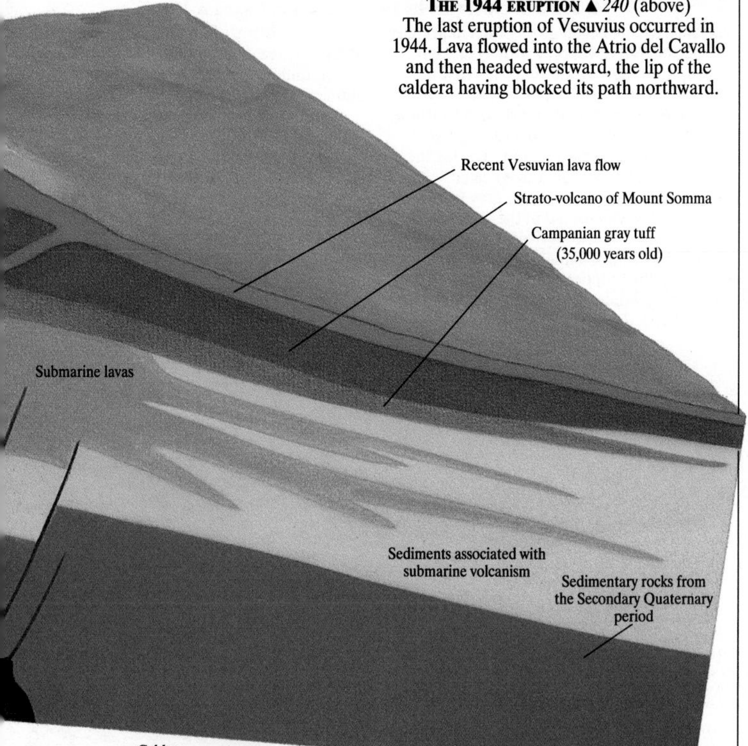

Recent Vesuvian lava flow

Strato-volcano of Mount Somma

Campanian gray tuff
(35,000 years old)

Submarine lavas

Sediments associated with
submarine volcanism

Sedimentary rocks from
the Secondary Quaternary
period

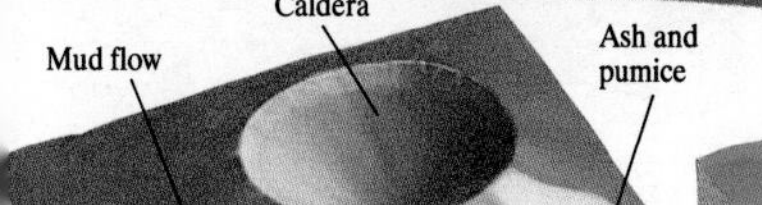

Caldera

Mud flow

Ash and
pumice

Lava
flows

Herculaneum

Pompeii

Torre del Greco

AD 79 ▲ 242
Following the opening up of the main volcanic vent, pumice and ash was spewed up. Eruptions followed, and the inner walls of the crater collapsed. A rain of ash and lapilli covered Pompeii, while glowing clouds and hot mud flows swallowed up Herculaneum.

VESUVIUS. From the 3rd century onward, eruptions and lava flows began again inside the caldera, building up a strato-volcano that slightly protruded over the previous one. The southern lip of the caldera was destroyed (or swallowed up) by the new cone.

■ THE PHLEGRAEAN FIELDS

The last eruption in the Phlegraean Fields took place in 1538. It threw up Monte Nuovo ▲ 205 (right) in the space of three days.

Visited since classical times for their hot springs and solfataras, the Phlegraean Fields consist of a vast volcanic area (93 square miles) with over fifty centers of eruption. Subsidences of volcanic origin, along with a rise in sea level in the Holocene epoch, have cut them off from the neighboring islands of Ischia and Procida, which are also volcanic.

BIRTH AND EVOLUTION OF THE PHLEGRAEAN FIELDS ▲ 198

Volcanic activity began during the Quaternary period, but it was only with a colossal eruption some 35,000 years ago that the Phlegraean Fields began properly to be formed. Magma abruptly reached the surface, and a mixture of gas and lava fragments escaped under great pressure. During the cooling process, crystals and volcanic "glass" solidified to form Campanian gray tuff. This substance is widespread in the area around Naples, and can be found even in numerous valleys of the Campanian Apennines. Following the eruption, subsidence of an area measuring 9 miles in diameter produced an enormous caldera, of which a portion is today under the sea. Subsequent volcanic activity was, initially, submarine (and therefore sub-aerial) and produced mainly tuff. Small volcanos and calderas were created by dramatic explosions and emissions of lava.

Cumae

Pozzuoli

Solfatara

Capo Miseno

Below: the Grotta del Cane (Roman ovens exploiting the characteristics of the Solfatara); sulfurous vapors in the Solfatara.

THE SOLFATARA ▲ 201

This is the crater of a half-extinct volcano some 4,000 years old, which emits fumaroles (sulfurous vapors) and boiling mud caused by seeping ground-water being heated deep down. The geothermic gradient has been gauged at 15° per 109 feet: this would situate the magma at a depth of some 2 to 4 miles.

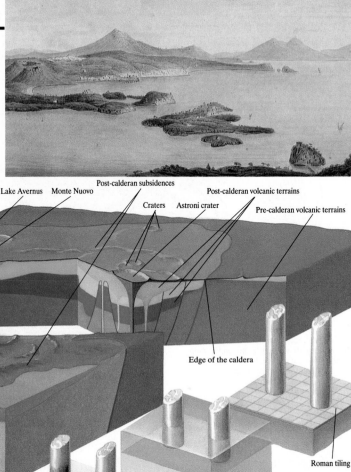

Lake Avernus   Monte Nuovo

Post-calderan subsidences

Craters   Astroni crater

Post-calderan volcanic terrains

Pre-calderan volcanic terrains

Edge of the caldera

Roman tiling

After sediment (possibly from an earlier subsidence) engulfed the lower portion of the columns, subsidence allowed the sea to flood in.

Sediment deposits

Present state (post-excavations)

Perforations over a length of 9 feet, made by marine shellfish

BRADYSEISM

Since ancient times, the ground level of the Pozzuoli zone has moved up and down on numerous occasions, a phenomenon called bradyseism. This is caused by a surge in the level of underground magma (which does not reach the surface) or to water heating, and so expanding, 1 to 2 miles underground. In 1538, following the eruption that formed Monte Nuovo, the ground level rose by 20 feet before dropping again by 13 feet. Between 1982 and 1984 the ground level rose by 6 feet, prompting fears of renewed volcanic activity.

A MEASURE OF BRADYSEISM

The columns of the Temple of Serapis ▲ *204* (below) at Pozzuoli were submerged beneath the sea in the 10th century, as can be seen from the perforations made by the marine species *Lithodomus lithophagus*.

ALEPPO PINE
This Mediterranean conifer colonizes areas
higher up the cliff, where it grows on the more
gentle slopes. It only really flourishes on
limestone soil, and is intolerant of
extreme cold.

**EUPHORBIA
ACANTHOTHAMNOS**
This attractive,
shrubby looking
euphorbia grows on
the bare rock. During
periods of drought, it
loses its leaves. When
the stalk is cut, a
milky juice (latex)
seeps out.

SEA FENNEL
This creeping plant
clings to the rock face
and can tolerate the
sea air. Its leaves have
a salty taste, while its
flowers give off a
scent reminiscent
of celery.

CHAMAEROPS HUMULIS
The only palm native to Italy, this shrub is
increasingly rare owing to the intensive
harvesting of its leaves, which are used to
make brushes and mats.

The limestone cliffs that plummet into the sea at Capri or along
the Sorrentine and Amalfi coasts are home to a remarkable
flora, ideally adapted to the wind, the thin soil and dry climate.
These plants have developed a root system that is able to take
hold in the smallest of rock crannies. In areas where the drop is
less precipitous, peasants have for centuries made use of cannily
constructed terraces, where olive trees can grow.

ALPINE SWIFT
Larger than the black
swift, this colonizing
species scans the rock
face for a suitable
spot to build its nest.
Returns during the
month of March.

SWIFT
Lives on rocky
outcrops overhanging
the sea and, in
groups, executes
spectacular sweeps
close to the sheer
cliff walls.

HERRING GULL
Mainly nests on the rocky islets along the
Amalfi Coast, especially those that tend to
remain undisturbed. Numbers of this species
are actually on the increase throughout the
Mediterranean, since it has managed to
benefit from diverse aspects of human
habitation (fishing, dumping grounds).

THE FLORA OF VESUVIUS

The flora of Vesuvius accounts for no fewer than 610 species, of which a number are endemic.

One of the most striking features is its diversity, in terms of the stages at which the volcanic rocks are colonized, depending on the age of the lava flow. Thus the *Stereocaulon vesuvianum* colonizes the most recent lava flows, while plants with colorful flowers, such as brooms, grow on the older substrata. Where more substantial layers of humus are found, shrubby species grow, thereby helping to hold the soil together.

SPANISH BROOM
The springtime flowering of this broom brings instant color, visible for miles around, to several hectares of the slopes of Vesuvius.

ETNA BROOM
This was introduced to Vesuvius during the last century by the Forestry Commission (the Forestale), and today it is perfectly naturalized.

RED VALERIAN
Thanks to a very deep root system, this pretty plant manages to grow on the poor substrata of lava flows.

"PTERIS VITTATA"
This fern with its fine arching leaves, found as far as the subtropical zone, likes well-shaded rocks.

HISTORY AND
LANGUAGE

8th century BC	Late 5th century. Occupation
Foundation of	of Capua, Cumae and Pozzuoli
Cumae	

| -5000 | -3000 | -2000 | -1000 | -500 | -300 |

2nd millennium BC	7th century BC	6th century BC	341 BC
Arrival of the Oscans, then	Foundation of	Etruscans seize	Roman occupation
the Marsyans, Samnites and	Naples and Paestum	Capua	of Campania
Lucanians.			

ANTIQUITY

THE FIRST GREEK COLONISTS

The Italic peoples of Indo-European origin (such as the Oscans and Samnites) who had occupied the region during the 2nd millennium were succeeded in turn by the Etruscans and the Greeks, who began to populate the coast from the 9th century BC. From the 8th century, Greeks who had been forced from their homeland, mainly because of internal politics, founded numerous colonies along the coasts of Naples and Salerno ● 67. The Eubian Greeks, who possessed a trading post on the island of Pithecusa (Ischia) ▲ 210 in the early 8th century, led the way by establishing the town of Cumae. This was probably the first Greek colony in the west. During the 7th century colonists from Cumae founded the town of Parthenope, on the hill of Pizzofalcone ▲ 188. The city expanded after its victory over the Etruscans in 474 BC, acquiring the name of Neapolis (meaning "new town"). Other sites were occupied, such as Pozzuoli ▲ 200 and Posidonia (Paestum) ▲ 296 to the south of the Gulf of Salerno, where a people from Sybaris, in Magna Graecia,

settled; in Velia, colonists from Phocaea established themselves. These diverse populations lived together, more or less harmoniously, in an area that was small but nonetheless well sited in terms of agriculture (mainly consisting of wheat cultivation) and trade. Despite the conflicts and rivalries that would occasionally flare up between them, excavations have proved that interbreeding between the indigenous peoples and their conquerors occurred very early on, in Etruscan towns as much as in Greek ones.

ETRUSCAN FOUNDATIONS

Throughout the 6th and 5th centuries BC, Campania was mainly dominated by the Etruscans, who were extending their domain southward while, at the same time, sparing the Greek towns. From Capua, they founded other cities such as Nola, Herculaneum ▲ 272 and Pompeii ▲ 246, and pushed as far south as Salerno. They thus unified the entire region within a confederation, made up of twelve cities, which had Capua as its capital. But being few in number against the indigenous peoples, they were halted during the course of the following century. Their defeat near the walls of Cumae in 474 BC signaled the start of their decline, to be hastened by dramatic population shifts.

82 BC
Soldiers led by Sulla
capture Naples

AD 79
Eruption of Vesuvius:
destruction of Pompeii
and Herculaneum

SAMNITE OPPOSITION

In the late 5th century the Samnites, established in the Abruzzi, began to descend from the mountains and settle on the coastal plain. In 430 they gained control of Capua, and in 420 of Cumae and Pozzuoli. They gradually swallowed up a large portion of Campania, which they organized into city federations: to the north, that of Capua extended as far as the slopes of Vesuvius; to the south, that of Nuceria enveloped the Sorrentine peninsula. The only towns to escape Samnite domination were the Greek coast-towns, although sources even indicate the presence of a Samnite colony inside Naples. Further south, Posidonia and Velia had to fend off the Lucanians ▲ 296. The Greek towns of Campania, impoverished by their encounters with seasoned invaders, appealed to Rome, who had repulsed the Etruscan kings and completed the conquest of Latium. An initial victory over the Samnites resulted in the capture of Capua in 334, while Naples, occupied in 328, was awarded the status of subject ally. Having vigorously resisted the thrust of the Roman army, the Samnites, now vanquished, surrendered in 290, bringing in their wake the southern Greek cities. The defeat of Pyrrhus, King of Epirus, who arrived ten years after to defend Tarentum and the cities of Magna Graecia, did nothing to delay the day of reckoning. Campania would again experience the desire for autonomy during Hannibal's Carthaginian expedition. Capua opened its gates to Hannibal and his army following the Battle of Cannae, which took place in 216 BC. In 211 the town was reconquered by the Roman army and sacked.

CAMPANIA WITHIN THE ROMAN EMPIRE

From the 3rd century BC, Campania formed part of the Roman Empire. Its fertile lands provided the region with a rich supply of grain, and Roman aristocrats would vacation in the lavish villas along the coast, of which excavations in Pompeii and Herculaneum have yielded ample evidence. However, civil wars in the 1st century BC were to shatter this tranquility. Naples was decimated by the soldiers of the dictator Sulla in 82 BC, and thousands of slaves, led by Spartacus, revolted, and settled at the foot of Vesuvius during 73 BC. Under the Empire, Naples managed to retain its original character, as befitted a former Greek city. The town became famous for its gymnasiums and schools. Men of renown elected to take up residence, such as Lucilius, a friend and correspondent of Cicero, and Virgil himself ▲ 192, who composed the *Georgics* there, and who was quite possibly also buried there. During the 1st century after Christ, the Emperor Tiberius settled on Capri ▲ 226. Nevertheless, by this time Campania's decline had already begun. The earthquake of AD 62, followed by the eruption of Vesuvius in 79 ▲ 243 (which buried not only Pompeii, but also Herculaneum and Stabiae) served only to aggravate the situation.

29

476 End of the Roman Empire in the West	6th century Reconquest of Italy by Justinian			763–1139 Duchy of Naples independent	
400	570	670	770	870	1030
410 Rome sacked by the Visigoths	455 Vandals raid Campania	7th century Lombard conquest of Italy	661–763 Duchy of Naples under Byzantine authority		1030 Aversa given to the Norman, Rainulf Drengot

THE INVASIONS

Until the early 5th century, Campania had been spared Germanic invasion, but the frontiers of the Empire collapsed in 406, and Naples and the surrounding region had to face the

Visigoths under Alaric, then the Vandals under Gaiseric. It was at Naples that the fate of the Empire was to be sealed. In 476 the German Odoacer deposed the last emperor, Romulus Augustulus, and imprisoned him in a villa situated on the site of the Castel dell'Ovo ▲ 190. In the 6th century, the Byzantine emperor Justinian began his

reconquest of Italy and tried to reinstate the provinces of the Roman Empire. Naples came under his sway (AD 536), but the political situation remained unstable: the Byzantines were succeeded by the Goths, then by the Lombards. They instated themselves at Benevento, and occupied most of Campania. The coast remained under Byzantine rule.

THE FEUDAL ERA

Between the 8th and 10th centuries the region's history is marked by a struggle between Lombards and Byzantines, to which was added both Franks (Charlemagne attempted to seize the Lombard Duchy of Benevento) and Saracens who, in the 9th century, set up a small emirate on the Garigliano. During the 10th and 11th centuries, the

dramatic impact of feudalism swept away the old political structures of Campania: the Lombard Duchy of Benevento was split into three autonomous principalities, centered around Benevento, Capua and Salerno, while the Byzantine duchies, virtually free from imperial control, continued to exist at

Gaeta, Naples, Sorrento and Amalfi. Furthermore, veritable monastic states began to emerge in northern Campania, based around the powerful Benedictine abbeys of Monte Cassino and San Vincenzo of Volturno. It was in the midst of this feudal turmoil that the Normans decided to try their luck.

THE NORMAN CONQUEST

The Normans began to arrive in southern Italy in the 10th century. First to

appear were pilgrims from Jerusalem; they were followed by mercenaries in the employ of various warring princes, or hired by the Byzantines in Sicily to fight against the Muslims. In the early 11th century the Duke of Naples, Sergius IV, engaged the Norman warriors led by Rainulf Drengot to fight against the Lombards of Capua. Thanks to the support of the Church, the Normans managed to expand their territory. Rewarded with the county of Aversa in 1038 (its fortress had been granted to them

by the Duke of Naples in 1030) they gained control of Capua with the assistance of the abbey of Monte Cassino. Further south, other Norman adventurers founded a capital at Melfi (requisitioned in 1041 by the Emperor in Constantinople, to defend Byzantine possessions in southern Italy against the Duchy of Benevento). Their leader, William Bras-de-Fer, came from Hauteville-la-Guichard in Normandy. There were twelve Hauteville brothers, who had set off to

wrest southern Italy from the Lombards and Byzantines, and Sicily from the Muslims. Following Robert Guiscard's conquest of the duchies of Salerno, and Amalfi, Capua and Naples by Roger II in 1139, southern Italy became a single state under Norman rule, with Palermo as its capital. To gain the support of the Church, the Normans paid homage to Pope Nicholas II for their Italian conquests, and agreed to pay a tax to the Holy See. The Kingdom of Naples was now a pontifical fiefdom.

NAPLES UNDER FOREIGN RULE

THE CAPITAL OF THE KINGDOM

The Norman dynasty ended in 1189 following the death of William II. After a period of turmoil during which various feudal princes attempted to seize his legacy, Emperor Henry VI claimed the kingdom of Sicily for his own (he had married Constance, daughter of Roger II) and came to the throne in 1194, founding the Swabian Hohenstaufen dynasty. Its most brilliant member was Frederick II who, lost in his imperialistic dreams, rapidly alienated the papacy. Upon his death in 1250, the dynasty was threatened in Naples. In 1263 Charles I of Anjou took possession of the kingdom of Sicily. Two successful battles at Benevento (1266) and Tagliacozzo (1268) eliminated the last remaining representatives of the House of Hohenstaufen, and ushered in an era of Angevin rule in southern Italy. In 1282, rioting Sicilian barons massacred the French and, throwing off the Angevin yoke, called upon the Aragonese for assistance. The "Sicilian Vespers" incident separated Sicily politically from the mainland, and Naples became the capital of an independent kingdom for six centuries. After numerous feudal revolts and upheavals at the palace, the Angevin period ended, in Naples, in 1442, just as the city began to emerge as a political entity.

THE HOUSE OF ARAGON

Alfonso the Magnanimous, turning internal dissensions to his advantage, seized the kingdom of Naples from King René, the last sovereign of the Angevin dynasty. From 1442 to 1707, Naples remained within the sphere of Aragonese and Spanish influence, becoming part of a vast empire. It was a key moment in the history of the city, which became one of the most important areas in the Western World. In the early 17th century, with a population of over 300,000, Naples was the largest town in Europe. Alfonso the Magnanimous imposed a direct tax, calculated by regular census, and a levy on transhumant herds moving between the Abruzzi and Apulia. His son Ferrante, a legitimized bastard, succeeded him, but clashed with a mutinous aristocracy who revolted on several occasions. In 1494 the King of France, Charles VIII, attempted to reconquer Naples and its kingdom. Charles had barely been crowned king (at Naples in May 1495) when he was compelled to hurry north again to France. By the following year, all trace of the French presence had been effaced. And although French troops returned to Naples in 1501, following a treaty concluded between Louis XII and Ferdinand of Aragon, they did not remain there for very long: in 1503 they were ejected by Spanish troops under the "Grand Captain", Gonzalo de Córdoba.

1503–1707 Spanish rule.
Spanish viceroys govern Naples

1707–34 Austrian rule

| 1500 | 1550 | 1600 | 1650 | 1720 |

1501 Treaty of Córdoba: Louis XII King of Naples

1503 Victory of Gonzalo de Córdoba at Cerignola and Garigliano

1647–8 Masaniello revolt

1656 Plague epidemic

1701–13 Wars of Spanish Succession

PROSPERITY

THE SPANISH VICEROYS

The 16th century was one of the most prosperous periods in Neapolitan history.

The Spanish viceroys who ruled the kingdom in the name of, first, Ferdinand of Aragon, then Charles V, then Philip II, reestablished order by subduing the local aristocracy. The uprisings that punctuated political life failed. In its way, Naples benefited from the discovery of the New World. Its population more than doubled in size.
Consequently, its walls had to be enlarged, and new districts were created, such as the famous Spanish area ▲ 149 of the city. The aristocracy built

sumptuous palaces for themselves within these walls; the Counter-Reformation Church, numerous churches and monasteries; and in the countryside, around Vesuvius, weekend residences sprang up. The port prospered, and galleys ensured free passage for Christian vessels threatened by Barbary pirates on the Tyrrhenian sea. Toward the end of the 16th century, Naples was even to become an outlying base on the "Flanders' route", supplying soldiers and money to the Spanish garrisons in the Low

Countries. This period of prosperity came to an end during the second quarter of the 17th century. The bankruptcy of Genoa, in 1622, severely disrupted the economic activity of the Spanish Empire, and of Naples in particular, where Genoese interests were considerable. Spain, engaged in ruinous conflicts, increased financial pressure, and Naples revolted in 1647 ● 38.

THE PLAGUE

The 17th-century crisis reached its climax in 1656 with the great plague epidemic which, in a matter of months, ravaged Naples and Campania. The capital lost nearly three quarters of its inhabitants, and economic vitality was crushed. The road to recovery was extremely long. When in 1707, during the turmoil of the War of Spanish Succession,

the kingdom passed under the authority of the Austrian emperor, Naples had

still not recovered its population level prior to the plague epidemic.

NAPLES IN THE AGE OF ENLIGHTENMENT

The kingdom of Sicily passed to the Bourbons in 1734 and its king, Charles, youngest son of Philip V of Spain, gave it the luster of an Enlightenment capital. The Capodimonte Palace, the Teatro San Carlo, the Biblioteca Nazionale and the Palazzo Reale at Caserta all illustrate his efforts. He also

initiated the first excavations of Pompeii and Herculaneum. The Bourbon dynasty was undeniably popular, the Neapolitans, finally, having a resident king. But in 1799, on the orders of Napoleon, General Championnet took Naples and proclaimed the Parthenopean Republic. The king

fled to Sicily. The liberal elites who then took control never enjoyed the support of the masses. As soon as the French troops retreated the regime collapsed, and King Ferdinand regained the throne, only to lose it again at the Battle of Austerlitz. The collapse of Austria deprived him of his principal ally.

Napoleon installed his brother Joseph, who was replaced, in 1808, by Joachim Murat. Despite reforms, such as the abolition of feudal laws, the new regime was only able to sustain itself through force. The growth of banditry and smuggling reflected the population's opposition to foreign rule.

1799 Parthenopean
Republic

1806–8 Joseph Bonaparte,
King of Naples

1848 Revolutions
in Europe

1740   1800   1820   1840   1860   1880

1734–1860
Bourbon
dynasty

1808–15 Joachim
Murat, King of
Naples

1815 Congress
of Vienna

1860 Garibaldi
in Naples. End of
the Kingdom of the
Two Sicilies

TOWARD ITALIAN UNIFICATION

The restoration of the Bourbons in 1815 brought Naples into the aristocratic and conservative Europe that had emerged with the Congress of Vienna in 1814. The revolutionary wave of 1848 that swept across southern Italy, and in particular Sicily, barely touched Naples. Ferdinand II temporarily conceded to the upsurge of liberalism, by authorizing the election of a Parliament, which was dissolved once revolutionary fervor had subsided. The last sovereigns of the dynasty were not particularly popular, but manipulated the plebeian classes against the liberal ideals of the intellectual and bourgeois elites. Thus Francis II's concession of a new constitution in 1860 provoked a popular insurrection on June 25, which had as its rallying cry, "Long live the King, down with the Constitution."

GARIBALDI IN NAPLES

The arrival in Naples of Giuseppe Garibaldi, marching up from Sicily and Calabria with his troops to complete the unification of Italy, was viewed with as much disquiet as enthusiasm. In Sicily, the violence of the revolutionary movement conducted by Garibaldi and the "I Mille" (the thousand) had routed the loyalist troops. In Naples, however, it was only after a *rapprochement* with the House of Savoy

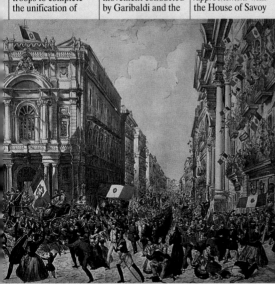

that Garibaldi was able to make his triumphal entry into the town on September 7, 1860. The loyalist Bourbon troops, however, still resisted. Their September 21 victory at Caiazzo, north of Caserta, was followed by violent struggles on the Volturno on October 1 and 2, 1860, during which Garibaldi emerged victorious. In the aftermath of this decisive victory, the population voted for the Kingdom of the Two Sicilies to join the Kingdom of Italy (in the referendum of October 21). Vittorio Emmanuele made his entry into Naples on November 7.

THE SOUTHERN QUESTION

Following unification, the pressing issue was that of the integration of the south into the north. For some, the "backward" character of the south was only underlined by its union with the north, which was industrialized. For others, the south was the victim of government policies geared toward the development of the north. Commerce, local trades and output declined following "legal" unification (1861). Agriculture was thrown into chaos by the extension of *latifundia* (large estates), and by laws that disregarded its interests and traditions, prompting a wave of emigration. Naples gained little from integration: once the capital of a vast kingdom, it had become a provincial city, losing its position as a pivotal center of international prestige. With the Great War, it declined still further, while the industrial north underwent substantial growth.

1900	1920	1950
	1922 Mussolini's march on Rome	**1943** Allied bombardments of Naples. Liberation of the town by American troops

THE 20TH CENTURY

Following the unification of Italy, the ruling classes in the south were unable, despite their efforts, to restore the city to its 18th-century glory. Naples lived in nostalgic remembrance of its brilliant past. It was at this time that the myths of Naples were born (the beautiful, sunny, carefree town, with her good and generous citizens), which spread throughout the world in its "song" and *sceneggiata*. These folkloric clichés simply masked the town's economic and political decline, but have become almost impossible to shrug off.

THE FASCIST PERIOD

The Fascist Regime swept aside the council elected by "popular block vote" in 1913, and sanctioned the return to power of the old Catholic and conservative elites, represented by Cardinal-Bishop Alessio Ascalesi. At the other end of the scale, anti-fascism found its most powerful voice in the person of Benedetto Croce (1866–1952). During this period, the town underwent profound changes. In 1927 it absorbed the border communes, and extended west along the coast of Chiaia toward Posillipo and the Vomero, and beyond Fuorigrotta toward Bagnoli and the Phlegraean Fields, where the Grand Overseas Fair was held, celebrating the glorious colonial achievements of the regime. A new airport (1936), funicular railways up to the Vomero, and a metro (*metropolitana*) and suburban system helped to rescue the town. But the campaign to destroy the *bassi*, the slums in the heart of the city, failed.

WORLD WAR TWO

Italy's entry into the World War Two helped boost the ports of Naples and Salerno as well as the armaments industries. From 1943, after the Allied landings in Sicily, Campania became a battle zone. To facilitate the advance of expeditionary troops from the south, the Allies disembarked south of Salerno, to the rear of the German army. The battles were bloody, but after a four-day revolt (September 26–30, 1943), the Neapolitan people expelled the Germans and opened the city to the Allies. The Allies were trapped around Monte Cassino for several months, until the French troops of General Juin liberated them. During this time, Naples was the seat of the temporary Allied government in Italy.

The whole region suffered badly in the battles. Aerial bombardments destroyed the port and old districts of Salerno, several districts of the old center of Naples and a large part of Caserta. The abbey of Monte Cassino, one of the most important sites of intellectual and religious consciousness in the West, was razed to the ground. A portion of the old archives of the kingdom of Naples was burned by the retreating German army. In his novel *La Pelle*, Curzio Malaparte describes these times of chaos that marked the liberation of Naples and the arrival of the American troops.

AFTERMATH OF WAR

When it came to rebuilding the town and its port, damaged by the 1943 bombings, industrial development seemed the only way to help the south integrate with the north and become fully modernized. Moreover, the conservative leaders, who had collaborated with the Fascists, managed to stay in power and again raised the old cry of southern independence. Thus, in a referendum on the Republic (June 2, 1946), Naples voted massively in favor of the monarchy, which did not, however, prevent it from giving Italy its first president of the Republic, Enrico de Niccola. The 1950's were marked by real estate speculation and the swift reconstruction of the marina. Under town councils dominated first by the monarchist shipping magnate, Achille Lauro, then by the Christian Democrats (Democrazia Cristiana), the region lacked the industrial development that it so badly needed. Naples still suffers from ill-planned investments, profiteering, public finance deficits and corruption: all the familiar evils that have come to characterize the administration of the Italian south.

THE NEAPOLITAN CAMORRA

The Camorra is less well known than the Sicilian Mafia, but nonetheless plays an important role in the social and economic life of Campania. Having taken over the trade in contraband cigarettes, it then turned to the fruit and vegetable markets of the Neapolitan hinterland (where it now controls distribution), then to the real estate market and the drugs trade. Defrauding European subsidies on agricultural produce, rackets and extortion and "settling debts" now constitute the basis of its criminal activities. The Camorra recruits its henchmen among the working classes, but has long enjoyed political protection at the highest level. Far from being a colorful piece of folklore, the Camorra is a very real blight on Neapolitan society.

SINCE THE 1980 EARTHQUAKE

Naples is a large conglomeration that stretches well beyond its ancient historical perimeters. In the old town, with its Mediterranean charm, the offices of large national and international firms or administrations rub shoulders with a poor population living off traditional crafts or the "underground" economy. The residential area stretches westward (Posillipo, the Vomero, Mergellina and Chiaia). The earthquake of November 23, 1980

▲ 40 brought about a considerable transformation. The town then spread its tentacles and dormitory suburbs toward the south and east (in the Nola hinterland and the belt of villages at the foot of Vesuvius), and toward the north, as far as Caserta, and along the coast. Since 1994, to play host to the Group of Seven summit, Naples has instigated a policy of regeneration, which has profoundly altered the appearance of the town.

35

The succession of numerous ruling houses over a period of six centuries has left Naples with a multicultural legacy. Its history may be read as one long love affair between foreign kings and a city rich in natural beauty and steeped in classical culture. Thanks to the generosity of its rulers, the city became a cosmopolitan center: the founding of a university under Frederick II raised Naples to the rank of centers of intellectual excellence such as Paris and Bologna, while under Angevin and Aragonese rule, it was enriched with prestigious monuments. Up until the Unification of Italy the ruling houses and the Spanish, Bourbon and Austrian dynasties sustained the town's reputation, so dear to Shelley's heart, as the *Elysian city*.

THE NORMANS
William (1042–59)
Robert Guiscard (1059–1127)
Roger II (1127–54)
William I (1154–66)
William II (1166–89)
Tancred of Lecce (1189–94)

ROGER II
Duke, then King, of Sicily, he founded the Norman state of Sicily, which united southern Italy with Sicily.

Center, *Coronation of Roger II.*

THE HOHENSTAUFEN
Henry VI (1194–7)
Frederick II (1197–1250)
Conrad (1250–54)
Manfred (1254–66)

FREDERICK II (left) Proclaimed king at the age of three and brought up by Pope Innocent III, he became King of Sicily and Germanic emperor. His reign is noted for the founding of the University of Naples (1224) and the enforcement of the "Constitutions of Melfi" (1231), the first attempt at establishing a code of law in the south.

Charles of Anjou, given the Kingdom of Sicily

Alfonso the Magnanimous

THE ANGEVINS
Charles I (1266–85)
Charles II (1285–1309)
Robert the Wise (1309–43)
Joan I (1343–81)
Charles III (1381–6)
Ladislas (1386–1414)
Joan II (1414–35)
René (1435–42)

THE ARAGONESE
Alfonso the Magnanimous (1442–58)
Ferdinand I (1458–94)
Alfonso II (1494–5)
Ferdinand II (1495–6)
Frederick (1496–1503)

CHARLES I
Pope Urban IV gave the kingdom to Charles of Anjou, brother of Saint Louis. Charles made Naples the capital of the kingdom, which he finally had to share with the Aragonese in 1282. From that time on, the Angevins governed over the peninsula while the Aragonese ruled Sicily.

ALFONSO THE MAGNANIMOUS
Taking the title of King of the Two Sicilies in 1442, Alfonso the Magnanimous settled in Naples, where he carried out major institutional reforms and modernized the machinery of State.

THE VICEROYS OF SPAIN
For over two centuries (1503–1707) the Kingdom of Naples was ruled by the Spanish and governed from Palermo, Naples and Cagliari by viceroys.

BONAPARTE AND MURAT
Joseph Bonaparte (1806–8)
Joachim Murat (1808–16)

Charles VII

THE BOURBONS
Charles VII (1734–59)
Ferdinand I (1759–1825), King of Sicily as Ferdinand III, and King of Naples as Ferdinand IV
Francis I (1825–30)
Ferdinand II (1830–59)
Francis II (1859–60)

CHARLES VII
Charles VII, King of Naples, became of Charles III of Spain in 1759. He was favored by economic circumstances and aided by advisors who were well versed in the new ideas of Enlightenment philosophy, so that his reign left its mark on Naples and the surrounding region.

On July 7, 1647, a popular insurrection broke out on the Piazza del Mercato in Naples. At this time, Spain, Italy's oppressor, whose army was surrendering on every battle front, was engaged in conflict with France; Portugal and Catalonia, for their part, had seceded, while Palermo had risen up in revolt in May. In Naples, where discontent among the common people, crushed by taxation, had been simmering since June, the imposition of a duty on fruit acted as a spark to the tinderbox. The rebels found a leader in the figure of Tommaso Aniello, a young fisherman who became a respected and well-heeded advocate of their cause.

JULY 7, 1647
The edict of January 3, 1647 imposed a new tax, which the fruit growers of Pozzuoli, coming to sell their produce on the Piazza del Mercato, refused to pay. On the morning of July 7 they were joined in support by the tradespeople, led by Masaniello. The tax-collectors were hounded out and the people's representative, Andrea Naclerio, fled to save his life. The demonstrators, demanding that the viceroy abolish the tax, clashed with the guards of the Castel Nuovo. That evening, the rebels set up an elected committee in the church of Santa Maria del Carmine.

THE DUKE OF ARCOS
The viceroy of Naples, Rodrigo Ponce de Léon, was a courageous soldier but an ineffectual politician. Unable to deal with the popular uprising and the demands of the Neapolitan bourgeoisie, he was removed from office by Don Juan of Austria, who arrived in Naples in October 1647. He was replaced by the Count of Oñate in 1648.

CARDINAL ASCANIO FILOMARINO
A charismatic figure, the archbishop of Naples played an essential role in mediating between the leaders of the revolt and the government. He sought, above all, to defend the interests of the church and the Holy See when the rebels sought to confiscate monastic property. His doubtful loyalties led to his disgrace and death in 1666.

THE DEATH OF MASANIELLO
On the instigation of the viceroy, and with the complicity of his own followers, Masaniello was beheaded on July 16. His enemies displayed his head on the end of a pike, and dragged his body through the town before throwing it to the dogs. On July 17, his followers retrieved the remains of his corpse.

MASANIELLO

Tommaso Aniello d'Amalfi was born in 1620. His family was well known in the working class districts of Naples. He succeeded in uniting the urban poor and the working classes, who were members of various corporations. However, goaded on by his troops to take increasingly extreme measures, he was assassinated on July 16, 1647.

THE FUNERAL

The strength of popular feeling led to Masaniello's corpse being paraded in triumph, with all the military honors owed to his rank as "Captain General" of the people. It seemed that an air of sanctity hung over his death; some even believed in his resurrection.

A POLITICAL CRISIS

What had begun as a straightforward and spontaneous uprising turned into a protracted political crisis. The ensuing anarchy rekindled the enmity between the bourgeoisie (some of whom joined the rioters) and the Neapolitan nobility. France saw this as an opportunity to weaken the power of Spain, and sent the Duke of Guise to Naples, who, on his arrival, proclaimed a Republic. The new viceroy, the Count of Oñate, reestablished order: the rebellion was crushed on April 6, 1648, Guise was captured, and the rebel chiefs were executed.

● THE SCOURGES OF NAPLES

"Under the purest of skies lies the most uncertain of soils": thus Goethe described the unpredictable Neapolitan land stretched beneath a sky of deceptive serenity. Its inhabitants have learned to live with the repeated telluric tremors and the devastating power of the sly, half-sleeping volcano. The densely crowded, haphazard population of Naples (numbering 42,000 inhabitants per square mile in the historical district of San Lorenzo), together with a tightly constructed urban fabric without an efficient sewerage system, has caused numerous and catastrophic epidemics. The powerless citizens look to their patron saints, and particularly to San Gennaro (Saint Januarius), for help, and live in fevered apprehension of ill omens.

CHOLERA
A controlled urban spread was hardly possible in Naples. Dwellings were simply thrown up to keep pace with a growing population. In overcrowded conditions, public hygiene deteriorated. The disasters, however, led to urban improvements: the cholera epidemic of 1884 resulted in a program of urban renewal and public health. The problems of sanitation were, nevertheless, far from solved, and Naples once again suffered a cholera outbreak in 1973.

THE 1980 EARTHQUAKE
The destruction of property (whole villages reduced to rubble) and the three thousand deaths caused by the earthquake of November 23, 1980 pointed an accusing finger at the anarchic urban sprawl, the disregard of safety regulations and the impotence and corruption of the political elite (funds for redevelopment had mysteriously vanished).

THE PLAGUE OF 1656

This epidemic was the worst Naples had known. After its outbreak in May there were 100 deaths a day; in early June, the count had reached 1,000, climbing to 2,000 by the end of the month; in July and at the beginning of August, 4,000 deaths a day were recorded. At this point the plague receded, but it was not over until October. Out of 350,000 inhabitants, 7 out of 10 had fallen victim. Poor sanitation and overcrowding help explain these staggering statistics. Naples fell into a decline that lasted a century.

THE VOLCANO ▲ *238* Since the AD 79 eruption ▲ *243*, over forty volcanic episodes have marked the history of the region. Neapolitans have learned to live with this constant threat, and have even managed to exploit the potential of their volcanos as a tourist attraction.

SANTA LUCIA
— BARCAROLA —

THE DIALECT OF DAILY LIFE

In spite of Italian unification, Neapolitan remains the dialect of everyday life. Far from being extinguished over the course of the centuries, it has continued to grow in richness and vigor.

THE ITALIAN DIALECT MOST FAMILIAR TO FOREIGNERS
From the early 19th century Neapolitan "song" disseminated the dialect around the world, with works that are still famous today (such as "O Sole Mio", "Marechiaro", and "Te Voglio Bene Assaje"); in the 20th century, the movies took over this role.

A UNIQUE PRONUNCIATION
An "e" whose pronunciation is, with very rare exceptions, identical to that of the English vowel sound in *heard*; a final "o" whose pronunciation has become so weak that it is now close to the silent "e" of, for example, mauve; and a median "o" approximating the sound "oo" in *hoot*; consonants that are doubled at the beginning (*lloco*) and middle (*tabbacco*, *tubbo*) of words; an "s" that becomes a "sh" in front of a voiceless consonant (*pasca*, *masculo*) and an initial "y" sound often transformed into a "g" (*jurnata/ghiurnata*).

A RICH VOCABULARY
Geography and history seem to have conspired to enrich its vocabulary with innumerable foreign imports. It was inevitable that Naples should be open to a wide range of

influences, situated as it was on the major maritime routes of the Mediterranean and having close links with the Levant. Added to this was a string of foreign occupiers. Other civilizations (and they were not always friendly) were thus grafted onto the Italic and Greco-Latin roots, with the waves of conquering peoples leaving their mark on both the language and the customs, thereby helping to make the dialect the richest in substrata in the whole of the peninsula.

A FEW ADOPTED WORDS
◆ *sciué sciué* (slowly, slowly) from *chouaï chouaï* (Arabic)
◆ *zizza* (breast) from *zitze* (German)
◆ *birbia* (din) from *briba* (Spanish)
◆ *tirabbbusciò* (corkscrew) from *tirebouchon* (French)

A JOURNEY TOWARD A WRITTEN LANGUAGE

For many centuries in the peninsula, a burning issue was the creation of a unifying written language; the principal dilemma was whether to choose Latin, or a vulgate form, in the guise of one of the local dialects. Coexisting alongside Latin were a number of vernacular languages, all of which more or less developed written forms and experimented with literary genres. Eventually, at the turn of the 16th century, Tuscan (prized since the 14th century because of the prestige conferred on it by its great writers) became the literary language of the peninsula.

However in Naples and throughout the kingdom, Latin remained the language of choice among humanists, although the language of the occupier was sometimes used as well (the 1352 statutes of the Order of the Knights of the Knot ▲ *191* bear witness, for instance, to the use of French). Texts of a practical nature were rarely produced in the vernacular, although such works were common in Italy under the Communes, owing to the complexity of current affairs. Literary texts were also rare. In the interim, while awaiting a "national" written language, the tendency was to avoid the more pronounced and strictly local dialectical forms. This was to remain the case until the mid-15th century.

Sul ma_re luccica l'astro d'ar_gen_to, pla_ci_da è

COMPETING LANGUAGES

COMPETING LANGUAGES

During the second half of the 15th century, Naples actively participated in the three simultaneous and parallel trends of the moment: a return to Latin by the humanists; the search for a poetry of popular inspiration (rich, for example, in dialectical forms) and the gradual adoption of the Tuscan model.

NEAPOLITAN HUMANISM

While Antonio Beccadelli, called "il Panormita" (1394–1471) is recognized as the founder of the humanist school in Naples, his friend and follower Giovanni Pontano (1426–1503), who established the Neapolitan academy, remains the finest representative of Neapolitan humanism. A confidant of the king, attached to the chancellery then to the state secretariat, Pontano produced a body of work entirely in Latin, in which treaties and philosophical discourses stand alongside poems that are largely inspired by the city of Naples, his adopted home.

GENTLEMEN'S POETRY

Inside a select coterie which, as in Florence, revolved around the prince (but which, in Naples, produced less of real consequence) was created a poetry that was popular in tone and inspired by dialectical forms.

LITERARY NARRATIVES

Masuccio Salernitano (c. 1410–75) wrote his *Novellino*, a collection of short stories, in polished Neapolitan but also included Tuscanisms; the work took Boccaccio's *Decameron* as its literary and linguistic model. Jacopo Sannazaro (1457–1530) published *Arcadia*, a pastoral novel that came out in seventy different editions during the 16th century, and demonstrated the triumph of Tuscan literature, since any Neapolitan turns of phrase were removed between the first and final editions.

NEAPOLITAN BECOMES ESTABLISHED

The awareness that a common literary language now existed enabled works in dialect to flourish from the 16th century onward. Standing out against the unifying language, vernacular writing could now seize upon the possibilities of dialect. The latter rapidly caught on in comedy, where it could produce unique characters and lend itself to an easy humor. Plays, poems, tragi-comedies, satires and parodies – the uses of dialect were nonetheless well defined. Literature written in dialect experienced two high points in the peninsula: one, in the 17th century, the other during the late 19th and early 20th centuries. Each time, Naples was to experience a writer of great talent. Between these two "moments", however, decades of new ideas elapsed.

NEAPOLITAN LITERATURE

Neapolitan literature of the 17th century was in some respects "like a masked ball, where the guests dress up as peasants" (Migliorini). It mainly produced works in verse, such as the poems by Giulio Cesare Cortese (1575–1627) and Giambattista Basile (1575–1632). The latter figure was best known as the author of *Lo Cunto de li Cunti o Pentamerone* (published in 1636), a collection of fifty popular stories in

literary form. This first great Neapolitan work inspired the fables of Tieck, the Brothers Grimm and Perrault, and was translated into Italian by Benedetto Croce. Two centuries later, Neapolitan literature was to thrive again with Naturalism. The poet Salvatore di Giacomo (1860–1934) depicted the world of the "small people" and cast a sympathetic gaze, tinged with humor and melancholy, over his native town.

BAROQUE ACHIEVEMENTS

VERBAL VIRTUOSITY
The principal literary current of the 17th century, called "Marinism", derives its name from a Neapolitan writer, Giovan Battista Marino, known as Cavalier Marino (1569–1625), whose most important work was the *Adone*. This movement, the most vivid expression of the Baroque in literature, laid emphasis on musicality, inventiveness and the skill of the poet, and carried verbal

virtuosity to its heights. Language was manipulated playfully, rather like an optical instrument that produces unexpected changes of perspective. In passages where literal and metaphorical meanings of words were strangely combined, the different levels of reality

were deliberately confused. Thus objective points of reference were dispensed with in favor of a literary genre whose sole aim was to dazzle the reader.

THEATRICAL AND VOCAL "TOURS DE FORCE"
From the mid-17th century, Neapolitan opera dominated Europe for the next hundred years. *Opera seria* took center stage, and its great masters were Alessandro Scarlatti (1659–1725) and the theoretician Metastase. Most often based on a

mythological or historical tale of intrigue, *opera seria* was characterized by alternate *recitativi secchi* (recitatives with a simple piano accompaniment) that would move the plot forward, and *arias* (*arie da capo*) in which a particular sentiment would be expressed. These *arias*, holding the normally inattentive audiences in raptures, tended to become mere pretexts for showing off the voice, allowing generations of singers to display their virtuosity. First among them were the *castrati*. *Castrati* received exceptional training in Naples' four conservatories, from which the greatest names of the 18th century were to emerge (Matteuccio, Gizziella, Farinelli, Caffarelli). Excelling in vocal "pirouettes" and adored by the town, *castrati* (who played all the roles, including the female ones) used these *arias* to improvise the most spectacular embellishments.

COMEDY AND TRAGEDY

Naples was also the birthplace of *opera buffa*, which grew out of *opera seria*. In order to provide a moment of relief, intervals were enlivened with dramatic interludes. Originally composed of ballets, the *intermezzo* was later to look to old Italian popular farces for inspiration, and to borrow its characters from the *commedia dell'arte*. With these totally unconnected entertainments, comedy began to punctuate the serious scenes. These *intermezzi* were soon to become completely independent forms of entertainment. Initially composed of situation comedies, with quid pro quos and the ubiquitous masks, *opera buffa* was to evolve alongside the developments in comic literature, led by Goldoni (author of a dozen librettos, set to music by Galuppi) to end up being a comedy of characters. The first masterpiece of the genre, *La Serva Padrona* by Pergolese, was to spark the "buffoons' quarrel" in Paris, and *opera buffa* was seen by the court as a vehicle for subversive bourgeois impulses. It was

hardly surprising that the characters were thereafter seen as mouthpieces, as long as the bourgeoisie remained subjects of public interest.

"LI CUNTI", OR FAIRY TALES

Only fifty years ago in the Campanian hinterland, the best storytellers would still gather on the day after Epiphany to exercise their talents for the next ten days and nights. The *cunto* is one of the chief vehicles of Naples' language, culture and tradition. While its main theme does not change, it can be lengthened or shortened, thus adapting itself to both time and place. Giambattista Basile (17th century) ● *44* was the first to record this oral tradition. In the 20th century, its interpreters include Italo Calvino, Michele Rak and Roberto de Simone, who summed up the principal threads of its narrative structure: dominating the *cunto* (and the native imagination) is the mother, or *mamma,* in various guises (ogress, dragon and siren, mother of the seven winds, mother of lightening and of thunder). She is benevolent, but inhuman; while she slays her children, she can also be their victim.

THE ANCIENT PHILOSOPHERS

Between 70 and 40 BC a Neapolitan tradition of philosophical enquiry, inspired by Epicurus, grew up. Its chief exponents were two philosophers of Syrian origin, Philodemus and Siron. Philodemus, on his arrival in Italy, gained the friendship and protection of Pison, father-in-law of Caesar. He followed his patron on numerous military campaigns before settling down in his magnificent villa at Herculaneum ▲ 272, where he founded an important library of philosophical works. The papyrus remains that have been discovered there are a testament to his studies of inductive

logic, theology, musical appreciation and literature. Cicero, his friend and contemporary, who settled at Pozzuoli, has left us with a record of the man: his personality, his role as philosopher, and the extremely unfortunate influence of his disciple Pison. Siron, on the other hand, was a man of integrity and severity. "We guide our sails toward the ports of happiness, to seek out

the learned lessons of the great Siron, and thus we will rid life of all anxiety": so wrote Virgil, after abandoning his studies of rhetoric to join the master in Naples. He lived in Siron's house after his death, which then became known as the "School of Virgil", after he transformed it into a meeting place for thinkers and poets, frequented, among others, by Horace.

MODERN AND CONTEMPORARY PHILOSOPHY

During the Middle Ages philosophical studies flourished in the north at the universities of Bologna and Padua, and in the south at the court of Frederick II at Palermo. While the south may boast an uninterrupted tradition of great thinkers, from Thomas Aquinas (1228–74) to Giordano Bruno (1548–1600) and Tommaso Campanella (1568–1639), it was not until the late 17th century that Naples played a major role in international philosophical terms: with his *Scienza Nuova*, Giambattista

Vico (1668–1744) initiated a veritable revolution in the concept of history, with his theory of *corsi* and *ricorsi* as recurring cycles of events. He is considered to be the forefather of historiography and the philosophy of history; his legacy was to influence the centuries to come. Neapolitan philosophy reemerged in the 19th century under Benedetto Croce (1866–1952), historian, philosopher and politician, who managed to combine all these disciplines with everyday existence. The

"historicism" of Croce had a major impact in both Europe and America where, even today, numerous organizations still use his name and ideas. Naples is still extremely active within the discipline of philosophy. For around twenty years now, the Italian Center of Philosophical Studies at the *palazzo* Serra di Cassano ▲ 188 has researched and disseminated philosophical thought with single-minded application, an endeavor that has been referred to as "unsurpassed world-wide".

ARTS AND TRADITIONS

● FESTIVALS OF THE BAY OF NAPLES

Festivals in the Bay of Naples, whether secular or religious, often have ancient origins and are occasionally colored by features deriving from pagan cults. As in classical times, festivals are a time of heady elation, joy and collective "letting off steam", an opportunity for Naples to forget all her problems. The festival is also a kind of street theater in which the crowd takes the principal role; even religious festivals have a theatrical flavor. Their sacred quality is lost in the hubbub and fireworks, while at every turn "lucky stalls" offer all sorts of treats, whose smells mingle with the odor of incense, burned for purification and luck.

END OF YEAR FESTIVALS

The end of the year is animated by the sound of bagpipes (*zampogne)* and the crackle of firecrackers and fireworks set off by the townspeople. Each family is preoccupied with its nativity crib, while the town is filled with stalls laden with honey cakes, fish and eels (*capitoni*). At every street corner can be found the *tronari*, or firecracker-sellers (left).

FEAST OF THE MADONNA OF THE ARC

This takes place in the village of Sant'Anastasia at the foot of Vesuvius, in commemoration of a 16th-century miracle. According to this, a painted Virgin in a fresco bled when an exasperated pall-mall player hit her with his ball. Since then, on every Easter Monday bare-footed men, known as *fujenti*, run through the streets asking for alms. The holy image is then carried in procession and, in earlier times, was followed by elaborately decorated floats. The crowd finally disperses into the countryside, where pagan bacchanalia are enacted to the sound of cymbals and castanets.

THE FESTIVAL OF PIEDIGROTTA

Celebrated on September 8 (the Virgin's birth), this festival was instituted in the middle of the 18th century by Charles III of Bourbon. In a grand procession, the court paraded along the Riviera di Chiaia to the Piedigrotta church ▲ *191*, which at that time was a simple sanctuary for fishermen and sailors. Before long the streets of Chiatamone, Santa Lucia and Toledo were animated with improvised dances (tarantellas, in particular) and covered with stalls and kiosks. Pasteboard floats appeared in the 19th century. Thus Piedigrotta, ostensibly a Christian festival, became the carnival of Naples; it was also the setting for a song contest. One of the high points of the Neapolitan calendar, the festival has sunk into oblivion.

LA TRIBUNA
illustrata

LA TRADIZIONALE FESTA DI PIEDIGROTTA A NAPOLI

GOOD FRIDAY AT PROCIDA

Behind a veiled statue of the dead Christ assembles a procession of men in the costume of Roman centurions, and children dressed in black and gold, their faces made up to represent angels of death. Hooded penitents follow the cortege, in a funerary rite dating back to the 16th century. The procession breaks up at the port, in front of a representation of the Tomb, in which flowers and wheat (symbolizing the Resurrection) are placed.

49

The best insight into the Neapolitan character is provided by its musical folklore, with its tradition, as rich as it is ancient, of songs, ballads and dances. These are often difficult to date, and have survived either because they conveyed a universal emotion, or because talented intellectuals raised them to the level of an art form. Neapolitan musical tradition has clearly been influenced by its contact with other cultures. Two significant features illustrate its popular origins: an anonymous authorship, and a choral dimension capable of reproducing the melodies, gestures, cries and colors of everyday life. And while Pulcinella is the chief symbol of Naples, the tarantella is the dance that officially represents the town.

THE TARANTELLA

Legend has it that this was created by the Graces in order to seduce Ulysses after his recent escape from the spell of the sirens' song. The focus of the dance is a couple engaged in an amorous debate, around which evolves a choir of dancers, accompanied by guitars and tambourines, who mark its rhythms with castanets. The effect is one of extreme lightness and grace.

THE "NDREZZATE"

These songs, for which the performers carry swords and batons, probably originated in the propitiatory fertility rites of classical times, celebrated in the spring. One of the most famous of these takes place at Ischia on the Monday before Easter.

TRADITIONAL DANCES

The TURKS' DANCE, performed at carnival time, involves five or six men dressed as Turks engaging in a grotesque rigmarole around a sultana, to the tribal beat of a tambourine. During the "Trescone" on Capri, four (or eight) couples dance into a circle by way of some superb formations.

'o Sole Mio!

THE INSTRUMENTS

Besides the tambourine, guitar and mandolin, four other instruments featured prominently: the *siscariello*, a kind of flute made out of elder; the *sectavaiasse*, composed of split canes to emit a piercing noise; the *triccaballacco*, a wooden instrument with two hammers on the side, which would hit a fixed hammer in the middle; and, finally, the *nacchere* (castanets).

THE "SONG"

The *iesco sole*, the song of the lavender ladies of the Vomero ▲ *184,* is the oldest known popular Neapolitan song (dating from the early 13th century). The *villanelle* (16th century), in dialect and accompanied by rudimentary instruments marking a basic beat, would often celebrate love and feminine beauty. The *massicce* songs were built around a simple thread, into which were woven numerous digressions.

SONGS AND MUSIC

In 1839 the song festival of Piedigrotta ● *49* presented "Te Voglio Bene Assaje", by Raffaele Sacco and apparently set to music by Donizetti, which became instantly famous. Since the end of the 19th century, with, notably, "O Sole Mio" (Giovanni Capurro, 1859–1920), "Torna a Surriento" (Giambattista de Curtis, 1860–1904) and "Funiculì-funiculà" ● *6* (1881, music by Schoenberg), Neapolitan song has traveled the world, thanks, in the main, to Enrico Caruso.

"ZINGARI". *Zingari*, a sort of "tragic fable", is one of the most important works by Roberto Viviani. Its most dramatic passages are, as in nearly all his comedies, emphasized by music and songs composed by the author.

ROBERTO DE SIMONE. He takes his inspiration from folklore and popular music. In his plays, both actor and spectator participate in a magical experience, from which they emerge transformed, as after the performance of a rite.

"Naples," it is often said, "is a theater." It would be more accurate to say "the theater is Naples," since today Italian theater is based in Naples. The main protagonist in the comedies of Eduardo Scarpetta, Raffaele Viviani, Eduardo de Filippo and Roberto de Simone (and the leading player in the highly popular *sceneggiate*) is, after all, Naples herself. This is so even when the theater tries to loosen those visceral ties that traditionally bind it to the town, and the attention of the spectator shifts to the relationship between gesture, music and words; that is, between Naples and its language.

PULCINELLA
The origin of this mask is uncertain and hotly debated. Some claim that it dates back to the "Maccus" of classical theater, a typical figure from the ancient Atellan farces, which were improvised performances introduced to Rome by Oscan theater. Others, such as Benedetto Croce, believe that Pulcinella was conceived in 1600, and that the name is derived from a certain Puccio d'Aniello.

> ## "I WANTED TO SHOW NAPLES AS SHE REALLY IS IN MY PLAYS: A DREAM OF INCOMPARABLE BEAUTY."
> RAFFAELE VIVIANI

"MASANIELLO". The reenactment of a historical scene dear to the Neapolitans ● 38, along with the creation of a mobile stage set onto which the public is invited, have made this spectacle an unforgettable event in the town's collective consciousness.

ENZO MOSCATO. Moscato, a major figure in contemporary drama, working on one of his best-known pieces, *Rasoi* (1991). Moscato's work constantly pushes the boundaries of the medium, in the Neapolitan theater, in his use of both gesture and language.

THE CONTRADICTIONS OF THE NEAPOLITAN SOUL
Simultaneously base and heroic, obscene and romantic, roguish, chaotic and philosophical, Pulcinella is all and nothing. Oppressed victim, he is above all his own worst enemy. Thus comedy is his only weapon.

RAFFAELE VIVIANI (1888–1950)
This actor-playwright is one of the greatest Neapolitan dramatists of this century. The common populace of the streets, whom he observes with affection and detachment, anger and irony, is the chief protagonist in his plays. Less well known than Eduardo de Filippo (because of the Brechtian motifs in his comedies and his use of dialect), he was ostracized by Fascism.

EDUARDO DE FILIPPO (1900–84)
Coming from the streets, he reestablished the Neapolitan theater within a tradition which, during the 19th century, had known its greatest interpreters in Antonio Petito and Eduardo Scarpetta. De Filippo was not interested in the "street" people who were dear to Viviani; instead, he slid into the houses and domestic milieu of the petite bourgeoisie. *Questi Fantasmi, Le Voci di Dentro* and *Filomena Marturano* are among his most celebrated works. Gifted with an incomparable talent as an actor, Eduardo rendered his comedies and masques unique in theaters worldwide.

● BELIEFS AND SUPERSTITIONS

PER EVITARE :
SPIACEVOLI JETTATURE, O
'RINFRESCHI' PER I TUOI MORTI.
TI CONSIGLIAMO : DI NON
SOSTARE IN QUEST'ANGOLO,
CONCEDERAI LA POSSIBILITA'
DEL PASSAGGIO VETTURE
NEL PALAZZO DI FRONTE..
EGL'INTERESSI SI RINGRAZIA

Beliefs and superstitions are still very much alive, and can be seen in the way Neapolitans from all walks of life go about their daily business. The slightest incident is seen as a good or bad omen. A familiar panoply of sayings, ritual gestures and charms is resorted to each day as a way of attracting or repulsing benevolent or evil occult influences. These customs are rooted in a past some two thousand years old: even Greek and Latin authors evoked some of these beliefs. But although the poet Lucretius refined the distinction between *religio* and *superstitio* as far back as classical times, Neapolitans have always confused the sacred and the profane.

THE CASTER OF SPELLS
The *jettatore* is the familiar figure of bad luck, an encounter with whom spells the most appalling misfortunes. Those who believe they have encountered a "spell caster" instinctively attempt to ward off the evil spirit by touching iron, or, more usually, a tiny horn of gold, silver or coral; they may "make horns" by pointing the index and forefinger toward the suspect, with the rest of the hand curled inward.

THE "MONACELLO"
The *monacello* is the spirit of the house, and most probably dates back to the cult of the Lares (above), the domestic spirits of the Roman household. Assuming the traits of a mischievous little boy who haunts the house, he occasionally appears among mortals. If he is dressed in white, he brings good luck; if dressed in red, he is a harbinger of misfortune.

THE EVIL EYE
The *malocchio* is the evil influence that springs from "envying" another. Envy, in this sense, is rooted in the etymological meaning of *invidiare*: to "pierce with one's glance" and, by extension, to cast an evil spell. To ward off the evil eye, you need only to touch a "horn" or perform a combination of ritual gestures, exorcising chants and signs of the cross that illustrate the gray area between magical customs and religious practices.

LOTTO AND THE SYMBOLISM OF NUMBERS

The game of lotto is a very old popular tradition. It is related to a belief in the symbolic power of dreams which, when translated into the language of numbers, allows one to "encode" and "decode" their images. This exercise is often a public event.

Incidents and misfortunes may be perceived by an entire community as supernaturally significant, and will then be transposed into numbers after lengthy and detailed discussion. This language of numbers has its own handbook, called the *smorfia*.

THE NEAPOLITAN CRIB

The crib scene appeared in Naples during the 14th century, evolving from the Nativity performances of Saint Francis of Assisi. In keeping with the Franciscan influence, emphasis fell on the humility and holiness of the Nativity, but from the 16th century onward, and particularly in the 17th century, decorative considerations gained supremacy over the religious message. The holy family were joined by shepherds, then the procession of the three kings, while all around a hilly landscape began to take shape. With the 18th-century taste for grand spectacles, the tendency toward heightened realism and increasingly complex scene constructions reached its peak. The crib scene, now wholly theatrical in concept, was populated by minor characters lifted straight from the streets, the port and surrounding countryside.

Great artists, such as Giuseppe Sammartino, who produced the *Veiled Christ* ▲ 144 in the Sansevero chapel, created and signed figures and miniatures for cribs.

FACES OF MORTALS AND FACES OF ANGELS
The skill of the figurine artists (*figurari*) was well suited to the expressive rendering of the common people, although at times this bordered on the grotesque. In contrast to this rather one-sided naturalism, the representation of saints, angels and figures of the aristocracy gave rise to studied, elegant poses and beautiful, idealized faces.

MINIATURES

From the 18th century to the early 19th century, the crib scene enjoyed a golden age that produced an entire craft devoted to miniaturization. Tools, kitchen utensils and musical instruments were all reproduced in extraordinary miniature detail. The creation, in wax, of minuscule baskets of fruits gave rise to fierce competition between craftsmen to achieve perfection.

SCENES FROM DAILY LIFE

From the 18th century onward, the Nativity cave no longer dominated the crib scene. Instead, it became just one element within a broader landscape in which the Neapolitan populace was brought to the fore. Butcher, chimney-sweep, fruit seller, blind man and cripple populated a scene inspired by the streets of Naples and the surrounding countryside. Increasingly, the designs incorporated self-contained "tableaux", each of which represented a scene from everyday life such as the fish market, *osteria*, and bands of itinerant musicians. The crib scene gained in popular realism what it lost in religious flavor.

Survival: this simple precept has, for centuries, driven the people of Naples to invent thousands of small jobs and trades. All kinds of services offered to the passer-by, together with impromptu performances, have animated the streets of this town for over two thousand years. While most of these small trades once existed in every preindustrial European capital, in Naples they still survive, and sum up the art of "scraping by" intrinsic to the Neapolitan mentality. Naples has thus preserved its original character, inherited from its ancient Greek past. For it is still the market town, where anything can be bought and sold on a street corner, and the town of street-theater, where at every crossroads an imaginative scene is being improvised.

THE WATER-CARRIER

The water-carrier is an ancient Neapolitan figure. Like his partner-in-trade the sorbet-seller, he would offer passers-by welcome refreshment in the stifling heat of the Neapolitan summer. The water was kept in terracotta flagons, known as *mummare*. Lemon, orange or elderberry juice would sometimes be added to it.

THE RAG MAN
Trading in all types of "rag and bone", swapping second-hand goods for old cloth, the Neapolitan rag man was the mouthpiece of cynical philosophy, reminding the people that they came from dust and would return to dust. A common figure in the last century, he has today all but disappeared.

THE OCTOPUS SELLER
Neapolitans (above all, the women) selling freshly caught octopus cooked in its juice, once crowded elbow to elbow in front of Santa Lucia ▲ *189*, and their pots would clutter up the sidewalk of Via Caracciola. Even today there are still a few octopus-broth sellers in the working-class district of Porta Capuana ▲ *157*.

A MARKET TOWN
Between the 17th and 19th centuries the small trades gradually took over the squares and streets of the town. Today, the street sellers (cigarette sellers, especially) still display their wares on makeshift stalls, giving certain districts a "market town" appearance.

THE TRAVELING STORYTELLER
This street-poet, accompanying his tales with song in the manner of the ancient minstrels, brought the great "chansons de geste" borrowed from Ariosto or Tasso to the imagination of a populace hungry for such epic tales. In the 19th century the street storyteller was replaced by the organ grinder.

● "WHITE" ART: PASTA AND PIZZA

Mozzarella

Water, flour and Neapolitan sunshine: these are the ingredients that go into the age-old art of pasta-making. This magical combination was, from the 19th century up until World War Two, at the root of an unprecedented economic boom. But when the sun and the air of Vesuvius were replaced by mechanized methods of drying and aeration, the weight of competition from factories in the north became unchallengeable. The history of pasta-making is essentially a family affair, with its jealously guarded secrets and recipes carefully passed on. It has led to such inventions as short and hollow pastas, and to the extraordinary variety of shapes which are now, with due pride and recognition, produced by the large manufacturing brands.

PIZZA
While it is far from certain whether pizza comes from Naples, it is an undoubted fact that it developed here, and from here it set out to conquer the palates of the world. The famous "Margherita", with its red, white and green Italian colors (tomatoes, mozzarella and basil), was created by the Neapolitans in honor of Queen Margaret of Savoy.

PASTA: A QUESTION OF WHEAT
The hard wheat from Russia is superior in quality and cheaper than Italian wheat. It was exempted from customs taxes by central government as it was essential to have wheat that was strong and free from mold. The grain was cut in order to check that its canes were straight and clean. It was then placed in the cylinder to be weighed, and to determine its weight in relation to its density.

"A *pastaio* must also be . . . an astronomer and a meteorologist; he must know the stars and the phases of the moon, the air pressure – but without a barometer – and the humidity levels – but without a hygrometer." (Maria Orsini Natale, *Francesca e Nunziata*).

THE DRYING PROCESS
● *3*
The pasta was placed on bamboo canes and carried outside for the first stage of the drying process. Once it had hardened, it was left in a cold room, where its residual humidity would rise to the surface. It was then transferred to a well-aired place for the last stage of the drying process, which was gradual and lengthy.

METHODS AND UTENSILS
Originally, the process was essentially manual. The pasta was kneaded, cut into strips or pieces, then worked with the fingers or with basic utensils. Technical advances allowed the whole process to be mechanized, including the drying. Thanks to mangles and presses, hollow pastas (*rigatone*, *zito*) could be produced, as well as long pastas (such as *vermicelli*, a type of spaghetti). From this time on, the industrial north took over the market, bankrupting the business of the south.

Cracked wheat, the basic ingredient in *pastiera*, is common to all the countries of the Mediterranean basin (Turkey, Lebanon and other regions of the Near East), and finds its way into numerous sweet and savory dishes. Wheat takes on highly symbolic significance at Easter; in the days leading up to its celebration, tiny pots of growing wheat are to be found in all the churches of the region. *Pastiera* is made in extremely large quantities, to be shared around each member of the family during the Easter festivities. It seems that the origins of this recipe date back to classical times, and can be linked with pagan celebrations of springtime.

1. The night before, mix the ricotta and the sugar. Place in a refrigerator overnight.

2. Soak the bulgar (cracked wheat) in water. When it has swollen, measure 2½ cups of (strained) bulgar. Over the heat, mix this paste with the milk, candied zests and a pinch of salt.

3. Cook for around 1 hour, until a creamy consistency is achieved. Then add a ⅓ cup of lard, the vanilla clove, the cinnamon and orange flower water. Add the ricotta to the mixture and leave to stand for about 10 minutes.

4. Add the 5 egg yolks together with 5 tsps of sugar and, lastly, the 5 whipped egg whites.

INGREDIENTS
Serves 12:
2¼ cups ricotta, 2 cups sugar,
1½ cups bulgar wheat, water,
25 floz milk, candied zests of
lemon, citron, squash and
grated orange, salt, ⅓ cup
lard, 1 vanilla clove, a small
amount of cinnamon, a small
quantity of orange flower
water, 5 eggs
FOR THE SHORTCRUST
PASTRY:
3½ cups flour, ⅔ cup lard,
2 eggs, ½ cup sugar, candied
zest of grated lemon

5. Prepare the shortcrust pastry by mixing the flour, lard, whole eggs, sugar and candied zest of grated lemon.

6. Knead the dough and leave to stand in the refrigerator for about 1 hour.

7. Roll out the pastry (keep a little to one side for the decoration) and arrange it in a tin approximately 14 inches across and 2 inches deep.

8. Spread the ricotta mixture. Make a lattice pattern on top with strips of shortcrust pastry.

9. Cook for 30 minutes in an oven at 350°F.

● SPECIALTIES

LUCKY CHARM
In a world where superstitions and spells abound, amulets are essential. They are often made of coral, most commonly in the shape of a horn, but can also be in the form of a hunchbacked man or a horseshoe . . . or a combination of all three.

COFFEE
What do Neapolitans take with them when they leave their home town? Coffee. Because of the refined torrefaction process, its aroma is unparalleled. The Neapolitan *cafetière* gives it its fullest flavor.

PASTRIES AND MOZZARELLA
Naples has a well-established pastry-making reputation. The *babà* and the *sfogliatelle* are best known, but a thousand other equally delicious pastries also exist. Mozzarella, a cheese made from buffalo milk (often mixed with cow's milk), can be found at Sorrento in a plaited form.

NEWSPAPERS
Il Giornale di Napoli, *Il Mattino* and *La Città* are the main newspaper titles in Naples, but several national dailies also have a special Neapolitan edition.

CORAL
Whether fashioned into necklaces, cameos, horns or earrings, coral is traditionally crafted at Torre del Greco ▲ 220.

REGIONAL WINES FROM AROUND NAPLES
The *Lacrima Christi*, from the vineyards of Vesuvius, is the best known, but Ischia and Capri also produce reputable varieties.

ARCHITECTURE

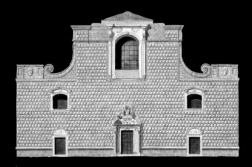

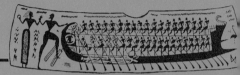

Terracotta fragment representing a Greek vessel.

Fueled by a desire to conquer new territory, or perhaps fleeing the political upheavals that were devastating their own country, Greeks began to settle along the coast plain of the "Great Mountain", as the Delphic Oracle had dictated. Grouped under the name Magna Graecia, the colonies that they founded in southern Italy and Sicily between the 8th and 6th centuries BC preserved many of the features of their mother-city (laws, urban layout), while remaining fully independent.

A

B

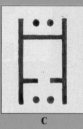

C

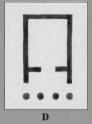

D

EVOLUTION OF THE PLAN
Religious architecture in the 7th century BC was characterized by the Doric style. Clean and strong, it aptly reflected the pioneering colonists, thirsty for novelty. The temple, originally made of wood, acquired an incontestable originality with stone, and gave rise to countless variations of the basic typology.

A. MYCENAEAN MEGARON
B. WITH SINGLE ANTAE
C. WITH DOUBLE ANTAE
D. PROSTYLE
E. AMPHIPROSTYLE
F. PERISTYLE

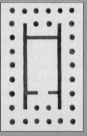

E (far left)
F (left)

THE GREEK TEMPLE ("TEMPLE OF NEPTUNE", PAESTUM ▲ 299)

The Greek temple, rectangular in plan, was surrounded by a portico (1). An antechamber, or *pronaos* (2) opened into the *cella* (3), where the deity was believed to abide and its statue was kept; the public was excluded. The offerings and treasure were stored in a room at the rear (the *opisthodomos*, 4). The temple stood on a stylobate (5). Between 16 and 20 flutes in sharp relief decorated the shaft of the columns (6). The central portion formed a definite *entasis* (outward curve), then, rising, was tapered, to compensate for the fact that from afar columns seem thinner in the middle. The capital (7) was composed of a circular echinus and square abacus. The entablature (8) was decorated with metopes (9) and triglyphs (10), and rested on the architrave (11). Acroteria adorned the roof corners and the apex of the pediment (12), which had a sculpted tympanum. Antefixes (13) surrounded the whole of the roof.

COLONIES ● 28

1. Naples ▲ *138, 188*
Cumae ▲ *208*
Ischia ▲ *210*
Pozzuoli ▲ *200*
2. Paestum ▲ *296*

3. Sybaris
4. Syracuse
5. Naxos
6. Messina
7. Croton

FOUNDING COUNTRIES AND CITY-STATES

A. Athens
B. Sparta
C. Samos

D. Cumae
E. Euboea
F. Chalcedon

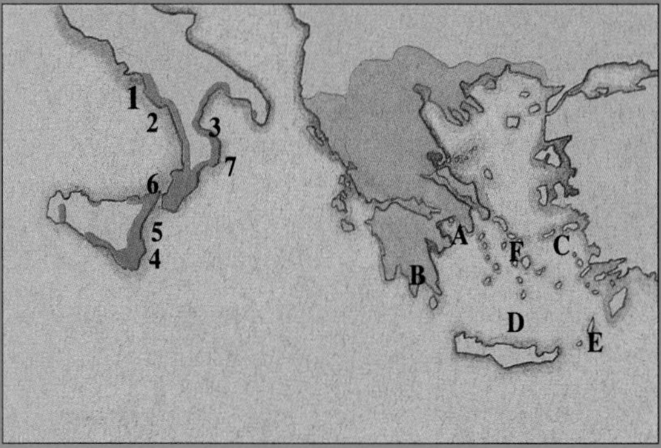

GREEK COLONIZATION

Plato believed that this was provoked by the political conflicts that were troubling Greece. According to Aristotle, it was linked to the extension of property-owning rights. Thucydides explained it within the context of the end of the Trojan War, and returning heroes having to confront usurpers at home.

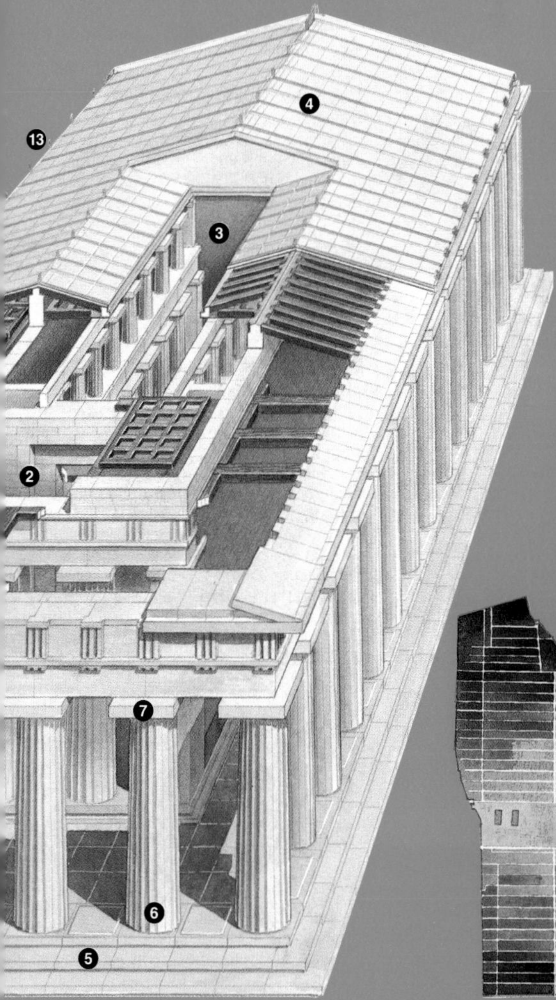

THE GREEK CITY

The city was planned as a regular grid of main streets: the *plateiai*, which ran from north to south; and the *stenopoi*, which ran from east to west. These divided the area into lots. The town was comprised of three zones: private areas, with different-sized residential buildings; sacred areas, characterized by the space around the temples, themselves often prominently sited; and public areas, used for political meetings and as a gathering place for the citizens (the *agora* to the Greeks; the forum to the Romans).

67

The curved rhythms of Roman arches and vaults replaced the horizontal and vertical divisions of Greek architecture. The volcanic region around Vesuvius offered a wide range of specialized building materials, namely tufas and *pozzolana*. Marble, used for decoration, was imported from neighboring or distant provinces. From the simple method of assembling bricks without mortar (*opus quadratum*), or with a rubble fill (*caementicium*), Roman builders developed a facing technique that was both cheaper and allowed for greater freedom.

1

VOLCANIC ROCKS
TUFA (**1–2**), a soft stone, whose color varies from yellow to black; peperino is ash-gray in color.

2

POZZOLANA (**3**) is a siliceous sand, named after Pozzuoli. It was used to make a highly resistant waterproof mortar.

3

MARBLE
Used primarily for facing, owing to its elevated cost. Its range of color made it a sought-after decorative material.

4

SARNO "LIMESTONE"
This tough, coarse-grained travertine conglomerate (4) of sediments from the Sarno area hardens when exposed to air.

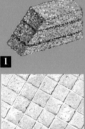

1

2

3

4

5

6

7

DIFFERENT BONDS
During the 2nd century BC, buildings were made of *opus caementicium* (stones and tufa rubble mixed with mortar, **1**), occasionally faced with tufa blocks (**2**). In the latter half of the century, the more refined *opus incertum* (**3**) was used, and the walls left

bare. During the 1st century BC stone was cut into regular-shaped blocks, producing *opus quasi reticulatum* (**4**). *Opus reticulatum* (**5**), smoother still, was widely adopted during the second half of the century. *Opus mixtum* (tufa and brick, **6**) was used to reinforce corners.

"OPUS CRATICIUM"
This consists of a wooden frame filled with stones and mortar. The finest example can be found at Herculaneum ▲ 275.

THE SUPPORT
Vaults and arches were built over solid wooden frames that formed a scaffold into which cement could be directly poured.

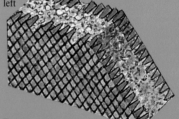

FACING
This masonry technique consisted of creating two walls of stone or brick. The gap between them was then closed with a fill of rubble mixed with lime mortar.

1 **2** **3**

BRICK

The Romans were the first to use baked brick (**1–2**) extensively. Brick was used to build *opus latericium* (**3**) walls, pavements (*opus spicatum*) and architectonic devices such as vaults and arches.

TERRACOTTA

Its impermeability made it ideal for use in water piping systems.

COLUMNS

Mostly these were made of brick, and then coated with stucco. Columns made of marble, a costly material, were most frequently used for public projects or in homes belonging to the very wealthy.

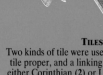

TILES

Two kinds of tile were used: the *tegula* (**1**), the tile proper, and a linking tile which could be either Corinthian (**2**) or Laconian (**3**) in style. Toward the end of the Roman era, Gaul ceased to manufacture the *tegula*, and retained only its cone-shaped counterpart, the "canal tile", or "Roman tile".

"OPUS SECTILE"

This geometric pattern of motifs in polychromed marble was used to decorate floors and walls. Herculaneum is home to some magnificent examples.

1 **2** **3** **4**

PLASTER AND FRESCO

The wall surface (**1**) usually received a first coat of coarse sand mixed with lime (**2**), striated to assist the application of a second, finer coat (**3**). This, once smooth, would in turn receive a final coat, often composed of pure lime, which would be carefully smoothed over. This layer, while still wet, would form a surface for the fresco pigments (**4**) ● *76*.

MOSAICS

TESSERAE

Opus tesselatum, a fairly simple technique, involved making a pattern using tiny cubes (tesserae) of stone, marble, terracotta or colored glass pastes. The more complex *opus vermiculatum* technique used smaller pieces.

Mosaics were essentially a floor decoration, but were also used to decorate walls and fountains. The mosaic was produced by glueing the tesserae onto a traced pattern or design. From simple pavings made of shards of terracotta and mortar (*opus signinum* was the most common form) the technique became increasingly refined, culminating in *opus tesselatum* (left), *opus vermiculatum* (right) and *opus sectile*.

69

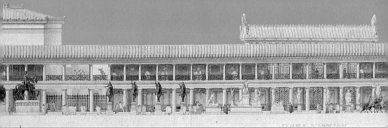

The forum, as the Greek *agora* had been before it, was both a meeting place and the political, economic and social nerve center of the city. Among the great Italic and Roman cities, the Forum at Pompeii ranks as both the most sophisticated and splendid. The principal façades of its buildings were not turned inward toward the square; instead, a continuous two-story colonnade surrounded it, linking the buildings within a unified space. The harmonious volumes and horizontal and vertical emphasis of Greek architecture were succeeded by an architectural concept of space, articulated by façades. The size of a building, whether large or small, was hidden behind the portico: it was only on entering it that its actual dimensions became apparent.

THE BASILICA
This exemplifies the Roman ability to reinvent ancient Etruscan and Greek forms. The word basilica means "royal" in Greek, and was used to describe the *stoa*, or portico, of the Hellenistic palaces. The basilica as a large three-aisled room probably originated in Pompeii, where it was no doubt an enclosed extension of the Forum, replicating its dimensions and colonnade. This was the economic hub of the city, where civil or commercial disputes could be heard.

THE CAPITOL (TEMPLE DEDICATED TO JUPITER, MINERVA AND JUNO)
As the only isolated element within the Forum, it dominated the whole square. To the Etruscan model, with its raised base, the Romans added Greek elements, displaying a marked preference for the Corinthian style. The use of a wall in the *cella* replaced that of a colonnade, which had been purely decorative.

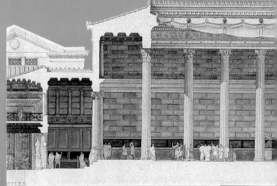

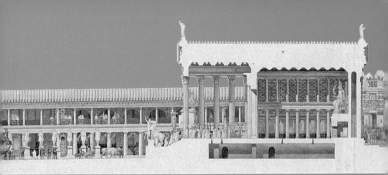

THE PORTICO

This served as an intermediate space between the square and the public buildings. The architecture of the square was conceived as a succession of volumes, ordered according to hierarchical importance and linked by such transitional areas.

THE BUILDINGS OF THE FORUM, ACCORDING TO FUNCTION

◆ RELIGIOUS AND COMMEMORATIVE
1. Capitol
2. Arch of Tiberius
3. Shrine of the Lares (guardian spirits of the city)
4. Temple of Vespasian
5. Temple of Apollo

◆ ADMINISTRATIVE
6. *Comitium* (voting area in which magistrates were elected)
7. Office of the *duumviri*, the senior magistrates of the city (local senate)
8. Office of the *aediles*, and city archives
9. *Curia* (Chamber of the Decurions)

◆ LEGAL AND COMMERCIAL
10. Basilica
11. *Macellum*
12. Building of Eumachia
13. *Mensa ponderaria* (counters into which standard measures were carved)
14. *Forum olitorium* (warehouses and cornmarket)

THE ADMINISTRATION

The magistrates who ran the city assembled in the three buildings along the southern side of the Forum (*tabularium*, *curia* and office of the *aediles*), and in the *comitium*.

BUILDING OF EUMACHIA

The seat of the *fullones* (fullers), or linen bleachers' corporation, was erected by Eumachia, their priestess. It probably also served as a wool market.

"MACELLUM"

This was the central market, with stores opening onto the square and sales counters tucked away inside. The markets of Naples ● *78* and Pozzuoli ▲ *204* are set out the same way.

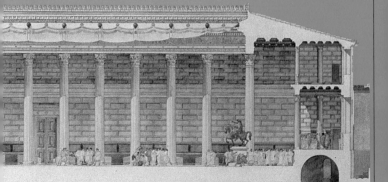

It was in Campania that the theater and amphitheater acquired truly monumental architectural proportions. In Rome, the politics of tradition and social correctness hindered the development of buildings for public entertainment. Until 55 BC amphitheaters were temporary wooden structures. In 154 BC the stone theater erected by Publius was destroyed on the orders of the Senate, who pronounced it "inopportune and contrary to the public interest".

THE THEATER
During the 1st century BC, Campanian architects invented new types of theater, and moved away from the Hellenistic traditions that were still being upheld in most of the other provinces of the Empire. The Greeks had already made use of natural slopes in the hillside to build their *cavea*. The chief innovation of Campanian builders was the creation of a structure that was independent of its topographical situation, and in bringing it inside the urban fabric.

AMPHITHEATER AT POMPEII (BELOW)
Given to the city by two *duumviri* between 76 and 65 BC, this is the best preserved of the ancient amphitheaters.

THE AMPHITHEATER
This structure was called "Spectacula" by the Romans, since it offered them the chance to get a "good view". Its elliptical shape did indeed solve the problem of poor visibility that had been a characteristic of the rectangular-shaped forum, in which wooden tiers had originally had been erected to provide a view of the games. The thirty-five rows of seats in the amphitheater at Pompeii could hold twenty thousand people, who were seated according to a strict social hierarchy.

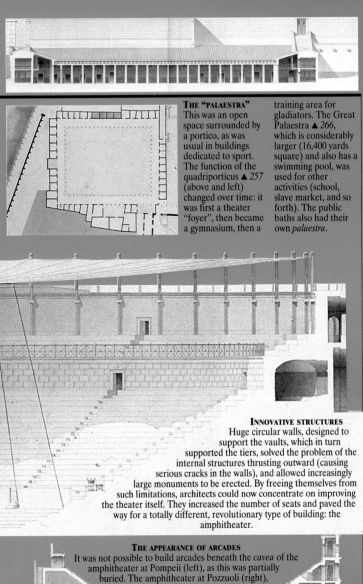

THE "PALAESTRA"

This was an open space surrounded by a portico, as was usual in buildings dedicated to sport. The function of the quadriporticus ▲ *257* (above and left) changed over time: it was first a theater "foyer", then became a gymnasium, then a training area for gladiators. The Great Palaestra ▲ *266*, which is considerably larger (16,400 yards square) and also has a swimming pool, was used for other activities (school, slave market, and so forth). The public baths also had their own *palaestra*.

INNOVATIVE STRUCTURES

Huge circular walls, designed to support the vaults, which in turn supported the tiers, solved the problem of the internal structures thrusting outward (causing serious cracks in the walls), and allowed increasingly large monuments to be erected. By freeing themselves from such limitations, architects could now concentrate on improving the theater itself. They increased the number of seats and paved the way for a totally different, revolutionary type of building: the amphitheater.

THE APPEARANCE OF ARCADES

It was not possible to build arcades beneath the *cavea* of the amphitheater at Pompeii (left), as this was partially buried. The amphitheater at Pozzuoli (right), however, constructed at a later date, was built with them.

THE BATHS

The first baths in Campania were probably built in the 2nd century BC, developing more rapidly here because of the numerous springs of the volcanic terrain. From the outset, thermal architecture made use of vaults built in *opus caementicium*, its flexibility providing unprecedented freedom from the constraints of a classical style of architecture that relied on rhythmic supports (balancing the vertical and horizontal with pilasters and architraves).

● The "Domus"

House of the Faun ▲ 253.

In the Roman cities of Campania, the primary urban residence was the *domus*, or single-unit family residence. It did not evolve into the tall communal apartment block, known as the *insula*, which characterized Rome and Ostia. Based on the Italic model, built around a central atrium, the *domus* grew larger and ever more opulent; its apotheosis was to be the imperial villa, with its vast proportions and leisure areas.

The Italic house
The rooms of the Samnite house ● 29, dating from pre-Roman times (4th and 3rd centuries BC), were arranged around a central atrium (1), originally without an *impluvium*. A wooden door provided access to the *tablinum* (2), and a small garden, or *ortus* (3) was laid out at the rear of the house.

A typical Pompeian house

1. Atrium
2. *Compluvium*, an opening in the roof to let in light. Rain water was collected in the *impluvium* (3).
4. *Cubicula* (bedrooms) and storerooms
5. *Triclinium* (dining room)
6. Kitchen, with a masonry worktop and perhaps a small oven
7. Latrines
8. *Tablinum* (master's room, where the family archives were kept, and dining room for houses without a *triclinium*)
9. *Lararium* (domestic sanctuary)
10. Dining room for entertaining (*oecus*)
11. Peristyle
12. Small private baths (in wealthy households)
13. Summer *triclinium*
14. Summer kitchen

The atrium
This was the heart of the Italic house, and the focus of family life. Its name derives from the color of its walls, which were blackened with soot from the fire kept burning there (*ater* means "black").

74

EVOLUTION OF THE "DOMUS"

This was marked by the extension of the house lengthwise, beyond the *ortus*, by the creation of one or two peristyles and the transformation of the atrium, to which Greek features were added. From being Tuscan in style (small, with no colonnade), it became tetrastyle or hexastyle (with four or six columns), giving it the look of a peristyle.

POMPEIIAN HOUSE

THE PERISTYLE

Between the 2nd and 1st century BC, the *domus* was enriched with a peristyle (from the Greek, meaning "surrounded with columns"). This was now an area enclosed by a colonnade, thus forming a type of interior garden decorated with fountains and statues. It became the focus of domestic life during the summer months.

THE "TRICLINIUM" (DINING ROOM)

Its name derives from the Greek three-seater benches which were copied by the Romans, who would lie on them to eat their meals. There would be three of these, arranged around a table on which the dishes were laid. Certain well-to-do owners also had a summer *triclinium* (below), open to the sky, which would have been arranged in the same manner.

THE "TABLINUM"

Originally the family archives were stored here, and the master received clients and conducted business. It became the chief living room, where important guests were received.

● FRESCOS

Painting and architecture merge within the *unicum* of the *domus*, thereby illustrating the continuous relationship between décor and space in Roman art. Painters, who at the outset simply imitated architectural features, were to invent illusionistic vistas that passed beyond the plane of the wall. From the 3rd century ornamentation became increasingly important, and the painted image freed itself from its architectural constraints, to the point where imaginary buildings would be depicted. The classic division into four historical styles helps highlight the trends within the evolution of Pompeiian painting.

THE FIRST STYLE (150–80 BC)

Sometimes called the "incrustation", or "structural", style, this was characterized by wall paintings in imitation of architectural features and facings. Widely practiced throughout the Hellenistic world, it rapidly caught on in Italy, and formed the basis of Roman painting.

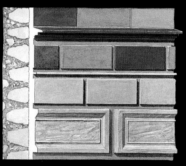

THE SECOND STYLE (1ST CENTURY BC– AD 62)

This style emerged as an original expression of Roman art. Toward the end of the period, the wall space was decorated with mythological scenes. No longer content with imitation, artists now created illusionistic spaces with the aid of perspective.

THE THIRD STYLE (END OF THE REIGN OF AUGUSTUS)

A more decorative, delicate and colorful style. Architectural motifs (frames, baldachins) are somewhat isolated, lacking realistic volumes, and are used purely as ornamental devices within the composition. It was enriched by Egyptian art and culture, and was later referred to as the Egyptian style.

THE FOURTH STYLE (END OF THE REIGN OF NERO–AD 68)

Also referred to as the "ornamental style", this was marked by an extraordinary taste for architectural vistas. Painted scenes redeployed the illusionism that had characterized the Second Style, together with the preciosity of the Third. Architectural forms regained their true volumes, but were used to create fantastic friezes. Now autonomous, they were closely linked to figures, without ever attempting to unbalance the composition.

COLORS

The reds and blacks that characterized painting at the end of Augustus' reign were now succeeded by a richer, brighter palette, dominated by yellows and golds. The Fourth Style became widespread in Campania, where the AD 62 earthquake prompted an extensive program of reconstruction.

● BASILICA OF SAN LORENZO MAGGIORE:
A PALIMPSEST OF THE HISTORY OF NAPLES

Unlike other classical cities of Campania, the ancient town was not abandoned in favor of an alternative site: Neapolis developed into Naples. The town conceals a remarkable series of archeological layers, with San Lorenzo itself constituting a perfect palimpsest of the town's history. On top of Greek foundations, the Romans built their market place, over which, in turn, a paleo-Christian basilica was erected. The latter was succeeded by the finest Gothic church in Naples.

THE FOUNDING LEGEND
The siren Parthenope (above), having failed to seduce Ulysses, was washed up on the shore, where a city was founded in her name. During the period of expansion that marked the 6th century BC, this became Neapolis, meaning "new town".

THE GREEK, THEN ROMAN, MARKET PLACE
The Roman *macellum* ● *71*, raised on a terrace, was built along a *cardo* during the second half of the 1st century BC. Excavations have identified structures some 23 feet below the Gothic church. The rectangular market place had in its center a *tholos*, similar to those found in Pompeii ▲ *251* and Pozzuoli ▲ *204*.

THE PALEO-CHRISTIAN BASILICA
This was erected during the 6th century AD, by the bishop John II, on a three-aisled plan with a semicircular apse. Roman columns and capitals were used, and then later incorporated into the nave of the Gothic church. Birds and flowers stand out among the geometric motifs of the mosaic pavement, with its magnificent sky-blue, orange, yellow and green tesserae.

8

7

4

3

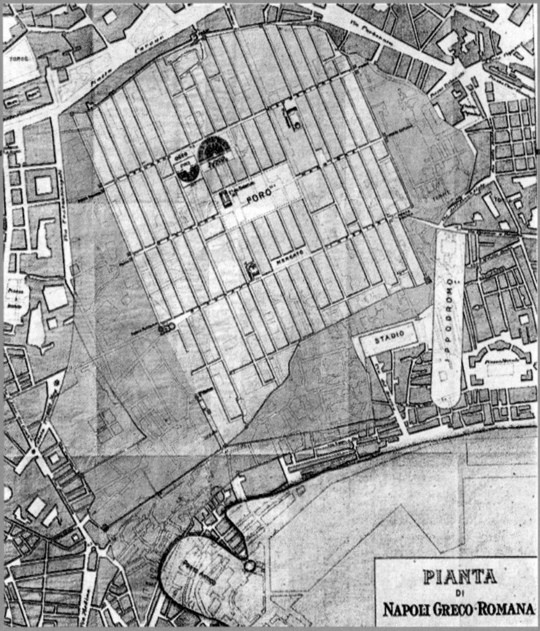

PIANTA
DI
NAPOLI GRECO-ROMANA

THE GRECO-ROMAN TOWN

The city was composed of a grid of main streets (the *cardi*, running from north to south, and the *decumani*, from east to west) which divided the area into plots of around 40 by 330 yards. The public areas were slotted in over several plots. The Greek city of Neapolis remained unchanged despite the arrival of the Romans, on whom it imposed its own roots and culture, and for whom it constituted the first contact with the Greek world.

THE BAROQUE TRANSFORMATION

The church, cloister and convent were completely renovated in the 18th century, mainly under the guiding hand of Cosimo Fanzago. In the 19th century the church was returned to its original Gothic appearance.

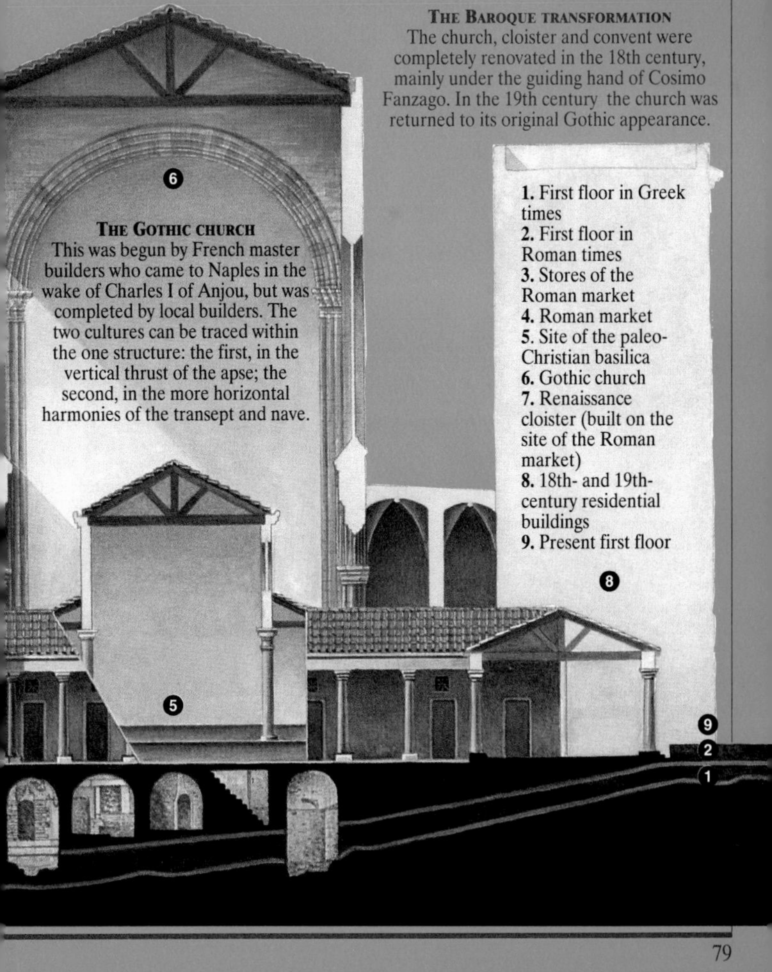

6

THE GOTHIC CHURCH

This was begun by French master builders who came to Naples in the wake of Charles I of Anjou, but was completed by local builders. The two cultures can be traced within the one structure: the first, in the vertical thrust of the apse; the second, in the more horizontal harmonies of the transept and nave.

1. First floor in Greek times
2. First floor in Roman times
3. Stores of the Roman market
4. Roman market
5. Site of the paleo-Christian basilica
6. Gothic church
7. Renaissance cloister (built on the site of the Roman market)
8. 18th- and 19th-century residential buildings
9. Present first floor

8

5

9
2
1

Charles I of Anjou (brother of the King of France) was summoned by the Pope to fight the Swabians, and became king of the realm in 1266. It was not long before Naples, which he made his capital, underwent a series of transformations that would strengthen its links with the Western world. Many Angevin projects were based on schemes initiated by the previous Norman and Swabian dynasties. And while religious edifices were concentrated in the old Greco-Roman town, new areas of urban development began to emerge. The spur was the construction of the Castel Nuovo, next to which aristocratic palaces were erected, and the enlargement of the the port, around which an urban fabric wove itself in a typically haphazard, medieval fashion. Here, workshops, guilds and branches of foreign banks simultaneously thrived.

CASTEL NUOVO
The presence of French artists in Naples, attested to by written sources, can only be detected through a few rare surviving remains (Sant'Eligio, certain chapels of the Duomo, and the apse of San Lorenzo). Secular buildings of Angevin influence are even rarer. The Palatine Chapel (1279–82) in the Castel Nuovo is the most important surviving reminder of the original quadrangular-shaped buildings of the French architects.

FUNERARY MONUMENTS
▲ 141, 161
(left, the tomb of Robert of Anjou)
Based on the works by Tino di Camaino ▲ 141, a typology can be seen to emerge.
The sarcophagus (itself of paleo-Christian origin) forms the central feature; the flagstone on top bears the portrait of the deceased. The sarcophagus is supported by caryatids or by columns resting on animal bases, in the medieval style. The tombs of prominent individuals possess, in addition, a baldachin supported by columns.

1. Castel Nuovo
2. Sant'Anna dei Lombardi
3. Santa Maria la Nova
4. Santa Chiara
5. San Giovanni
Maggiore
6. San Domenico Maggiore
7. San Lorenzo
8. Duomo
9. San Pietro Martire
10. Sant'Agostino alla
Zecca
11. Sant'Eligio
12. San Giovanni a Carbonara
13. Castel Capuano
14. Santissima Annunziata

THE "TAVOLA STROZZI"

With the exception of a handful of large secular buildings, it was the churches, with their soaring edifices, that dominated the urban landscape during the Angevin period, as the *Tavola Strozzi* ● 90 shows. Subsequent alterations make it hard to even detect the original Provençal Gothic style. It can nonetheless be seen clearly in the radiating structure and strong vertical emphasis of the polygonal apses of Sant'Eligio, Santa Maria Donnaregina and San Lorenzo.

SAN LORENZO ● 78, ▲ 152
While the apse, with its ambulatory and radiating chapels, is Gothic in conception, the principal nave, whose chapels were constructed during the time of Charles II, reveal a marked Cistercian influence.

Opposite and above: elevation and ground plan of the apse of San Lorenzo.

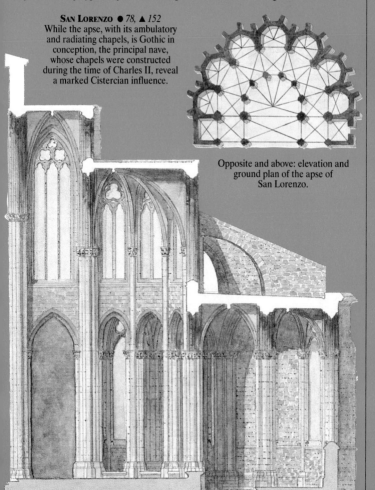

It was under the Aragonese (1442) that the cultural rebirth, using antiquity as its point of reference, took place in Naples, some fifty years after the birth of the Renaissance in central Italy. While Angevin architecture had been mainly religious in function, Aragonese works were predominantly secular. Buildings in the pure Renaissance style are rare in Naples, where Tuscan influences tend in turn to be marked by the Spanish tradition.

REARRANGEMENTS OF THE CASTEL NUOVO ▲ 13

The interior is a testament to the power of classical Tuscan models, but also reveals the influence of Catalan art, notably in the Hall of Barons, with its high double-veined ribbed vault. The triumphal arch of Alfonso of Aragon (left), a masterpiece of Renaissance style, was erected to commemorate the entry of the king into Naples in 1443 (1). The attic story is composed of niches displaying Virtues (2), while the tympanum contains two river gods (3). The ensemble is crowned with a statue of Saint Michael.

THE ARAGONESE ENCEINTE

In addition to the mighty peperino towers on Via Marina, Corso Garibaldi and Via Cesare Rosaroli, there are two gateways along the eastern wall: the Porta Nolana and the Porta Capuana ▲ 157 (above).

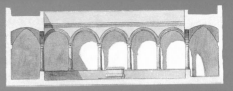

THE CLOISTERS
These were not always built at the same time as the church to which they were adjoined. In the early Renaissance period they were characterized by rounded arches supported by marble columns. The cloister of San Giacomo (above), constructed between 1596 and 1599, and attached to the church of Santa Maria la Nova ▲ *147*, itself of Romanesque origin, is a good illustration of this. Thereafter, columns were replaced by square peperino pilasters, whose greater strength allowed an upper story to be added to the cloister.

THE SPANISH DISTRICT (above)
Above the Via Toledo (opened in 1536), which followed the line of the Aragonese enceinte, viceroy Don Pedro of Toledo created an area for the Spanish troops. This was built with narrow, checkerboard streets, whose layout is still apparent within the present urban fabric.

PALAZZO CUOMO ▲ *145*
This is the most Tuscan of the Renaissance palaces, with its three (front and sides) bossed stonework façades. The rusticated stonework of the base contrasts with the smooth rendering of the upper story. Few Renaissance palaces survive in Naples, as many of them were subsequently altered during the Baroque period (for example, the palaces of Corigliano, Filomarino, Sansevero and Maddaloni).

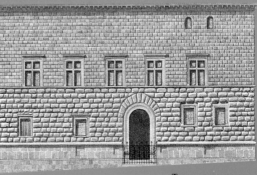

THE PALAZZO OF DIOMEDES CARAFA
▲ *145*
The rectangular bossed tufa stonework and classical marble doorway are in marked contrast to the interior, which is characterized by low Catalan vaulting and late-Gothic polystyle pilasters. This mixture of Tuscan and Catalan styles is typical of Neapolitan *palazzi* (Cuomo, Penna...).

MAJOLICA
Blue, yellow and green faience tiles cover the walls or cupolas in churches and aristocratic residences. One of the finest expressions of this tradition of craftsmanship is the cloister of Santa Chiara, transformed by Domenico Antonio Vaccaro in 1742.

Over and above any urban program, the Baroque town was altered in accordance with the wishes, scenographic or otherwise, of the viceroy in charge, ever keen to applaud himself. During the 17th century, the elements which characterized the Baroque (the reinterpretation of the classical orders, the fusion of architecture, sculpture and painted décor, and the absorption of detail into a spectacular and theatrical whole) fulfilled their celebratory function most successfully within a religious context which, more than any other, demanded participation.

THE COUNTER-REFORMATION CHURCH OF GESÙ NUOVO
Exemplifying Baroque reinterpretation, the diamond-embossed stone façade of the Renaissance palace (1470) was changed to make its new role as mother-church of the Neapolitan Jesuits more explicit.

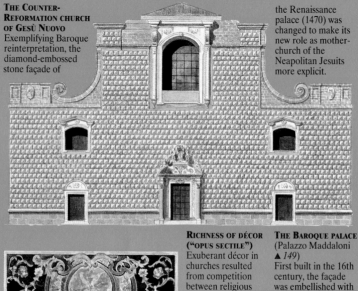

RICHNESS OF DÉCOR ("OPUS SECTILE")
Exuberant décor in churches resulted from competition between religious orders and between marble workers. The altar was often inlaid with marble, lapis-lazuli, agate and onyx.

THE BAROQUE PALACE
(Palazzo Maddaloni ▲ 149)
First built in the 16th century, the façade was embellished with exuberant stuccowork and corner balconies, as well as a rusticated doorway (the work of Cosimo Fanzago) in the 17th century.

FOUNTAINS

The sculpted décor of fountains, usually in marble and peperino, was modeled on the triumphal arch, a dominant landmark of decreed public holidays.

Cross-section of the Guglia della Immacolata.

BAROQUE REINTERPRETATION

Stucco, marquetry, wrought iron, marble and majolica tend to characterize décors of the Baroque period, and often seem to take precedence over the architecture. Baroque devices were applied to doorways and façade décors. The hallmarks of the Renaissance, based on the classical orders, were subverted in favor of a naturalistic and anthropomorphic style. The symbol of the skull was its most dramatic emblem.

TEMPORARY STRUCTURES

From the 17th century up until the mid-18th century, "greasy poles" and pyramids made of wood and board were erected on feast days held in honor of a religious or political name. Before long, sculptors and architects would experiment with works of a more permanent nature.

STONE SPIRES

The spires of San Gennaro, San Domenico and the Immacolata (left) were the stone counterparts of the temporary structures erected on public holidays. They were highly elastic in their conception, and were made of tufa blocks into which bricks were sometimes inserted. The whole was splendidly clad in marble.

Charles of Bourbon's arrival in 1734 led to a series of urban and regional schemes being launched, with the dual aim of helping to redress economic and social imbalances, and celebrating the new regime. Chief among the artists brought to Naples by the Spanish sovereigns were Luigi Vanvitelli and Ferdinando Fuga. During the 19th century, the urban landscape of the old town was dissected by broad thoroughfares, which formed the principal arteries of communication. Grand architectural and urban schemes were launched during French rule, some of which were completed. The neoclassical taste was established in Naples during this period.

THE MAIN THOROUGHFARES
1. Corso Vittorio Emanuele II (1853)
2. Riviera di Chiaia (1781)
3. Corso Napoleone (now Duca Amadeo d'Aosta) ▲ *178*. Driven through in 1810, under French rule, it linked the Via Toledo with Capodimonte.
4. Via Toledo (1536)
5. Capodimonte
6. Corso Umberto I ("Rettifilo"), 1889
7. District of Santa Lucia

THE BOURBON PALACES
Ever concerned with appearances, the Bourbons renovated the Palazzo Reale and, in 1738, started to build a royal residence at Capodimonte ▲ *172* (above).

VILLA COMMUNALE

In 1778 Ferdinand IV entrusted Carlo Vanvitelli with a project to create a public promenade along the Riviera di Chiaia. Opened in 1781, this Villa Reale ("royal") was the first public garden in Naples. The Riviera di Chiaia is one of the streets to have been most influenced by neoclassicism. It is bordered by the Villa Acton (now the Villa Pignatelli) and the Villa Communale, created when the Villa Reale was extended.

CONTINUITY

Upon their return to power, the Bourbons continued with the schemes begun by the French. They also paved the way for new projects, thus confirming the 19th-century shift in tastes.

THE "TEMPLES OF SCIENCE AND CULTURE"

In the 19th century, buildings devoted to the sciences such as already existed in Europe began to spring up in Naples, among these the Observatory ▲ 171 (below), the Botanical Garden ▲ 171 and the Aquarium ▲ 191. It was here that the neoclassical taste was fully to express itself.

THE POST-UNIFICATION PERIOD (AFTER 1870)

The most striking projects to be initiated after 1870 were the creation of the Corso Umberto I and the construction of two covered galleries, in wrought iron and glass: the Galleria Principe di Napoli ▲ 165 (1870–83) and the Galleria Umberto ▲ 134 (1887–90), considerably larger and modeled on the gallery in Milan. In the early 20th century the elegant residential district of Santa Lucia ▲ 189 was created, built by the sea on the embankment constructed in the late 19th century.

● THE SANFELICE STAIRCASE

In the early part of the 17th century the Baroque acquired a wholly original dimension in Naples. Two markedly different men came to the fore: Domenico Antonio Vaccaro, a grand master of religious architecture, and Ferdinando Sanfelice, an important figure in secular architecture. The daringly spectacular staircases designed by Sanfelice can be found at the back of numerous Neapolitan *palazzi* courtyards.

OPEN STAIRCASE
▲ *164, 165*
Already under the Angevins, the staircase had been an essential feature in numerous Neapolitan palace courtyards. With Sanfelice, its importance as a scenographic feature was reinforced. The open staircase at the back of the courtyard was to become more highly valued than the

principal façade. By reinforcing the solid parts of the wall, while at the same time allowing the space between the pillars to widen, the architect managed to create an impression of transparency. And by laying the emphasis on the angle of the stairs running from one landing to another, he succeeded in creating an object of magnetic fascination. In the blink of an eye, the structure reveals what it appeared to conceal. Ornamentation was redundant: the architecture alone provided sufficient surprise.

NAPLES
AS SEEN BY PAINTERS

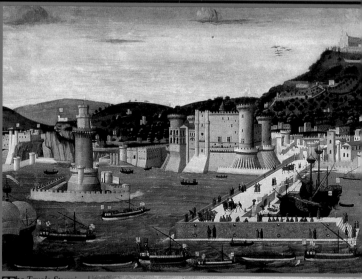

The *Tavola Strozzi* (1) is the first complete view of Naples and is a commemorative "portrait" of the town as it celebrates the victorious return of the Aragonese fleet, following the Battle of Ischia in 1465. Of uncertain date and attribution (it could be by either Francesco Pagano or Francesco Rosselli), the panel served as a model for later depictions of the town from a "bird's-eye view". The sea becomes a privileged viewpoint for a "panoptic" vision of the urban fabric, from which Sant'Elmo ▲ *185*, San Martino ▲ *184* and the Castel Nuovo ▲ *134* emerge in all their monumental splendor. The arc-shaped depiction of the Bay of Naples (2), painted in around 1560 by Peter Bruegel (1525–69), while being more intensely emotional, is actually less truthful, since it introduces imaginary elements and urban topographies taken from other sites.

1. Anonymous, *Tavola Strozzi, View of Naples and return of the Aragonese fleet* (late 15th century).
2. Peter Bruegel, *Harbor of Naples* (c. 1560).

VESUVIUS AS NATURAL SPECTACLE

The "sublime" spectacle produced by the violence of natural forces fed an important cultural and esthetic phenomenon in the 18th century, which was to presage 19th-century Romanticism. Vesuvius in eruption was to prove one of its richest sources of inspiration, and Pietro Jacopo Volaire (1729–92) was to be its most passionate and lucid interpreter. In *Vesuvius erupting, seen from the Bridge of the Maddalena*, his nocturnal vision of the active volcano as nature in absolute chaos, contrasting with the tranquil countryside bathed by the cold light of the moon, was to become a recurrent motif in oil and gouache canvases and watercolors of the period. This image reflected the new sensibility of those Grand Tour travelers in search of exalted or "picturesque" emotions. It was in complete contrast to the sensibilities of the previous century, for whom this "awful subject" gave rise, instead, to portrayals of a sacred and devotional nature, associated with the figure of a patron saint capable of saving the endangered town. Indeed, Vesuvius erupted in 1631 ▲ *238*, having lain dormant for several centuries. From this point, it became the focal point in depictions of Naples; the disconcerting backdrop that lorded over the crowded and frenetic urban scenes, punctuated by parades and processions.

During the second half of the 18th century, while artists such as Vernet, Volaire and Wright of Derby attempted to capture the emotions and "sublime" effects of landscape, another artistic current was emerging, with Luigi Vanvitelli as its chief exponent, which was bent on incredibly precise, almost topographical representations of Naples and her surroundings. Partial or panoramic views, observed from a variety of angles, document the changing urban pattern which, by this time, had spread beyond the limits of the walls built by the viceroys. Practiced by local artists or foreign painters on extended stays, view-painting became the ideal genre for celebrating a town which, by now, ranked as a cultivated and fashionable European capital. The influence of Enlightenment ideals is evident in the intentions of Giovanni Carafa, Duke of Noja, who produced a precise topographical map that would enable the area to be studied and ordered within the context of a concerted program of urban planification. The painter Pietro Fabris (probably of English origin), working in Naples between 1754 and 1804, demonstrates a similar analytical, documentary and topographical awareness, in his refined depictions of life at court, or everyday episodes in the slum districts. In 1776 he produced a series of gouaches destined to illustrate a volume on the Phlegraean Fields, edited by Sir William Hamilton ▲ 244, the British Ambassador in Naples. The scientific nature of these illustrations, as demonstrated by the painting *The Phlegraean Fields from Mount Epomeo* (**1**), blends harmoniously with his ability to evoke a visual response in the viewer and create a particular atmosphere. View-painting became the official pictorial genre at court with the Prussian Philipp Hackert, who was nominated painter of the Royal Chamber through the influence of Queen Maria Carolina. Hackert produced a series of tempera paintings for the Queen, of which *View of Anacapri at the foot of Monte Solaro* (**2**) is an example. His realistic and documentary style, based on the direct observation of nature (whose forms and flora are minutely analyzed, and in which the human element simply becomes part of an organic whole) constituted the visual counterpart of the literary and philosophical current sweeping through Europe at that time, of which Goethe (his friend and sincere admirer) was the leading exponent.

| 1 |
| 2 |

The Romantic Landscape

1. A. Sminck Pitloo, *Temple at Paestum.*
2. A. Sminck Pitloo, *Cava de' Tirreni.*

Anton Sminck Pitloo (1791–1837) breathed new life into the "view-painting" genre in the 19th century. Breaking away from pure Naturalism, he replaced it, instead, with a looser sensibility, alive to the effects of light and following in the footsteps of recent pre-Impressionist experiments in France and, above all, England. Neapolitan view-painting thus became a topic worthy of academic teaching establishments and the subject of painterly experiments. Pitloo (**1** and **2**), professor of landscape painting at the Royal Institute of Fine Art, headed a whole generation of artists (Mattei, Duclère, Smargiassi, Gigante, Fergola, Carelli . . .) who practiced in Naples during the first half of the 19th century, known as the School of Pausilippo. Giacinto Gigante, a follower of Pitloo (later to influence him), was inspired by the paintings of Corot and Turner, which he used to develop his own style. This was free from the documentary concerns that were typical of Hackert and relied, instead, on a lyrical and romantic interpretation of the Neapolitan landscape that was stripped of all convention.

NAPLES AS SEEN
IN THE MOVIES

● Totò

Antonio de Curtis, alias Totò (1898–1967), slots into the great Neapolitan tradition of comic theater ● 58, starting out as a variety performer at a very young age. When he first appeared on screen in 1937, he was already well known throughout the peninsula. For nearly twenty years he managed an unbroken theatrical and screen career with varying degrees of success. Although acclaimed for his stage roles, he nonetheless had to wait until the 1950's to achieve real success in the movies, which owed more to his performance as an actor than to the inherent quality of the movies. Indeed, in every movie (over 120 titles) Totò exploited his unique physique (his pointed chin, especially) and talents of mimicry to create a "type", or "masque". His facial expressions (grimaces, rolled eyes), the elasticity of his body (akin to the jerky movements of an uncoordinated string puppet), his clothes (bowler hat and threadbare, oversized suit) made him, in a way, the "Italian Charlie Chaplin". Totò demonstrated the same versatility in his command of language, playing endlessly on words as well as linguistic register (moving from polished Italian to Neapolitan). But he was often trapped in the caricaturized roles he played, and the endless stereotypical backdrops (the milieu of Naples and southern Italy, in particular). It was by working with directors such as Pasolini, Lattuada and Monicelli, above all, that enabled him to finally lift the mask and fully express his range of talents. Among his "Neapolitan" movies, the best remembered are *The Gold of Naples* (**4**), *Misery and Nobility* (**1**), *A Neapolitan Turk* (**2**), and *Totò in Color* (**3**).

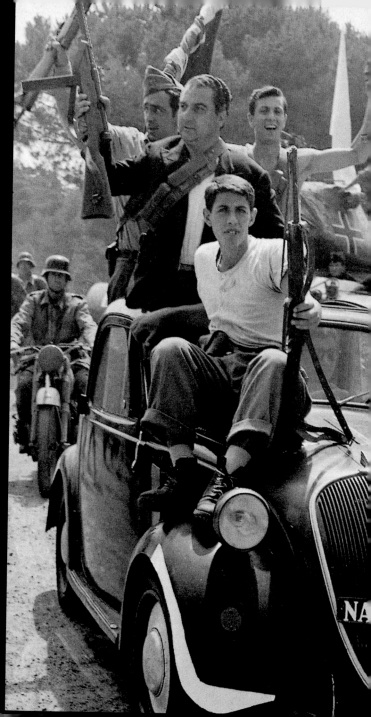

On the strength of its theatrical and musical tradition, Naples became, with the advent of silent movies, an important center of artistic creation for the emerging movie industry. Her output was not confined to folkloric depictions of the town, but was distinguished, instead, by a thread of realism well in advance of its time. The most famous example is *Assunta Spina* (Gustavo Sereni, 1915), a melodrama set in the working-class districts of Naples. Even when Naples lost its position as a production center, it remained the preferred backdrop for numerous movies by Italian directors, who continued to depict the town without recourse to artifice or clichés. The dark years of World War Two presented these directors with an opportunity to explore the social realities of the town, over and above the straightforward historical narrative. First to do this was Roberto Rossellini with, in the second episode of *Paisà* (1946) (2), which recounted the meeting between a young shoe-shiner and a black soldier, one of the most moving tableaux of Naples during the conflict. With documentary objectivity, the father of Neo-realism produced a heartrending account of the suffering and survival of a humiliated people, nowhere more so than in the final scene, where the soldier discovers the precariousness of the young child's existence. In 1962 Nanni Loy brought a new dimension to the realistic representation of the Parthenopean city. In *The Battle of Naples* (1) he documented the Neapolitan uprising against the German army in 1943 ● *34* and, paying

homage to the dead of the "four days of Naples", managed to find an even balance between epic élan and documentary truthfulness. To these "war tableaux" can be added the adaptation of Curzio Malaparte's novel *La Pelle* by Liliana Cavani in 1981 (3 shows the poster for the French version, *La Peau*). With piercing realism, Cavani lifts the veil on the misery of a town struggling with all its might to survive in the face of corruption, the black market, prostitution and other such social evils.

In the 1960's the Italian movie industry, rediscovering social reality, was marked by an increasing politicization. These were the years of the economic miracle and a new

generation of committed writers intent on denouncing the abuses of contemporary society. The Neapolitan Francesco Rosi **(2)** devoted numerous movies to the hidden and almost institutionalized power that was corroding southern Italy: the Mafia.

His first movie, *The Challenge* (1958), dealt with the struggle within the Camorra for the control of the fruit and vegetable market in Naples. *A Grip on the City* **(3)**, which he made in 1963, attacked speculative machinations and revealed the close connection between the real estate business and the world of politics. Winner of the Golden Lion award at Venice, this harsh summation had

the effect of a bombshell. Rosi took his inspiration from a real-life event, which he chose to depict in normal surroundings with, for the most part, non-professional actors, thereby emphasizing the documentary element. He nonetheless states in the opening credits, "the people and events are fictitious, but the events that produced them are authentic." Twenty years later (1985), Lina Wertmÿller would also express an interest in this scourge of Neapolitan society. In *Camorra* **(1)**, she describes, with "anger and passion" and unflinching realism, a Naples "poisoned" by drugs and the Camorra's maneuvers.

1

2

3

(who died prematurely in 1994) revealed himself as the last descendant of Pulcinella ● 52, without adopting his narrow "napolitude". The movie recounts the difficulties experienced by a Neapolitan in exile in Florence, with a comic finesse combined with self-criticism. Troisi was from the outset hailed by critics and audiences alike as the new comic genius of the 1980's. In his depiction of three Neapolitans caught between traditional values and an irrepressible appetite for life, the iconoclastic director of *Libera* (1991) **(2)**, Pappi Corsicato, deployed humor, scorn and provocation in a style that was pushed to the limits.

The 1980's were marked by a renewal of traditional culture in the musical and theatrical milieu: a new generation of artists sought, without renouncing their roots, to present an out-of-the-ordinary image of the town. The movie played its part in this rediscovered vitality. Salvatore Piscicelli and Massimo Troisi **(1)**, initially, then Mario Martone and Pappi Corsicato expressed, each in their own way, the malaise of a society in the throes of change, and painted a portrait of the everyday life of Neapolitan youth. From his first movie, *Ricomincio Da Tre* (1980), Troisi

Naples
AS SEEN BY WRITERS

STREET LIFE

THE "LAZZARONI"

Writer and esthete Harold Acton (1904–94) was born in Italy and returned to live there after an English education and travels throughout the world. His works include several historial studies of Italy.

❝In glaring contrast with [the nobles] and with the army of mixed clergy . . . there was the formidable city populace, which became world-famous under the name of *lazzaroni*. Since Masaniello's rebellion in 1647, this class had given rise to fantastic legends; during the eighteenth and well on into the nineteenth century, foreign travellers were quite as curious about the *lazzaroni* as they were about Vesuvius and Pompeii. The reason is not far to seek, for these were as fascinating in their way as the landscape; and their open-air life was a constant source of amusement and interest – a perpetual comic opera, for those who did not peer too close. Their voluble presence enhanced the atmosphere of seaside festivity and masquerade which the tourist expected of Naples. They were children of nature, sturdy, excitable, apparently cheerful and carefree, proliferating in primitive simplicity, sufficient unto the day, the passing minute, walking and sporting on the sea-shore naked, with no more shame than Adam in his primal innocence, and thanks to the climate, content with little and sleeping under the stars most of the year.

Squeamish Président de Brosses called them 'the most abominable rabble, the most disgusting vermin which has ever crawled on the surface of the earth'; and under the Spanish regime the hordes of ragged beggars must have been frightening, as the name *lazzaroni* implies; probably the Abbé Galiani was correct in deriving it from the lepers, whose patron was Saint Lazarus and who were segregated in hospitals called lazarets in consequence. They became a byword for all that was thieving, treacherous, seditious, lazy and corrupt. 'There is not such another race of rogues as the common people of Naples,' Henry Swinburne concluded. But as Goethe observed with greater sympathy, the Northerner mistook for idlers those who did not toil all day.❞

HAROLD ACTON,
THE BOURBONS OF NAPLES,
METHUEN AND CO. LTD, LONDON, 1957

BLACK MARKET KIDS

London-born poet Gavin Ewart (1916–95), served in North Africa and Italy in World War Two, and wrote "Cigarette for the Bambino" while in Naples at the end of May, 1944.

❝Hey, Joe! Cigarette! Cioccolat'!
Egg and chips?
Wanna eat? wanna drink?
Vermouth a very good
Very nice
Wanta girl? Wanta woman?

> **"THE STREETS ARE ONE CONTINUED MARKET, AND THRONGED WITH POPULACE SO MUCH THAT A COACH CAN HARDLY PASS."**
> THOMAS GRAY

> In the filthy streets of handsome towns
> Black Market kids accost the soldiers –
> Under the pictures of the Virgin Mary
> Whores give themselves for tins of bully
> And still amidst a starving population
> The priests ecclesiastically waddle
> As fat and sinister as any gangster.
> Catholicism, black market of the soul,
> That holds this wretched country down,
> Corrupted state, corrupted crown,
> Dangles its tarnished tinkling Heaven
> Above this maze of medieval squalor.
>
> Gone all the good of European culture
> The hangover of 'taste' in tawdry chapels,
> Fat cherubs and madonnas puffed like clouds,
> A throbbing, over-sexed and maudlin music –
> O, that the centuries should show so little!
>
> The beauty of the girls and children
> Shining through rags, their friendliness,
> The easy kindness of a Latin people,
> Lacking the hardness of the French,
> Brutality of the conceited German,
> Deserve a better heritage than this.
> GAVIN EWART, "CIGARETTE FOR THE BAMBINO", 1944
> IN *THE COLLECTED EWART*, HUTCHINSON, LONDON, 1980

A COPIOUS LANGUAGE
In the spring of 1844, Charles Dickens (1812–70) went to live in Italy, and with characteristic curiosity and keen observation of city life, visited Rome, Naples, Florence and Venice.

> Why do the beggars rap their chins constantly, with their right hands, when you look at them? Everything is done in pantomime in Naples, and that is the conventional sign for hunger. A man who is quarrelling with another, yonder, lays the palm of his right hand on the back of his left, and shakes the two thumbs – expressive of a donkey's ears – whereat his adversary is goaded to desperation. Two people bargaining for fish, the buyer empties an imaginary waistcoat pocket when he is told the price, and walks away without a word: having thoroughly conveyed to the seller that he considers it too dear. Two people in carriages, meeting, one touches his lips, twice or thrice, holding up the five fingers of his right hand, and gives a horizontal cut in the air with the palm. The other nods briskly, and goes his way. He has been invited to a friendly dinner at half-past five o'clock, and will certainly come.
>
> All over Italy, a peculiar shake of the right hand from the wrist, with the forefinger stretched out, expresses a negative – the only negative beggars will ever understand. But in Naples, those five fingers are a copious language.
> CHARLES DICKENS, *PICTURES FROM ITALY*,
> ANDRÉ DEUTSCH, LONDON, 1973

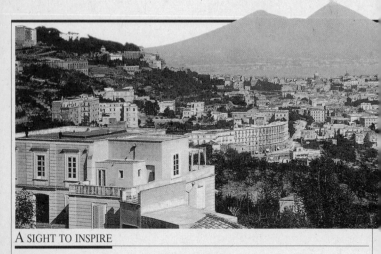

A SIGHT TO INSPIRE

THE LANDSCAPE

Edward Lear (1812–88) was a widely traveled artist, writer and humorist. Born in London, he finally settled in Italy, finding there ample inspiration for his landscapes.

❝October 2. – Vietri di Basilicata appears full of really fine scenery and material for good landscape, and left a strong impression of beauty on our minds, though every succeeding hour brought fresh charms to view. It is hardly possible to find a more beautiful day's drive in any part of the Regno di Napoli than this, the road passing through a constant succession of lovely scenes till it reaches Eboli. At sunset the blue gulf of Salerno was visible, and we soon reached the convent-inn of Eboli; which ten years ago I can recollect thinking a horrible place, though it seems to me now rather à comfortable inn.

October 4. – Yesterday we passed at Paestum: – the morning drive by the beautiful Persano and its plain; the hours of lingering among the bright solitudes of ancient Posidonium; the return at evening when the western sun was golden, and the mountains fading red; the bustling and noisy Salerno by night.❞

EDWARD LEAR, "JOURNALS OF A LANDSCAPE PAINTER",
IN *EDWARD LEAR IN SOUTHERN ITALY*, WILLIAM KIMBER, LONDON, 1964

THE BAY

William Beckford (1759–1844), a passionate traveler, extravagant collector and connoisseur, is chiefly remembered for his eccentric literary career.

❝The sky was cloudless when I awoke, and such was the transparence of the atmosphere that I could clearly discern the rocks, and even some white buildings on the island of Caprea, though at the distance of thirty miles. A large window fronts my bed, and its casements being thrown open, gives me a vast prospect of ocean uninterrupted, except by the peaks of Caprea and the Cape of Sorento. I lay half an hour gazing on the smooth level waters, and listening to the confused voices of the fishermen, passing and repassing in light skiffs, which came and disappeared in an instant.

Running to the balcony the moment my eyes were fairly open (for till then I saw objects, I know not how, as one does in dreams) I leaned over its rails and viewed Vesuvius, rising distinct into the blue æther, with all that world of gardens and casinos which are scattered about its base; then looked down into the street, deep below, thronged with people in holiday garments, and carriages, and soldiers in full parade. The shrubby, variegated shore of Posilipo drew my attention to the opposite side of the bay. It was on those very rocks, under those tall pines, Sannazaro was wont to sit by moonlight, or at peep of dawn, composing his marine

eclogues. It is there he still sleeps; and I wished to have gone immediately and strewed coral over his tomb.**

WILLIAM BECKFORD, *ITALY, WITH SKETCHES OF SPAIN AND PORTUGAL*,
RICHARD BENTLEY, LONDON, 1834

THE LAND OF THE ANCIENTS

James Boswell (1740–95) is most famous as a journal-writer and biographer of Samuel Johnson. He traveled the continent on the Grand Tour between 1763 and 1766.

My dear Johnston, – If a man's mind never failed to catch the spirit of the climate in which he breathes, I ought now to write you a most delicious letter, for Naples is indeed a delicious spot; *praeter omnes ride*t ['Which smiles beyond all others' (Horace, *Odes*, II. vi. 13–14)]. I have been near three weeks here and have been constantly employed in seeing the classical places all around. Is it possible to conceive a richer scene than the finest bay diversified with islands and bordered by fields where Virgil's Muses charmed the creation, where the renowned of ancient Rome enjoyed the luxury of glorious retreat and the true flow of soul which they valued as much as triumphs?

JAMES BOSWELL, LETTER TO JOHN JOHNSTON,
IN *BOSWELL ON THE GRAND TOUR*,
WILLIAM HEINEMANN LTD, LONDON , 1955

THE CITY

Percy Bysshe Shelley (1792–1822) left England in 1818 and spent the rest of his life in Italy. The political ode "To Naples" was written during his most creative period.

**Naples! thou heart of man which ever pantest
  Naked beneath the lidless eye of heaven!
Elysian City which to calm enchantest
  The mutinous air and sea; they round thee, even
  As sleep round Love, are driven!
  Metropolis of a ruined Paradise
    Long lost, late won, and yet but half regained!
  Bright altar of the bloodless sacrifice
    Which armed Victory offers up unstained
    To Love, the flower-enchained!
Thou which wert once, and then did cease to be,
Now art, and henceforth ever shall be, free,
  If Hope, and Truth, and justice can avail,
    Hail, hail, all hail!**

PERCY BYSSHE SHELLEY,
ODE TO NAPLES, 1820

TRADERS AND ARTISANS

MARKET LIFE

Hans Christian Andersen (1805–75) was born in Odense, Denmark. Having won international fame for his fairy tales, he journeyed widely throughout Europe. "A Prospect from my window in Naples" carefully documents the market life of the city.

66It is Piazza Florentina we see, – a place just as broad as a common street with us in the North, and the length is in proportion to the breadth. Opposite to this, and close by a narrow crooked street, extends the *façade* of a little church, over the open entrance to which the neighbouring dames have hung all their clothes out to dry, from the mysteries which should not be seen, to the variegated gowns that should be seen. Two young priests reading their book of the Evangelists, walk up and down the entrance hall. Outside sits an old woman selling money. She is the poor man's money-changer; the open place is her office; the little table, whose leaf is a box with brass wires across, is her cash chest; and therein lie the small coins which she, for a percentage, sells for the larger ones. But the trade does not answer well. Close by her stands a fruit shop, variegated like a picture cut out of an A B C book, with oranges and lemons. The picture above the door, where Madonna quenches the thirst of souls in purgatory, is a very suitable sign. The whole place is paved with broad lava stones; the poor horses cannot keep their footing, and are therefore beaten with screams and shouts. Not less than sixteen shoemakers sit and sew there to the left; the two nearest the door have already lighted their candles; they pull the cap off that poor boy, and throw oranges at him; he seems to protest against their being applied externally. In all the houses, the ground-floors are without windows, but with broad, open shop doors. Outside one they are roasting coffee, outside another they are boiling a soup of chesnuts and bread, and the man has many customers. Fellows dressed in rags eat out of broken pots. In the highest stories of the houses each window has its balcony, or else it goes along the whole story, and has a flourishing garden, in which are large tubs, with oranges and lemon trees. The ripe fruit amongst the green leaves shines like the Hesperian friut. An Englishman, in his dressing-gown, has his rocking chair out there. Now the chair falls backwards, and the Briton strikes the stars with his proud head. But far above the church and houses rises the rock of St Elmo, with its fortress; the evening sun shines on the white walls, towers, and telegraph. Now the sun is down and the bells ring to Ave Maria. People stream into the church; the lamps within shine through the windows. The tavern keeper puts lights in his white paper lantern; the shoemakers have each his lamp; it is a complete illumination. The little old woman shuts up her money shop, and her boy lights her home with a candle in a paper pottle. There is song in the church, and there are noises in the streets; they harmonize strangely together. But what is that? There is a procession coming from the narrow street. White figures, each with a large candle in his hand; four men likewise in long white frocks, with hoods over their heads, bear on their shoulders a bier with red drapery; a young girl dressed like a bride, with a veil and wreath of white roses around her brow lies on the bier. Every one takes his hat off for the dead, and the shoemakers kneel.

The procession is now in the church, and the same noise is heard in the streets as before.

That little square is a faithful picture of this large Naples; yes, a very true one; for the poet sat at his window, and drew every feature of what he saw below.99

HANS CHRISTIAN ANDERSEN, *A POET'S BAZAAR*,
RICHARD BENTLEY, LONDON, 1846

CHRISTMAS FARE

Hester Thrale (1741–1821), later Hester Piozzi, was a lively and intelligent woman and the author of several published works. She was an intimate friend and confidante of Dr Johnson until their relationship soured upon her marriage to Italian musician Gabriel Piozzi..

❝The Christmas season here at Naples is very pleasingly observed. The Italians are peculiarly ingenious at adorning their shops, I think, and setting out their wares. Every grocer, fruiterer, etc., now mingles orange and lemon and myrtle leaves among the goods exposed at his door, as we do greens in the churches of England, but with infinitely more taste; and this device produces a very fine effect upon the whole, as one drives along la Strada del Toledo, which all morning looks showy from these decorations, and all evening splendid from the profusion of torches, flambeaux, etc., that shine with less regularity, indeed, but with more lustre and greater appearance of expensive gaiety, than our neat, clean, steady London lamps. Some odd, pretty movable coffee-houses, too, or lemonade shops, set on wheels, and adorned, according to the possessor's taste, with gilding, painting, etc., and covered with ices, orgeats, and other refreshments, as in emulation each of the other, and in a strange variety of shapes and forms, too, exquisitely well-imagined for the most part, help forward the finery of Naples exceedingly. I have counted thirty of these *galante* shops on each side of the street, which, with their necessary illuminations, make a brilliant figure by candlelight, till twelve o'clock, when all the show is over, and everybody put out their lights and quietly lie down to rest .

THE NEAPOLITAN CRIB

❝There is a work of art peculiar to this city, and attempted in no other, on which surprising sums of money are lavished by many of the inhabitants, who connect or associate to this amusement ideas of piety and devotion. The thing when finished is called a *presepio*, and is composed in honour of this sacred season, after which all is taken to pieces. . . . [The figures are] managed by people whose heads, naturally turned towards architecture and design, give them power thus to defy a traveller not to feel delighted with the general effect; while if every single figure is not capitally executed and nicely expressed beside, the proprietor is truly miserable, and will cut a new cow, or vary the horse's attitude, against next Christmas, coute que coute. [. . .] One of these playthings had the journey of the three kings represented in it, and the presents were all of real gold and silver finely worked; nothing could be better or more livelily finished.❞

HESTER PIOZZI, *GLIMPSES OF ITALIAN SOCIETY IN THE EIGHTEENTH CENTURY*, SEELEY AND CO., LTD, LONDON, 1892

NEAPOLITAN PASSIONS

THE LOTTERY

Charles Dickens wrote "Pictures from Italy" in 1844, between "A Christmas Carol" and "Dombey and Son". Although not a work of fiction, it was nevertheless suffused with the evocative depictions of ordinary citizens' lives that had colored his novels.

❝There is one extraordinary feature in the real life of Naples, at which we may take a glance before we go – the Lotteries.

They prevail in most parts of Italy, but are particularly obvious, in their effects and influences, here. They are drawn every Saturday. They bring an immense revenue to the Government; and diffuse a taste for gambling among the poorest of the poor, which is very comfortable to the coffers of the State, and very ruinous to themselves. The lowest stake is one grain; less than a farthing. One hundred numbers – from one to a hundred, inclusive – are put into a box. Five are drawn. Those are the prizes. I buy three numbers. If one of them come up, I win a small prize. If two, some hundreds of times my stake. If three, three thousand five hundred times my stake. I stake (or play as they call it) what I can upon my numbers, and buy what numbers I please. The amount I play, I pay at the lottery office, where I purchase the ticket; and it is stated on the ticket itself.

Every lottery office keeps a printed book, an Universal Lottery Diviner, where every possible accident and circumstance is provided for, and has a number against it. For instance, let us take two carlini – about sevenpence. On our way to the lottery office, we run against a black man. When we get there, we say gravely, 'The Diviner.' It is handed over the counter, as a serious matter of business. We look at black man. Such a number. 'Give us that.' We look at running against a person in the street. 'Give us that.' We look at the name of the street itself. 'Give us that.' Now, we have our three numbers.

If the roof of the theatre of San Carlo were to fall in, so many people would play upon the numbers attached to such an accident in the Diviner, that the Government would soon close the numbers, and decline to run the risk of losing any more upon them. This often happens. Not long ago, when there was a fire in the King's Palace, there was such a desperate run on fire, and king, and palace, that further stakes on the numbers attached to those words in the Golden Book were forbidden. Every accident or event, is supposed, by the ignorant populace, to be a revelation to the beholder, or party concerned, in connection with the lottery. Certain people who have a talent for dreaming fortunately, are much sought after; and there are some priests who are constantly favoured with visions of the lucky numbers.

I heard of a horse running away with a man, and dashing him down, dead, at the corner of a street. Pursuing the horse with incredible speed, was another man, who ran so fast, that he came up, immediately after the accident. He threw himself upon his knees beside the unfortunate rider, and clasped his hand with an expression of the wildest grief. 'If you have life,' he said, 'speak one word to me! If you have one gasp of breath left, mention your age for Heaven's sake, that I may play that number in the lottery.'❞

CHARLES DICKENS, *PICTURES FROM ITALY*,
ANDRÉ DEUTSCH, LONDON, 1973

THE OPERA

Michael Kelly (1762–1826) was born in Dublin, where he became celebrated for his singing voice. He toured Europe, and sang in the first performance of Mozart's "Marriage of Figaro." His "Reminiscences" are full of theatrical gossip.

❝At San Carlo's are performed grand serious operas, (the other three theatres are for the opera buffa,) the first I saw there was Metastasio's Olimpiade, the music by Metzlevisic, a German of great musical celebrity. I thought it very fine, and the performance exquisite.

The celebrated Marchesi, the first soprano, performed the part of Megacle; his expression, feeling, and execution in the beautiful aria, 'Se cerca se dice l'amico

dov'e', were beyond all praise. Ansani, then the finest tenor voice in Europe, was there; and Macherini his wife, was the principal female singer; she had a very sweet voice, but small and of limited compass; the Neapolitans called her 'La cantante con la parruca,' from her wearing a wig, in consequence of her h ead being shaved during illness, previous to her engagement; but they liked her in spite of her wig!

Nothing could surpass the splendour of the spectacles they produced, or the beauty of their ballets. Le Pique was their first ballet master, Rossi the second, – both great artists. Madame Rossi was the principal female dancer amongst a crowd of talent.

The first ballet I saw, was Artaxerxes. Le Pique, the Arbaces; Madame Rossi, Mandane; and Artabanes, by Richard Blake, an Irishman, who went abroad very young, and had become a very fine pantomime actor, and was considered the best grotesque dancer of his day. The decorations of this ballet were magnificent. [. . .] I cannot conceive why, on our theatres, it might not be equally so, except, indeed, that the stage at San Carlo is of an immense size, capable of bearing and working any machinery, and besides, opens at the back towards the sea, and because it seems that the English theatres would not risk the expense. . . .

Four times in the year this magnificent theatre is illuminated; viz. on the evening of the birth-day of the King of Spain, and on those of the King, Queen, and the Prince Royal of Naples.

In this vast edifice there are seven tiers of boxes; in the front of each box is a mirror, and before each of those, two large wax tapers; those, multiplied by reflexion, and aided by the flood of light from the stage, form a blaze of splendour perfectly dazzling.

Each box contains twelve persons, who have commodious chairs, &c.; at the back of each of those, on the principal tiers, is a small room, where the confectioner and pages of the proprietor wait, and distribute sweetmeats and ices to the company in the boxes, and any of their friends in the pit, whom they choose to recognize.

There are sixteen rows of seats in the pit, forty seats in each row; they are fitted up with stuffed cushions and rests for the arms, like chairs. When any one takes a place for the night, he receives a key of it, and when he leaves the theatre, he locks the seat up again, and returns the key.

On all gala days, the King, Queen, and all the Court attend in full dress; at which times, the coup d'oeil is magnificent. **99**

MICHAEL KELLY, *REMINISCENCES*,
CASSELL AND COMPANY, LONDON, 1956

RUINS

THE PHLEGRAEAN FIELDS

Born in Cambridge, Rose Macaulay (1881–1958) was a novelist, essayist and travel-writer, whose novels were noted for their wit, urbanity and mild satire. Of her works of non-fiction, "The Pleasure of Ruins" is perhaps the most famous.

❝Diocletian's is one of the few Roman imperial villas now standing moderately intact; it is also the largest. But it lacks, with its huge formidable military-camp air, the delicious amenities of the palaces and villas that crowd the gulf of Naples, the Phlegraean fields so beloved of patrician Romans, poets, statesmen and emperors. . . . where every one in Rome who was any one had his villa or his palace to retire to from the Roman dog-days. We see their ruins now, or many of them; scattered down the mountains that run down to the sea, themselves too running into the sea, *villes englouties*, drowned as well as wrecked, for some who lacked enough room on the shore (so great was the competition for house-space) thrust out, as Horace jeered, into the sea... : but the cause of their drowning was that the sea of the bay, so often convulsed by volcanic motions, rose twenty feet above its old level [. . .] Palaces, fishponds, lampreys, swimming-pools on the tops of houses, all were perished, leaving only their ruins under water or in caves. Alas, there is always, or nearly always, something in the past of ruins which displeases, and probably one should not know too much of their late owners. Of the imperial palaces down this golden coast and on its islands, those of Nero, Caligula, Tiberius and the rest, there remain a few temples, great baths, cisterns, the fragments jutting from the sea, and the seaweed-green pavements dimly seen through clear blue water. You can still swim about among palace walls, though now you have to hire a cabin and swim from a crowded bathing beach or rocks brown with sprawling bodies.❞

ROSE MACAULAY, *THE PLEASURE OF RUINS*, WEIDENFELD AND NICOLSON, LONDON, 1953

POMPEII

London-born Samuel Rogers (1763–1855), commissioned Turner as illustrator for an edition of his "Italy", for which he had followed Childe Harold's footsteps as a tribute to Lord Byron.

> **"POMPEII LIKE ANY OTHER TOWN. SAME OLD HUMANITY.**
> **ALL THE SAME WHETHER ONE BE DEAD OR ALIVE.**
> **POMPEII COMFORTABLE SERMON. LIKE POMPEII**
> **BETTER THAN PARIS."** HERMAN MELVILLE, 1857

"We had no intimation of what was coming – when, alighting at a small, door, we descended a few paces, & found ourselves in the forum, the columns of its portico standing, & on some of them scrawled by the people names, a horse galloping in red chalk – then came the theatres, the basilica, the temples, the streets – after passing the Apothecary's, who can stand at the fountain – Ganimede – where the three ways meet paved with lava – & look up & down near the oil-merchant's door & the miller's, & not feel a strange & not unpleasing sadness. Who can walk thro' the better houses – one of these is bounded by Vesuvius itself – particularly those in the borgo, their baths, & courts & gardens unmoved?"

SAMUEL ROGERS, *ITALIAN JOURNAL*,
FEBRUARY 20, 1815

AN EDUCATION
Mother of Anthony and Thomas, Frances Trollope (1780–1863) was herself a writer and a woman of inexhaustible energy. She traveled in America and throughout continental Europe, writing on the native peoples she found there.

"In nothing has my ignorance led me wider astray in every idea I had formed beforehand, than in the case of Pompeii. I had fancied a (comparatively speaking) small excavation, to which we were probably to descend by steps. But, instead of this, a gate was opened to us which led into an enclosure on a level with the road without. [. . .] for of all the walks I ever took, this was decidedly the most pregnant in interest . . . and till somebody or other will be kind enough to make a *scavo* to the extent of another mile or two, I can never hope for such another.

I may tell you that the sort of excitement produced by being able to wander thus through streets, and into dwellings, whose latest inhabitants were antique Romans, is strangely delightful, and the whole spectacle infinitely more redolent of all we have read of this proud, voluptuous, artificial race, than I had expected to find it. . . . It is so easy too, from the very similar arrangement of all the dwellings, however different in size and stateliness, to follow their manner and style of existence. Before the first two hours' walk was ended I felt possessed of an immensity of classic knowledge, not of words, but of things. No wonder the race are so rarely represented as having any of those dear domestic qualities which make even the littlenesses of human life amiable! . . . The very smallest of their dwellings shows much more preparation for public receiving, and display, than for home comforts; and as for the quiet, I might almost call it the sacred retreat, that all classes possessing the decencies of life enjoy in modern days, namely the portion of a dwelling called a *bed-room*, it evidently came not into their calculation of necessities. In place of these we see cells, – decorated indeed, but still cells, – having no ventilation, or

light either, save by means of the door. [. . .] The streets with the impression of carriage wheels still visible upon them. . . the commodious fountain wherever four streets meet. . . the well-used curb-stone, against which the ear almost fancies it can catch the grating of a Roman chariot wheel. . . the oil shop. . . the baker's shop. . . the startling '*cave cane*' at the poet's door. . . all bring dead days to life again, with a power almost as mysterious as that which brought back Saul."

MRS TROLLOPE,
A VISIT TO ITALY,
RICHARD BENTLEY, 1842

VESUVIUS

A GULF OF FLAMES

Fynes Moryson (1566–1617) was born in Cadeby, Lincolnshire, and was educated at Cambridge. Between 1591 and 1597 he traveled round Europe, and wrote historic and lengthy accounts of his voyages.

66 This Mountaine Somma [Vesuvius] is most high, and upon the top is dreadfull, where is a gulfe casting out flames, and while the windes inclosed, seeke to breake out by naturall force, there have been heard horrible noises and fearefull groanes. The rest of the Mountaine aboundeth with vines, and Olives, and there growes the Greeke-wine, which Pliny calles Pompeies wine; and of this wine they say, this place is called Torre di Græco. The greatest burning of this Mountaine brake out in the time of the Emperour Titus, the smoke whereof made the Sunne darke, burnt up the next territories, and consumed two Cities, Pompeia, and Herculea, and the ashes thereof covered all the fields of that territory. It brake out againe in the yeere 1538 with great gaping of the earth, and casting downe part of the Mountaine. 99

FYNES MORYSON, *AN ITINERARY*, JAMES MACLEHOSE AND SONS, GLASGOW, 1908

THE BURNING MOUNTAIN

"Voyage of Italy" (1670), by Richard Lassels (?1603– 1668), was hailed by politician and journalist John Wilkes as "one of the best accounts of the curious things of Italy".

66 Having thus seen the towne itself, you must then see the wonders of Nature which are about it. And horseing betimes in the morning, you may go to see Vesuvius the burning Mountaine, some seven miles distant from Naples. Your guide will shew you the last spoyle it made, some twenty four yeares agoe, in its last eruption, which covered the rich country round about it with barren ashes above two yards thick. So that Iam cinis est ubi tellus erat. Then he will shew you the vast stones which overchargeing the stomack of this hill had caused it to vomit them up with such boaking [sic] that Naples thought the day of doome had been at hand. Then he will shew you a channel in which from that spewing hill, had runn a filthy green matter mingled together of brimstone, alum, iron, water, Salpeter and Sulphur. The manner of it was thus: first the Hill beganne to smoake more vehemently than ordinarily it used to do. Then it begann to flame and cast out a clowd of ashes, which (had the wind layd towards the towne) it had covered all Naples. Then it beganne to roare, as if nature had been in Labour. Thunder was put [sic] pistol crack to this noyse: a mouth of a Canon two miles wide must needs make a great report. It bellowed and thundered againe. The ground swelled; the aire shivered for feare, whiles Vesuvius tearing its owne entralls with huge violence, was brought to bedd of a world of great stones and a flood of Sulphurious matter which ranne into the Sea. The long inscription at the foot of this hill upon the road, will tell you more, if youl stay to read and write it out in your table booke as I did.

Being thus instructed youle grow more desirous to see this hill, and therefore leaving the guide with your horses, you must climbe up it afoote for a mile together. The first wonder that I observed there was this: that one hill should be so hoat within as to burne, and be so cold without as to be covered with snow and as I mounted, I could not but compare it to an old man with a white head and beard boyling within with the flames of love.

At last comeing to the topp of the hill, and looking the vast hollow, you will finde this hill to be like a vast chauldron two miles in compasse, a mile deep, and about a quarter of a mile in diameter. Having thus peeped rather than gazed into into this concavity (remembering Pliny's accident here) and seen the young hill (which is now growing up in the very bottom of the hollow cave of this great hill) which smooketh allwayes, as the rest of the hollow cave doth, you may return downe againe, and come to Naples."

RICHARD LASSELS AND "THE VOYAGE OF ITALY" IN THE SEVENTEENTH CENTURY,
IN EDWARD CHANEY, *THE GRAND TOUR AND THE GREAT REBELLION*,
SLATKINE, GENEVA, 1985

LAVA STREAM

Whimsical and satirical writer and essayist Washington Irving (1783–1859) lived in Europe for seventeen years following the death of his fiancée.

"We could now plainly percieve the course of the lava which had merely run down the crater and collected in a small valley, at the foot of it. Quitting this place we ascended along the edge of the lava to attain the crater, but this was by far the most fatguing part of the excursion. The ascent was exceeding steep. The ashes so soft & loose that we slipped back two thirds of each step, and the eddies of wind frequently brought volumes of sulphurous smoke upon us [that were] almost stifling.

Our throats were sore from inhaling it. On our way the guides pointed out to us a spot where the lava seemed to spume out of a hole – being conducted from the crater to that place in a kind of coverd aqueduct formed by the cold lava's being incrusted over it. A little higher up was a hole that vomited up smoke & sparks. The cicerone took us on the lava about twelve feet higher up than the hole and told us to regard it steadfastly till the wind blew the smoke another way. We did so – and saw the lava rushing along in it like a torrent, by the direction of it we found it passed under the very spot on which we stood, the lava having there coold & formed a kind of coverd way.

It even began to feel very hot to our feet and we evacuated the place with precipitation – The guides seemed diverted with our apprehensions being themselves habituated to the scene. About ten yards further up was a small eminence or hillock in the lava out of which sulphurous flames issued with a violent hissing noise. We were toiling up the crater nearly in a parallel line with this object when the wind sat directly from it and overwhelmed us with dense torrents of the most noxious smoke. I endeavor to hold my breath as long as possible in hopes another flow of wind would carry it off but at length I was obliged to draw in my breath and inhale a draught of the poisonous vapour that almost overcame me. Fortunately for us the wind shifted as I sincerely believe that in a little time we should have shared the fate of pliny & died the martyrs of imprudent curiosity."

WASHINGTON IRVING, *JOURNALS AND NOTEBOOKS, 1803–6*,
UNIVERSITY OF WISCONSIN PRESS, MADISON, 1969

ERUPTION

Norman Lewis spent a year in Naples in 1944 as an officer in the US army.

"Today Vesuvius erupted. It was the most majestic and terrible sight I have ever seen, or ever expect to see. The smoke from the crater slowly built up into a great bulging shape having all the appearance of solidity. It swelled and expanded so slowly that there was no sign of movement in the cloud which, by evening, must have risen thirty or forty thousand feet into the sky, and measured many miles across. The shape of the eruption that obliterated Pompeii reminded Pliny of a pine tree, and he probably stood here at Posillipo across the bay, where I was standing now and where Nelson and Emma Hamilton stood to view the eruption of their day, and the shape was indeed like that of a many-branching tree. What took one by surprise about Pliny's pine was that it was absolutely motionless, not quite painted – because it was three-dimensional – but moulded on the sky; an utterly still, and utterly menacing shape."

NORMAN LEWIS, *NAPLES '44*, WILLIAM COLLINS, GLASGOW, 1978

THE ISLANDS OF THE BAY

ISCHIA

Irish philosopher George Berkeley (1685–1753) traveled in Italy in the early part of the 18th century. While there he lost the first draft of the second part of "The Treatise Concerning the Principles of Human Knowledge", and never attempted to rewrite it. Here he describes the delights of the isle of Ischia to his friend Alexander Pope.

❝The island . . . is an epitome of the whole earth containing within the compass of eighteen miles, a wonderful variety of hills, vales, ragged rocks, fruitful plains, and barren mountains, all thrown together in a most romantic confusion. The air is, in the hottest season, constantly refreshed by cool breezes from the sea. The vales produce excellent wheat and Indian corn, but are mostly covered with vineyards intermixed with fruit trees. Besides the common kinds, as cherries, apricots, peaches, &c., they produce oranges, limes, almonds, pomegranates, figs, water-melons, and many other fruits unknown to our climates, which lie every where open to the passenger. The hills are the greater part covered to the top with vines, some with chestnut groves, and others with thickets of myrtle and lentiscus. The fields in the northern side are divided by hedgerows of myrtle. Several fountains and rivulets add to the beauty of this landscape, which is likewise set off by the variety of some barren spots and naked rocks. But that which crowns the scene is a large mountain rising out of the middle of the island, (once a terrible volcano, by the ancients called Mons Epomeus). Its lower parts are adorned with vines and other fruits; the middle affords pasture to flocks of goats and sheep; and the top is a sandy pointed rock, from which you have the finest prospect in the world, surveying at one view, besides several pleasant islands, lying at your feet, a tract of Italy about three hundred miles in length, from the promontory of Antium to the cape of Palinarus: the greater part of which hath been sung by Homer and Virgil, as making a considerable part of the travels and adventures of their two heroes . . . The inhabitants of this delicious isle, as they are without riches and honours, so they are without the vices and follies that attend them; and were they but as much strangers to revenge as they are to avarice and ambition, they might in fact answer the poetical notions of the golden age.❞

GEORGE BERKELEY, *LETTER TO ALEXANDER POPE*,
OCTOBER 22, 1717

. . . AND PROCIDA

Historian Arnold Toynbee (1889–1975) was born in London. His major achievement, "A Study of History", surveys the great civilizations of the world, examining cycles of cultural creativity and decay. "Between Niger and Nile" was one of several books he produced as an enthusiastic traveler.

❝I thought I saw a man-o'war
Making from Naples Bay;
I looked again and saw it was
The Isle of Ischia.
Poor thing, I said, poor silly thing,
It can't get under way.

"CAPRI IS NOT THE PLACE FOR MORALIZING."
NORMAN DOUGLAS, 1952

That is how Lewis Carroll might have put it if he had seen Ischia and Procida from our plane when he was writing Sylvie and Bruno.**
ARNOLD TOYNBEE, BETWEEN NIGER AND NILE, 1965

CAPRI
The debauched antics of the notorious Roman emperor Tiberius, documented by Gaius Suetonius Tranquillus (AD c.70–c.140) and Tacitus (AD c.55–after 115), in his "Annals", established a reputation for Capri that has proved hard to shed.

**So he took refuge on the island of Capreae, separated from the tip of the Surrentum promontory by three miles of sea. Presumably what attracted him was the isolation of Capreae. Harbourless, it has few roadsteads even for small vessels; sentries can control all landings. In winter the climate is mild, since hills on the mainland keep off gales. In summer the island is delightful, since it faces west and has open sea all round. The bay it overlooks was exceptionally lovely, until Vesuvius' eruption transformed the landscape.

On the island, then, in twelve spacious, separately named villas, Tiberius took up residence. His former absorption in State affairs ended. Instead he spent the time in secret orgies, or idle malevolent thoughts.**

TACITUS, *ANNALS*,
TRANS. MICHAEL GRANT, PENGUIN,
HARMONDSWORTH, 1956

On retiring to Capri he made himself a private sporting-house, where sexual extravagances were practised for his secret pleasure. Bevies of girls and young men, whom he had collected from all over the Empire as adepts in unnatural practices, and known as spintriae, would perform before him in groups of three, to excite his waning passions. A number of small rooms were furnished with the most indecent pictures and statuary obtainable, also certain erotic manuals from Elephantis in Egypt; the inmates of the establishment would know from these exactly what was expected of them. He furthermore devised little nooks of lechery in the woods and glades of the island, and had boys and girls dressed up as Pans and nymphs posted in front of coverns or grottoes; so that the island was now openly and generally called 'Caprineum', because of his goatish antics.

SUETONIUS, *THE TWELVE CAESARS*,
TRANS. ROBERT GRAVES, PENGUIN, HARMONDSWORTH, 1957

CAPRI
Axel Munthe (1857–1949) was a Swedish-born doctor whose memoir, "The Story of San Michele", was an international bestseller describing the building of a dream villa on Capri.

**Old Mastro Vincenzo was still hard at work in his vineyard, digging deep furrows in the sweet-scented soil for the new vines. Now and then he picked up a slab of coloured marble or a piece of red stucco and threw it over the wall, 'Roba di Timberio' said he. I sat down on a broken column of red granite by the side of my new friend. Era molto duro, it was very hard to break, said Mastro Vincenzo. At my feet a chicken was scratching in the earth in search of a worm and before my very nose appeared a coin. I picked it up and recognized at a glance the noble head of Augustus, 'Divus Augustus Pater.' Mastro Vincenzo said it was not worth a baiocco, I have it still. He had made the garden all by himself and had planted all the vines and fig-trees with his own hands. Hard work, said Mastro Vincenzo showing me his

119

large, horny hands, for the whole ground was full of roba di Tiberio, columns, capitals, fragments of statues and teste de cristiani, and he had to dig up and carry away all this rubbish before he could plant his vines. The columns he had split into garden steps and of course he had been able to utilize many of the marbles when he was building his house and the rest he had thrown over the precipice. A piece of real good luck had been when quite unexpectedly he had come upon a large subterranean room just under his house, with red walls just like that piece there under the peach tree all painted with lots of stark naked cristiani . . . with their hands full of flowers and bunches of grapes. It took him several days to scrape off all these paintings and cover the wall with cement, but this was small labour compared to what it would have meant to blast the rock and build a new cistern, said Mastro Vincenzo with a cunning smile.**99**

AXEL MUNTHE, *THE STORY OF SAN MICHELE*,
JOHN MURRAY, LONDON, 1950

THE BLUE GROTTO

Besides his novels and short stories, Henry James (1843–1916) wrote several volumes of travel sketches, concentrating upon his favorite theme of the American in Europe.

66The creaking and puffing little boat, which had conveyed me only from Sorrento, drew closer beneath the prodigious island – beautiful, horrible, and haunted – that does most, of all the happy elements and accidents, towards making the Bay of Naples, for the study of composition, a lesson in the grand style. There was only, above and below, through the blue of the air and sea, a great confused shining of hot cliffs and crags and buttresses, a loss, from nearness, of the splendid couchant outline and the more comprehensive mass, and an opportunity – oh, not lost, I assure you – to sit and meditate, even moralize, on the empty deck, while a happy brotherhood of American and German tourists, including, of course, many sisters, scrambled down into little waiting, rocking tubs and, after a few strokes, popped systematically into the small orifice of the Blue Grotto. There was an appreciable moment when they were all lost to view in that receptacle, the daily 'psychological' moment during which it must so often befall the recalcitrant observer on the deserted deck to find himself aware of how delightful it might be if none of them should come out again. The charm, the fascination of the idea is not a little – though also not wholly – in the fact that, as the wave rises over the aperture, there is the most encouraging appearance that they perfectly may not. There it is. There is no more of them. It is a case to which nature has, by the neatest stroke and with the best taste in the world, just quietly attended.**99**

HENRY JAMES, *COLLECTED TRAVEL WRITINGS: THE CONTINENT*,
THE LIBRARY OF AMERICA, NEW YORK, 1993

ITINERARIES IN THE CITY AND BAY OF NAPLES

▲ Neapolitan smiles.

▲ Cigarette vendor.   ▼ Religious devotion, Capri.

▲ Temple of Athena (known as Ceres), Paestum. ▼ Forum at Pomp

▼ House of the Deer, Herculaneum.

NAPLES

The urban structure of Naples is rich in dimensional and morphological contrasts. On the one hand, landscaped roads lead to the waterfront, open squares break up the densely built framework of buildings, and large monuments occupy the most visually strategic locations; by contrast, on the other, streets, flights of steps and narrow alleys form part of a fairly fragmented urban fabric consisting of five- or six-story blocks built on small plots of land. The richness of this architectural and urban structure is the result of the construction and expansion carried out during different periods of the city's history. Evidence of this can be found in the great monuments, as well as the less important buildings, and in the districts, characterized by their relative position within the city and the specific traits of their particular type of architecture. To appreciate fully its particular characteristics and its very specific beauty, the city of Naples must be considered in its entirety. It was to this end that, under the leadership of three directors (Antonella di Luggo, Riccardo Florio and Fulvio Rino), a talented team of architects and historians from the University Federico II of Naples constructed the view of Naples entitled *Napoli in Assonometria* (Electa Napoli, Naples 1992). The form and structure of Naples is above all characterized by its variety; and it is the general relief of the landscape that has made it possible to combine a wide diversity of often contrasting realities in a city of unparalleled formal beauty.

Adriana Baculo Giusti,
Professor of
Relief Architecture,
University Federico II,
Naples

ITINERARIES IN NAPLES

◆ The monumental center, containing the city's most important buildings.
◆ The urban structure based around the Spaccanapoli, the lower *decumanus* of the Greco-Roman city.
◆ The oldest part of the city, between the Piazza Dante and the Piazza Bellini.
◆ The upper districts of the city, between the Museo Archeologico Nazionale and the Albergo dei Poveri.

◆ The north–south axis that runs across the city from the sea to Capodimonte.
◆ The Quartieri Bassi, dissected at the end of the 19th century by the Corso Umberto I, linking the monumental center to the Piazza Mercato and Piazza del Carmine districts.
◆ The Vomero.
◆ The waterfront, from Mergellina to Santa Lucia.

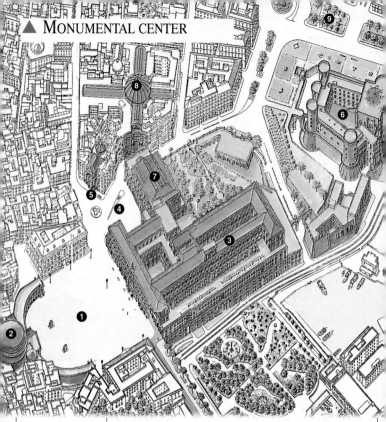

PARADES ON THE LARGO DI PALAZZO
The Largo di Palazzo, today occupied by the Piazza del Plebiscito, was once the site for official ceremonies and military parades.

At the end of the 13th century, Charles I of Anjou's decision to abandon the Castel Capuano and build another castle (the Castel Nuovo) further west, on the waterfront, significantly affected the urban development of the city. Naples became the capital of the kingdom, while this area of the city was established as its political and administrative center, a role that it still retains. Here the successive rulers of Naples left their monumental mark: the kings of Anjou and Aragon built and rebuilt the Castel Nuovo, the Spanish viceroys reflected the splendor of the Madrilenian dynasty in the Palazzo Reale, while the Bourbons of the Two Sicilies gave the royal palace the dimensions worthy of a great European capital. It also became the home of the military command, the city hall and, more recently, the Regional Council of Campania.

Piazza Plebiscito

A monumental piazza. This is one of the most orderly and symmetrical squares in Europe. Its buildings represent the four centers of power, with the Church and the Kingdom of Naples at either end of the main axis, and the military command and government on the transverse axis. Equestrian statues of Charles III and Ferdinand I stand in the center of the piazza, bordered to the south by the 18th-century Palazzo Salerno (its exact counterpart), the Palazzo della Prefettura (1818) to the north, and the façade of the Palazzo Reale to the east.

Church of San Francesco di Paola. The church of San Francesco di Paola stands at the center of the hemicycle. It was founded in 1817 by Ferdinand I, King of the Two Sicilies, as an act of thanksgiving following his reconquest of the kingdom (from which he had been driven by the Napoleonic wars ▲ 33). The massive drum, surmounted by a low dome, and the Ionic portico were inspired by the Roman Pantheon. Its neoclassical design, by the architect Pietro Bianchi, blends perfectly with the Tuscan Doric colonnade built by Leopoldo Laperuta, in 1809, at the request of Joachim Murat.

Palazzo Reale

In 1598 the new king of Spain, Philip III, made Fernández Ruiz de Castro viceroy of Naples. The latter, wishing to build a palace that would represent the glory of Spain, engaged the services of the architect Domenico Fontana, in 1599. By 1616, the main body of the façade building and part of the courtyard were completed and inhabited. But it was not until the accession of Ferdinand IV, in 1759, that the State Wing was constructed, under the direction of Ferdinando Fuga. The palace was completed by Gaetano Genovese after a fire in 1837, when the façade of the Belvedere was built overlooking the sea. The palace was extensively restored after the bomb damage sustained in 1943. The second-floor royal apartments, accessible from the state courtyard, have retained their decoration and give an insight into the history of the palace and its sovereigns from the 17th to the 19th century.

Statue of Vittorio Emanuele II, on the façade of the Palazzo Reale.

Treasures of the Biblioteca Nazionale
The Biblioteca Nazionale occupies the State Wing of the Palazzo Reale. It was founded in 1919, at the instigation of Benedetto Croce ▲ 142, the then Minister for Education, and its early (pre-1500) printed collections make it one of the richest libraries in Italy. It has more than two million volumes, including some remarkable 15th- and 16th-century miniatures and the manuscript of *L'Infinito* by Giacomo Leopardi.

THRONE ROOM

This is one of the most beautiful rooms in the palace: its baldachin dates from the 18th century and the ceiling reliefs represent the twelve provinces of the Kingdom of Naples. The royal portraits on the walls include paintings of Ferdinand I in the costume of a knight of San Gennaro, by Vincenzo Camuccini, and Vittorio Emanuele III, by Enrico Marchiani (1874). The throne, installed for the Bourbons in 1850, was retained by the house of Savoy, which merely added its eagle in 1860.

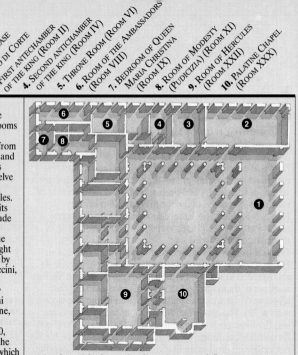

The Grand Staircase leads to the second-floor apartments (now a museum) formerly inhabited by the Bourbons.

FIRST ANTECHAMBER OF THE KING. The ceiling of the chamber (also known as the "antechamber of the diplomatic corps") was painted by Francesco de Mura (1738) for the marriage of Charles of Bourbon and Maria Amalia of Saxony. The tapestries representing fire and air were made in the Gobelin factory in Paris.

SECOND ANTECHAMBER OF THE KING. The frescos by Belisario Corenzio (early 17th century) represent the triumph of the house of Aragon. Rooms VIII and XI also have ceilings from the same period depicting the glory of the Spanish sovereigns and the conquest of the Kingdom of Naples.

BELVEDERE TERRACE. The bedroom of Queen Maria Christina, the first wife of Ferdinand II, opens onto a terrace garden that overlooks the sea and offers a magnificent view of the Gulf of Naples, Vesuvius and Capri. This is where the so-called Belvedere wing begins.

ROOM OF MODESTY (PUDICIZIA). The room is named after the *Allegory of Modesty* tapestry that was woven in 1766 by the royal manufactures of Caserta for the bedchamber of Ferdinand I. The ceiling by Battistello Caracciolo depicts the conquest of Calabria by the first viceroy of Naples.

ROOM OF HERCULES. The room contains tapestries, woven by the royal manufactures of the House of Bourbon, dating from the second half of the 18th century. The *lys d'or* (golden lilies) of the house of Bourbon, obscured in 1860 ● *31*, were made good during the restoration work carried out in 1994.

PALATINE CHAPEL. The chapel, by Francesco Antonio Picchiatti (1640), has a marble and gilt bronze altar by Dionisio Lazzari (1674). The altar had a magnificent *Immaculate Conception* by Guiseppe Ribera. The Neapolitans, shocked at the artist using his daughter as its model, removed the painting during the plague of 1656. It was taken back to Spain by one of the viceroys and burnt during the Spanish Civil War.

ROOM OF THE
AMBASSADORS (top).
The room has a
ceiling depicting the
great deeds of the
Spanish royal house,
painted by Belisario
Corenzio and
Massimo Stanzione.
GRAND STAIRCASE
(left). The double
staircase by Francesco
Antonio Picchiatti
(1651) was
considered "the finest
in Europe" by
Montesquieu.
TEATRO DI CORTE
(above).
The theater was
designed by
Ferdinando Fuga, in
1768, in 18th-century
style. Partly destroyed
during the bombing
in 1943, it has now
been beautifully
restored.

Piazzo del Municipio (right).

NEAPOLITAN LITERARY RENDEZVOUS
The Gambrinus, the famous Edwardian *café-concert* on the Piazza Trieste e Trento, was the favorite rendezvous of Neapolitan literary circles. It has retained its stucco, silk and paper decorations.

GALLERIA UMBERTO ● 87: A MASTERPIECE OF IRON AND GLASS ★
This impressive covered gallery, with its glass roof reaching to a height of 187 feet, was built behind the church of San Ferdinando at the end of the 19th century. It stands on the site of an apartment block, demolished after the cholera epidemic of 1884, and is a monumental

manifestation of the "modernity" of a united Italy ● *33*. Cafés, stores and a theater were established in what soon became one of the busiest meeting places in early 20th-century Naples. Today its cafes and stores, which include Barbaro, outlet of the top Neapolitan designer, and Eboli, an established family jeweler's, still make the Galleria Umberto a fashionable rendezvous.

PIAZZA TRIESTE E TRENTO. Formerly known as San Ferdinando, the piazza's present name derives from the accession of the house of Savoy. In spring Neapolitan brides gather for their traditional wedding photograph, taken against the backdrop of the piazza's majestic palaces. In the center of the piazza, the CHURCH OF SAN FERDINANDO (1622–65), owned by the Jesuits until they were expelled in 1767, has a rich collection of frescos, stuccowork and funerary monuments.

CASTEL NUOVO ● *80*

A ROYAL FORTRESS. The dark and impressive bulk of the castle, punctuated by massive towers, overlooks the port and the Piazza del Municipio. Begun in 1442 under Alfonso and Ferrante of Aragon, it was built on the ruins of the Maschio Angioino ("Dungeon of Anjou"), a name still used to refer to the castle. All that remains of the fortress, built by Charles I of Anjou (1279–82) is the Gothic nave of the CAPPELLA PALATINA dedicated to Santa Barbara. The restoration work carried out in the early 20th century, under the direction of Gaetano Filangieri, eliminated the many later additions and restored the fortress to its former glory, as it appears in 15th-century miniatures. The geometric decoration at the base of the towers and the two-story loggia (a reminder that the Castel Nuovo was also a royal residence) on the façade overlooking the sea are the only elements to alleviate the gray austerity of the high, peperino walls. The flower market, set up at dawn at the foot of the castle, adds a welcome splash of color.

ARCO DI TRIONFO ● *82*. The monumental, white marble triumphal arch (far right), set between two massive towers, forms the entrance to the courtyard of the castle. A masterpiece of Italian Renaissance sculpture, it commemorates the victory of Alfonso the Magnanimous over the Angevins in 1443 ● *31*. Many Italian and Spanish sculptors worked on its decoration between 1445 and 1468. Above the arch, which is surmounted by a loggia, a bas-relief

shows the triumphal entry of Alfonso the Magnanimous into Naples. In the courtyard are the old bronze gates of the castle's triumphal entrance, by Guglielmo Monaco da Parigi and Pietro di Martino. The six panels of the gate, cast between 1462 and 1468, celebrate the victories of Ferrante of Aragon over the Angevins in 1462 ● *31*. There is also a cannon ball embedded in the metal.

INTERIOR. Today municipal council meetings are held in the SALA DEI BARONI ● *82* where, in 1487, Ferrante of Aragon had all the barons who supported the Angevin cause ● *31* assassinated during a marriage celebration. The sala's magnificent ceiling, with its Catalan-inspired octagonal vaults with intersecting ribs, is by the Majorcan architect Guglielmo Sagrera (15th century). Most of the paintings and sculptures (15th–19th century) housed in one of the building's two museums, have come from the city's old churches.

PIAZZA DEL MUNICIPIO

This long, rectangular square (above), bordered by the north wing of the Castel Nuovo and with Vesuvius in the background, slopes gently toward the sea. Since the 15th century it has provided a link between land and sea, between the west and east of the city.

PALAZZO MUNICIPALE. The Palazzo Municipale (formerly "San Giacomo") stands at the top end of the square, with the Castel Sant'Elmo ▲ *185* and the Certosa di San Martino ▲ *184* outlined in the distance. The palace, now the city hall, was built by Stefano and Luigi Gasse in 1816–17 as a PALACE FOR THE MINISTERS SERVING UNDER THE BOURBONS. The new structure incorporated the façade of the church of SAN GIACOMO DEGLI SPAGNOLI, commissioned from Ferdinando Manlio, in 1540, by the viceroy Don Pedro de Toledo for the Spanish community in Naples.

TEATRO MERCADANTE
The construction of the former Teatro del Fondo was financed by the sale of confiscated Jesuit wealth. In order to compete with the nearby Teatro San Carlo ▲ *136*, it specialized in comedy and burlesque theater. The façade, which overlooks the Piazza del Municipio, was completely rebuilt in 1892, when the theater took its present name.

The Arco di Trionfo (Triumphal Arch) of Alfonso the Magnanimous.

135

▲ TEATRO SAN CARLO

Charles of Bourbon wanted his new opera house, built to replace the Teatro San Bartolomeo, which had become far too small, to rival the other Italian musical capitals (Venice and Rome) and establish the reputation of Neapolitan opera abroad. He employed the services of the architects Giovanni Antonio Medrano and Angelo Carsale who, in less than three hundred days, built an impressive monument designed to symbolize the reign of the Bourbons. The Teatro San Carlo, considered at the time to be the largest and most beautiful opera house in the world, opened on November 4, 1737 with a performance of *Achille in Scirro* by Domenico Natale.

THE FIRE OF 1816

The theater, destroyed by fire on February 12, 1816, was rebuilt in less than a year by Antonio Niccolini, thanks to its director Domenico Barbaia ▲ *149.* A year later, it re-opened under the direction of Domenico Barbaia and Gioacchino Rossini with a performance of *Il Sogno di Partenope*, by Simone Mayr, with Isabella Colbran (who became the wife of Rossini) in the role of *prima donna.*

"PRIMA DONNA"

The *prima donna* (the title stipulated in the contract) occupied an elevated position, enjoyed certain prerogatives in the interpretation of her role and was venerated by the opera-going public. Renata Tebaldi (above) was one of the great *prima donnas* of the 20th century.

> "ON SPECIAL OCCASIONS, THE CANDLES BURNING ABOVE EACH BOX CREATE THE IMPRESSION THAT THIS VAST, DARK AUDITORIUM . . . IS SOMEHOW ALIVE."
>
> ALEXANDER DUMAS, FILS

THE OLDEST ITALIAN OPERA HOUSE
The six levels of (184) boxes provided the framework for the royal box, a veritable salon with some fifteen or so seats, each surmounted by a huge crown. The thousands of candles burning between the rows of boxes were reflected in the mirrors. Today the Teatro San Carlo is still the largest theater (3,000 seats) in Naples.

AN ENCHANTING EXPERIENCE
The theater's chandeliers, draperies, gold, silver and blue decorations, as well as a stage that could be opened onto the gardens of the Palazzo Reale, were guaranteed to enchant all those who crossed its threshold.

The Spaccanapoli is one of
Naples' oldest districts and is
still steeped in the atmosphere of
Neapolitan popular life. It takes its name
(which literally means "Split-Naples") from the
street that bisects the city center from the hill of
San Martino to the district of Forcella. This itinerary
explores Greco-Roman Naples and follows the line of
the southern *plateia*, one of the three straight arteries
intersected at right angles by a network of narrow streets
(*stenopoi*) and a fine example of the
checkerboard layout of Greek
urban colonies. The structure has
survived intact in the
regular pattern of the
apartment blocks,
even though the
appearance of the
streets has changed
significantly since the
13th century. When
Charles I of Anjou
decided to make
Naples his capital, the
impressive churches
he built along this
ancient street were
much taller than the
houses that bordered
it during antiquity.
The constructional
framework was
further altered in the

Guglia (spire) della
Immacolata.

15th century when the aristocracy built palaces on the Spaccanapoli (this itinerary has some of the finest Renaissance residences in Naples) and the narrow street became enclosed between these high buildings. But behind the façades, only a few yards from the noise and bustle of the street, are luxuriant, well-kept gardens, a legacy of the Roman *domus* ● 74, which turned its back on the street and opened onto shady green courtyards decorated with fountains.

The Spaccanapoli.

PIAZZA GESÙ NUOVO

THE PIAZZA. The Piazza Gesù Nuovo (below) is irregular in shape, evolving, unplanned, over the centuries. It is bordered by palaces of yellow-ocher tufa and "Bourbon" brick red, whose coloring creates a sense of warmth. During Roman times, it was the open area outside the Porta di Cumae, and was later incorporated into the city by the new walls built by the Angevins, pierced at this point by the Porta Reale ("royal gate"). From then on the *largo* marked the city's west entrance. In 1526 Ferrante Sanseverino, Prince of Salerno, demolished the houses he had just bought from the nuns of Santa Chiara ▲ 140 to clear the area in front of his beautiful palace. In the mid-16th century the viceroy Don Pedro de Toledo moved the city walls further west. The gate was demolished and the piazza became the link between the old city and the new Spanish districts.

GUGLIA DELLA IMMACOLATA ● 85. The Jesuits used donated funds to erect this amazing Rococo monument on the site of an equestrian statue of Philip V (destroyed during a popular uprising in 1707). Its pinnacle, inspired by Egyptian obelisks, was built between 1747 and 1750 by Giuseppe Genuino. Its rich and strongly theatrical decoration is a direct reflection of the preferences of the Jesuit order, which used the lavish Rococo style as a symbol of its power and an effective vehicle for religious propaganda.

PULCINELLA ● 52 During the pre-war period, one of Naples' principal puppet theaters stood at the foot of the Guglia della Immacolata. The puppet theater, an extremely popular and often irreverent form of Neapolitan entertainment, was responsible for the creation of the well-known character, Pulcinella, who represented the man in the street.

CHURCH OF GESÙ NUOVO ★ ● *84*. In 1584 the Jesuits took over the palace of the Sanseverino princes ▲ *139* that Ferrante, in disgrace with the Spanish Crown, had been forced to abandon in 1552. The architect and Jesuit father, Giuseppe Valeriani, was given the task of transforming the palace into a church, with a view to establishing the seat of the order in Naples. He retained the magnificent embossed façade of the Renaissance palace, with its diamond-point extrusions, and the two lateral marble portals. Behind the façade he designed a vast structure in the form of a

Greek cross, surmounted by a high dome that could be seen all over the city. The church was named Gesù Nuovo to distinguish it from the church of Gesù Vecchio ▲ *146*, the city's first Jesuit establishment. The dome of the church, rebuilt after the earthquake of 1688, was once again in danger of collapsing at the end of the 18th century. This symbol of the decline, in Naples, of the Society of Jesus (expelled from the kingdom by Ferdinand I in 1767), was leveled at the beginning of the 19th century. The richly decorated interior (above) is a fine example of the virtuosity of the Neapolitan artists who worked on it from the end of the 16th to the mid-18th century.

Portal of the church of Gesù Nuovo.

CONVENTO DI SANTA CHIARA

In 1310 the new King of Naples, Robert (the Wise) of Anjou, built a vast convent for the Clarisses at the request of his wife, Sancia di Maiorca, who was their patroness.

A PANTHEON.

The church's vast dimensions reflect the fact that it was designed to house the tombs of the Angevin dynasty. The work was carried out under the direction of Gagliardo Primario who, in 1328, completed the high Gothic nave with its naked framework, inspired by the Franciscan rejection of ornamentation. This simplicity was not appreciated by Charles of Anjou, the king's son and Duke of Calabria, a sophisticated and anti-establishment intellectual who preferred the elistism of the Carthusian order and compared the church with a stable. The royal tombs were entrusted to the famous sculptor from southern Italy, Tino di Camaino ● *80*. The church's original appearance was significantly altered in the 18th century by the addition of a false Baroque vault. On August 4, 1943 the church was bombed and devastated by fire. When the damage was assessed two days later, it was found that the Rococo additions, the roof and the medieval frescos had been destroyed and some of the tombs were very badly damaged. Today the edifice has regained its former Gothic purity as a result of major restoration work. The grandiose tomb of Robert the Wise (at the far end of the choir), by the Florentine sculptors Giovanni and Pacio Bertini, has been very badly damaged by fire. The FUNERARY MONUMENT OF CHARLES, DUKE OF CALABRIA, and the TOMB OF HIS WIFE, MARIE DE VALOIS (to the right of the altar), are both the work of Tino di Camaino. The tombs of the sovereigns of the Neapolitan house of Bourbon are in the last chapel on the right. A vestibule on the right of the transept leads into the CHIOSTRO DELLE CLARISSE, the vast cloister from where the nuns took part in the services. Its intersecting ribs are inspired by the French Gothic style. Behind the altar are the surviving fragments of the frescos attributed to Giotto which decorated the Gothic church.

CHIOSTRO DELLE CLARISSE: WISTERIA AND MAJOLICA TILES ★.

In the 18th century Domenico Antonio Vaccaro created a rustic garden in the huge 14th-century cloister, which still has its original Gothic arcades. The arbors shading the two walkways are beautifully decorated with blue, yellow and green majolica tiles (right) ● *84* by Giuseppe and Donato Massa. The benches are decorated with pastoral scenes, and garlands of vines and wisteria create a trompe-l'oeil effect as they wind around the octagonal pilasters that support the real vines and wisteria of the pergola. The cloister leads into the refectory. On the second floor, the 18th-century dormitory by Ferdinando Fuga has retained its original wooden structure. The cells open onto broad terraces whose ancient vines still produce a good dessert grape. Archeological excavations on the site of the convent have revealed the remains of Roman baths which stood at what was then the western limit of the city. These remains, as well as the ancient marbles re-used in the church, and medieval and Renaissance sculptures that were not

VOTIVE OFFERINGS OF GESÙ NUOVO
The CHAPEL OF THE VISITATION houses the relics of San Giuseppe Moscati (1880–1927), a renowned doctor and biochemist who was canonized in 1987. His self-denial aroused intense popular devotion even during his lifetime, as is evident from the many votive offerings lining the chapel and the rooms containing mementos of the saint.

The façade and spire of San Domenico Maggiore.

destroyed by fire, can be seen in the recently opened museum.
CAMPANILE. The Campanile, built on the site of the ancient Roman gate, marks the western end of the Spaccanapoli. It was rebuilt after the 1456 earthquake.

SANTA CHIARA TO SAN DOMENICO MAGGIORE

VIA BENEDETTO CROCE. Immediately on the left is the beautiful Baroque portal of the Palazzo Filomarino. The palace, built in the 14th century, was transformed in the 16th, damaged during Masaniello's rebellion (1647) ● *38* and extensively renovated in the 18th century. It was the home of Benedetto Croce, who gave his name to this section of the ancient thoroughfare linking Santa Chiara and San Domenigo Maggiore. Here, among Renaissance palaces (PALAZZO PETRUCCI, PALACE OF THE VENETIAN AMBASSADORS) and secret gardens, the ancient crafts of jewelry-making (pieces set in gold and coral) and paper-making (tissue paper, parchment, marbled paper) have been carried on by families of artisans for centuries. The PALAZZO PETRUCCI, with its Renaissance portal and the Catalan arches of its beautiful courtyard (15th century), partly echoes the structures of the earlier (Balzo) palace, destroyed by an earthquake in 1456. It was bought and rebuilt by Antonello Petrucci, the grand seneschal of King Ferrante of Aragon. He did not live to enjoy it, however, since he was accused of taking part in the baronial conspiracy ● *31* and executed in 1486.

PIAZZA SAN DOMENICO MAGGIORE. The high apse of San Domenico Maggiore, festooned with crenelations, dominates the piazza, whose café terraces, performances, concerts and exhibitions make it one of the busiest squares in Naples. It is also one of the few examples of Renaissance urban intervention. At the beginning of the 15th century, the area (the site of the west wall of the Greek city in the 5th century BC) was still partially occupied by gardens. The Aragonese sovereigns made San Domenico their royal church and duly set about opening up the approaches and modifying the existing structures to create a suitable setting for their ceremonies. The square assumed its present form in the 17th century when the aristocracy (especially the various branches of the Sangro family) built impressive palaces on the piazza: the PALAZZO SANGRO DI CASACALENDA, PALAZZO CORIGLIANO (today the Oriental Institute of the University) and the PALAZZO DEI SANGRO DI SANSEVERO, the home of Carlo Gesualdo. To the right of the monumental apse is an elegantly sculpted, 15th-century balcony decorated with the arms of the Carafa

"HOW COMFORTING IT IS TO FEEL ONESELF GATHERED TO THE BOSOM OF THESE ANCIENT BUILDINGS, WATCHED OVER AND PROTECTED BY THEIR FAMILIAR PROFILE."

BENEDETTO CROCE

family. In the center of the piazza the Baroque Guglia di San Domenico ● 85 was erected by the inhabitants of Naples to mark the end of the plague of 1656 ● 32.

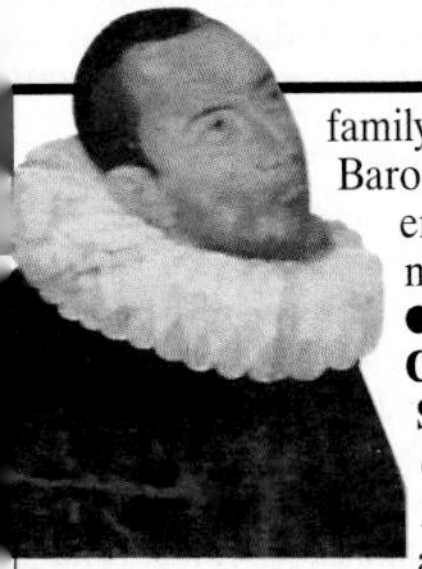

CHURCH AND CONVENT OF SAN DOMENICO MAGGIORE. At the end of the 13th century Charles II of Anjou built a vast, austere church and a convent for the mother house of the Dominican order. The new edifice incorporated the older church of Sant'Angelo a Morfisa, which was transformed into a huge side chapel. To improve access to the basilica, the Aragon sovereigns built a monumental staircase linking the piazza to the side entrance of the chapel. Many modifications, the last in neo-Gothic style (1850–3), have unfortunately obliterated all traces of the original Gothic architecture. The CAPPELLA BRANCACCIO (second on the right) contains early 14th-century frescos, attributed to Pietro Cavallini. The CAPPELLONE DEL CROCIFISSO, named after a 13th-century painting of the Crucifixion, and the CARAFA DI RUVO CHAPEL (1511), with its beautiful Renaissance decoration, are also worth a visit. The balustrade of the high altar, the marble pulpits set against the pilasters of the choir (Cosimo Fanzago, 1640-6) and the polychrome tiling (Domenico Antonio Vaccaro, 1732) are all Baroque additions. The right transept leads to the Sacristy where the frescoed vault (Francesco Solimena, 1709) illustrates the triumph of the Dominican order. On a gallery above the presses lining the walls, forty-five elaborately decorated and recently restored coffins contain the remains of two kings (Ferrante I, d. 1494, and Ferdinand II, d. 1496) and a number of princes of Aragon, as well as court dignitaries (including Antonello Petrucci, even though he was executed by order of the king). Saint Thomas Aquinus was among those who taught in the Convent's faculty of theology (1272), while its students included the philosopher Giordano Bruno, sentenced in Rome to be burnt at the stake for heresy, and the poet Giovanni Pontano ● *43*, ▲ *151*.

CARLO GESUALDO, PRINCE, MUSICIAN AND MURDERER

(c. 1560–c. 1613) During the night of October 16–17, 1590 Carlo Gesualdo, Prince of Venosa (left), caught his wife with her lover, Fabrizio Carafa. He had them both killed and fled Naples. However, because he enjoyed the protection of the viceroy, he was able (after a period of traveling) to return to the city with complete impunity. The incident did not affect his musical genius and this virtuoso of the lute is one of the best-known composers of madrigals. He introduced the anguish of his crime into his music and composed "his first piercing notes". (Jean-Noël Schifano, *Chroniques napolitaines*, 1984)

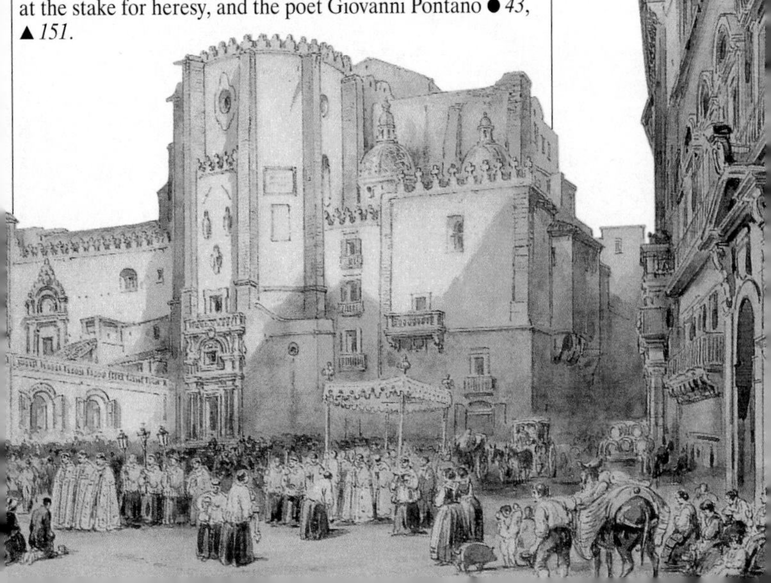

The tiny Piazza Sant'Angelo a Nilo is named after the antique statue of the Nile (right), extensively restored during the Baroque period, that stands at its eastern end. In ancient times, Naples had a large Alexandrian community for whom the river was the object of great veneration. The statue became identified with the city and acquired its popular name: Corpo di Napoli ("Body of Naples").

"PUDICIZIA"
During his visit to Naples (1765–6) the famous French astronomer, Joseph Jérôme Lalande, was enraptured by Corradini's veiled statue of *Modesty*: ". . . you see the figure as if through a veil, fine enough to reveal its nudity: the gracefulness of the face and softness of the features also give the impression that you are seeing them revealed".

SAN DOMENICO TO THE VIA DUOMO

CAPPELLA SANSEVERO ★. The chapel was built in 1590 to house the tombs of the Sangro family. The esthete and alchemist, Raimondo di Sangro (1710–71), Prince of Sansevero, is responsible for the chapel's sinister reputation. He is said to have used evil spells to petrify the blood of two young men while they were still alive. The two écorchés, veritable anatomical figures, are preserved in the crypt. The prince decorated the chapel with indecipherable symbols and sculptures on which the representation of veils, bodily detail and wet drapery effects are particularly striking: *Disillusion* by Francesco Queirolo, *Modesty* by Antonio Corradini and the *Dead Christ* by Guiseppe Sammartino (1753).

CHURCH OF SANT'ANGELO A NILO. This small church contains one of the city's first works of Renaissance sculpture, the remarkable Tomb of Cardinal Rinaldo Brancaccio,

commissioned in 1427 from the Florentine sculptors Michelozzo and Donatello.

VIA SAN BIAGIO DEI LIBRAI ★. Beyond the *largo* of the Corpo di Napoli, the Spaccanapoli becomes the Via Biagio dei Librai, a reminder that this was once the street where books for the nearby university were printed and sold. Alongside the bookish tradition, the religious devotion of the people of Naples is expressed in its most ancient and modern forms, from workshops restoring 18th-century statues of saints and religious figures to a kitsch religiosity represented by neon halos and psychedelic comets. The single, embossed Renaissance façade of the 15th-century PALAZZO CARAFA (no. 121) is pierced by a beautiful marble portal whose architrave is decorated with antique busts. The portal, which has retained its original wooden doors, still bears the coat of arms of the Carafa family. In the courtyard of the palace is a large terracotta horse's head, a copy of the famous "ancient" bronze head given to Diomedes Carafa by Lorenzo the Magnificent. The original has been in the Museo Archeologico Nazionale since 1809. The PALAZZO MARIGLIANO (no. 39) stands on the right, beyond the busy intersection of the Via San Gregorio Armeno. This masterpiece of 16th-century architecture, designed by Giovanni Donadio, contains one of the "secret gardens" of Naples, reached via a flight of steps at the far end of the courtyard. The many jewelers' stores in this section of the Via San Biagio dei Librai once sold jewelry from the nearby Monte di Pietà (pawnbroker's) which has stood on the corner of the street and the *vico* San Severino since the end of the 16th century. It was set up to help those in debt to the city's moneylenders, who were expelled from the kingdom in 1540. In the courtyard of the impressive building, the Cappella della Pietà contains a pietà by Michelangelo Naccherino and two statues (*Charity* and *Constancy*) by Pietro Bernini, illustrating the aims of the Monte di Pietà.

VIA DEL DUOMO TO SANTI SEVERINO E SOSSIO

Via del Duomo was built in 1860 following a decree issued by Garibaldi. It was the first new street to be opened through the old urban fabric of the Greco-Roman city.

FORCELLA. Beyond Via del Duomo lies the busy district of Forcella. It is the preserve of the Camorra families who, for decades, have controlled the fortunes of this "city within a city". The city's fine arts department recently had to call for police support in order to demolish an illegal structure built against the apse of the tiny church of Sant'Agrippino.

CHURCH OF SAN GIORGIO MAGGIORE. This ancient church, originally dedicated to San Severo, was almost completely destroyed by fire in 1640. It was rebuilt in Baroque style by Cosimo Fanzago. All that remains of the early Christian basilica is the apse ★ (now the entrance to the new church), with its arches and Roman columns surmounted by Corinthian capitals. The church's right-hand aisle and façade were badly damaged during the construction of Via del

FILANGIERI MUSEUM
The museum is housed in the Palazzo Cuomo ● *83*, near the church of San Giorgio Maggiore. The beautiful embossed façade of the palace, built between 1464 and 1490 for a family of rich Florentine pyrotechnicians, is reminiscent of the palaces of the Tuscan city. During the construction of Via del Duomo the palace was dismantled, stone by stone, and rebuilt 20 yards away. In 1882 it received the collections of Prince Gaetano Filangieri the Younger (1824–92) which he bequeathed to the city of Naples upon his death. The museum's fine collection of antique weapons includes a 15th-century Aragonese culverin, once used to defend the Castel Nuovo ▲ *134*. The display cases contain medals, coins, pieces of crockery, ceramics and porcelain, and the walls are hung with paintings by Giovanni Battista Caracciolo, Andrea Vaccaro, Mattia Preti and Luca Giordano.

CHIOSTRO DEL PLATANO ★
The convent is built around three cloisters. The largest of these is the beautiful, 16th-century Chiostro del Platano, which takes its name from a plane tree said to have been planted by Saint Benedict. Although the tree was felled in the 1950's, the old roots have sent up new shoots. Two wings of the cloister are decorated with frescos by Antonio Solario (early 16th century), illustrating the life of Saint Benedict in twenty episodes.

Duomo. (Turn right into Via dell'Arte della Lana which takes you through the southernmost districts of the ancient city. During the Greco-Roman period, these districts formed a natural terrace overlooking the sea.)

CONVENT OF SANTI SEVERINO E SOSSIO. This former Benedictine convent today houses the State Archives, established by order of Ferdinand IV of Bourbon with a view to bringing the kingdom's administrative documents (kept from the time of the Angevins) together under one roof. It is one of the most important collections of archives in Europe. Its three hundred rooms contained over one million documents and ten thousand parchments. Unfortunately part of the collection was destroyed in 1943 when the most valuable documents, transferred to a villa near Nola, were burnt by the Germans. The FONTANA DELLA SELLARIA, built by the viceroy Inigo Velez de Guevara in 1649, stands in the tiny square (above) in front of the convent. The CHURCH OF SANTI SEVERINO E SOSSIO, adjoining the complex, was founded by the Benedictines in 902, rebuilt in 1490 and completed in 1537 by Giovan Francesco di Palma. The façade (1731) has an elegant gallery.

GESÙ VECCHIO TO SANTA MARIA LA NOVA

CHURCH OF GESÙ VECCHIO. Not far from Santi Severino e Sossio, the church of Gesù Vecchio, the first Jesuit establishment to be founded in Naples (1564), is today incorporated into the university. The church houses paintings by Marco Pino, Giovanni Battista Caracciolo and Francesco Solimena, and statues by Cosimo Fanzago and Matteo Bottiglieri. (Cross the Chiostro del Salvatore, which houses the university library, and turn into Via Mezzocannone.)

CHURCH OF SAN GIOVANNI MAGGIORE. The church was founded in the 4th century, probably on the site of a Roman temple built by the Emperor Hadrian in honor of his favorite, Antinus. It was the first of the great Neapolitan parish churches, and although it was modified in 1685 by Dionisio Lazzari, it has retained the great apse of the early Christian

church, with its arches and columns. Inside is the tombstone of Pope Sylvester II (999–1003).

CAPPELLA PAPPACODA. The richly carved Gothic portal of the chapel, founded in 1415 by Artusio Pappacoda, the grand seneschal of the Angevin court, opens onto the Piazza San Giovanni Maggiore. The 15th-century bell tower that stands to one side is one of the few Neapolitan campaniles of the period to have survived the subsequent earthquakes intact. Opposite the chapel the elegant Palazzo Giusso, dating from the Neapolitan Renaissance period, today houses the internationally renowned Oriental Institute of the university.

VIA DEI BANCHI. This was the banking and trading district where deals were struck and commercial contracts negotiated around the *banchi*, or "counters". The Palazzo Penna, at no. 24, was built in 1406 by the king's secretary, Antonio Penna. Its magnificent Renaissance façade has a regular checkerboard pattern of flat and rectangular bosses, decorated alternately with feathers, the family symbol (*penna* means "feather") and fleurs de lys, the symbol of royalty. Directly opposite is the Baroque Palazzo Palmarice (18th century), by Ferdinando Sanfelice. It has a distinctive embossed portal and a fine octagonal flight of steps.

CHURCH OF SANTA MARIA LA NOVA. The church, a dependency of the adjacent Franciscan convent, was completed by Angelo Franco in 1599. It has an elegant Renaissance façade and is built in the form of a Latin cross with a rectangular apse. The magnificent coffered ceiling in gilt wood (1598–1600) is decorated with forty-six paintings by the greatest Neapolitan artists of the period. When Naples was under Spanish rule, the church was a favorite with the nobility, as is evident from the many aristocratic tombs in the chapels and cloisters. The Chiostro San Giacomo is a fine example of the Florentine Renaissance style that can be seen in Naples ● *83*.

VIA AND PIAZZA MONTEOLIVETO

The end of Via Monteoliveto is bordered by the right wing of the beautiful POST OFFICE BUILDING (1933–6) by Giuseppe Vaccaro.

FONTANA DI MONTEOLIVETO
The fountain was built by the viceroy Don Pedro Antonio of Aragon and financed (according to custom) by the local inhabitants. It is surmounted by a statue of the Spanish king, Charles II of Hapsburg, which was begun when the king was eight years old and was not completed until he was eighteen.

The entire district of Guantai Nuovi, between the Via Monteoliveto and the Via Toledo, was demolished and rebuilt during the inter-war period. All that remains of the old district is the ancient cloister of Sant'Anna dei Lombardi, behind the Post Office. To the right, in the Via Monteoliveto (no. 3), the façade of the PALAZZO GRAVINA (1513–49) has retained traces of its Renaissance origins (embossed diamond-point extrusions). Today it houses the Faculty of Architecture.

CHURCH OF SANT'ANNA DEI LOMBARDI ★.
Begun in 1411, Sant'Anna dei Lombardi became the favorite church of the Aragonese court during the second half of the 15th century. Its dignitaries made it a veritable Renaissance museum by employing leading artists from the main centers of Italian art to work on the chapels and tombs. The altar in the PICCOLOMINI CHAPEL is decorated with a bas-relief of the Nativity by Antonio Rossellino (1475), while the TOLOSA CHAPEL has a glazed terracotta decoration executed in Florence either by Giuliano da Maiano or by the Della Robbia studio. The altar of the TERRANOVA (or Correale) CHAPEL reflects the esthetic principles of Brunelleschi and has a magnificent bas-relief of the Annunciation (1489), sent from Florence by Benedetto da Maiano. The art of Ferrara is represented in the CHAPEL OF THE HOLY SEPULCHER (or Cappella Orilia) by the *Pietà*, a remarkable terracotta group by Guido Mazzoni (1492). The SACRESTIA VECCHIA (Old Sacristy) has a frescoed vault by Giorgio Vasari (1544) and intarsia stalls by Fra Giovanni da Verona (1506–10) with some very realistic views of Naples.

VIA TOLEDO

BY ORDER OF DON PEDRO DE TOLEDO. This elegant street, named after Don Pedro de Toledo, the viceroy of Naples from 1532 to 1553, was built as part of an ambitious project to restructure and develop the city. This involved extending it westward, onto the slopes of San Martino, using a checkerboard layout similar to that of the ancient city ● 79.

BANCO DI NAPOLI
This is one of Italy's oldest credit institutions. It was founded in 1539, originally as a pawnbroker's, and was followed by the establishment of a number of other public banks: the Banco del Popolo (1589), Banco dello Spirito Santo (1591), Banco di Sant'Eligio (1592), Banco di San Giacomo (1597), Banco dei Poveri (1600) and the Banco del Salvatore (1640). These institutions brought the letter of credit introduced by pawnbrokers into general use. In 1808 Joachim Murat succeeded in forming them into a single bank: the Banco delle Due Sicilie. In 1861, after the unification of Italy, the bank became known as the Banco di Napoli.

This was how the SPANISH DISTRICTS ● *83* came into being. The street was designed as a link between these new western districts and the old city, and noblemen and bankers from all over Europe had impressive mansions built on Via Toledo. This magnificent succession of wealthy residences was much admired by foreign visitors. In the 18th century President De Brosses described it as "the most beautiful street of any city in Europe" and, in the following century, Stendhal expressed the wish that he would always remember "the most beautiful city in the universe". Herman Melville gave a different view: "Great crowds. Could hardly tell it from Broadway." The high dome of the CHURCH OF THE SPIRITO SANTO (1774), by Mario Gioffredo, marks the end of Via Toledo.

PALAZZO DORIA D'ANGRI. The palace (on the corner of Via Toledo and the Piazza VII Settembre) was built in 1755 by Luigi Vanvitelli. After the conquest of Naples, on September 7, 1860 ● *33*, Giuseppe Garibladi stood on its balcony to proclaim the unification of the Kingdom of the Two Sicilies with Italy.

PALAZZO MADDALONI ● *84*. The palace (no. 46), built by Cesare d'Avalos in 1582, was bought in the 17th century by the Carafa di Maddaloni family. They had it extended by Cosimo Fanzago who created the beautiful loggia above the magnificent portal that opens onto the Via Maddaloni. Its *saloni* were beautifully decorated by Giacomo del Po, Francesco de Mura and Fedele Fischetti.

CHURCH OF SAN NICOLA DELLA CARITÀ. This late 17th-century church is one of the rare architectural works by the renowned Neapolitan artist Francesco Solimena. The interior has paintings by Paolo de Matteis.

PALAZZO BERIO. The palace (no. 256), built in the 16th century by the Portuguese financier Simon Vaez, Count of Mola, was redesigned (1772) by Luigi Vanvitelli for the Tomacelli family. It was subsequently bought by Giovan Domenico Berio, Marquis of Salza, whose guests included the sculptor Canova, Gioacchino Rossini and Stendhal. It stands opposite the Palazzo Barbaia where Rossini composed his *Otello*.

ROSSINI CONFINED TO QUARTERS
Among the Neapolitan experiences recounted in *Le Corricolo*, Alexandre Dumas (fils) tells how Domenico Barbaia, the Milanese director of the Teatro San Carlo ▲ *136*, asked Rossini to compose

an opera for the famous opera house. So that Rossini would not have any material worries while he was composing, Barbaia placed his palace, servants and tradesmen at his disposal. But Rossini, who enjoyed the good life, used and abused his host's hospitality for several months without writing a single note. Two weeks before the premiere Barbaia, at his wits' end, is said to have locked his "guest" in his room in an attempt to force him to compose the opera. This he did, with legendary speed, and produced the libretto and music for *Otello* on time.

▲ PIAZZA DANTE
TO PIAZZA BELLINI

1. PIAZZA DANTE
2. S. PIETRO A MAIELLA
3. S. MARIA MAGGIORE
4. S. MARIA DELLE ANIME DEL PURGATORIO
5. S. PAOLO MAGGIORE
6. S. LORENZO MAGGIORE
7. S. GREGORIO ARMENO

This itinerary follows the ancient *decumani* of the Greco-Roman city and enables you to experience the "real" Naples, where poverty exists alongside nobility, and the beauty of the monuments and the proliferation of works of art provide a striking contrast to the general deterioration of the environment. These old streets are pervaded by the intense vitality, tolerance and irony of the Napoletani: weapons used to combat fortunes that have left their scar on this part of the city.

PIAZZA DANTE TO SAN PIETRO A MAIELLA

PIAZZA DANTE. In 1757 Charles of Bourbon engaged Luigi Vanvitelli to build a monumental palace, the Foro Carolino. The architect chose the site of a small market, near the Port'Alba exit,

to create a large hemicycle opposite the church of
San Domenico Soriano (below).

CHURCH OF SAN PIETRO A MAIELLA. This tiny church (late
13th-early 14th century) was dedicated to San Pietro
Angeleri, the hermit-monk from the mountains of Maiella
(Abruzzes) who renounced the pontificate following his
election as Pope Celestine V. The French Gothic church was
extended between 1493 and 1508, renovated in Baroque style
in the mid-17th century and restored to its original medieval
style between 1888 and 1927. The chapel to the left of the
choir has some beautiful, 15th-century enameled tiling. On
the ceiling of the nave and the transept is a major series of
paintings by Mattia Preti (early 17th century), illustrating the
life of San Pietro Angeleri. The campanile, to the left of the
church, stands at the end of the Via Tribunali.

VIA TRIBUNALI, TOWARD SAN LORENZO

Via Tribunali follows the line of the ancient *decumanus
maximus*. It is bordered on one side by high porticos which
have always served as a market place and provided a setting
for the events of everyday life. On the other, the sacred
monuments originally dedicated to pagan gods have been
transformed in response to changing architectural styles and
new forms of religion.

CAPPELLA PONTANO. This small Renaissance chapel was built
(1492) at the request of Giovanni Pontano ● *43*, ▲ *143* as a
funerary chapel for his family. It is the most important edifice
of its kind in southern Italy and was inspired by the temple of
Fortuna Virilis in Rome. Inside, the delicate faience paving is
strongly influenced by Islamic and Byzantine art, while the
walls are decorated with Latin epigraphs dictated by the
renowned humanist.

CHURCH OF SANTA MARIA MAGGIORE, "LA PIETRASANTA".
Legend has it that, in the 6th century, the Holy Virgin
appeared in a dream to Bishop Pomponius and advised him
to build a church on this site to drive away the Devil who
appeared, each night, in the form of a pig. And
so the bishop built a Christian basilica on the
remains of a Roman edifice. The impressive
Baroque church (1653–67) that can be seen
today is the work of Cosimo Fanzago, who
used the slender dome (right) resting on a
tall drum supported by four pilasters

PORT'ALBA (below)
The gate was built in
1625 by the viceroy of
Naples, Don Antonio
Alvárez de Toledo.
It opens onto the
Piazza Dante and
stands at the end of
the busy Via
Port'Alba, which is
lined with old
bookstores.

**CONSERVATORY OF
SAN PIETRO A
MAIELLA**
Since 1828 the
former convent of
San Pietro a Maiella
has housed one of
Italy's most famous
conservatories. It
was formed by the
amalgamation of
four institutions
established during
the 17th and 18th
centuries as children's
(particularly
orphans') homes.
The boys were made
castrati and received a
musical, historical
and literary
education. As adults
they sang as sopranos.
Carlo Broschi, alias
Farinelli (1705–82),
was the most famous.
He performed
throughout Europe,
particularly at the
Spanish court of
Philip V, from where
he was expelled
following a number
of scandals.

151

to highlight the centralized layout. He also preserved the block of stone carved with a cross that consecrated the early church. It is from this that the present church's popular name, "Pietrasanta" ("Holy Stone"), is derived. On the parvis, the Romanesque campanile of the former 11th-century basilica is one of the few medieval bell towers still standing in Naples.

CHURCH OF SANTA MARIA DELLE ANIME DEL PURGATORIO. The church is dedicated to the secular worship of the dead, which still has a large following in Naples. The pilasters of the entrance are surmounted by bronze skulls. Inside, a staircase leads to the hypogeum ★, as vast as the church itself, containing the much-venerated remains of the dead.

PIAZZA SAN GAETANO. The Piazza San Gaetano (left) occupies part of the site of the ancient *agora* and forum at an intersection on the *decumanus maximus* of the Greco-Roman city. Over the centuries it has retained its symbolic value as one of the city's main meeting places. Today the stalls set up by small traders in the square and under the surrounding porticos serve as a reminder of the market held from the Greek period. Overlooking the piazza is the BASILICA OF SAN PAOLO MAGGIORE. It was built on the ruins of a medieval church which itself incorporated the Roman temple of the Dioscuri (1st century AD). The present basilica, whose vestibule echoed the *pronaos* of the pagan temple, was built (c. 1583) according to plans by the Theatine father, Francesco Grimaldi. However the pediment and the central columns of the temple collapsed during the earthquakes of 1631 and 1688. Only two columns survived and were incorporated into the new façade in 1773. The nave has some remarkable frescos, illustrating the lives of Saint Peter and Saint Paul, by Massimo Stanzione (1644), while those in the sacristy, decorated with gilt stuccowork, are the work of Francesco Solimena (1689–90). The 18th-century CHIOSTRO GRANDE (access behind the choir) is built on an impressive fragment of the stage of a Roman theater, which could still be seen at the end of the Middle Ages.

SAN LORENZO MAGGIORE ★ ● 78

The Franciscan basilica (one of Naples' most impressive medieval churches) and the adjoining convent were built on the site of what was once the Greek *agora* and then the Roman forum. It is a unique complex, in terms of its archeological, architectural and artistic stratification, as well as the wealth of its historical associations.

THE BASILICA. In the 6th century an early Christian church, dedicated to San Lorenzo, was built on the site of the Roman forum. Its layout is shown

AQUEDUCT
San Paolo Maggiore gives access to a dense network of underground galleries carved out of the tufa. A section of the Renaissance aqueduct, which brought water to the city's wells from Sarno along 105 miles of conduits, is open to the public.

Beneath the city of Naples a network of underground passages forms a subterranean urban system, a city beneath a city known only to the initiated.

Basilica of San Paolo Maggiore (above and right).

> ## "THOSE WHO WANT TO SEE SOME FINE PIECES OF ARCHITECTURE SHOULD VISIT THE CHURCHES AND ADMIRE THEIR PORTALS, CHAPELS, ALTARS AND TOMBS."
> MAXIMILIEN MISSON

by the brass outline on the tiled paving of the present church. At the end of the 13th century Charles I of Anjou had the church rebuilt by French master-craftsmen. The apse, in pure French Gothic style, dates from this period. The transept and nave, built several years later by local craftsmen, re-used ancient columns and are stylistically very distinct from the apse. The edifice, weakened by subsequent earthquakes, was strengthened and renovated in Baroque style in the 17th and 18th centuries. In 1743 Ferdinando Sanfelice rebuilt the façade, although he retained the beautiful marble portal (1324), which still has its original doors. The restoration work carried out between 1882 and 1944 did not affect the façade and, by removing the Baroque additions from the interior, restored it to its original Gothic form. The church houses some fine 14th- and 15th-century funerary monuments and the remains of some early 14th-century frescos. In the choir, to the right, the TOMB OF CATHERINE OF AUSTRIA (d. 1323), surmounted by a delicate, inlaid marble canopy with wreathed columns, contains a finely decorated coffin supported by two caryatids. Statues of San Lorenzo, San Antonio and San Francesco stand against the rich marble composition of the HIGH-ALTAR by Giovanni da Nola (first half of the 16th century). In the lower register, three panels illustrate episodes from the lives of the three saints, against a backdrop of 16th-century Naples.

CONVENT OF SAN FRANCESCO. The narrow façade of the convent entrance is set in between the bell tower (1487–1507) and the church. The 18th-century cloister (with its clearly visible archeological excavations) has a large well by Cosimo Fanzago. Opening off the cloister is the chapter house. The former refectory, on the right, dates from c. 1230 and is preceded by a small portico with re-used columns from the Roman period. From 1442 the parliament of the Kingdom of Naples met in the great hall of the convent where, in 1443, Alfonso I of Aragon recognized his natural son, Ferdinand, Duke of Calabria. In 1879, in recognition of its political role, the

THE ANCIENT TREASURES OF SAN LORENZO Excavations have revealed an extraordinary superposition of historical periods: terraced walls, Roman streets and a

porticoed Byzantine edifice. San Lorenzo was built on the site of the Greek *agora*, later the Roman forum. In the cloister of the convent you can see part of the *tholos* of the *macellum*, the Roman market. Below it are Roman streets with a row of stores and several rooms with benches where people shopping in the market could rest.

The Duomo.

Vestibule of the convent of San Gregorio Armeno (right).

"PRESEPI"
Even under its carriage entrances, Via San Gregorio Armeno is lined with the stores and stalls of the craftsmen who make the figures for the traditional Neapolitan *presepi* (cribs) ● 56. Store windows and

stalls are full of terracotta figurines and religious figures, fountains, miniatures, moss and cork for backgrounds. In December the narrow street becomes a veritable mecca for Neapolitans in search of creative and imaginative ideas for the family crib.

terracotta coats of arms of the various nobiliary assemblies (*sedili*) that once governed the districts of Naples were hung above the convent entrance.

VIA SAN GREGORIO ARMENO ★

The former *cardo* of the ancient city is spanned, near the convent of the same name, by a solidly built bell tower in red roughcast (18th century).

CHURCH AND MONASTERY OF SAN GREGORIO ARMENO ★. In the 8th century a group of nuns fled to Naples to escape iconoclastic persecution in Constantinople, taking with them the relics of Saint Gregory, Bishop of Armenia. They re-established their community near the present church of San Gregorio Armeno and founded a convent which was built between 1574 and 1580 by Giovanni Battista Cavagna, according to the rules of the Counter-Reformation. During services, two galleries separate the nuns from the congregation. The first overlooks the choir, while the second, the "winter choir", was installed (1757), unusually, above the wooden ceiling of the nave, painted (1580–2) by the Flemish artist Teodoro di Enrico. The church is one of the finest examples of Baroque decoration in Naples, with the rich gilt stuccowork and the polychrome decorations of the frescos, inlaid paneling and painted wood providing a striking contrast with the shadowy half-light of the nave. The iconographic theme is inspired throughout by the worship of relics, of which the church has many: the head of

San Gregorio, the blood of San Giovanni Battista, the arm of San Lorenzo and the body of Santa Patrizia. A magnificent portal (which still has the two bronze wheels of the "hatch" used to pass provisions and other items to this reclusive order of nuns) leads into the CONVENT, which was entirely rebuilt at the end of the 16th century. The superb cloister, planted with a citrus orchard, has a fountain in curved and scrolled marble flanked by statues of Christ and the Samaritan woman by Matteo Bottiglieri. Opening onto the cloister is the refectory with its ancient oven where the nuns, expert pastry cooks, made the famous *sfogliatelle* (small shell-shaped pastries filled with ricotta cheese).

VIA TRIBUNALI, TOWARD THE DUOMO

CHURCH OF GIROLAMINI. The church, the seat of the Oratorians, was built at the end of the 16th century by Giovanni Antonio Dosio. The dome and façade were designed by Dionisio Lazzari in the mid-17th century. In 1780 Ferdinando Fuga revised the design by adding two lateral bell towers. The Oratorians, who wanted to be seen to be promoting art, culture and education, entrusted the decoration of their church to illustrious Italian (Pietro da Cortona, Guido Reni) and local (Luca Giordano, Francesco Solimena) artists.

THE DUOMO

Ensconced between two palaces and set back from the street, the cathedral stands on a site that has probably been occupied by religious buildings since the Greco-Roman period.
THE FORTUNES OF CONSTRUCTION. Either Charles I of Anjou or his son Charles II, the Lame, ordered this huge French Gothic cathedral to be built on the site of the early Christian basilicas of Santa Stefania and Santa Restituta, and four baptistries. Earthquakes (1349, 1456), Renaissance modifications, Baroque additions and some unfortunate 19th-century restorations have significantly altered the cathedral's Gothic structure. The façade, redesigned by Enrico Alvino in 1876 and later modified by Giuseppe Pisanti, has retained the three Gothic portals (1407) of the Angevin cathedral.
INTERIOR. Inside the cathedral, built in the form of a Latin cross, sixteen piers, incorporating re-used antique columns, separate the principal nave from the two lateral naves. In the 17th century the vault was sealed off by a beautiful gilt and painted coffered ceiling and, at the end of the century, a Baroque decoration was painted above the pointed arches. Some of the chapels leading off the transept still have clearly visible traces of the original Gothic style. The CAPPELLA SAN LORENZO (left side of the transept) has a fresco, painted in the first half of the 14th century and attributed to Lello da

155

CAPPELLA SAN GENNARO ▲ *158* (right aisle)
The huge chapel of Saint Januarius is a masterpiece of Neapolitan Baroque art. It was built between 1608 and 1637 in fulfillment of a vow made by the Napoletani, in 1527, during a plague epidemic. It was constructed, in the form of a Greek cross, in place of three side chapels. It is surmounted by a frescoed dome and was decorated by the greatest Neapolitan artists of the 17th and 18th centuries.

Orvieto, representing the tree of Jesse. The CAPELLA TOCCO (right side of the transept) is lit by a high gemmate window in French Gothic style. Frescos attributed to Pietro Cavallini (first half of the 14th century) have recently been discovered. In the CAPPELLA MINUTOLO, adjoining the apse at the end of the right side of the transept, the structure and decoration of the original Gothic cathedral (the majolica paving with animal designs, and the late 13th-century frescos by Montano d'Arezzo on the left-hand wall) have been entirely restored. It also contains the funerary monuments (early 14th century) of the Minutolo family: the tombs of Orso and Filippo and the sepulcher (1402–5) of Cardinal Arrigo, whose Gothic canopy surmounts the altar. In the left-hand aisle, the CAPPELLA SANTA RESTITUTA, the only surviving vestige of the 4th-century Christian basilica, was modified and lost its façade when the cathedral was built. All that remains of the original edifice are the antique columns and a few fragments of tiled paving. At the far end of the chapel, on the left, the BAPTISTRY OF SAN GIOVANNI IN FONTE (late 4th century) ★ is decorated with magnificent 4th- and 5th-century mosaics. Finally, beneath the choir, the CRYPT OF THE SUCCORPO, an elegant Renaissance structure by Tommaso Malvito (1497–1506), contains the bones of San Gennaro.

VIA TRIBUNALI, TOWARD CASTEL CAPUANO

PIAZZA DEL CARDINAL RIARIO SFORZA. In the center of the piazza stands the beautiful Baroque spire of the Guglia San Gennaro, surmounted by a statue of the saint. It was built by Cosimo Fanzago (1637) in fulfillment of the vow made by the Neapolitans in 1631, during the eruption of Vesuvius ▲ *238*.
PIO MONTE DELLA MISERICORDIA. This charitable institution was founded in 1601

by seven Neapolitan nobles, with a view to performing the
seven works of mercy. On the high altar of the adjoining
church, a masterpiece by Caravaggio (c. 1607) illustrates these
seven acts of Christian charity. The institution, where the
seven governors have met every Friday morning since it was
founded, has an interesting *pinacoteca* on the second floor.
HOSPITAL OF SANTA MARIA DELLA PACE. A remarkable
pointed portal forms the entrance to the former mansion
(15th century) of Gianni Caracciolo, converted into a hospital
in the early 17th century by the Knights Hospitalers of Saint
John. The sick were cared for in the vaulted, frescoed hall on
the second floor. A gallery running the length of the hall
enabled visitors to avoid contagion. To the right of the palace
stands the church of Santa Maria della Pace, named after the
peace treaty signed between France and Spain (1659).
PALAZZO RICCA. In 1617 the Monte dei Poveri, a charitable
institution founded in 1599, acquired the 16th-century
Palazzo Ricca. The interior staircase is the only surviving
feature of the Renaissance period. In 1770 Gaetano Barba
completely rebuilt the façade and a large part of the buildings.
The chapel at the far end of the courtyard houses paintings by
Luca Giordano (1673) and Francesco Solimena (1686).

CASTEL CAPUANO

This impressive fortress was built by William I, the
Bad, in 1165. According to legend, Virgil's
"golden fly", a talisman supposed to ward off
the flies that infested the surrounding marshland,
was kept in the castle. When it lost its magical
powers the citizens turned to
Santa Maria di
Constantinopoli, the
"Madonna of the Flies",
to protect the town.

PORTA CAPUANA ● 82
The Porta Capuana
stands on the piazza
behind the Castel
Capuano, next to the
Renaissance church
of Santa Caterina a
Formiello. Ferdinand
II of Aragon had a
white marble
triumphal arch built
between two massive,
dark peperino towers.
The arch, by Giuliano
da Maiano, stands
above one of the city's
main entrances. The
district around the
Porta Capuana,
especially the tiny
piazza in front of the
18th-century church
of Sant'Anna a
Carbonara, is one of
the busiest in Naples
and teems with small
businesses and
market stalls.

The Neapolitan soul and spirit have been formed and nourished by two extremes embodied by San Gennaro (Januarius) and Vesuvius, representing blood and fire, spiritual protection and temporal threat. Gennaro (250–305), Bishop of Benevento, executed at Pozzuoli during the reign of Diocletian, is the city's patron saint. His is an ancient cult, deeply rooted in the popular consciousness. Neapolitans see the miracle of the blood of San Gennaro as the symbol of a city several times doomed, but which has always risen from the ashes

PROCESSION
The miracle of the blood occurs three times a year: on the first Saturday in May, the day of the translation of the relics; on September 19, the anniversary of the saint's execution; and December 16, the anniversary of the threatened eruption of Vesuvius in 1631. The manifestations are celebrated in the Duomo ▲ 155 and by an impressive procession along the Roman road between the Duomo and Santa Chiara ▲ 140.

RELIQUARY OF SAN GENNARO
The silver-gilt reliquary bust (1305), made by a French silversmith, contains the saint's skull. In the base, designed by Carlo Fanzago, are the phials containing his blood.

THE EARLIEST IMAGE OF SAN GENNARO (5TH CENTURY)
The fresco, which bears the inscription "Sancto Martyri Ianuario" (Catacombe di San Gennaro ▲ 178), provides a valuable indication of the age and intensity of the cult of San Gennaro, as evidenced by the letters alpha and omega (a monogram symbolizing Christ), inscribed in the halo encircling the saint's head.

THE MIRACLE OF THE BLOOD

Twice a year the congealed blood of San Gennaro, preserved in two glass phials, liquefies before the very eyes of an ecstatic congregation. A rapid liquefaction is considered a good omen, while failure or delay indicate grave misfortunes. On the front row, the old women of Naples intone popular hymns in dialect which, although sometimes incomprehensible and even disrespectful, always end by praising the Holy Trinity.

TOMB OF LADISLAS
Although the pinnacles and trefoil arches of the 60-foot high tomb (by Marco and Andrea da Firenze) are typically Gothic, it has early Renaissance features.

COURT OF JUSTICE. The castle, extended by Frederick II of Swabia and later restored by Charles I of Anjou, became the city's Court of Justice (La Vicaria) under the viceroy Don Pedro de Toledo. The façade still bears the Hapsburg coat of arms and an inscription commemorating the transfer of the law courts. Inside, the CAPPELLA DELLA SOMMARIA, where the judges and magistrates attended mass before pronouncing sentence, contains many fine examples of 16th-century art, with frescos depicting scenes from the New Testament by the Spanish Mannerist, Pedro Rubiales. The COURT OF APPEAL

The monument is supported by four Virtues and is decorated with the enthroned statues of Ladislas and Jeanne II. The gisant on the coffin depicts the king being blessed by a bishop and two deacons.

(1770) is decorated with allegorical figures representing the provinces of the Kingdom of Naples.

SAN GIOVANNI A CARBONARA ★

VIA SAN GIOVANNI A CARBONARA. The street opened onto an area that lay outside the city walls and was used, until the end of the Middle Ages, as a garbage dump (*ad carbonatum*). It leads from the Castel Capuano to the religious complex of

San Giovanni a Carbonara, preceded by a double staircase (Ferdinando Sanfelice, 1707).
AUGUSTINIAN RELIGIOUS COMPLEX. In 1343 the Augustinians began to build a church and convent on donated land. Work was completed in the early 15th century, during the reign of Ladislas. At the top of the monumental staircase, the beautiful Gothic portal of the CHAPEL OF SANTA MONICA (14th

century) attests to the original style. The chapel contains the tomb of Ruggero Sanseverino, by Andrea da Firenze (1443). The church, whose façade was obscured in the 16th century when the Cappella Somma was built, can be reached through the south portal.

THE CHURCH. The nave of this rectangular church has visible timberwork and the ribbed vault of the choir is preceded by a pointed arch. The chapels house funerary monuments that constitute one of Naples' most interesting collections of sculpture. At the far end of the choir the TOMB OF LADISLAS (1424), surmounted by an equestrian statue of the king, introduces the esthetic principles of the Renaissance. Built against the left wall of the nave and facing the entrance, the early 16th-century TOMB OF THE MIROBALLO FAMILY (Jacopo della Pila and Tommaso Malvito) has some remarkable statuary. Opening onto the choir, the CAPELLA CARACCIOLO DEL SOLE (1427), whose the entrance is between the two caryatids on the Tomb of Ladislas, contains the uncompleted tomb of Gianni Caracciolo, the ambitious dignitary and lover of Jeanne II who was stabbed to death in 1432. The chapel has some superb majolica paving. To the left of the choir, the early 15th-century CAPPELLA CARACCIOLO DI VICO (Tommaso Malvito) is in pure Renaissance style. The church opens onto the 15th-century cloister, a gift from Ladislas to the Augustinians. (Retrace your steps to Via San Giovanni a Carbonara and turn down Via Santa Sofia, the eastern end of the ancient north *decumanus*.)

Monumental Tomb of Queen Mary of Hungary (Santa Maria Donnaregina Vecchia).

Street vendor selling *taralli*, small savory snacks in the shape of a crown, made from lard, pepper and almonds.

TOWARD VIA ANTICAGLIA

CHURCH OF THE SANTI APOSTOLI. The church, which was probably founded in the 5th century on the site of a temple to Mercury, is dedicated to the Apostles. It was completely modified (1610–30) by Francesco Grimaldi and Giovanni Giacomo di Conforto. The 17th-century stuccowork and frescos that decorate the interior make it a sophisticated example of the Neapolitan Baroque architectural style.

CHURCH OF SANTA MARIA DONNAREGINA ★. The late 8th-century church and convent of Santa Maria Donnaregina were partially destroyed by the earthquake of 1293. In the early 14th century Mary of Hungary, Queen of Charles II of Anjou, financed the reconstruction of the complex. In 1620 a new church was built against the old one, engulfing the medieval apse. Restoration work carried out in the 1930's separated the two churches and freed the beautiful Gothic apse of SANTA MARIA DONNAREGINA VECCHIA with its high gemmate windows. The nave of the church, covered by a carved, gilt-wood ceiling, was raised to create a gallery for the nuns, separate from the congregation. Against the left wall is the monumental TOMB OF QUEEN MARY OF HUNGARY (1325–6), by Tino di Camaino ● 80. The series of frescos (first half of the 14th century) on the upper register of the walls is generally considered to be the most beautiful and most complete in Naples. Those in the gallery are attributed to Pietro Cavallini and his pupils

▲ PIAZZA DANTE TO PIAZZA BELLINI

The red façade of the convent of Sant'Antoniello a Port'Alba overlooks the busy Piazza Bellini with its many brightly colored café terraces.

SCHOOL OF RESTORATION
The conventual buildings of Santa Maria Donnaregina were given to the city of Naples after the dissolution of the monasteries in 1861. Since 1969 they have housed the University's school for the restoration of monuments.

In the past match-sellers were a common sight on the streets of Naples ● 58. Today they have been replaced street vendors selling cigarettes and lighters.

(far right). The CAPPELLA LOFFREDO, to the right of the nave, has fragments of 14th-century frescos. The interior of the Baroque church of SANTA MARIA DONNAREGINA NUOVA (by Giovanni Guarini), overlooking the piazza, is richly decorated in polychrome marble.

TOWARD PIAZZA BELLINI

ARCHBISHOP'S PALACE. The palace (construction began in 1289) was built on the site of the earliest Christian basilica in Naples. Recent excavations have uncovered the remains of a quadriporticus.
CHURCH OF SAN GIUSEPPE DEI RUFFI. A double staircase leads to the atrium (an early 18th-century addition) of the church. Built in 1669, according to plans by Dionisio Lazzari, it was founded by four Neapolitan noblemen (two of whom were members of the Ruffo family) who decided to withdraw to the convent.
VIA ANTICAGLIA. The Piazza Avellino, named after Camillo Caracciolo, Prince of Avellino, lies at one end of Via Anticaglia, which in turn derives its name from the "antiques" (*anticaglia* in the Neapolitan dialect) bought and sold there over the centuries. During the Greco-Roman period, this section of the *decumanus* separated the sacred part of the city (*acropolis*) from the lower part, where the principal public buildings were located. These included the two theaters (the great open-air theater and the *odeum*) and the monuments of the forum. The two massive arches that span the street originally linked the baths (on the right) with the great theater (on the left). The theaters formed an important architectural complex whose remains, still partly

visible at the end of the Middle Ages, were incorporated into later structures. Partial excavations, carried out between 1881 and 1884, revealed tiered seats, which made it possible to imagine the *cavea* of the great theater, where the Emperor Nero appeared. Via Armanni, on the right, leads to the monumental courtyard of the hospital of SANTA MARIA DEL POPOLO DEGLI INCURABILI where the old pharmacy is open to the public.

VIA PISANELLI. Via Anticaglia leads into Via Pisanelli which follows the line of the ancient *decumanus* and runs past the high wall of the CAPUCHIN CONVENT, also known as the "Convent of the Thirty-Three" (the number of nuns who lived there). The narrow *vico* Gaudioso that borders the CONVENT OF SANTA MARIA REGINA COELI leads to the nearby church of SANTA MARIA DELLE GRAZIE A CAPONAPOLI. The name "Caponapoli" ("end of Naples") bears testimony to the fact that, during the Greco-Roman period, this hill represented the outermost part of the city.

VIA SANTA MARIA DI CONSTANTINOPOLI. The street, which follows the line of the ancient walls, was built between 1533 and 1547 when the viceroy, Don Pedro de Toledo, ordered the city walls to be extended. Today the elegant public and religious buildings that line this broad, sunny street have been joined by a number of traditional craft and antique stores. Clearly visible at the far end of the street are the colored tiles of the dome of SANTA MARIA DI CONSTANTINOPOLI (Fra Nuvolo, late 16th century), while midway along stands the ACCADEMIA DI BELLE ARTI (1857), a fine example of the neo-Renaissance style by Enrico Alvino. A little further on, the impressive 18th-century façade of the CHURCH OF SAN GIOVANNI BATTISTA DELLE MONACHE stands opposite the church of SANTA MARIA DELLA SAPIENZA.

PIAZZA BELLINI. The piazza, which lies at the south end of Via Santa Maria di Constantinopoli, bears the traces of several very distinct historical periods. The remains of the Greek city walls can still be seen at the foot of the statue of the composer, Vincenzo Bellini. Where the street opens onto the piazza, the PALAZZO CONCA, one of the most important buildings in 15th-century Naples, was annexed in 1637 to the CONVENT OF SANT'ANTONIELLO A PORT'ALBA (16th century). Today it houses a university department. On the opposite side of the square, the PALAZZO FIRRAO was rebuilt in Baroque style, in the early 17th century, according to plans by Cosimo Fanzago.

PHARMACY OF SANTA MARIA DEL POPOLO DEGLI INCURABILI
The former pharmacy is reached via the courtyard of the hospital of Santa Maria del Popolo degli Incurabili. Rebuilt in 1744, its old walnut shelves hold a magnificent collection of 18th-century apothecary's jars.

Detail of the frescoed gallery of Santa Maria Donnaregina Vecchia, attributed to Pietro Cavallini and his pupils.

ACCADEMIA DI BELLE ARTI
Founded as an academy of art by Charles of Bourbon in 1754, it was transferred from San Carlo alle Mortelle ▲ *187* to Via Constantinopoli during the rebuilding of the Fosse del Grano district. During the second half of the 19th century, the masters of Neapolitan painting studied and taught there.

This itinerary explores the busy popular districts of the borghi dei Vergini and della Sanità, whose narrow streets wind up the hillsides of Capodimonte ▲ 172 and the Miradois. During the Greek period these hillsides gradually became a vast necropolis, and the burial vaults constructed during the early Christian period perpetuated this funerary tradition. In the early 18th century, when the rules of urban development allowed construction beyond the ancient city walls, the city spread rapidly onto these pleasant slopes. Churches and Baroque palaces were built on the Greek and early Christian remains, with the imaginative Rococo geometry of such architects as Sanfelice providing a striking contrast with the solemn austere style of Luigi Vanvitelli. Everywhere porches, courtyards, luxuriant hanging gardens, stairways and terraces favored communication between street and interior.

MUSEO ARCHEOLOGICO TO THE BORGO DEI VERGINI

MUSEO ARCHEOLOGICO NAZIONALE ★ ▲ 166. Magnificent collections of sculptures, mosaics, paintings and everyday objects from antiquity make this one of the most beautiful museums in the world. The vast museum building was originally a cavalry barracks. It was subsequently occupied by the University (1616–1777), before being extensively modified when Ferdinand IV decided to mark his reign by opening a huge museum that would house all the royal antique collections. Numerous pieces from Pompeii, Herculaneum, Stabiae (Castellamare di Stabia) and the increasing number of sites excavated in the late 18th century were added to the Farnese collection, originally kept at Capodimonte ▲ 172. The conversion of the building to a museum was completed in

THE BAROQUE GEOMETRY OF SANFELICE
Ferdinando Sanfelice (1675–1748) bequeathed some fine examples of civil architecture to the borghi dei Vergini and della Sanità, in which he made brilliant use of the potential of a complex geometrical style. The Palazzo dello Spagnolo (1738), on the Largo dei Vergini, is famous for its double, openwork staircase. Huge, transparent bays capture the light from a vast rear courtyard where there was once a garden.

1818 and from then on the Museo Archeologico became one of the meccas of European cultural tourism.

AROUND THE PIAZZA CAVOUR. Formerly the Largo delle Pigne that ran along the north wall of the city from the Porta San Gennaro, the Piazza Cavour lies to the right of the museum. Overlooking the piazza is the beautiful 18th-century façade of the CHURCH OF THE MADONNA DEL ROSARIO ALLE PIGNE, preceded by a double, elliptical staircase. To the left of the church is the Salita di Via Stella. Beyond the impressive PALAZZO SANNICANDRO, a flight of steps on the left leads to the 16th-century CHURCH OF SANTA MARIA DELLA STELLA, by Camillo Fontana. The single-naved church was modified several times, in particular by Cosimo Fanzago, during the 17th century. Back on the piazza is the PORTA SAN GENNARO, rebuilt on its present site in the 15th century when the city walls were extended. In line with the gate and beyond the (now non-existent) city walls lies the Borgo dei Vergini ("district of the Virgins").

LARGO DEI VERGINI. This long, narrow, rectangular piazza is bordered by beautiful Baroque buildings. On the left, the 18th-century CHURCH OF SANTA MARIA SUCCURRE MISERIS, by Ferdinando Sanfelice, stands on the remains of an earlier Gothic church (14th century). On the other side of the square is the CHURCH OF THE MISSIONARY FATHERS (1758–60, façade 1788), whose large, elliptical spaces were designed by Luigi Vanvitelli. Next to it, the CHURCH OF SANTA MARIA DEI VERGINI stands on the site of a 14th-century conventual complex. Although very badly damaged during World War Two, it is still possible to appreciate the architectural quality of the simply designed façade.

PALAZZO SANFELICE. Ferdinando Sanfelice built the palace (nos. 2 and 6, Via della Sanità), between 1724 and 1726, for his own family. The main body of the building is centered around an octagonal courtyard in which a complex, double staircase ● 88 creates a beautiful scenographic effect. A second larger, rectangular courtyard is separated from an interior garden by an openwork staircase which anticipates the more audacious version used in the Palazzo dello Spagnolo ▲ 164.

GALLERIA PRINCIPE DI NAPOLI ● 87
Opposite the Museo Archeologico is the Galleria Principe di Napoli, built between 1870 and 1883. Based on the galleries of Paris and London, it was the first example of an iron and glass structure in Naples. Its modernity marked the beginning of a phase of major architectural works. The new masters of the united Italy used this new wave of urban development to reinforce their control over the city.

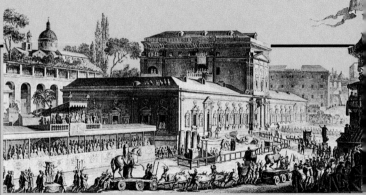

Since the Palazzo Reale di Portici was not large enough to hold all the archeological treasures from Pompeii and Herculaneum, Ferdinand IV decided to combine them with the Farnese collection, the library and the academies of art and house them in an "encyclopedic" museum in Naples. At the beginning of the 19th century Ferdinand fled to Palermo, taking the best pieces from his collections. In Naples, Napoleon Bonaparte and Joachim Murat continued to add to the museum, since which time it has been constantly enriched, particularly by the continuous flow of pieces from the excavations of Pompeii and southern Italy. It is devoted entirely to archeology and constitutes the largest collection of classical antiques (especially paintings) in the world.

BLUE VASE
Blue glass vase in the form of a wine amphora, discovered in a tomb in Pompeii. The vase was used for wine, and the cameo decoration depicts vine shoots and small cupids gathering grapes.

THE TRIUMPH OF ANTIQUE ART

The project for the foundation of the museum took shape in 1777. This engraving (1778) is an illustration of antiques being transported from Portici to Naples. However, the event, depicted as the triumphal procession of a Roman general, never actually took place. It took fifty years to bring all the pieces together in the museum.

"THE RAPE OF EUROPA"

Unlike their modern counterparts, the artists of antiquity were not concerned about originality. This fresco, from a house in Pompeii, is a 1st-century Roman work based on a Greek work from the 4th century BC. "The Rape of Europa", one of the better-known ancient myths, provided a link between Greece and the Orient. The fresco shows the Phoenician princess, Europa, being carried off to Greece by Zeus in the form of a bull. The composition is centered around a column (which adds a sacred dimension) and set against a mountain landscape with a tree.

ALEXANDER MOSAIC ▲ 252

The Alexander Mosaic, *Darius and Alexander at the Battle of Issus*, is a true masterpiece, in terms of its size (19 x 10½ feet), the fineness of its technique (*opus vermiculatum* ● 69) and the scope of its composition. It is undoubtedly based on a painting by a grand master of the Hellenistic period. The scene depicts one of the battles between Alexander the Great (left, at the head of his cavalry) and Darius III (right, fleeing in his chariot).

"TORO FARNESE"

The *Farnese Bull* was part of the rich Farnese collection that Charles III inherited from his mother. Until the Museo Archeologico Nazionale was founded it was kept in Rome. Like the famous *Farnese Hercules*, the sculpture was discovered in the Baths of Caracalla where it decorated the palaestra and was possibly used as a fountain. It is one of the most monumental groups bequeathed by antiquity, which is why it became known as the *Marble Mountain*. Dirce, tied to a bull by the sons of Antiope, is being made to pay for the suffering she inflicted on their mother.

GOLD NECKLACE
Necklace from
Ruvo di Puglia
(6th century BC),
decorated with heads
of Silenus, acorns and
lotus flowers. It
is thought to be an
Etruscan piece.

TOMB PAINTING FROM RUVO
Although many funerary paintings have been
discovered in Puglia and Campania, the
composition of this particular painting makes
it truly unique. It depicts a funeral dance of
mourners led by three young children, and
came from a tomb dating from the second
half of the 4th century BC.

PERSIAN KRATER
Vase discovered at Canosa
di Puglia, in the tomb of a
horseman (a horse's bit was
found among the funerary
paraphernalia of weapons
and magnificent painted
vases). The monumental
krater is both a masterpiece
by the "artist of Darius"
(active c. 330 BC) as well as
of Italiot ceramics. The
Persian king, who inspired
the name attributed to the
artist, is seated on his
throne, surrounded by
advisers.

HYPOGEUM OF THE CRISTILLANI
(Borgo della Sanità) This is the best preserved of the cemeteries that extended across the hillside to the north of the ancient city. Its barrel vault, bed-like sarcophagi and sculpted and painted decorations date from the 4th century BC.

CEMETERY OF THE FONTANELLE
(Via Fontanelle 77) Until the end of the 18th century, former tufa quarries were used as burial grounds. At the end of the 19th century, the arrangement of the bones in impressive piles (right) coincided with the development of a popular cult that saw these anonymous bones as the remains of souls in purgatory who were in need of help and prayer. Many skulls were "adopted" and placed in wooden caskets which sometimes bore the name and the imaginary history of the dead person.

BORGO DELLA SANITÀ

CHURCH OF SANTA MARIA DELLA SANITÀ. The church, built by the Dominicans (1602–13) according to plans by Giuseppe Donzelli (known as Fra Nuvolo), is the true heart of the district. Its fine dome, covered with glazed yellow and green tiles, is today dominated by the Ponte della Sanità, built in the early 19th century to link Capodimonte ▲ *172* with the city center. Beneath the raised high altar is the huge, 5th-century CHAPEL OF SAN GAUDIOSO and the entrance to the early Christian CATACOMBS where the saint was buried. The bodies were placed in the strange, seat-shaped niches in the walls of the burial chambers, where they remained until they decomposed. The galleries are still decorated with 6th-century paintings and some curious 17th-century funerary effigies. Below the skulls set in the wall, the painted clothes and attributes of the frescoed bodies indicate their rank. Beyond the bridge lies the Fontanelle district.

CHURCH OF SAN SEVERO A CAPODIMONTE. In the 17th century the Franciscans had a single-naved church (transformed between 1680 and 1690 by Dionisio Lazzari) built on the site of the small 4th-century church that marked the entrance to the Catacombe di San Severo. The second chapel leads to one of the galleries of the ancient catacombs that is still partly decorated with 5th-century frescos.

HILLSIDE OF THE MIRADOIS

SALITA CAPODIMONTE. This steep street was cut out of the tufa, through ancient quarries and antique burial sites. The first floor of most of the houses are hewn out of the rock. The *palazzo* at no. 10 is by Ferdinando di Sanfelice (1746). Its broad, elliptical staircase ● *88* leads to a brightly lit, arcaded loggia and a hanging garden planted with citruses and overlooked by an Angevin tower that once defended the city entrance. (Make your way back down the hillside via the winding Salita Moiariello where flights of steps offer some magnificent views across the city. Turn right at the bottom of the *salita*.)

OBSERVATORY ● *87.* This fine building by Stefano Gasse, one of the uncontested masters of Neapolitan neoclassicism, was begun in 1812 and completed in 1819. It houses a rich collection of 19th-century scientific instruments. (Return to the Salita Moiariello where steps leads to the busy Miracoli district.)

SANTA MARIA DEI MIRACOLI. The Franciscan convent and adjoining church were built by Francesco Antonio Picchiatti (1662–75) with a legacy bequeathed by a dignitary of the royal court. The buildings were transformed into a girls' orphanage in the early 19th century and today house a school. (Turn into Via Foria bordered by 18th- and 19th-century palaces.)

VIA FORIA, TOWARD THE ALBERGO DEI POVERI

BOTANICAL GARDENS. The gardens, founded in 1807 by Joachim Murat, cover an area of 30 acres and contain three glasshouses. The largest is in neoclassical style and dates from 1813. Occupied by the Germans during World War Two, it has been painstakingly restored by A. Merola, a well-known botanist and the director of the botanical gardens.

ALBERGO DEI POVERI. The Albergo dei Poveri stands at the end of Via Foria. It was built by Ferdinando Fuga (1751 onward), by order of Charles of Bourbon, to house the poor of the Kingdom of Naples.

171

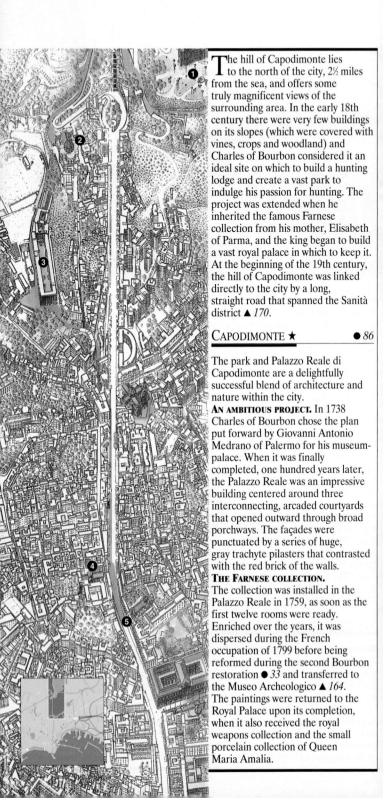

The hill of Capodimonte lies
to the north of the city, 2½ miles
from the sea, and offers some
truly magnificent views of the
surrounding area. In the early 18th
century there were very few buildings
on its slopes (which were covered with
vines, crops and woodland) and
Charles of Bourbon considered it an
ideal site on which to build a hunting
lodge and create a vast park to
indulge his passion for hunting. The
project was extended when he
inherited the famous Farnese
collection from his mother, Elisabeth
of Parma, and the king began to build
a vast royal palace in which to keep it.
At the beginning of the 19th century,
the hill of Capodimonte was linked
directly to the city by a long,
straight road that spanned the Sanità
district ▲ *170*.

CAPODIMONTE ★ ● 86

The park and Palazzo Reale di
Capodimonte are a delightfully
successful blend of architecture and
nature within the city.

AN AMBITIOUS PROJECT. In 1738
Charles of Bourbon chose the plan
put forward by Giovanni Antonio
Medrano of Palermo for his museum-
palace. When it was finally
completed, one hundred years later,
the Palazzo Reale was an impressive
building centered around three
interconnecting, arcaded courtyards
that opened outward through broad
porchways. The façades were
punctuated by a series of huge,
gray trachyte pilasters that contrasted
with the red brick of the walls.

THE FARNESE COLLECTION.
The collection was installed in the
Palazzo Reale in 1759, as soon as the
first twelve rooms were ready.
Enriched over the years, it was
dispersed during the French
occupation of 1799 before being
reformed during the second Bourbon
restoration ● *33* and transferred to
the Museo Archeologico ▲ *164*.
The paintings were returned to the
Royal Palace upon its completion,
when it also received the royal
weapons collection and the small
porcelain collection of Queen
Maria Amalia.

When the park was modified in 1840, under the direction of F. Dehrardt, many exotic species were planted.

MUSEO E GALLERIE DI CAPODIMONTE. Although the famous Farnese collection was later transferred to the Museo Archeologico Nazionale ▲ *164*, the palace continued to be used as a museum. Today it has some of the richest collections of paintings, ancient weapons and porcelain in Europe.

PARCO DI CAPODIMONTE. The 306-acre park surrounding the palace is enclosed by a high wall pierced by three gates. Five broad avenues fan out from the Porta di Mezzo and are intersected by paths cutting across them at right angles. This wooded section of the park was created by Ferdinando Sanfelice in 1742. A dense covering of vegetation combining tall trees (holm-oaks, limes and maples) and shrubs (laurels, hollies and myrtles) was planted to offer shade and shelter for game. In the center of the "fan" stands the so-called Princes' Pavilion built in 1828 by Francis I. The section of the park near the Palazzo Reale was extensively modified, from 1840 onward, in the English landscape style. It was cleared to create vast lawns surrounded by pines and interspersed with cedars, eucalyptus and magnolias.

State room of the Palazzo Reale.

In 1957 the Palazzo Reale di Capodimonte became a museum once again, the function attributed to it by the Bourbons in the 18th century. Apart from the Royal Apartments, it houses medieval and modern art previously kept in the Museo Nazionale. Its original nucleus, the Farnese collection, which includes the great Italian and European schools of painting from the Middle Ages to the 17th century, has been further enriched with works acquired under the Bourbons and after Italian unification. Also of interest are the Borgia museum collections of medieval Oriental and Western objets d'art, and the section devoted to the development of the arts in Naples from the 13th to the 19th century.

"FRANCESCO GONZAGA" (c. 1460)
Cardinal Francesco Gonzaga as a young boy in ecclesiastical dress, by Andrea Mantegna (1431–1506). The boy's brightly lit profile is clearly defined against the dark background, in the purest tradition of the medallists, and particularly of the most representative in this field, Antonio Pisanello.

"DANAË" (1544–6)
Painted for the private apartments of Cardinal Alessandro Farnese, this is one of the best-known paintings in the Museo di Capodimonte. It represents the culmination of Titian's study of light. Michelangelo himself is said to have admired Titian's supple and vital style as he painted the canvas in which Danaë, daughter of the King of Argos, is being seduced by Jupiter in the form of a golden shower of rain. Such is the erotic intensity of the work that it was withdrawn from public display at the beginning of the 19th century and placed in the so-called "obscene" collection.

"CRUCIFIXION" (1426)

The painting, bought in 1901, was the focal point of the polyptych painted by Masaccio (1401–28) for the Chiesa del Carmine in Pisa. The other panels are today dispersed in museums in London, Berlin, Malibu and Pisa. The low-angle view creates the powerful foreshortening of the figures, situated in a spatial perspective against a gilt background.

"MARRIAGE OF SAINT CATHERINE" (1518)

This small painting is a fine example of the development of the serene classicism of Correggio (c. 1489–1576), who enhanced the lesson learnt early in his career from his contact with the work of Mantegna and the Ferrara school by drawing inspiration from the works of Leonardo da Vinci and Raphaël's Roman period.

"PORTRAIT OF ANTEA" (1530–5)

The painting from the later works of Parmigianino (1503–41) is a masterpiece of Italian Mannerism. It shows a young woman, probably the artist's mistress, who traditionally identified with the famous Roman courtesan Antea. Detail (below)

"FLAGELLATION"
(1607–10)
The painting, which was placed with the Museo di Capodimonte for safekeeping, came from the Cappella di Franchis in the church of San Domenico Maggiore ▲ *142*, where it was replaced by a copy by Andrea Vaccaro. Caravaggio (1571–1610) painted the work in 1607, but added the figure of the torturer on the right in 1609, when he returned to Naples on his way back from Sicily. The impressive structure of the composition, set in a completely deserted, dark and desolate place, heightens the dramatic impact of the artist's vision. Together with *The Seven Works of Mercy*, his other masterpiece created for the Pio Monte della Misericordia ▲ *156*, the *Flagellation* provides an insight into the development of the Parthenopean pictorial tradition toward Naturalism.

"MADONNA OF THE BALDACHIN" (C. 1686)
One of Luca Giordano's (1635–1707) best works. In this monumental composition he uses formulae inspired by Baroque sculpture and reveals, in his borrowing from Bernini, his affinity with the work of his contemporary Gaulli.

"SAINT SEBASTIAN" (1657)
Transferred from the church of Santa Maria dei Sette Dolori, the painting was one of a series painted by the Calabrian artist, Mattia Preti (1613–99), during his four-year stay in Naples after the plague epidemic of 1656. He adapts Caravaggio's technique by introducing intersecting planes of light to heighten the naked strength of the saint, highlighting the angles of the twisted body and investing it with great artistic strength.

CAPODIMONTE
PORCELAIN
In 1739 Charles of
Bourbon founded
the Real Fabbrica
delle Porcellane,

REAL FABBRICA DELLE PORCELLANE. The former buildings of the royal porcelain manufactury, founded by Charles of Bourbon (1739) in the Parco di Capodimonte, today house the national training institute of the ceramics and porcelain industry. Opposite the manufactury Ferdinando Sanfelice built the elliptical CHAPEL OF SAN GENNARO (1745) as a place of worship for the workers and their families. It still houses 18th-century religious objects. Near the church, a grain storehouse bears testimony to the former agricultural activity carried out on the hillside. It is now used for exhibitions.

VIA CAPODIMONTE AND CORSO AMEDEO DI SAVOIA

During the period of French rule, the hill of Capodimonte, which for a long time had remained fairly inaccessible, was linked directly to the city by a long, tree-lined avenue known as the Corso Napoleone ● 86. The project involved major construction works: to obtain a gentle, regular slope, the hillside was excavated and a bridge built across the Sanità district ▲ 170. This long avenue (now Via Capodimonte, Corso Amedeo di Savoia, Via Santa Teresa degli Scalzi), opened in 1809 by Joachim Murat, was extended in 1836 by the addition of a magnificent flight of steps, by Antonio Niccolini, leading to the approaches of the Royal Palace. The opening of the new road brought about the rapid expansion of the district's urban development and, over the years, housing spread up to and around the boundaries of the park. The CHURCH at the end of the avenue, on Via Capodimonte, is a grandiose pastiche of St Peter's in Rome. It was built by the architect Vincenzo Veccia and consecrated in 1960. The street to the left of the church leads to the BASILICA OF SAN GENNARO EXTRAMŒNIA, built in the 5th century on the site of the catacombs that, until the 19th century, contained the body of the patron saint of Naples ▲ 158.

CATACOMBE DI SAN GENNARO

The catacombs, carved out of the hillside in what is now the Sanità district, form one of the largest underground necropolises of the early Christian period. They were created around the hypogeum of an important pagan family (2nd century AD), and became extremely important in the 5th century when they received the remains of San Gennaro ▲ 158. They began to decline based on the French royal porcelain manufactures. The chemist Livio Ottavio Schepers was given the task of developing a new type of paste. This was finally achieved by his son Gaetano, who discovered the formula for a *pâte tendre* (soft paste), using the kaolin mined near Cosenza, which had a good resistance during firing.

The manufactury, whose maker's mark was the golden lily of the house of Bourbon, was closed in 1805.

in 831 when Sicardo, Prince of Benevento, seized the remains of the martyr. However the bishops of Naples continued to be buried there until the 11th century.

NECROPOLIS. The necropolis has two stories of galleries, of a width rarely found in other early Christian burial vaults. In places the walls have some extremely interesting paintings and mosaics: a Baptism of Christ in the lower chamber, *Adam and Eve* (3rd century) in the upper chamber, and mosaic busts of the early bishops of Naples (5th century) in the crypt. The paintings in the upper gallery include the earliest known images of San Gennaro ▲ *158*.

OSPIZIO SAN GENNARO DEI POVERI. This vast building, now a hospital, was built after the plague epidemic of 1656 to house the city's beggars.

SANT'AGOSTINO AND SANTA TERESA DEGLI SCALZI

On the way back down to the city, the avenue becomes Via Santa Teresa degli Scalzi below the Tondo (circus) di Capodimonte. To the right is the *vico lungo* Sant'Agostino degli Scalzi, named after the nearby church.

CHURCH OF SANT'AGOSTINO

The church was built on a hill (1603–27) by Giovanni Giacomo di Conforto. It has a beautifully decorated stuccowork interior and houses a collection of paintings by the 17th-century Neapolitan school (Massimo Stanzione, Luca Giordano, Domenico Antonio Vaccaro and Giacomo del Po). (Return to Via Santa Teresa degli Scalzi, past the PALAZZO CIMITILE, built in the 18th century by Carlo Vanvitelli and modified at the beginning of the 19th century.)

CHURCH OF SANTA TERESA DEGLI SCALZI. Before the avenue was built, the façade, by Cosimo Fanzago, opened onto the street. The interior of the church (1602) has a rich Baroque decoration of polychrome marble and stuccowork. The present high-altar, by Giuseppe Sammartino (1750), came from the church of Divino Amore, and the sacristy contains the beautiful *Ecstasy of Saint Teresa*, by Luca Giordano.

This itinerary takes you through the *quartieri bassi* (poor districts) along the waterfront that, during the Greco-Roman period, lay outside the city walls. Charles I of Anjou was the first to develop these districts by extending the city walls (1270–85) and making them a major center for commercial and craft activities. This development was accompanied by the construction of many charitable institutions. The Aragonese continued his work, pushing the city walls further toward the sea and strengthening them with twenty huge towers. Densely packed housing, with very mediocre sanitary conditions, developed haphazardly behind the walls and repeated cholera epidemics led to the urban fabric of the area being extensively modified at the end of the 19th century. Entire districts were opened up to make way for a network of broad streets. The waterfront and the few surviving remains of the ancient city walls were bombed during World War Two.

PIAZZA MERCATO

PIAZZA MERCATO. The Piazza Mercato (market place) has witnessed a number of historical events. It was here that Masaniello's rebellion ● *38* broke out, it was the site of public executions from the Middle Ages onward and it has been the market place since the time of the Angevins when Charles I transferred the market from the ancient Greek *agora* (Piazza San Gaetano ▲ *152*). In 1781 Francesco Securo reorganized the irregular area to create a scenography that was reminiscent of a stage set. The buildings, which open onto the back of the piazza via four passageways that form the "wings", describe a perfect semicircle. At the back of this amphitheater stands the church of SANTA CROCE AL MERCATO, with its dome of colored tiles (currently being restored).

EXECUTIONS ON THE PIAZZA MERCATO
In 1268 Charles I of Anjou ordered the execution of Conradin of Swabia and seven of his companions on the Piazza Mercato (market) for attempting to recapture the Kingdom of Naples from the Angevins. Inside the church of Santa Croce al Mercato is the porphyry column surmounted by a marble cross that once stood on the site of Conradin's scaffold.

SANT'ELIGIO ● *81.* The building, commissioned at the end of the 13th century by Charles I of Anjou, was, like the adjoining church, intended as a charitable institution: the Ospedale dei Poveri ("hospital of the poor"). In the 16th century the viceroy Don Pedro de Toledo had a new orphanage built on the site. Only the richly decorated portal of the church attests to the original French Gothic style. The beautiful adjoining clock tower (15th century) used to overlook the street leading to the Piazza Mercato, of which it marked the entrance.

SANTA MARIA DEL CARMINE

By contrast to the Piazza Mercato, the nearby Piazza del Carmine was distinctively monumental in appearance and commemorative in function. The 14th-century Castello del Carmine (now destroyed) stood next to one of the city gates, overlooking the piazza.

CONVENT OF SANTA MARIA DEL CARMINE. The convent and church of Santa Maria del Carmine stand on the piazza. The convent, founded in the 12th century by the Carmelites, was rebuilt from 1270 using money donated by Margaret of Burgundy, the second wife of Charles I of Anjou, and Isabella of Bavaria, mother of Conradin of Swabia. The latter dedicated the ransom demanded by Charles I of Anjou (which had arrived too late to save the last heir in the Hohenstaufen line) to the Carmelite convent where her son's tomb was built. The GOTHIC CHURCH has been extensively modified over the centuries. Between 1753 and 1756 it was decorated in elaborate Baroque-Rococo style. At the intersection of the transept, a suspended structure houses a much-venerated wooden crucifix (second half of the 14th century) contained in a tabernacle. Behind the high-altar is the resplendent *Madonna Bruna*, a small Byzantine-style icon (14th century) which is also the object of popular veneration.

"HAND OVER THE CITY!" ▲ *102*
The 1943 bombings completely destroyed the ancient buildings separating the Piazza Mercato from the waterfront. In the 1960's a property deal that epitomized post-war building speculation resulted in the construction of a huge apartment block that looked completely out of place in this old urban district. Francesco Rosi described the episode in his movie *Le Mani sulla Città* (*Hand over the City!*, 1963).

CAMPANILE OF SANTA MARIA DEL CARMINE
The church of Santa Maria del Carmine is flanked by a beautiful (246-foot) campanile, whose first three stories were rebuilt between 1456 and 1458. The tower was completed during the first half of the 17th century by an octagonal drum, surmounted by a strange spire decorated with majolica tiles. Every year on the Madonna del Carmine festival (July 16), the bell tower is lit up by a firework display commemorating the fire that destroyed it.

▲ PIAZZA MERCATO TO VIA MEDINA

CONVENT FOR WOMEN OF ILL REPUTE
Only a few steps from the Annunziata, the church of Santa Maria Egiziaca and the adjoining convent were founded, in 1342, by Queen Sancia di Maiorca as a Magdalen hospital. The church, which has an unusual oval nave, was completely renovated (1684) in Baroque style by Dionisio Lazzari. On the altar and in the side aisles, the works of Andrea Vaccaro and Luca Giordano illustrate episodes from the life of Santa Maria Egiziaca (the Egyptian), the former prostitute to whom the church was dedicated.

Corso Umberto I.

PORTA NOLANA ● 82

Every morning a scenic fish market (above and opposite) is held in the VIA SOPRAMURO ("on the walls"). The street, which follows a long section of the Aragonese city wall, leads to the 15th-century PORTA NOLANA. Above the gate's horseshoe arch, flanked by two huge, cylindrical trachyte towers, is a bas-relief depicting Ferdinand I of Aragon on horseback.

CORSO UMBERTO I ● 86

The Corso Umberto I is a long, straight avenue (which is why it is also known as the Rettifilo) linking the station (Piazza Garibaldi), in the east, with the western districts of the city. The façades of the Rettifilo, described by Matilde Serao as a "screen", are the result of the policy of opening up urban districts that became fashionable in Italy at the beginning of the 19th century. The composite style of the 19th-century buildings creates a homogenous whole that exists alongside interesting ancient monuments.

CHURCH OF SAN PIETRO AD ARAM. Rebuilt in 1650 by Pietro de Marino on the site of an Angevin convent, the church stands on the very spot where, according to tradition, Saint Peter is said to have celebrated mass before baptizing Saint Candida and Saint Asprenus.

THE ANNUNZIATA. These buildings (now a hospital) and the adjoining church used to belong to a charitable institution, founded at the beginning of the 14th century, for abandoned children. The so-called "Foundlings' Wheel", the tower where abandoned babies were left, can still be seen to the left of the entrance. The church was destroyed by fire in 1757 and rebuilt, between 1760 and 1782, by Luigi and Carlo Vanvitelli.

CHURCH OF SANT'AGOSTINO ALLA ZECCA. The church was built during the Angevin period and modified, in Baroque style (1641), by Bartolomeo Picchiati. It was named after the nearby Zecca (Mint).

UNIVERSITY. Beyond the Piazza Nicola Amore, which forms a circus at the intersection of the Rettifilo and the Via del Duomo, the Corso leads to the impressive neoclassical palace of the University (1887–1908).

Behind the present building are a number of edifices, including the former Jesuit convent (1593).

CHURCH OF SAN PIETRO MARTIRE. Opposite the University are the church of San Pietro Martire and the adjoining Dominican monastery (now the Faculty of Arts). They were built by order of Charles II of Anjou in an attempt to clean up this district, characterized by its lime kilns, which had become a hotbed of robbery and prostitution. The church's Rococo decoration (1750) is the work of Giuseppe Scala, a mason who specialized in staff-work. The third chapel on the left contains a late 15th-century painting on wood depicting scenes from the life of San Vincenzo Ferreri, a major work from the Neapolitan school by Colantonio. During a visit to the monastery (then occupied by the royal tobacco manufactury) in 1812, the French Romantic poet, Alphonse de Lamartine, fell in love with one of the manager's servants, Maria Antonia Iacomino, who became the famous "Graziella" of his works.

PIAZZA BOVIO. The PALAZZO DELLA BORSA stands on the Piazza Bovio, at the western end of the Rettifilo. Opened in 1895, the building's sophisticated eclectic style is the work of Alfredo Guerra. The left-hand side of the *palazzo* engulfs the 8th-century church (transformed in the 17th century) of Sant'Aspreno (Asprenus). In the center of the piazza is the FONTANA DEL NETTUNO, designed in 1601 by Domenico Fontana, which once stood at the entrance to the Arsenal. The sculptures are by Pietro Bernini and Michelangelo Naccherino.

VIA MEDINA

Below the street is the medieval church of SANTA MARIA INCORONATA, built by Jeanne I of Anjou, in 1352, to commemorate her coronation. It was pillaged in the 17th century and has recently been beautifully restored. The interior has a series of remarkable frescos (1352–4) by Roberto Oderisi.

CHURCH OF THE PIETÀ DEI TURCHINI. The church, founded in 1592, was named after the color *turchino* (deep blue) of the clothes worn by the orphans who were taken in and given a musical education. The orphanage was, like similar institutions dedicated to music, absorbed at the beginning of the 19th century by the conservatory of San Pietro a Maiella. Alessandro Scarlatti (1660–1725), Francesco Durante (1684–1755) and Giovanni Paisiello (1740–1816) were among the pupils of the Pietà dei Turchini.

THE FIRST BISHOP OF NAPLES
Sant'Aspreno is commemorated at both ends of the Rettifilo. Near the Piazza Garibaldi, the vestibule of San Pietro ad Aram has a 12th-century altar at which, according to legend, Saint Peter baptized Saint Asprenus and the early Christians of Naples. On the Piazza Bovio the 8th-century church, engulfed by the Palazzo della Borsa, attests to the ancient cult of the saint. In the basement, an oratory has been installed on the remains of ancient Roman baths.

The campanile of the Annunziata (above, left) dates from 1524. At the foot of the tower, a remarkable 16th-century portal by Tommaso Malvito leads to the former orphanage.

183

Well (16th century) in the Chiostro Grande of the Certosa di San Martino.

Until the 19th century the hillside of the Vomero had only a few isolated dwellings, scattered farms and small villages (Vomero Vecchio and Antignano). At the top of the hill, the villas of the Duke of Salva, the Prince of Belvedere, the Duchess of Floridia and the Princess of Palazzolo were set in vast parks and enjoyed a magnificent view of the Bay of Naples and the islands. On the summit (820 feet), overlooking the city, stood the Castel Sant'Elmo and the Certosa (Carthusian monastery) di San Martino. The Vomero was linked to the city by a series of tracks intersected by flights of steps. During the second half of the 19th century the construction of the Via Tasso and the Corso Vittorio Emanuele led to the rapid expansion of a new and fashionable district on the slopes of Sant'Elmo. Villas and small Stile Liberty apartment blocks, surrounded by gardens, were built along the regular grid system formed by the new roads. Post-war property speculation destroyed the district's elegant Edwardian image by replacing villas and gardens with more densely built housing.

CERTOSA DI SAN MARTINO ★

In Naples, the Carthusian order, which was the cultural elite of the Church of the period, enjoyed the protection of Charles of Anjou, Duke of Calabria. In 1325 Charles began to build a monastery worthy of their status on this magnificent site. The conventual buildings and church, dedicated to Saint Martin, Bishop of Tours, were completed in 1368 during the reign of Jeanne I. During the second half of the 16th century, with the Counter-Reformation well underway, the original Gothic complex was extended and modernized according to the new canons of religious architecture. The Angevin structures were covered with a Mannerist-style revetment. From 1623 onward, Cosimo Fanzago played an important part in the modification of the monastery complex, which explains the clearly Baroque influence.

THE CHURCH. The church, preceded by a *pronaos,* stands in the courtyard of the entrance. The original triple-naved interior was modified by the Florentine, Giovanni Antonio Dosio, and then by the Neapolitan, Giovanni Giacomo di Conforto. By partitioning off the secondary naves, they created a series of large side chapels opening directly off the central nave. Adjoining the church are several rooms used for religious purposes: on the right, the CHAPTER HOUSE, with its beautiful 17th-century wood paneling, and the MONKS' CHOIR, whose stalls date from 1510; on the left, the Sacristy, with its late 16th-century inlaid presses, and the richly decorated TREASURY containing paintings and frescos; above the altar, Ribera's *Descent from the Cross* (below) and Luca Giordano's vault-fresco depicting Judith.

THE MONASTERY. The monastery is centered around two cloisters. The CHIOSTRO GRANDE, where Fanzago included a small rectangular cemetery decorated with marble skulls, was surrounded by the monks' cells. The smaller CHIOSTRO DEI PROCURATORI used to be reserved for the lay brothers. Between the two cloisters is the Prior's Apartment decorated with frescoed landscapes (1640) and beautiful 18th-century majolica tiling. A magnificent staircase, by Cosimo Fanzago, links it to the gardens whose several terraces are shaded by a vine-covered pergola and offer one of the finest view of the city and the Bay of Naples.

MUSEO NAZIONALE DI SAN MARTINO. The museum, with its rich collections of art and historical artefacts, has been housed in the monastery since 1886. The Neapolitan history and art section includes a large crib ● 56 and a remarkable collection of 18th- and 19th-century religious figures ★.

The rich decoration of the church of San Martino makes it a prime example of 17th- and 18th-century Neapolitan art. It includes key works by Stanzione, Lanfranco and Ribera.

CASTEL SANT'ELMO

FORT OF ROBERT OF ANJOU. In the 10th century a small church dedicated to Sant'Erasmo (which became Eramo, Ermo and then Elmo) stood on the summit of the hill. In the 14th century Robert of Anjou built a fort on this dominant site and surrounded it with strong ramparts. The castle, called Belforte, towered above the city for the next century.

▲ The Vomero

THE PRISONS OF
SANT'ELMO
Over the centuries
the cells of the Castel
Sant'Elmo housed a
great many prisoners,
the most famous being
Tommaso Campanella
(1568–1639), who was
held there between
1604 and 1608. With
the outbreak of
Masaniello's rebellion
● *38* (1647), the then
viceroy, the Duke of
Arcos, sought refuge
in the castle where he
held out against the
attacks of the populace.
It was here that the
Neapolitan republic
● *32* was proclaimed,
in 1799, and the first
"tree of liberty"
erected. During the
subsequent repression,
the handful of
intellectuals and
nobles who had led
the revolutionary
movement were
imprisoned in the
fort. The castle was
used as a military
prison until 1952.

A MILITARY CITADEL. Between 1537 and 1546 the viceroy Don
Pedro de Toledo employed the Valencian, Pier Luigi Scrivà,
one of the leading fortifications experts of the period, to
strengthen the
Angevin fortress.
A six-pointed star
fort, surrounded by
high, bastioned
ramparts and a deep
moat, was built
around the original
structure. The Castel
Sant'Elmo became
one of the kingdom's

most impressive fortresses, a veritable military citadel with its
own castellan, chaplain, garrison, court and prison. In 1587
the powder store was struck by lightning, killing 150 people
and destroying the church and the castellan's apartments
(subsequently rebuilt). Today, the restored buildings are used
for exhibitions and conferences.

THE VOMERO DISTRICT

The Vomero district, with its checkerboard urban grid system
centered around the Piazza Vanvitelli, lies at the foot of the
Castel Sant'Elmo. This residential and commercial district is
linked to the lower part of the city by two funicular railways
which run from Via Cimarosa to Via Toledo and the Chiaia
district.

VILLA FLORIDIANA. The magnificent Villa Floridiana (above)
stands in a vast park and opens onto Via
Cimarosa. It was built by the
architect Antonio Niccolini
(1817–19) at the request of
Ferdinand I for his
morganatic wife Lucia
Migliaccio Partanna,

Duchess of Floridia. Niccolini took account of the steeply sloping site, making extensive use of paths and belvederes, and placing artificial ruins, fountains, glasshouses and even a small open-air theater among the vegetation.

ON THE HILLSIDE

Just beyond the Villa Floridiana lies Via Aniello Falcone, one of the city's most scenic streets, bordered by small Stile Liberty buildings. It leads into Via Tasso which runs down into the Corso Vittorio Emanuele, built (1853–60) midway up the hillside between Mergellina in the west, and the Piazza Mazzini in the east. This long, terraced avenue follows the relief of the hillside and offers some truly magnificent views across the city and the Bay of Naples.

CHURCH OF SANTA MARIA APPARENTE. The church was founded in 1581, at the same time as the adjacent convent of the Order of the Reformed Church.

SAN CARLO ALLE MORTELLE. The conventual complex was built (c. 1616), by the Barnabites, among fields and gardens. In 1738 Charles of Bourbon established the royal tapestry and hard stone manufactures in a building adjoining the church.

CONVENT OF SUOR'ORSOLA BENINCASA. From the Corso Vittorio Emanuele a steep slope, on the left, leads to the entrance of this impressive convent. A lift takes you up to the terrace, from where you plunge into a dark, winding passage which suddenly opens onto a vast, well-lit and brightly colored cloister offering magnificent views of the Bay of Naples. When the original convent was founded by Suor'Orsola Benincasa at the end of the 16th century, it included a hermitage for women "incarcerated" in the convent. This was extended between 1656 and 1669. In 1869 Suor'Orsola became a girls' boarding school for the daughters of the Neapolitan bourgeoisie. Today it houses a University institute.

MUSEO NAZIONALE DELLA CERAMICA
In 1910 the State bought the Villa Floridiana to house the faience, porcelain and glassware bequeathed by Don Placido di Sangro, Duke of Martina. This legacy was subsequently complemented by acquisitions and donations. The collection includes some extremely beautiful Oriental pieces, especially Chinese (Ming), and 18th-century European porcelain (Capodimonte, Limoges, Meissen, Sèvres).

Beyond the colonnade of the Piazza del Plebiscito, the tightly packed buildings encroach haphazardly upon the slopes of Mount Echia. The summit, Pizzofalcone, offers a sweeping view across the Bay of Naples. It was on this hillside, in c. 7th century BC, that the Greeks founded a town named after the siren Parthenope who, according to legend, was washed ashore and buried on the beach at the foot of the mountain. The itinerary then follows the *lungomare* along the wealthy façades of the Riviera di Chiaia to the panoramic hillside of Posillipo.

PIZZOFALCONE

CHURCH OF SANTA MARIA DEGLI ANGELI A PIZZOFALCONE. The 17th-century church, by Francesco Grimaldi, is surmounted by a very high dome offering a magnificent east-west panorama of Naples. The balance and proportions of its three naves give the interior an impressive and sober appearance.

PALAZZO SERRA DI CASSANO. This is undoubtedly one of the most beautiful Baroque palaces in Via Monte di Dio, the street which very probably follows the line of the ancient Greek Parthenopean way (Via Partenope). The residence, built according to plans by Ferdinando Sanfelice, once opened onto Via Egiziaca a Pizzofalcone, lower down the hill. In 1799 Prince Serra ordered the great portal to be closed following his son's arrest, by order of the Bourbons, for having taken part in the revolutionary uprisings of the short-lived Parthenopean Republic ● 32. The square courtyard with its rounded corners has a magnificent double staircase with a trachyte revetment. (From here, turn right into Via Generale Parise.)

CHURCH OF THE NUNZIATELLA. The interior of the church, designed by Ferdinando Sanfelice, is richly decorated with rare marbles. It has some remarkable vault-frescos and wall paintings on the inside of the façade by Francesco de Mura, and altar sculptures by Giuseppe Sammartino. Next to the church is the military college, built in 1588 as a Jesuit novitiate and transformed by Sanfelice in 1736. (Walk up Via Egiziaca a Pizzofalcone.)

PIZZOFALCONE. The hill of Pizzofalcone was the site of the first Greek colony, initially known as Parthenope and then Paleopolis ("old city"), as opposed to Neapolis ("new city"). It appears that, some time later, the hill was also chosen as the

"COLMATA A MARE"

After the cholera epidemic of 1884, it was decided to improve living conditions in the districts of Porto, Pendino and Mercato. The rubble from the demolition work was transported to Santa Lucia and thrown into the sea to form a *colmata*, or "fill", which was subsequently covered with luxury buildings and given a new *lungomare* ("promenade"), Via Nazario Sauro. The operation was hypocritically presented as an attempt to clean up the Pallonetto of Santa Lucia, a collection of shacks clinging to the slopes of Mount Echia. In reality it was a skillful property deal.

site of Lucullus' villa. Its slopes are covered with the shacks of the old waterfront district of Santa Lucia and fishermen still gather today in the narrow, crowded streets of the Pallonetto. (Return to the Piazza del Plebiscito and turn right or take the steps that lead down from Pizzofalcone to Santa Lucia.)

SANTA LUCIA

VIA GUZMANA, "ROAD OF THE VICEROYS". At the end of the 16th century, the viceroy Enríquez de Guzmán, Count of Olivares, employed the Roman urban architect, Domenico Fontana, to construct a road that ran round Mount Echia, in order to encourage the development of the city to the west, along the delightful Riviera de Chiaia. Several important families (such as the Carafa and the Macedonio) built palaces along Via Guzmana.

CHURCH OF SANTA LUCIA. The church of Santa Lucia, the patron saint of sight, is a place of great popular devotion, especially for seafarers. The church represents three historical periods: the new church, built by Eusebia Minadoa (1588) on the 9th-century foundations, was completely rebuilt in 1845 and restored after the 1943 bombings.

VIA GUZMANA
The road, built between the hillside and the sea, was originally decorated with a number of fountains which were later removed. For example the FONTANA DELL'IMMACOLATELLA (1622–9, below), built for the viceroy Antonio Alvárez de Toledo and attributed to Pietro Bernini, father of Gianlorenzo Bernini, now stands on the corner of Via Nazario Sauro and Via Partenope; the FONTANA DI SANTA

LUCIA (1606), by Michelangelo Naccherino, was moved to the Villa Comunale ▲ *190* in 1898; while the SEBETO FOUNTAIN (1635–7), by Cosimo Fanzago, now stands on the Largo Sermoneta.

VIRGIL THE MAGICIAN
The Castel dell'Ovo is named after the magic egg that Virgil is said to have locked in an iron cage hung from the vault of a secret room. If the egg broke, it was the sign of imminent catastrophe. Believing Virgil to be buried in the castle, a medieval traveler, Conrad de Querfourt, wrote with a certain uneasiness, in 1194: "If Virgil's bones are exposed to the air, the sky grows dark, the sea begins to foam and boil and, suddenly, a roaring tempest rises. This is what we have seen and witnessed."

CASTEL DELL'OVO

The Castel dell'Ovo ("Castle of the Egg") stands on the tufa rock of the ancient island of Megaris, once a fortification of the Greek colony of Parthenope. During the early Middle Ages, a community of monks of the Order of Saint Basil settled there and cut several hermitages out of the rock. It was transformed into a castle by the Normans and, under the Angevins, became the Palacium Magnum, the prestigious palace of Joan I until the Castel Nuovo ▲ *134* was completed. In the 16th century the castle became a fortress, complete with casemates and bastions. It was bombarded by the Bourbons, occupied by the populace in 1799 and later used for military purposes, before being restored in the 1970's and opened to the public as a venue for cultural events.

BORGO MARINARO. The district came into being in 1885, when the *colmata* of Santa Lucia ▲ *188* was built. It consists of a collection of buildings still inhabited by fishermen. The busy new bars and restaurants in many of the apartment blocks offer an opportunity to sample the local specialties.

VILLA COMUNALE ● 87

The park of the Villa Comunale stretches from the Piazza Vittoria to the Piazza della Repubblica and is bordered, on one side, by Via Caracciolo and, on the other, by the Riviera di Chiaia with its magnificent 18th- and 19th-century palaces. The latter's crescent-shaped beach was used as a landing place by fishermen until 1697, when the viceroy, the Duke of Medinacoeli, had a double row of trees planted and thirteen fountains built along the shore. In 1778–80 Ferdinand IV commissioned the architect Carlo Vanvitelli and the botanist Felice Abate to construct a "public park" in which five parallel avenues led to the central fountain. The park was designated a "royal site", which

Seafood vendor.

meant that "liveried servants, the poor, beggars and improperly dressed persons" were forbidden to enter. The Farnese bull (now in the Museo Archeologico Nazionale ▲ 168) was placed at the center of the famous park, so that it could be seen from the end of each of the avenues. In 1825 it was replaced by the Paparelle fountain. In the park are the CASINA POMPEIANA (1870), the CASSA ARMONICA (built to plans by Enrico Alvino, 1878) and the ZOOLOGICAL STATION (Oscar Capocci and Adolf von Hildebrand, 1873). Inside, the library (decorated with frescos of marine and equestrian scenes from southern Italy, by the German Hans von Marées and Von Hildebrand) and the Aquarium are open to the public. The latter has some two hundred species of underwater flora and fauna from the Bay of Naples.

VILLA PIGNATELLI. Set in a vast park, the façade of this neoclassical villa (Piero Valente, 1826) incorporates a magnificent portal. Since 1960 it has housed the MUSEO PRINCIPE DIEGO ARAGONA PIGNATELLI CORTES. The decoration on the first floor has remained unchanged and visitors can experience the atmosphere of a true nobiliary residence. There is a CARRIAGE MUSEUM in the park.

"LE QUATTRO GIORNATE DI NAPOLI". In the center of the Piazza della Repubblica stands Mazzacurati's Monumento allo Scugnizzo (1969) commemorating the city's four-day uprising against the Nazi occupation ● 34. This episode has been immortalized in Nanni Loy's movie, Le Quattro Giornate di Napoli (The Four Days of Naples, 1962) ▲ 101.

CHURCH OF SANTA MARIA DI PIEDIGROTTA. The church used to be the focal point for the famous Festival of Piedigrotta, held on September 8 ● 49. On the high altar is a wooden figure of the Madonna, by the Siena school (14th century).

PARCO VIRGILIANO. The park lies behind the Church of Santa Maria di Piedigrotta and contains the tombs of Giacomo Leopardi and Virgil. The latter is in fact an anonymous Roman *columbarium*. Nearby is the mouth of the Grotta Vecchia (or Crypta Neapolitana),

Castel dell'Ovo (left).

GROTTA VECCHIA OR "CRYPTA NEAPOLITANA" In his *Satiricon*, Petronius recalls that the entrance to the cave (located, at the time, in an isolated spot some distance from the city) was the scene of orgiastic rites held in honor of Priapus, god of fecundity and fertility. In *Il Segno di Virgilio*, Roberto Simone associates the cave with the solar mythology. According to medieval tradition, the cave was supposed to have been created magically, by a single gesture from Virgil, along an east-west axis. On two days of the year, at the end of October and the end of February, the setting sun shines right along it, a phenomenon that gives those using the tunnel a feeling of protection and security.

a tunnel (776 yards long) dug by the Roman architect Lucius Cocceius Auctus, in the 1st century BC, to link Neapolis (Naples) with Puteoli (Pozzuoli) and the Phlegraean Fields.

MERGELLINA

A walk along the bay of Mergellina, to the cries of *taralli* ▲ 161 and seafood vendors, takes you past the yachts in the port to the Largo Sermoneta, the bay's most scenic point.
CHURCH OF SANTA MARIA DEL PARTO. This small church (1529) is well worth a visit, if only to see the *Diavolo di Mergellina* by Leonardo da Pistoia (first altar on the left). It shows Saint Michael defeating a demon unusually bearing the features of a woman. According to legend, the saint is said to represent Cardinal Diomedes Carafa, Bishop of Ariano, and the demon, a woman who tried to seduce him. Having resisted her charms, the cardinal had the following words inscribed on the painting: "FECIT VICTORIAM ALLELUIA, 1542, CARAFA". The church also houses the tomb of the Neapolitan poet and humanist, JACOPO SANNAZARO ● 43, a masterpiece of Renaissance style decorated with a bucolic scene evoking the Arcadian myth.

POSILLIPO

The Romans chose the Capo di Posillipo as the site for their vacation (*otium*) villas. Here, between countryside and sea, rich patricians discovered the refinements of Neapolitan Greek culture. The largest of these villas, Pausilypon, later gave its name to the entire hillside, still the most elegant residential district in modern-day Naples.
PALAZZO DI DONN'ANNA ★. This extraordinary palace, built in 1642 by Cosimo Fanzago for the vicereine, Anna Carafa, was never completed. Its massive tufa structure, now partly ruined, is attractively reflected in the sea.
VILLA ROSEBERY. The former residence of the brother of King Ferdinand II of Bourbon, Louis Charles Marie (who used it for his amorous rendezvous with the dancer Amina Boschetti), is today one of the official residences of the Italian President. (Take Via Marechiaro which runs down from Posillipo to the sea and leads to the tiny fishing village of the same name, celebrated by

> **"When the moon shines down on Marechiaro,**
> **In Marechiaro, my love smiles**
> **down from a balcony."**
>
> Marechiaro

Salvatore di Giacomo and Francesco Paolo Tosti in the famous Neapolitan song *Marechiaro*, 1885 ● 42.

Villa of Lady Elizabeth (Villa Rae). The villa was the property of Lady Elizabeth Berkley, margravine of Brandenburg, who, at the beginning the 19th century was a key figure on the Neapolitan social scene. The villa was sold several times before it was finally bought by Charles James Rae, in 1924, after whom it is now named.

Villa Pausilypon. This idyllic villa was given the evocative Greek name – Pausilypon – by Publius Vedius Pollio, its owner during antiquity. The infamous Pollio, a native of Benevento, had made his fortune in Asia with the help of Augustus. But his friendship with the emperor was short-lived. When Pollio's cupbearer broke a murrhine drinking cup, his master ordered him to be fed to the moray eels. Augustus was outraged by his host's attitude and ordered the entire collection of murrhine cups to be broken. On his death, in 15 BC, Vedius bequeathed his fortune to Augustus, on condition that the latter had a funerary monument erected in his honor. Augustus refused to honor the condition and even had the dead man's Roman palace razed to the ground. The Villa Pausilypon was spared as it blended perfectly with the other imperial villas on the Bay of Naples. Its buildings skillfully echoed the relief of the delightful countryside between the bays of La Gaiola and Trentaremi. The most interesting building discovered on the site was a theater (2,000 seats) whose stage was a long pool. Opposite are the ruins of a smaller theater which was undoubtedly an *odeum*.

Two bays

At the end of the Capo di Posillipo is the Park of Remembrance (Rimembranza), which offers a magnificent view of the bays of Naples and Pozzuoli.

Nisida. Although the island of Nisida is linked to the mainland by a causeway, boat is the only way to visit Porto Paone, a creek on the edge of an extinct volcanic crater, and the so-called rocks of the Ponente (West) and the Levante (East). Brutus, Julius Caesar's assassin, had a villa on the island where he was visited by Cicero.

Palazzo di Donn'Anna.

"School of Virgil"
The underwater excavations carried out at the foot of the ruined Villa Pausilypon have revealed the *pilae* of a small private port and the remains of colonnades and *nymphaea* as well as the structures of the fish ponds for which the villa was renowned. The ruins still seem to be pervaded by the spirit of Virgil who is said to have performed the miracles attributed to him by medieval tradition on the rock known as the "school of Virgil".

ROYAL APARTMENTS
In the Old Apartment, the artist Fedele Fischetti used his fertile imagination to create a profusion of flowers and fruit. By contrast the Study of Ferdinand, the Library and the so-called "Crib Room" (containing a Neapolitan crib ● *56* composed of more than 1,200 figures) are decorated with the works of northern artists, including Philipp Hackert ● *95* who painted the canvases depicting the ports of the Kingdom of Naples. The decorations of the New Apartment, in the taste of Joachim Murat, recount the Homeric wars and pay obvious homage to the Napoleonic campaigns. The creation of the Throne Room (1845) marked the completion of work on the palace, celebrated by Maldarelli's painting commemorating the laying of the first stone.

To the north of Naples lies the *campania felix* described by the ancients, the fertile plain (renamed Terra di Lavoro) whose capital is Caserta. Charles of Bourbon was an enlightened monarch, who tried to transform the State by adopting an entrepreneurial approach and encouraging the development of such establishments as the porcelain manufactury of Capodimonte ▲ *178,* the hard stone manufactures of the Mortelle and the silk manufactury of San Leucio (near Caserta), and he wanted to add to the splendor of his reign by building a replica of Versailles, in the heart of the Italian countryside, devoted to leisure and hunting. This palace was the favorite residence of Italian monarchs until 1859.

PALAZZO REALE

A MASTERPIECE BY VANVITELLI. To help him achieve his ambition, Charles of Bourbon employed the services of Luigi Vanvitelli who already had the Foro Carolino ▲ *151* and the church of the Santissima Annunziata in Naples ▲ *182* to his credit. Vanvitelli, whose father, the artist Gaspar van Wittel, had been one of the leading *vedutisti* in Rome, was a master of *vedute* ● *95*. He had also assimilated the Baroque style of Bernini

THE PARK
Vanvitelli created this
magnificent view by
alternating pools,
monumental fountains
and cascades along a
central axis. The
architect also wanted
the rigid formality of
the flowerbeds to
provide an elegant
setting for the themes
of the Italian garden,
the mazes and other
Baroque features,
including the French-
style rockery.
Although the gardens,
like the palace, were
modified after the
architect's death by his
son Carlo and
Gaetano Genovese,
the iconographic
theme of water and
hunting was retained.
The four great
fountains, the Fontana
Margherita, Fontana
di Aeolo, Fontana di
Cerere, and the
Fontana di Venere
(Venus and Adonis),
symbolize the four
natural elements. The
fountain at the far end
of the axis represents
the theme of death
via the myth of Diana
and Acteon (below),
with death being
symbolically
transcended by the
ascent toward the top
of the cascade. The
English Garden to the
right of this fountain
was commissioned by
Marie-Caroline,
Ferdinand's
queen.

and studied architecture with Juvarra, who had given him his
taste for scenography. Work on the royal palace was begun in
1752 and then abandoned for many years when Charles of
Bourbon returned to Madrid. Vanvitelli's creation which, in
the 18th century, inspired the admiration of Raphael Mengs,
the Abbé de Saint-Non and Vivant Denon, was described by
Stendhal and Dumas, a century later, as little more than a
barracks built on an extremely unattractive site. With the
king's permission, Vanvitelli had given his very
personal stamp to the edifice in which he combined
the austerity of the exterior with the studied elegance
and refinement of the interior.

THE APARTMENTS. The five-story rectangular
building is centered around four main
courtyards and has some 1,200 rooms.
The State Staircase leads to the large,
octagonal vestibule. The PALATINE CHAPEL,
opposite, is directly inspired by the chapel
of the Palace of Versailles. This is followed
by the GUARD ROOM, the ROOM OF THE
HALBARDIERS and the ROOM OF
ALEXANDER whose decoration is inspired by
the legend of Hercules and the "heroic
age", one of the three philosophical stages
in the history of Giambattista Vico, so
dear to the hearts of Charles and
Vanvitelli. The furniture and decoration

CASERTA VECCHIA
This small, hilltop village (1,300 feet), about six miles to the northwest of the new town, has retained its medieval character. It was founded in the 8th century by the Lombards of Capua and remained a lively community until Charles of Bourbon built his palace (1752), displacing the center of attraction toward the plain. The 12th-century cathedral (above) overlooks a paved *piazzetta* surrounded by nobiliary residences.

of the ROYAL APARTMENTS (the Old Apartment and the New Apartment) constitute a veritable museum illustrating the development from Rococo to the neoclassical style. On the left of the second courtyard, the PALATINE THEATER was built at the instigation of Ferdinand IV who, unlike Charles, did not like hunting. The lavish decoration of the horseshoe-shaped auditorium creates a trompe-l'oeil effect (an illusion within an illusion) by using papier-mâché to imitate marble and disguising silver as gold by means of a varnish colored with saffron and walnut stain. The theater has another delightful detail: the stage can be opened up onto the park immediately behind it, thus creating a natural backdrop framed by Antonio Joli's beautiful curtains.

CASERTA VECCHIA

THE CATHEDRAL. The Cathedral's strange beauty stems from the blend of Romanesque architecture and Byzantine, Moorish and Norman decorations. The triangular tympanum of the façade is framed by small columns supported by lions, and windows with white marble surrounds. Inside, antique columns of varying heights (compensated by Corinthian capitals, each different from the other) run the length of the three naves. The windows of the principal nave are framed by a horseshoe-shaped archivolt, and the transenna, pulpit and paschal candlestick are decorated with magnificent majolica tiles. The interior of the 13th-century dome, on which a starry sky is finely depicted in gray tufa and white marble, is a masterpiece of Moorish art.

CHURCH OF THE ANNUNZIATA. The small Gothic church of the Annunziata (late 13th century), with its Baroque marble portal, stands on the street leading out of the village from the *piazzetta*. The nearby esplanade offers a fine view of the Terra di Lavoro.

CAMPANILE
The pointed archway (105 feet high) of the cathedral's beautiful 14th-century campanile spans the street. Its decoration echoes the intertwined arcades of the façade and the white marble surrounds of the window openings.

BAY OF NAPLES

▲ PHLEGRAEAN FIELDS

The reputation of the Phlegraean Fields, or Campi Flegrei ("burning fields") owes as much to the region's rich and varied history as to the strange volcanic phenomena that affect it. In c. 1500 BC Mycenaean navigators weighed anchor in the Bay of Naples. The Homeric and Virgilian epics of the *Odyssey* and the *Aeneid*, and the legend of the siren Parthenope ● *78*, reflect the memory of these navigational exploits. These mythical accounts were overlaid by the factual account of the Greek colonization in the 1st millennium BC. It was the early Greek settlers who gave the name Phlegraean Fields (from the Greek *phlegein*, "to burn") to this "burning" land. According to the historians of

antiquity, Cumae was the oldest Greek colony in the Western world. For several centuries its fortunes were linked to those of Capua, the Etruscan metropolis of the southern hemisphere ● *28*, and then Rome. The center of the Phlegraean Fields was later displaced to Puteoli (Pozzuoli) which became the largest trading port in the western Mediterranean. Rome strengthened its hold on the region when it became increasingly fashionable for the aristocracy to build luxurious villas overlooking the bay. During the Roman Empire, the imperial court often stayed in Baia, while the neighboring town of Misenum was used as a naval base to ensure the control and safety of the maritime routes. But the seismic phenomenon known as bradyseism ● *23* caused land levels to fall and ports and villas to be submerged, with the result that the trading counters were gradually transferred to Ostia, which became the main Roman port. Towns were depopulated as the inhabitants sought refuge on the healthier and more easily defended promontories, while a large part of the region was abandoned to the marshes until it was rediscovered with the advent of humanism.

NAPLES TO THE SOLFATARA

AGNANO TERME. Agnano has been a spa since antiquity, as the remains of its *thermae*, dating from the time of Trajan (98–117), bear witness. The springs emerge from the side of a rugged caldera known as the crater of Agnano, which was formed as a result of a series of volcanic eruptions.
ASTRONI. The extraordinary Parco degli Astroni, another extinct volcano, is one of the few conservation areas in the Naples region. It was established as a royal hunting reserve by Alfonso the Magnanimous in the 15th century, and remained a protected area until the 19th century, long enough for the city to have developed in other directions. On the left of the road from Astroni to Pozzuoli is the CONVENT OF SAN GENNARO, built in 1580 on the site where, according to tradition, San Gennaro (Saint Januarius) was beheaded ▲ 158. At the entrance to the Solfatara di Pozzuoli ▲ 201, an esplanade offers a magnificent view of the Bay

PARCO DEGLI ASTRONI
The Parco degli Astroni can be reached from the edge of the crater (which offers some magnificent views) or by following the hunting track, inside the crater, that leads to the lake. The magnificent forest surrounding the lake is teeming with game.

199

of Pozzuoli and the Phlegraean Fields, with the promontory of the Rione Terra in the foreground.

POZZUOLI

The "capital" of the Phlegraean Fields is a busy commercial center. Over the centuries it has been affected by the seismic phenomenon known as bradyseism which has often forced the population to flee the town (as in 1970). It has always managed to recover, however, and even expand, mainly because of its monuments and the general public's fascination for these dramatic natural phenomena.

HISTORY. The strategic position occupied by the promontory of the Rione Terra on the Bay of Naples explains why the Romans chose it as the site of their oldest colony, founded in 194 BC as the headquarters of the military contingent that controlled this part of the coast. Ceramic fragments discovered suggest that the site was occupied from the 8th or 7th century BC by a maritime fortress subject to Cumae (which at the time controlled the bay) and, some time later, by Greek colonists from Samos who founded Dikaearchia ("town of justice"). The most recent excavations confirmed that the urban fabric is much the same as that of the Roman town, whose paved streets and façades of the *insulae* have either been preserved beneath the foundations of the present buildings or visibly incorporated into their structure.

RIONE TERRA. Beyond the Great Amphitheater ▲ *202* lies the oldest part of the town and the cathedral of San Procolo. Consecrated in the 11th century, it retained and incorporated a large part of the Roman capitol, which was rebuilt during the Augustan period. The temple became known as the Temple of Augustus owing to an erroneous interpretation of the inscription on the façade whereby the name of the dedicatee, Lucius Calpurnius, was associated with the title "Aug(ustalis)". In 1964 a fire revealed the ancient face of the monument, which was that of a classical Greek temple built of marble. Beneath the podium was another, belonging to a temple, built during the Roman Republic using tufa blocks set directly on the rock. A program of archeological, architectural and environmental restoration is being carried out on the Rione Terra, which has been inhabited since 1971. A museum will house the remarkable marble sculptures from the Roman period and the remains of the antique town.

"SERAPEUM" AND RIPA PUTEOLANA. The only visible evidence of what were once the harbor districts of Puteoli is a magnificent edifice which was wrongly named the Serapeum ("Temple of Serapis") following the discovery of a small statue of the Egyptian god on the site. The so-called Serapeum ("Temple of Serapis) is in fact one of the finest surviving examples of a *macellum* (market hall) ● *71*.

The Greeks and Romans believed that the Solfatara was inhabited by the god of fire, and that volcanic activity was a manifestation of his presence.
The Greeks therefore called it the *agora Ephaistu* (market place of Hephaestus) and the Romans the *forum Vulcani* (market place of Vulcan).

THE SOLFATARA ● 22

In the crater of a volcano that has been extinct for some 4,000 years, jets of steam (fumaroles) emerge from pools of boiling mud. The volcanic rocks are swathed in sinister clouds of acrid, sulfurous vapor as the bubbling gases rise to the surface. These features, typical of volcanic regions, are caused by the infiltration of surface water that is heated deep beneath the center of the Phlegraean Fields (the magma could still be present at a depth of 2½ to 3½ miles). The steam rises to the surface, along with gas and various chemical elements, including sulfur. Numerous chemical reactions lead to the crystalization of minerals and the distortion of the volcanic rocks. The temperature of these fumaroles has sometimes reached more than 200°C. They also transform volcanic ash into mud which, at certain points throughout history, has filled the bottom of the crater. In the northeastern section of the crater are ancient Roman steamrooms known as the Grotta del Cane (Grotto of the Dog), at the bottom of which toxic gases (carbon dioxide and hydrogen sulfide) collect in lethal concentrations.

The inhabitants of Campania and Rome, as well as many foreign visitors, would crowd into the amphitheater to see the games. The wealth of Pozzuoli and the development of new construction techniques (combining cement and mortar) enabled the inhabitants to build one of the first amphitheaters in Italy. It was used until the middle of the 1st century, when population growth led to the construction of new amphitheaters. Although it is not known whether the Pozzuoli theater was built before or after the Coliseum in Rome, they are both fine examples of the technical sophistication of Roman architecture.

THE "CAVEA"
The *cavea* ("enclosure") had 39 rows of tiered seats (8 on the first level, 16 on the second and 15 on the third), with an overall capacity of 40,000. The emperor himself had laid down a series of rules to ensure the orderly access of the spectators, with the seats of honor allocated to the higher social ranks (senators and patricians).

GLADIATORIAL COMBATS
By the Roman period, the original value of religious games held in honor of the dead had long been lost. The games, which were contests between gladiators (*munera*) or between gladiators and wild animals (*venationes*), had become nothing more than a spectacle. The crowds went into a frenzy of excitement when their heroes entered the arena and infatuated women collected their blood, one of the most powerful love charms.

GLADIATOR'S HELMET

There is no doubt that the owner of this Pompeiian helmet fought at Pozzuoli. The gladiator belonged to the Thracians, originally recruited among the prisoners of Mithridates' army. He fought against other Thraces (Mirmillones or Hoplomachi) using a round buckler and a short, curved dagger.

STRUCTURE. The amphitheater was built on three, superposed levels crowned by an attic level, according to the plan widely used during the imperial period. Four main entrances, at the ends of the axes of the elliptical arena, and twelve secondary entrances enabled spectators to enter and leave the theater quickly and easily, while twenty flights of stairs led to the upper and attic levels.

The amphitheater of Pozzuoli was the third largest in Italy, after the Coliseum and the amphitheater of Capua.

SUBSTRUCTURES

Opening off the wide, underground corridors were rooms containing equipment, stage machinery, scenery and the wild animal cages. These cages were raised into the arena through trap doors. The hydraulic system consisted of a conduit which chaneled the rainwater collected in the vast *cavea* into the sea.

PHLEGRAEAN FIELDS

AN UNUSUAL "GAUGE"
The three cipolin columns of the *sacellum* (shrine) have been eaten away by a species of shellfish (*Lithodomus lithophagus*), indicating that they have at some time been submerged. These tiny holes made it possible to gauge the extent of the bradyseism ● 22 caused by the rise and fall of the subjacent molten magma.

LAGO DI AVERNO
The Lago di Averno occupies the bottom of an almost circular crater (over half a mile in diameter) formed nearly 3,800 years ago during an extremely violent eruption. The Greek name *Aornos* is generally taken to mean "without birds", because of the gaseous fumes given off by its dark, muddy waters. In Virgil's *Aeneid* the entrance to Hades was located on the shores of the lake.

"Thermae" at Baia.

Serapeum was built between the end of the 1st and beginning of the 2nd century AD and restored during the dynasty of the Severi (3rd century). The stores were arranged around a large porticoed courtyard paved with marble. At the far end, opposite the entrance, was a *sacellum* (shrine) dedicated to the market's tutelary deities and the emperors. The hall stood in the harbor district, the famous Ripa Puteolana, which extended as far as Portus Julius and consisted of a series of harbors, surrounded by stores, that alternated with blocks of housing, temples and *thermae*.

ROMAN NECROPOLIS. Via Puteoli-Capuam (or Via Campana) was the main highway in the region's road network. It linked the flourishing trading counter of the Phlegraean Fields with Capua, described by Titus Livius (at the time that Hannibal was sampling its delights) as "the largest and richest city in Italy" and baptized the "second Rome" by Cicero. It is hardly surprising that the aristocracy and merchants of Puteoli built their necropolis on either side of this road. Although the route has been much frequented since the Middle Ages, the monuments bordering Via Celle (*celle* are funeral chambers) and Via di San Vito were not destroyed. They were, of course, stripped of their statues and other valuable decorative elements, and have been variously used as barns, places of refuge, stables and wine cellars. However, in spite of all this, their structures still attest to the widely varied repertoire of funerary architecture. An impressive Roman necropolis is being excavated on Via Neapolis-Cumae, between the Solfatara and the great amphitheater.

LAGO DI AVERNO

During the Roman civil wars, at a point when a military leader from the army of Sextus Pompeius threatened to take control of the sea, the Triumvirate realized that it was vital to have the support of an efficient naval base to defend the Italian coast and the port of Pozzuoli. In 37 BC Agrippa and Octavius (the future Augustus) chose Lake Avernus, until then a place of pilgrimage dedicated to the gods of the Underworld, and the coastal Lucrine lake which, at the time, was studded with oyster beds and fish ponds. The Lucrine lake was larger than it is today, since it was partly filled in during the terrible earthquake of 1538, which also threw up the crater of Monte Nuovo. The coastal dunes separating the Lucrine lake from the sea were opened up to create an outer port, while a canal built between the two lakes transformed Lake Avernus into an inland harbor where the arsenals and possibly the high command of the fleet were installed. A tunnel dug beneath the ridge of Monte Grillo (under the direction of the architect Lucius Cocceius) led from the harbor of Lake Avernus to the center of Cumae, while a second gallery, beneath Monte di Cumae, opened onto the port. This impressive system, centered around the towns of Pozzuoli and Cumae, made a naval blockade impossible. The port structure was engulfed by Monte Nuovo, which subsided as a result of the bradyseism ● 23, and can only be seen from the air. The Lucrine-Avernus system, known as Portus Julius, was only used for a short time, most probably because of the silting caused by the onset of bradyseism. When the fleet was transferred to Misenum, the lakes became the elegant suburbs of Baia and were covered with villas and *thermae*.

BAIA

From the 2nd century BC to the end of the Roman Empire, Baiae, named after Baios, the navigator of Odysseus, who died near these shores, was the most fashionable resort on the Bay of Naples. The most prominent members of the Roman aristocracy had luxurious villas built here and the expression *more baiano* ("in the style of Baiae") was used to describe terraced structures, built on several slopes or, as a result of the progress made in the technique of cementing in water, even on the water's edge,

THE "CENTO CAMERELLE" (below)
The Cento Camerelle formed several
reservoirs belonging to a Roman villa.

**PLASTER
COPIES**
On the second floor
of the archeological
museum, fragments
of plaster statues
from the Roman
period are on display,
copied from original
classical Greek
bronzes. They were
used as models
between the 1st
century BC and the
2nd century AD by
the sculptors of a
studio in ancient
Baiae.

Statue of
Ulysses found
in the early
1980's off the
coast of
Baia.

to enable them to take full advantage of this extraordinary
landscape. But, above all, Baia was renowned for the
thermae (considered by Roman physicians to be an
ideal remedy for all kinds of ailments) that
abounded in this volcanic region. Huge
thermal establishments (dedicated to
Mercury ★, Sossandra, Venus and
Diana) sprang up around the sources.
Today only their huge domes attest to the
vastness of these structures. The opinion
expressed in the ancient medical texts was
pursued during the Middle Ages when the
therapeutic properties of the *thermae* of Baia were
rediscovered. In the 13th century Frederick II had several
establishments re-opened, as did the Spanish viceroys in the
17th century.

CASTELLO DI BAIA. Inside the walls of the impressive
Aragonese castle is the recently founded archeological
museum of the Phlegraean Fields, which will house the
pieces found on the sites of Baia and Misenum. On the first
floor of the northwest tower is a permanent exhibition of
pieces from the *sacellum* (shrine) of the Augustali in
Misenum, which was an important monument dedicated to
the cult of Augustus and built during the
Emperor's reign in the forum of ancient
Misenum. The shrine was restored in the mid-
2nd century, during the reign of Marcus
Aurelius, with the help of a donation made by
one of the *curatores Augustali*. The façade was
given cipolin columns, beautiful capitals and a
lintel bearing the dedication. The marble
pediment, with busts of the donors
surrounded by a crown of oak leaves
supported by two figures of Victory,
is of great iconographic and
artistic interest.

BACOLI AND MISENUM

BACOLI. Bacoli (the
ancient Roman town
of Bauli) is today a
fishing village and
holiday resort. The
old part of the
town stands on a
promontory,
while the modern
development
extends along the
shores of the Lago di
Miseno (the Mare
Morto), with the result that
Bacoli and Misenum, once
two clearly distinct towns,
now form a single urban
and regional unit. The
TOMB OF AGRIPPINA,
which stands on the

"MISENUS, FROM HIS HIGH OBSERVATORY, SOUNDS THE SIGNAL ON HIS BRAZEN TRUMPET."

VIRGIL

The austere Aragonese castle, overlooking the port of Baia.

STATUES OF THE "SACELLUM" OF THE AUGUSTALI
The shrine was decorated with sculptures donated by the *curatores Augustali*. Under the Flavians two statues of the emperors Titus and Vespasian, represented as naked Greek heroes, were placed in the temple. The bronze equestrian statue erected outside the shrine in honor of their successor, Domitian, is the only statue of a rearing horse to have survived from antiquity. When the emperor was executed, and his memory dishonored, his face was removed from the statue and replaced by that of the new *princeps*, Nerva.

shore at the entrance to the village, is in fact a small theater which was once part of a Roman villa (now destroyed). Nearby is the reservoir known (because of its many galleries) as the Cento Camerelle. The PISCINA MIRABILE ★ was another vast reservoir at the end of the Serino aqueduct, built to supply the Roman fleet stationed at Misenum. The vast structure, mainly hewn out of the tufa, produces some remarkable acoustic effects. It is divided into five naves supported by forty-eight pillars.

MISENUM. During the reign of Augustus, when an alternative had to be found for Portus Julius, Misenum was the obvious choice. The site was named after Misenus, another of Ulysses' companions, or (according to Virgil) the trumpeter of Aeneas. To create the new port, which, like its predecessor, consisted of two basins, the spit of land separating the two basins had to be opened up. The depth of the outer basin, a volcanic crater, was such that there was no risk of it silting up. The quays and arsenals were built on the shores of the Mare Morto and a small colony was founded on the headland to the south of the outer harbor with a view to servicing the naval base. It was also the site of the residence of the admirals of the fleet, of whom the most famous, the naturalist Pliny the Elder, died during the eruption of Vesuvius in AD *79* ▲ *243* as he was trying to help the town of Stabiae. The *classis praetoria Misenatis* was the largest fleet of the Roman Empire. Although little remains of the port and town of Misenum, the only official excavations to be carried out on the site discovered the *sacellum* of the Augustali ▲ *206*. It is extremely difficult to visit the ruins of the theater, which are situated on private property.

The Capo Miseno (548 feet) commands a magnificent view.

CAPO MISENO. At the foot of the Capo Miseno is the GROTTA DRAGONARA, another large Roman reservoir, excavated in the tufa and supported by twelve pillars. It was probably used to supply the fleet or the villa of Lucullus which, according to an ancient text, was situated on the headland overlooking "the Sicilian Sea, on the one hand, and the Tyrrhenian Sea on the other".

LAGO DI FUSARO
This non-volcanic lake is linked to the sea via three canals: the Foce Vecchia (or di Torregaveta), which runs beneath a tunnel pierced during the Roman period and completed in 1645; the north canal, opened by Ferdinand II (1856); and the central canal (1939). In 1794 Ferdinand IV opened the lake to oyster-culture and had a hunting lodge, the CASINA DEL FUSARO ★, built by Carlo Vanvitelli on one of the islands.

ARCO FELICE
(Via Provinciale, Cumae)
This brick archway (late 1st century AD) once formed the entrance to the town.

CUMAE

HISTORY. Little is known about the oldest Greek colony in the Western world, founded in c. 750 BC by Greeks from Euboea who had settled on the island of Ischia ▲ 210. It is primarily known for its beautiful vases, discovered in vast numbers in its necropolises during the 18th and particularly the 19th century, and today dispersed in museums throughout Europe. The excavations carried out in recent decades have been centered around the acropolis where a large section of the massive enclosure wall, restored during the war between the Byzantines and Goths (6th century), has been unearthed.

ACROPOLIS. Two huge temples from the Greek period of Cumae's history were transformed into basilicas in the 5th and 6th centuries, when a small village was founded among the ruins of the classical city (destroyed by the Saracens in 915). The first, on the lower esplanade of the acropolis, was dedicated to Apollo. It is reminiscent of the "vast temples" described by Virgil in Book VI of the *Aeneid* and dedicated to Apollo, the god of light, by Daedalus on his escape from the labyrinth of the Minotaur. The podium bears the traces of the Roman renovation carried out during the reign of Augustus, when the Ionic pediment was moved to the longest side of the temple so that it overlooked the forum. The remains of the octagonal baptistry of the early Christian basilica are also visible. The second, dedicated to Jupiter, stands on the upper terrace of the acropolis. The oldest remains are Greek (5th century BC) and Samnite, but these are scarcely recognizable; the Roman and early Christian periods, however, are better represented. The most famous monument, which is also most evocative of the city's ancient history, is the Cave of the Cumaean Sibyl ▲ 209, at the foot of the acropolis.

THE LOWER CITY. Recent excavations have confirmed that the area at the foot of the acropolis was inhabited very early on in history. The area, surrounded by an enclosure wall that extended to the ridge of Monte Grillo, was only partly explored between 1938 and 1953, so that the excavations of the Samnite and Roman forum, which almost certainly overlies the remains of the Greek *agora*, remained incomplete. The most impressive monument is the Temple of

Jupiter, which dates from the Hellenistic period (3rd century BC) and was probably built on the site of an earlier temple. Transformed into a Roman capitol, it was restored several times before being finally converted, during the imperial period, into a prostyle building with six Corinthian columns and a triple-naved *cella* containing three colossal marble statues (now in the Museo Archeologico Nazionale in Naples ▲ *166*). All that remains of the portico of the forum is its basic outline, on the south side of the square, and fragments of a beautiful Hellenistic tufa lintel, decorated with a frieze of weaponry motifs. Beyond the portico lies a sanctuary, which probably dates from the imperial period and whose layout is reminiscent of edifices in Pompeii ▲ *246* and Herculaneum ▲ *272*: a courtyard surrounded by columns on three sides and a high podium at the far end of the sanctuary. The forum also included the Temple of the Forum (dating from the Roman Republic and restored during the classical period), on the northwest side of the forum, and the Temple of the Giants, to the east, which dates from the imperial period and is now partially covered by farm buildings. The latter was named after a bust of Jupiter which became known as the "giant of the palace" after it was placed near the Palazzo Reale in Naples ▲ *131*. A third, much older complex (known as the Cave of the Cumaean Sibyl) stood further east, on the paved road leading to Monte Grillo. This road was recently discovered behind the existing road, at the intersection with the street leading to the Acropolis. Outside the ancient city, near the Villa Virgiliana, stands an amphitheater (2nd century BC), one of the oldest in Campania and the Roman world. Although the edifice (restored during the imperial period) is in the process of being excavated, the outline of the areas not yet cleared are already visible. Several inscriptions painted on the walls of Pompeii refer to the games held in this amphitheater, and graffiti found in Pozzuoli refer to a woman crucified here. A temple of Isis has recently been discovered in the harbor area, with its podium, and purification fountain, surrounded by a small portico paved with precious marble. It was destroyed at the end of the classical period by the Christians who decapitated the statues of the gods and the sacred symbols of the Ptolemaic religion (Isis, a priest with a model temple and a sphinx) and threw them into the fountain.

CAVE OF THE CUMAEAN SIBYL ★
It was in the vast, triple-niched, vaulted chamber (*oikos*), at the end of the long rock-cut corridor (*dromos*), that the Cumaean Sibyl, the priestess of Apollo, is said to have delivered her oracles during the classical period. According to Virgil she predicted the fate of Aeneas during one of her prophetic trances. However, it is by no means certain that there was ever an Apollonian oracle at Cumae, although an inscription on a bronze plaque refers to an oracle associated with Hera. It is more likely that the cave was used for military purposes.

▲ ISCHIA

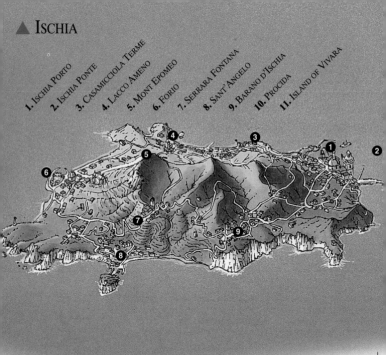

1. ISCHIA PORTO
2. ISCHIA PONTE
3. CASAMICCIOLA TERME
4. LACCO AMENO
5. MONT EPOMEO
6. FORIO
7. SERRARA FONTANA
8. SANT'ANGELO
9. BARANO D'ISCHIA
10. PROCIDA
11. ISLAND OF VIVARA

I schia lies at the western end of the Bay of Naples, opposite the Phlegraean Fields. With the neighboring island of Procida and the tiny island of Vivara, it forms the Phlegraean archipelago and is part of the same volcanic system. Its rugged, 21-mile coastline is laced with bays, sheer cliffs and coves that can only be reached from the sea. Although the volcano is now extinct, the island's many mineral springs, whose therapeutic properties have been renowned since ancient times, are a permanent reminder of its origins.

HISTORY

TOURIST PARADISE
Today Ischia is a tourist paradise, renowned for its healthy climate, thermal springs and, of course, the beauty of the sea, which is in perfect, albeit delicate, harmony with the fertile landscape.

PITHECUSA. Greeks from Euboea colonized Ischia, which they called Pithecusa (from *pithekòs*, "Island of Monkeys"), during the first half of the 8th century BC, before they settled on the mainland at Cumae ▲ *208*. They colonized the northern part of the island, near Lacco Ameno, as is evident from the thousands of objects found in the necropolis of San Montano and the ceramic debris on the acropolis of Monte Vico. The island subsequently came under Neapolitan and then Roman control, until Augustus exchanged it for Capri ▲ *226*.

THE AGE OF INVASION. After the fall of the Roman Empire, Ischia was controlled by the Byzantines, the Normans, the Swabians and the Angevins. After the last eruption, in 1302, the inhabitants sought refuge in Baia ▲ *205* and did not return until four years later when they gathered on the rock of the Castello, a location imposed by the continual invasions suffered by the island since the fall of the Empire. In 1438, under the island's new master, Alfonso of Aragon, the Castello became the town of Ischia and the island was completely protected by a system of towers, near which rural communities were established. On the coast opposite the rock, and linked to it by a bridge, the fishing village of Ischia Ponte flourished and became the starting point for the island's urban development. In the 16th century it was continually attacked by pirates, but as these attacks decreased (notably as a result of strengthening the fortifications), the inhabitants of the Castello began to settle in the coastal village that became the center of Ischia.

ISCHIA

ISCHIA PORTO. The port is a tiny jewel set in a volcanic crater, created in the 4th century BC. In 1854 Ferdinand II had a canal cut through the rock to link it to the sea. The town opens out onto the Piazza del Redentore, dominated by the neoclassical church of SANTA MARIA DI PORTOSALVO, built to protect the new port. There are also two interesting thermal establishments: the ANTICHE TERME COMUNALI, built in 1854 above the springs of the Fornello and the Fontana, and the Terme Militari, also built by the Bourbons and frequented by Ferdinand II.

ISCHIA PONTE. This old fishing village is named after the bridge (Ponte Aragonese) built by Alfonso of Aragon to link it to the Castello d'Ischia on its offshore rock. The 14th-century CHURCH OF THE ASSUNTA (modified during the Baroque period) is now the island's cathedral. In the Castello are the remains of the former CATHEDRAL OF THE ASSUNTA (built in 1301, modified in the 18th century and partially

"In the female sex, the passion for finery is almost superior to all others, and notwithstanding any effect the genial warmth of the climate may have on the constitution of a Neapolitan woman, I doubt whether she would not nine times out of ten prefer a present to a lover."
Henry Swinburne,
Travels in the Two Sicilies in 1777–1780

MONTE EPOMEO
Monte Epomeo, which consists of green volcanic rock (tufa), dominates the Bay of Naples from a height of 2,585 feet. Its vine-covered slopes produce the wine of the same name. Just below the summit are the hermitage and church of San Nicola (1459).

Via Roma, the main street, is bordered by serried ranks of houses, cafés and restaurants. Its continuation, the equally touristic Corso Vittoria Colonna, links Ischia Porto and Ischia Ponte.

destroyed by the English in 1809), of the FORMER CONVENT OF THE CLARISSES and of SAN PIETRO A PANTANIELLO (1547). The BELVEDERE OF CARTAROMANA offers a magnificent view of the garden of the Nymphs, the Guevara tower and the beach of Cartaromana. On the summit of the Castello stands the impressive bulk of the ARAGONESE FORTRESS.

TOUR OF THE ISLAND

CASAMICCIOLA TERME. The resort of Casamicciola Terme, renowned for its mineral springs and climate, lies in a setting of lush hillsides scored by deep valleys. The Castiglione, one of the island's best-known springs, nestles among the vegetation of a natural depression that slopes gently toward the sea.

LACCO AMENO. This elegant resort is on a par with that of Casamicciola Terme. It was here, on the summit of Monte Vico, that the first Greek colonists settled. Remains from this period can be seen in the MUSEO ARCHEOLOGICO, housed in the beautiful 18th-century Villa Arbusto. The most famous pieces include the so-called CUP OF NESTOR, a terracotta kotyle decorated with geometric motifs, found in the tomb of a child (late 8th century BC). Its three-line epigram, the earliest example of a written Greek poetic text, was composed at the same time as the poems of Homer. The museum has a vast range of ancient Greek ceramics from the tombs of the necropolis of San Montano, as well as decorative objects of Oriental origin. The mushroom-shaped volcanic rock (the FUNGO) overlooking the natural harbor of Lacco Ameno has become its emblem. About one mile to the west, the beautiful BAY OF SAN MONTANO lies below Monte Vico, ensconced between two rocky walls.

FORIO. Forio is a wine-producing town and elegant resort on the island's west coast. Its old, historic center is surrounded by ramparts reinforced by towers. One of its principal monuments, the church of Santa Maria del Soccorso, once belonged to the Augustinian convent

> **"THE GIRLS IN THE NORTHERN VILLAGES OF ISCHIA ... ARE MOSTLY PLAIN, BUT HERE IN THE NITROLI REGION YOU MAY SEE MANY OF RARE BEAUTY – NYMPH-LIKE CREATURES ... WITH FLASHING MAENAD EYES."**
> NORMAN DOUGLAS (1931)

(14th century). Its white outline, in the center of a broad viewing platform, makes it one of the most beautiful and romantic churches on the island. The narrow road leading to Monte Epomeo is bordered by vines and rock-cut troglodyte dwellings. Also worth a visit are the fumaroles of Cuotto and the so-called gardens of Neptune, a spectacular thermal complex in the bay of Citara. The town is also Ischia's leading wine-producing center.

SERRARA FONTANA. These two hillside hamlets now form a single community which also includes Monte Epomeo and the village of Sant'Angelo. Fontana (1,483 feet) is the departure point for the ascent of Monte Epomeo. The CHURCH OF SANTA MARIA DELLA SACCA (1374) is a reminder of Fontana's medieval origins.

BARANO D'ISCHIA. Barano d'Ischia, perched on an inland promontory, is the island's most picturesque village, both in terms of setting and traditions. One of its natural springs, the Nitrodi (renowned since antiquity for its therapeutic and cosmetic properties), can be reached from the beach of the Maronti, only 1½ miles from Barano.

CASTELLO D'ISCHIA
In 474 BC the rocky islet was apparently inhabited by the soldiers of the tyrant Hiero of Syracuse, who had defeated the Etruscans at Cumae. Hence it was known for a long time as the Castel Girone (Hiero). In 1036 the fortress that protected the islet was occupied by Marino Melluso, Count of Ischia. In 1438 Alfonso of Aragon had a massive complex built on the foundations of the fortress. It was linked to Ischia by a bridge that was a continuation of the access road to the islet and was partly cut out of the rock. Crossing the bridge from Ischia, you come to the walls of the fortress and enter a broad gallery that houses the tiny chapel dedicated to San Giovanni Giuseppe della Croce.

SANT'ANGELO
This delightful fishing village, with its multicolored houses perched above the vivid blue sea, is extremely popular with holiday-makers. The main reason for this is probably the beautiful beach of the Maronti (about 1½ miles long) with its elegant thermal establishments.

Procida is an island in miniature, its coastline laced with bays formed by volcanic craters.

"After slowly climbing four or five hundred steps, we found ourselves in a small, terraced courtyard surrounded by a gray stone parapet. At the far end of the courtyard were two dark archways which seemed to lead to a cellar. Above these massive arches, two depressed, rounded arcades supported a roof terrace, bordered by pots of rosemary and basil.

The tiny island of Procida lies at the entrance to the Gulf of Naples, between Ischia and the mainland. The island is formed by a high plateau whose sheer, striated cliffs plunge into the sea. Perched on the Monte San Michele, the rocky promontory in the north of the island, is the medieval town of Terra Murata. To the east and west are the natural harbors of Sancio Cattolico, which shelters the port ★, and Corricella with its flourishing fishing village.

Beneath the arcades, we could see a rustic gallery where shining clusters of corn hung like golden chandeliers shot with moonlight."
Lamartine,
Graziella

HISTORY

Very little is known about the early settlement of Procida. Recent excavations on the tiny island of Vivara have revealed the remains of Mycenaean settlements dating from the late Bronze Age. The island was later inhabited by the Romans, before becoming a place of refuge for the coastal populations fleeing from the barbarian invasions that precipitated the collapse of the Roman Empire. In the 7th century the Benedictines founded the abbey of Terra Murata, which became an urban center during the Angevin and Aragonese dynasties. Between the end of the 16th and the beginning of the 17th century, an increase in the island's prosperity and population led to the urbanization of Sancio Cattolico and Corricella, and the construction of the palace of Avalos. During the 17th and 18th centuries Procida's navy fulfilled a role of national importance and the island became a favorite royal resort. The hunting lodges of the court enhanced its reputation and the privileges granted by the king

Women from Procida.

increased its wealth. It entered a period of decline in the 19th century which lasted until World War One. Today Procida, whose hotel infrastructure is less developed than that of Ischia and Capri, is trying to establish its identity and encourage tourism.

TOUR OF THE ISLAND

The coastline of Procida is studded with tracks leading down to small beaches and reefs, while inland walks offer beautiful landscapes and magnificent views, and the island's main road is bordered by aristocratic residences (18th and 19th century) with terraced gardens leading down to the sea. Of particular historical and architectural interest is the ABBEY CHURCH OF SAN MICHELE, which stands in Terra Murata on the island's highest point (328 feet). The amphitheater of tiered, waterfront housing in the harbor town of Corricella is a fine example of this popular but picturesque architectural tradition that is found throughout the entire island, especially in the old districts of the HARBOR OF SANCIO CATTOLICO, the interior courtyard of the Casale Vascello and the fishing village of Chiaiolella.

VIVARA. The tiny island of Vivara is linked to Procida by a bridge. Since 1974, it has been a nature reserve and has a center for the study of migratory birds. It has a rich variety of Mediterranean flora.

Harbor of
Sancio Cattolico.

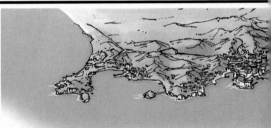

MIGLIO D'ORO
The beauty of the landscape and magnificence of the Baroque villas (known as Vesuvian villas) on the stretch of coast from San Giovanni a Teduccio to Torre del Greco have earned it the name of the Miglio d'Oro (golden mile). Today poverty and deprivation alternate with reminders of past glory. One of the first residents was Charles of Bourbon who had a palace built at Portici in 1738. Within the space of a few years other sumptuous residences, set in luxurious parks with direct access to the sea, sprang up between the towns of San Giovanni a Teduccio, Barra, San Giorgio a Cremano, Portici, Ercolano and Torre del Greco, which all lay on the royal route of Calabria. Architects included Vaccaro, Nauclerio, Sanfelice and Fuga, the tenors of Neapolitan Baroque architecture.

The towns on this itinerary, which ventures onto the lower slopes of Vesuvius, were in a sense founded twice. Buried during the eruption of AD 79, ▲ *243*, they have re-emerged over the centuries, either as industrial towns or holiday resorts. The history of the peninsula of Sorrento, at the far end of the Bay of Naples, was quite different since it was less seriously affected by the volcanic activity. During Roman times the coast between Naples and the peninsula of Sorrento was dotted with vacation (*otium*) villas whose skillfully designed layout enabled each room to enjoy the surrounding landscape to the full. In the 18th century the Neapolitan aristocracy fell in love with the setting and built luxurious villas surrounded by equally exotic gardens. It should be said that, in addition to its natural beauty, the region between Vesuvius and the sea had the added attraction of the discovery of Herculaneum ▲ *272* by Prince d'Elbeuf.

PORTICI

Leave Naples via Via delle Calabria, the former route of the Bourbons (today the Statale 18) which linked the Parthenopean capital with the rest of the kingdom. The medieval town of Portici experienced its golden age in the 18th century, following the construction of the Bourbon palace, when the Neapolitan nobility chose it as their favorite resort. In 1773 a port was built and, in 1839, a railroad line linking it with Naples (below).
VILLA BUONO. Prince Della Riccia, Bartolomeo of Capua, built this villa on a truly grand scale. The outbuildings were arranged in a semicircle, across the road from the palace, and a church was built in the center. Although the palace and gardens were destroyed, the exedra has survived, in spite of

being partly
demolished when
Via Diaz was built.

CHURCH OF SAN CIRO. The street, bordered
with 18th-century buildings, leads to the Piazza San Ciro.
Overlooking the piazza, the church of the same name (rebuilt
in 1642) houses a Birth of the Virgin and a Portrait of San
Felipe Neri by Luca Giordiano. (Follow the Corso Umberto I
down to the Granatelli and the Piazza San Pasquale.)
VILLA D'ELBEUF. This magnificent villa, designed by
Ferdinando Sanfelice for Prince d'Elbeuf, Emmanuel
Maurice de Lorraine, cavalry general of the kingdom of
Naples, was one of the first to be built on the coast, in 1711.
It incorporated some magnificent archeological pieces from
the excavations of Herculaneum ▲ 272. In 1741, Charles of
Bourbon bought it as a dependency, with access to the sea,
for his palace at Portici. The Bagno della Regina ("queen's
baths"), a small neoclassical building, was added later by
Ferdinand II. In spite of its great historical and artistic
interest, it was not spared by the railroad which passes
close to the rear façade. (Leave the Piazza San Ciro along
Via Università.)

**SPLENDOR AND
POVERTY OF THE
MIGLIO D'ORO**
During the reign of
Joachim Murat
(1808–16), the Miglio
d'Oro (golden mile)
was extended as a
result of the Prince's
frequent visits. It
began to decline in
1839, when the
opening of the
Portici-Naples rail
link (Italy's first
railroad) destroyed
the continuity of the
landscape and cut the
villas off from the sea.
(There is a National
Railway Museum at
Pietrarsa.) The main
reason for this
decline, however, was
industrialization,
which increased the
town's population,
drove out the
aristocracy and
destroyed the
environment.

VILLA CAMPOLIETO
Outside the villa, a huge curved portico, surmounted by a terrace-walkway, is linked to the upper story by a double staircase.

PALAZZO REALE. In 1738 Charles of Bourbon employed the architects Antonio Medrano and Antonio Canevari to build a palace in the center of a park stretching from the slopes of Vesuvius to the sea. They constructed it in two separate sections, the lower facing the sea and the upper looking toward Vesuvius, with the royal route of Calabria passing through the dividing courtyard. The building became a veritable museum of antiquities, since the pieces excavated on the sites of Herculaneum, Pompeii and Stabiae were brought together and exhibited in the palace. Since 1873 it has housed the Faculty of Agronomics of the University of Naples.

VILLA MALTESE. The villa was built in 1730 according to plans by the architect Antonio Domenico Vaccaro. The restoration work carried out at the end of the 19th century respected the original layout and structure of the buildings. The park, formerly one of the most popular rendezvous of the Bourbon court, is still decorated with terracotta fountains and statues.

ERCOLANO

Until the end of the 19th century, Ercolano, built partly on the site of ancient Herculaneum, was a resort for the Neapolitan aristocracy, as can be seen from the nobiliary residences on the Corso Resina.

VILLA DI BISOGNO CASALUCE (no. 189). In spite of its poor state of repair, the elegant stuccowork panels that once decorated the façade are still visible. Beyond the villa, the urban fabric is less dense (although land speculation has left its mark) and the Miglio d'Oro proper begins.

VILLA APRILE (no. 296). The villa, built during the second half of the 18th century for Gerolamo Riario Sforza, the Count of Imola and Forli, was extensively modified during the 19th century. In particular, characteristic elements from the Romantic period were incorporated into the garden.

LA FAVORITA
(below)
The villa's architectural design, by Ferdinando Fuga, distinguishes it from other Vesuvian Baroque buildings.

Broad straight pathways sloping gently down to the sea offered a view of the villa and park, with Vesuvius rising above the vegetation, on the one hand, and the beach (reached via a series of terraces and exedras) on the other.

VILLA CAMPOLIETO ★ (no. 283). The villa was constructed in 1755 for Luzio di Sangro, Duke of Casacalenda, according to plans by Luigi Vanvitelli, and is centered around a vast, covered atrium. A monumental staircase links the first floor to the upper story, in which Vanvitelli incorporated a magnificent room surmounted by a central dome. Today cultural exhibitions are held in the recently restored villa.

The main façade of the Villa Campolieto, like most of the Vesuvian villas, overlooks its park and the sea.

VILLA FAVORITA (no. 291). The Villa Favorita (below) is set in a vast park studded with kiosks, and with the Villa Campolieto is one of the two most prestigious monuments on the Miglio d'Oro. Toward the end of the 18th century, the villa was the residence of Ferdinand IV, who received it from the Prince of Jaci. His son Leopold had the woods landscaped and stables built in 1829. It was restored in 1854 by the architect Enrico Alvino and bought in 1879 by Ismail Pasha, who sold it in 1893.

TORRE DEL GRECO

The name of the town is taken from the Turris Octava, the defensive tower erected by Frederick II of Swabia against the Saracens. Torre del Greco, a fief of the Carafa family, bought its freedom in 1699. The event is commemorated, during the second week after Trinity, at the Festa dei Quattro Altari when four altars are erected at the four points of the compass in the town. Torre del Greco has suffered a number of volcanic eruptions, the most devastating in 1631 and 1794 ▲ 239. The town is famous for its coral, mother-of-pearl and ivory craftwork that has been practiced here for hundreds of years.

THE CORAL OF TORRE DEL GRECO
This rare and beautiful coral has

VILLA PROTA. (Via Nazionale no. 1109) The villa is preceded by a magnificent portal, whose two balconies and gateway form the frame for a delightful view of the façade at the end of the driveway. The villa's vaulted staircase is another

important feature in the overall scenography. On the front façade (left), the pendant arch linking the two third-floor wings forms a belvedere looking toward the slopes of Vesuvius.

TORRE ANNUNZIATA (OPLONTIS)

been used in jewelry-making since the beginning of history. It was probably used for talismans because its red color evoked the blood of life. For centuries Torre del Greco was one of the major centers for fishing, working and selling Mediterranean coral. In recent decades the discovery of other types of coral has revitalized a declining market. There is a coral museum in the Istituto d'Arte which has taught coral-carving since 1878.

Torre Annunziata, famous in Roman times as a thermal resort, went into a period of decline before recovering in the 14th century. Since 1964 a series of archeological digs have partially excavated two grandiose villas, conventionally known as Villas A and B.

VILLA OF POPPAEA ★. The villa is believed to be that of Poppaea, the second wife of Nero. A number of reception and service rooms constitute part of the rear section of the villa, which overlooked a rectangular pool and a vast garden. The pictorial decorations of the rooms are among the most remarkable in the region of Vesuvius. They were executed by local craftsmen who, with unrivalled elegance and sensitivity to color, drew upon the entire repertoire of the art of Roman wall paintings in vogue between the middle of the 1st century BC and the 1st century AD. They represent imaginary architecture embellished with masks, peacocks, baskets of fruit and glass vases. A series of rooms on either side of a vast passageway between the garden and pool offer a skillful combination of architecture and painting. Frescos, representing imaginary gardens painted on a yellow background, frame the windows on the far walls and create a magnificent trompe-l'oeil effect. The villa, which was being restored when it was buried in the eruption of AD 79 ▲ *243*, was also partially inhabited. Domestic furnishings were discovered along with several marble sculptures, including the group of Pan and Hermaphrodite, centaurs and a magnificent neo-Attic krater depicting naked warriors performing an armed dance.

VILLA OF L. CRASSIUS TERTIUS. The villa was named following the discovery of a bronze seal bearing the name of L. Crassius Tertius. The huge rustic building (2nd century BC), probably used for selling wine, is centered around a monumental peristyle with a double order of Doric columns made of tufa. Many amphorae were found in the rooms opening off the peristyle.

CASTELLAMARE DI STABIA (STABIAE)

Castellamare di Stabia is nestled in the Bay of Naples along the coast between Vesuvius and the Monti Lattari. Today it is a famous thermal resort.

HISTORY. Ancient Stabiae was buried at the same time as Herculaneum and Pompeii ▲ *243*, but re-emerged and prospered from the end of antiquity. The Castrum ad Mare de Stabiis (which gave the town its name) was built in the 9th century to defend a source. Charles I of Anjou surrounded it with a defensive enclosure wall, which did not prevent it being sacked in subsequent centuries. Charles of Bourbon founded a glassworks and opened up the surrounding countryside in his bid to excavate the ancient city.

THE RUINS OF STABIAE (Via Archeologica). During the Bourbon dynasty (1749–82), six luxurious vacation (*otium*) villas were discovered on the hill of Varano, as well as ten agricultural villas built on farmland. These were all buried again in 1782, and it was not until the end of World War Two that four of the six villas built on the bay, bearing the conventional names of San Marco, Arianna, Pastore and Il Complesso, were partially re-excavated. Thirty-five other villas were excavated in the surrounding area. This large number of villas confirms the reports in ancient texts of the importance of ancient

SHIPYARDS OF CASTELLAMARE DI STABIA
The shipyards founded by Ferdinand IV are still operational today and have something of the town's modernity.

MONTE FAITO

Botanists will enjoy the excursion from Castellamare di Stabia to Monte Faito (3,710 feet). The road leading from the Villa Quisisana, the Casina Reale of the Bourbons, to the top of the mountain passes through woods of holm-oaks and durmast-oaks, and then vast chestnut groves, before reaching the fine beech groves of the summit. The northern exposure of these slopes means that the shady side of the mountain is covered in a luxuriant forest vegetation that is absent from the (south-facing) slopes opposite. On the way down to Vico Equense, the landscape changes abruptly: vast expanses of whitish rocks seem to be tumbling down to the sea. The sparse vegetation that has taken root among the stones (rosemary, broom, thyme and helichrysum) exudes pungent Mediterranean scents.

TASSO

Sorrento was the birthplace of Torquato Tasso (1544–95), author of the famous *Gerusalemme liberata*. A statue erected to Tasso (1870) by Gennaro Calì, stands on the piazza that today bears his name.

Stabiae, renowned for the fertility of its soil, the mildness of its climate and the abundance of its drinking water. It has been possible to reconstruct the living accommodation as it was after the town was destroyed by Sulla, in 89 BC, to punish the inhabitants for their part in the rebellion of the Italian peoples against Roman domination. Stabiae re-emerged as an agglomeration of villas and a large number of *rusticae* (farms).

VICO EQUENSE TO SORRENTO

From Castellamare di Stabia, the Statale 18 follows the coast of the Sorrentine peninsula to the thermal and coastal resorts of TERME DELLO SCRAIO and, immediately afterward, VICO EQUENSE. The former Etruscan city of Aequa occupies a bank of tufa overlooking the sea and is today an extremely popular holiday resort. Its *antiquarium* contains the remains of a necropolis (7th–4th century BC) and an interesting museum of mineralogy. The scenic coast road continues to Meta (above), another holiday resort perched on a clifftop overlooking the sea, and then climbs to PIANO DI SORRENTO and SANT'AGNELLO. Unlike the sheer, vertiginous coastline of Amalfi ▲ *284*, the Sorrentine riviera is characterized by broad, intensively cultivated plains. The citrus plantations that once dominated the landscape are now much less common.

Perched on top of a sheer bank of tufa rising steeply from the sea, Sorrento looks out over a coastline laced with natural coves. The town's reputation as a tourist resort, which attracted many 19th-century Romantic artists, is earned by its wealth of monuments, pleasant climate and magnificent vegetation. In early spring the citrus plantations are a truly wonderful sight and the scent of the orange and lemon blossom is literally intoxicating. The very specific nature of the region's agriculture molds the landscape: branches laden with fruit are supported by chestnut-wood pergolas, and wooden stakes support the movable matting used to protect the fruit against frost and sun, allowing it to remain on the tree as long as possible. Today these traditional structures, handed down through generations of Sorrentine peasant farmers, are beginning to disappear.

PIAZZA TASSO

The town is built on the original Greco-Roman structure, when it was divided into *insulae* by *cardi* and *decumani* running eastward from the present Piazza Tasso. The piazza, the real heart of Sorrento, is traversed by the long Corso Italia, the town's main thoroughfare, bordered at this point by elegant stores.

CHURCH OF SANTA MARIA DEL CARMINE. The porticoed church was probably founded between 230 and 240 to commemorate the early Christian martyrs. The single-naved edifice has been modified in Baroque style and contains late 18th-century stuccowork.

VIA DELLA PIETÀ. The monuments of Via della Pietà, which leads off the Piazza Tasso, make it one of the town's most interesting medieval streets. They include the 13th-century PALAZZO VENIERO (no. 14), a fine example of the late Byzantine and Islamic period; the 15th-century PALAZZO CORREALE (no. 24), which still has the original portal, and two beautiful gemmate windows, along with a single window, on the second floor; and the Baroque CHURCH OF SANTA MARIA DELLA PIETÀ.

CORSO ITALIA

SEDILE DOMINOVA (Piazza Reginaldo Giuliani). This is Campania's only surviving example of the 15th-century loggias used as meeting places by the nobility. Its 16th-century dome is covered with yellow and green majolica tiles.

THE DUOMO. The lateral portal dates from the 15th century when the edifice was rebuilt. The Duomo houses, in particular, paintings by the Neapolitan school (18th century), a marble archiepiscopal throne

THE SORRENTO LEMON
The lemons for which Sorrento is famous were being grown in Roman times, but their large-scale cultivation was developed by the Arabs. The Sorrento lemon is a specific variety: it is a large, intensely fragrant fruit with particularly thick, white pith. As it is not very acid, it is sliced and eaten with sugar. The finely sliced zest is used to make the delicious liqueur known as *limoncello*.

THE BAY OF NAPLES.—Fountain in Sorrento.

(1573) and, in the choir, some remarkable intarsia stalls by Sorrentine artists. To the left of the Duomo is a campanile supported by four ancient columns.

VIA SERSALE. Behind the Duomo, the narrow Via Sersale passes under a ROMAN ARCH corresponding to the south gate of the ancient city, the Porta Parsano (4th–3rd century BC). The gate was incorporated into the 16th-century enclosure wall built on the site of the Greco-Roman walls.

MUSEO ARCHEOLOGICO DI VILLA FIORENTINO. The recently opened museum houses ceramics and bronzes from the necropolises of the town and peninsula of Sorrento, as well as from the famous temple of Athena on the Punta della Campanella.

TOWARD THE MARINA GRANDE

Via Tasso is well worth a visit, if only to see its two churches. The CHURCH OF SAN FELICE BACOLO (known as the Santissimo Rosario), probably erected during the reign of Constantine (310) on the remains of a pagan temple, was the cathedral of Sorrento from the 12th to the 15th century. A little further on is the CHURCH OF SAN PAOLO, richly decorated with stuccowork and 18th-century paintings. From the bottom of a winding flight of steps, Via Marina Grande leads to the fishing community of the Marina Grande and the site of the old gateway of Sorrento.

MARINA PICCOLA
A narrow, winding street leads down to the Marina Piccola from the Piazza Sant'Antonio. The bay is protected by a long quay where the Naples-Capri ferries dock.

Toward the Marina Piccola

VILLA COMUNALE. The villa opens onto a terrace which overlooks the bay and offers a magnificent view of Naples, the islands and Vesuvius.

CHURCH OF SAN FRANCESCO D'ASSISI. The 16th-century church has a carved door dating from the same period. The adjoining convent (first half of the 13th century) is partially occupied by the Istituto d'Arte. Two of the four wings of the cloister have Moorish interlaced arches, dating from the end of the 14th century, while the other two have semicircular arches supported by octagonal pillars. There are also fragments from ancient temples.

BASILICA OF SANT'ANTONIO. The church dates from the 11th century and incorporates several ancient elements, probably taken from Roman villas. Inside, a magnificent 18th-century creche ● *56* and votive offerings from the survivors of shipwrecks are particularly worthy of note. (Return to the Piazza Tasso and take Via Correale, on the left.)

Museo Correale di Terranova

Behind the white façade of the 18th-century Palazzo Correale is a magnificent garden planted with lemon trees ★ whose belvedere is perched high above the sea. At the beginning of the 20th century, the counts of Terranova Alfredo and Pompeo Correale donated their rich collections to the town.

Around Sorrento

Of the many vacation (*otium*) villas built in the region, the most famous is the Villa di Pollio Felix (whose ruins are known as the BAGNO DELLA REGINA GIOVANNA), which occupies a magnificent site on the Capo di Sorrento. The villa has a large peristyle, supported by a cryptoporticus set in the rock, and a small port formed by a natural inlet.

MUSEO CORREALE
The museum has a beautiful collection of Greek and Roman marbles found in the town and surrounding area. Particularly worthy of note are the Greek classical sculptures covered in inscriptions in Doric dialect; the famous Sorrento Base (1st century BC) decorated with bas-reliefs depicting episodes from the religious policy of Augustus; Attic and Campanian vases and lapidary inscriptions. The museum also has some fine examples of minor 17th- and 18th-century arts (furniture, faience and porcelain, marquetry), as well as a collection of paintings by the Neapolitan school.

▲ Capri

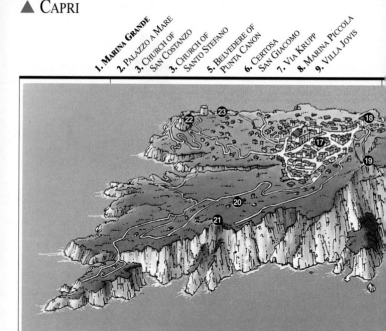

1. Marina Grande 2. Palazzo a Mare 3. Church of San Costanzo 3. Church of Santo Stefano 5. Belvedere of Punta Canon 6. Certosa San Giacomo 7. Via Krupp 8. Marina Piccola 9. Villa Jovis

COLOR AND FRAGRANCE

"All the artistry of color would not [be able to] render this harmony" (Goethe). Capri is indeed an wonderful expression of the triumph of color (the yellow of broom and thistles, the pale blue of campanula, the pink of roses and jasmine) and fragrance (pine-covered slopes, myrtle bushes and lentiscus), which the local spirit of enterprise has tried to capture in its famous perfumes. Capri is also an amazing contrast of indented coastlines washed by an azure sea, deep grottos and scented scrub, where everything colludes with the magical quality of the light.

C apri lies in the blue waters of the Bay of Naples, about 3 miles from the Punta della Campanella and opposite the tip of the Sorrentine peninsula. Since Roman times the island, "which combines, in a granite basket, all the most colorful and fragrant species of Mediterranean flora", has been a "land naturally dedicated to the repose of the mind and the delight of the senses, [an] *Insula Beatorum*, [a] floating Garden of Eden." (Alberto Savinio)

History

SIGNS OF EARLY HABITATION. Little is known of the origins of Capri. There is some evidence of a Paleolithic settlement (stone tools, animal remains) on the island, which was still linked to the Sorrentine peninsula by an isthmus during ancient times. The name "Capri" suggests that there were once wild boars (*kapros* in Greek) on the island, and fragments of pottery indicate the existence of some form of human habitation from the time of the first Greek colonies. **GLORY AND DECLINE.** Returning from his campaigns in the Orient, in 29 BC, Augustus was captivated by Capri and is thought to have exchanged the larger and more fertile island of Ischia for it (along with Naples). The island became a popular resort, reaching the height of its prosperity under Tiberius, who spent the last ten years of his life there. He continued to rule by means of a courier service, fueling fierce rumours about his dissolute lifestyle. The island began to decline after his death, in 37 BC. During the Middle Ages it became, like the rest of Campania, the theater for the battles between the Lombards and Byzantines ● *30*. In 1131 it was captured, along with Amalfi, by the Normans under Roger II. The Angevin and Aragonese monarchies gave the island's development a substantial and decisive boost by concentrating civil and religious buildings around the Piazzetta. It was during this period that the Certosa di San Giacomo (1371–4) was built, thus marking the beginning of Carthusian domination of the island. In the 17th century it suffered a plague epidemic under Spanish rule and then passed under Bourbon control. During the Napoleonic wars, the French and English fought over Capri, which reverted to the Neapolitan Bourbons before being annexed to the Kingdom of Italy.

THE MYTH OF CAPRI. Capri's reputation as a tourist resort was established in the 19th century with the discovery of the Grotta Azzurra (Blue Grotto) ▲ 236. During the Romantic period the island was extremely popular with writers, poets and artists from other countries (especially Germany) in search of all-consuming passions, who saw it as an image of the paradise of lost sensuality. The construction of the funicular railway in the 20th century cemented the island's destiny as an international tourist venue.

"PARADIS ARTIFICIELS"
One of the best examples of the pleasure-seeking society that inhabited Capri at the beginning of the 20th century was

undoubtedly Baron Fersen ▲ 232, a dandy who lived with his private secretary and lover in the villa he had dedicated to their love. In 1923 he committed suicide by adding a strong dose of cocaine to a glass of champagne. At the age of forty-four he could not bear the thought of growing old.

227

"This isle reunites such a variety of beauties and advantages that it is a matter of wonder to me why so few of our mysanthropic countrymen resort to it."
Henry Swinburne (1785)

NARROW STREETS AND STORES
The town of Capri, whose narrow streets wind through a complex, whitewashed labyrinth, has a wide range of interesting stores, restaurants and hotels.

MARINA GRANDE TO LA TORRICELLA

MARINA GRANDE. Travelers arriving at the Marina Grande, with its commercial and tourist ports, can see the rocky bulk of Monte Solaro to the west, and the hill of San Michele, dominated by Monte Tiberio, to the east. On the saddle between the two mountains lies the town of Capri. The center of the Marina Grande, which originally consisted of old fishermen's houses (now converted for commercial and tourist use), is a typical example of the spontaneous architecture which gradually developed along the port.

PALAZZO A MARE. A road leads from Via Cristoforo Colombo, to the west of the Marina Grande, to the Palazzo a Mare (the former palace of Augustus) and the so-called Baths of Tiberius, the maritime section of the villa. A few isolated fragments are all that remains of this Roman archeological site. (Return to Via Cristoforo Colombo.)

CHURCH OF SAN COSTANZO. San Costanzo, the oldest church in the Marina Grande and formerly the island's cathedral, is a fine example of Byzantine architecture (10th–11th century). During its partial reconstruction, in 1330, the entrance was moved to the right-hand side, the ancient portico was walled up and a vast choir added. The church housed the relics of San Costanzo, the patron

> "ANCIENT BREATH OF THE SEA,/SEEMING ONLY TO BREATHE
> FOR THE PRIMORDIAL ROCK,/PURE SPACE SURGING AND
> GUSTING FROM AFAR . . ."
>
> RAINER MARIA RILKE

saint of the island, who "had come from distant, golden Byzantium and arrived at the island in a barrel". (Alberto Savinio)

SCALA FENICIA. This flight of over eight-hundred steps is said to have been hewn out of the rocky hillside of Monte Solaro by the Greeks. Until 1877 it was the only link between the Marina Grande and Anacapri.

LA TORRICELLA. This Moorish-style villa, surrounded by a garden and terraces, was built in the early 20th century, as was the tower after which it is named.

CAPRI

VIA MARINA GRANDE. The road climbs through terraced vegetable gardens, vines and flower-filled gardens and then opens onto some breathtaking landscapes. It continues to the intersection of the Due Golfi, at the center of the saddle, which offers a magnificent view of the coasts of the Marina Grande and Marina Piccola on the opposite side of the island. From here, roads lead to Anacapri, Marina Piccola and Capri.

PIAZZA UMBERTO I. The Piazza Umberto I, also known as the Piazzetta (small square), is the island's social center and a major tourist attraction. It is also the heart of the medieval town, crossed by narrow winding streets which follow the

THE "SALONE" OF CAPRI: PIAZZA UMBERTO I
Capri's Piazzetta is overlooked by the clocktower that stands against the medieval ramparts, while a Gothic-style arch is all that remains of the town's former gateway. The Piazzetta, with its multicolored sunshades, has been the meeting place of Capri's high society since the Romantic period and is still the island's *salone* and showcase. After a tour of the island, what better way to relax than to sit at one of the many café tables and watch the world go by . . .

relief of the site. To the left of the CLOCKTOWER is the FORMER ARCHBISHOP'S PALACE (now the town hall), built in the 17th century when the church opposite was reconstructed.

CHURCH OF SAN STEFANO. The church was designed by Francesco Antonio Picchiatti and built (1683) by Marziale Desiderio, a master builder from Amalfi. It was built above the level of the square on the site of a former cathedral, of which only the clocktower (right, formerly the campanile) remains. The main façade looks onto the Palazzo Cerio, linked to the Piazzetta by a short flight of steps. Inside the church, at the foot of the high altar, is a fragment of polychrome inlaid pavement from the Villa Jovis ▲ *232*.

> **"**[The women of Capri] use their heads more readily than their hands. In fact the heads of these hard-working, patient island women constitute a veritable means of transport. They proudly bear large, heavy and perfectly balanced loads as they walk, single file, along the myriad tracks across the fields, the paths through the villages, the short-cuts hewn out of the rocky hillsides, the ancient "Phoenician" road that climbs from the shore, near the ancient church of San Costanzo, the patron of Capri, to Anacapri.**"**
>
> Alberto Savinio, *Capri*

PALAZZO CERIO. The palace consists of a series of buildings from different periods. The original nucleus, opposite the church, was built in 1371 by Count Andrea Arcucci. It subsequently became the palace of Count Jacopo Arcucci, the castle of Queen Jeanne I of Anjou, and passed through the hands of a number of other owners before becoming the property of Ignazio Cerio. The renowned physician and naturalist carried out a series of excavations on the island at the beginning of the 20th century. Today the palace is the seat of the Cerio Foundation and houses an ARCHEOLOGICAL MUSEUM, library and conference room.

VIA MADRE SERAFINA. This narrow street, which opens out beneath the arcades of the Palazzo Cerio, links the Piazzetta with the CONVENT OF SANTA TERESA. The long, covered section that follows the line of the old ramparts is lit by a series of light-wells.

CHURCH OF SAN SALVATORE. The convent and church were founded in the 17th century by Madre Serafina, who was also responsible for the construction of the church of San Michele ▲ *234* in Anacapri. The church of San Salvatore (one of the architects involved was Dionisio Lazzari) was never completed and the convent, abandoned by the nuns, was sold. Today it is privately owned.

VILLA NARCISUS. Villa Narcisus stands to the left of the church, at nos. 29–31. It was built in the late 19th century, on the site of a 15th-century building, in eclectic Moorish style by the architect and patron of the arts, Charles Cyril Coleman.

BELVEDERE OF PUNTA CANONE. Via Castello climbs to the belvedere which overlooks Via Krupp and offers a magnificent view of the bay of the Marina Piccola, the Punta Tragara and the Faraglioni. To the right the CASTIGLIONE, a former medieval castle built to defend the inhabitants of Capri, is today privately owned.

PIAZZA UMBERTO I TO MARINA PICCOLA

CERTOSA DI SAN GIACOMO. From the Piazza Umberto I, Via Vittorio Emanuele and then Via Federico Serena lead to the Certosa di San Giacomo, nestling in the valley between the Castiglione and Monte Tuoro. The sober and monumental style of the conventual buildings, set in a vast park, is a fine example of Capri's medieval and monastic architecture. The Carthusian monastery was founded in 1371 by Giacomo Arcucci, a member of one of the island's rich and powerful families. As secretary to Queen Jeanne, he shared her tragic fate and died at the monastery, stripped of his wealth. The monastery became the economic centre of the island and was sacked and burnt, in 1553, by the corsair Dragut before being restored and extended ten years later.

It subsequently prospered from individual bequests and the commercial initiatives of the monks, until the religious institution was dissolved by order of Joseph Bonaparte in 1807. The layout of the Certosa di San Giacomo is similar to that of the Certosa di San Martino ▲ *184*, in Naples, with its church, prior's apartment and two cloisters. The smaller 15th-century cloister has a central, circular well and a series of arcades with Romano-Byzantine capitals. The monks' cells open onto the larger 16th-century cloister. The refectory houses the DIEFENBACH MUSEUM with paintings by the German artist Wilhelm Diefenbach and four Roman statues of marine deities.

Certosa di San Giacomo.

GARDENS OF AUGUSTUS AND VIA KRUPP. From the monastery Via Matteotti leads to the GARDENS OF AUGUSTUS ★, a magnificent terraced park where trees and flowers grow in profusion. In one corner of the gardens stands a monument

The winding Via Krupp.

to Lenin who, during his exile, stayed on the island at the villa of Maxim Gorky. The vertiginously steep and narrow Via Krupp ★ attests to the German steel-heir's indestructible passion for Capri. The road, hewn out of the rock, winds its way down to the Saracen tower and the Marina Piccola.
MARINA PICCOLA. The Punta di Mulo, a rocky extension of the Monte Solaro, defines the limit of this delightful bay overlooked by the Scoglio delle Sirene (Sirens' Rock). In the 1950's and 1960's the resort played an important role in the rise of the island's tourist industry.

FRIEDRICH ALFRED KRUPP (1854–1902)
In 1902 Krupp committed suicide after being accused of taking part in orgies in one of the island's grottos. It was never discovered whether the scandal was a political plot or based on fact.

SALTO DI TIBERIO
To the right of the entrance of the Villa Jovis (or of Tiberius) is the Salto di Tiberio, an almost vertical rock (975 feet high) from which the emperor is said to have precipitated his victims. "On the island of Capri is the place of execution, from where he ordered his victims, after prolonged and skillful torture, to be precipitated into the sea before his very eyes; below a company of sailors beat them with boathooks until the life was crushed from their bodies."
(Suetonius, *Tiberius*)

Arco Naturale.

FROM THE PIAZZETTA TO VILLA JOVIS

VIA SOPRAMONTE. This narrow street, which runs along the slopes of San Michele, is reached from Via Longano. At the Della Croce intersection Via Tiberio, on the left, runs past of the CHAPEL OF SAN MICHELE (or Della Croce). Built at the end of the 14th century, the chapel's modest outline is a rupestral example of the Byzantine tradition. The road climbs to Monte Tiberio, one of the most beautiful excursions on the island, past vegetable gardens, gardens and magnificent residences (VILLA LO PITTORE, VILLA LA MONETA) and ends in steps hidden amid the vegetation. (At the Villa la Moneta, take Via lo Capo.)

VILLA FERSEN. The villa, situated in a vast park, is reminiscent of the Stile Liberty very much in vogue at the beginning of the 20th century. (Retrace your steps to Via Tiberio.)

VILLA JOVIS AND MONTE TIBERIO ★. The villa is thought to be one of the twelve residences built on the island for the Emperor Tiberius. The buildings, which espouse the contours of the promontory, are centered around vast rainwater cisterns. The imperial apartments lay to the north, the thermal complex to the south, and the servant's quarters to the west. On the summit of Monte Tiberio stands the tiny rustic church of SANTA MARIA DEL SOCCORSO (first half of the 17th century), from where there is an unrivalled view of the Bay of Naples, the islands of Ischia and Procida, Cape Miseno and Vesuvius. To the right are the Punta della Campanella (at the tip of the Sorrentine peninsula), the Li Galli rocks and part of the Gulf of Salerno.

TOWARD THE FARAGLIONI

From the Della Croce intersection in Capri, Via Matromania leads to a square that in turn leads to the ARCO NATURALE.

ARCO NATURALE ★. This huge archway in the rock resulting from centuries of erosion stands in an extraordinarily beautiful setting.

GROTTA DI MATROMANIA. A long, steep flight of steps, on the right, leads down to this natural cave which, as its name

> "THE FARAGLIONI . . . WASHED BY THE SEA, HUGE,
> PEREMPTORY, FIRMLY ENSCONCED IN THE LANDSCAPE,
> LIKE THREE APARTMENT BLOCKS, LIKE THREE HATS
> ON A SIDEBOARD" FÉLICIEN MARCEAU

suggests, is supposed to have been the scene of orgiastic practices linked to the cult of the Mater Magna (more generally known as Cybele). This magical cave, in the bowels of Monte Tuoro, contains traces of Roman mosaic and stucco decorations.

PUNTA MASULLO. The road continues through woodland to the rocky outcrop of Punta Masullo and the VILLA DI CURZIO MALAPARTE, a vivid red building, with a long solarium, which blends harmoniously with the rock. In January 1938, Curzio Malaparte, author of the famous novel *La Pelle* fell in love with this arid, windswept headland. He bought it and decided to build a villa in this inhospitable but infinitely beautiful setting. The design was produced by the rationalist architect Adalberto Libera, the figurehead of Rome's artistic set, but it was apparently vastly different from the end product. The writer did not like Libera's design and is said to have changed the plans during construction. He is responsible, in particular, for the amazing trapezoidal staircase leading down to the sea: the only means of access to the villa.

PUNTA TRAGARA. The path, bordered by luxuriant vegetation, continues upward, through Pizzolungo to the Punta Tragara. There are some truly magnificent views of the Faraglioni en route. The Punta Tragara was used as a landing point during Roman times.

THE FARAGLIONI ★. Opposite the Punta Tragara stand these gigantic rocks: enigmatic, pale-ocher colossi that cast their reflection upon the sea, they are symbolic of Capri. In bygone ages, marine erosion separated "these renowned Gothic cathedrals whose spires and steeples rise proudly above the sea" (Alberto Savinio) from the island, creating caves, grottos and beautiful natural archways. With luck you might even see the rare, endemic species of lizard, with its characteristic blue stomach, that lives among the rocks.

"LE MÉPRIS"
Jean-Luc Godard's most classic (certainly in terms of form) film *Le Mépris* (*Contempt*) (1963) was mainly shot on Capri. It starred Brigitte Bardot, then in her prime and at the height of her career, Michel Piccoli, Jack Palance and Fritz Lang and was set in and around the Villa di Malaparte, perched high on its rocky headland. Based on the novel by Alberto Moravia, with a magnificent score by Georges Delerue, the film is a festival of color that pays homage to the sea, the cliffs, the villa and, of course, Bardot herself.

MONTE SOLARO
SEGGIOVIA

TORRE DI MATERITA
There is a bus that runs from the Piazza Caprile, in Anacapri, to the park where the Torre di Materita stands in splendid isolation. It was built, in the 15th century, by the monks of the Certosa di San Giacomo ▲ 230 to defend their vast estates against the Saracen raids. At the beginning of the 20th century, it was bought and restored by Axel Munthe, who lived here between 1910 and 1943. The road continues to the lighthouse and the Punta Carena.

Casa Rossa.

ANACAPRI

Anacapri lies at 902 feet above sea level and is the island's second urban center. Formerly known as the upper citadel, it was linked to the Marina Grande by the Scala Fenicia. The Romans standardized the citadels of Capri and Anacapri, which only began to experience any form of real urban development from the 16th century onwards. The town's altitude and distance from landing points made it an agricultural, forestry and pastoral center. Today the small town is a quiet and elegant resort.

CASA ROSSA ★. The Casa Rossa stands above Via G. Orlandi, the main thoroughfare of Anacapri, amid the low houses of the town center. It was built, between 1876 and 1899, around an Aragonese defense tower. Today it houses a museum and is decorated with various remains from the excavations carried out in the vicinity of Anacapri, commissioned by the villa's American owner, C.C. MacKowenlors.

CHURCH OF SAN MICHELE. The Baroque church on the Piazza San Nicola was built in 1719 by Domenico Antonio

Vaccaro on the initiative of Madre Serafina ▲ 230. The interior has an extraordinary majolica pavement (*Story of Eden*), executed in Naples (1761) by Leonardo Chiarrese. (Follow Via G. Orlandi to the Piazza Armando Diaz.)

CHURCH OF SANTA SOFIA. The church, built in 1510 on the site of an earlier church, was extensively modified until 1765, when the façade (left) was finished. The church stands in the oldest part of Anacapri, whose most interesting street is Via Boffe.

PIAZZA VITTORIA TO MONTE SOLARO

VILLA SAN MICHELE ★. Via Axel Munthe, bordered by traditional craft stores and sumptuous villas, leads to the Swedish doctor's residence and magnificent gardens. Axel Munthe arrived in Capri in 1876 and bought the ruins of the chapel of San Michele and a farm, which he later transformed (1896) into this white building. The villa is a curious patchwork of styles, with loggias, terraces and pergolas filled with statues and works of art. The interior is furnished with an incongruous mixture of 18th-century and antique pieces. You leave the villa gardens via the former gateway of Anacapri, at the top of the Scala Fenicia. The terrace offers an unparalleled view, described by

BELVEDERE DI MIGLIARA
On the south coast of the island, the Belvedere di Migliara reaches a height of 958 feet. A tortuous path follows the line of the precipice to the Torre della Guardia, a medieval watchtower rebuilt by the English as part of the defense against the French troops of Joachim Murat.

VILLA SAN MICHELE
di Axel Munthe

Il più bel posto da visitare
A lovely place to visit
Ein wunderschöner Platz
Une merveille à visiter
5 minuti

ANACAPRI

The Swedish doctor, Axel Munthe, was passionately fond of Capri, which he describes poetically in his biographical novel *The Story of San Michele* (1929). The work, translated into more than fifty languages, tells the story of a great love: the encounter between Nordic

romanticism and the land, sun and one of the most beautiful jewels of the *Campania felix*.

Alberto Savinio: "From these heights, the gaze passes directly from the land to the sea, the naked, deserted, spectral sea."

CASTELLO DI BARBAROSSA. A mule track that runs beside Via Axel Munthe leads to the remains of a Byzantine edifice dating from the 9th century. The castle is said to have been destroyed in 1535 by the Algerian pirate Barbarossa, the admiral of Suleyman Khair ud-Din, after whom it was named. (Return to the Piazza Vittoria.)

MONTE SOLARO ★. A chair-lift runs to the summit of Monte Solaro, the highest point on the island (1,932 feet). Nearby are the ruins of a small fort built by the English (1806) on medieval foundations. From Monte Solaro there is an unparalleled view across the island to the sea and the mountains of Calabria beyond. If you return on foot to Anacapri, you can visit Santa Maria Cetrella overlooking the Marina Piccola. The church and small hermitage were built on this isolated site in the 14th century, in late Gothic style, and rebuilt in the 17th century.

GROTTA AZZURRA
·CAPRI·

❝It was as if I had been transported into one of those fairy-tale settings that seem so real to children. The world and the light have suddenly vanished and you find yourself beneath the vast vault, in the blue twilight of an electrical fire. Wavelets lap softly and bubbles rise to the surface, sparkling like dazzling emeralds, fiery rubies and myriads of carbuncles emerging from the depths. The ghostly blue walls are as mysterious as fairy castles. There is, in this strange natural setting with its strange effects, a truly wondrous enchantment that is both supernatural and familiar.❞
Gregorovius, in Norman Douglas, *Siren Land*

ANACAPRI TO THE GROTTA AZZURRA

VILLA DI DAMECUTA. There is a bus from Anacapri (leaving from Via Pagliaro) to the Grotta Azzurra (a distance of 2 miles). En route, Via Amadeo Maiuri leads to the archeological site containing the remains of the Roman villa of Damecuta. The villa, supposedly one of the residences of Tiberius, is magnificently situated on a rocky ledge overlooking the vault of the grotto.

GROTTA AZZURRA. This famous grotto was discovered in 1826 by two tourists, the German poet August Kopisch and his friend, the Swiss artist Ernest Fries, accompanied by a fisherman from Capri, Angelo Ferraro. It was not only known during Roman times, but was the marine *nymphaeum*, decorated with statues, of the Roman villa of Gradola, situated immediately above it. However, although past residents of the island knew of the grotto's existence, they

Cross-section of the Grotta Azzurra
1. Entrance
2. Gallery of the Pilastri

preferred to avoid it, believing it to be an enchanted, evil place. It is possible to enter the grotto by boat via a fissure in the rock, remembering to duck as the opening is 6½ feet wide and only 3½ feet high. According to a 19th-century English poet: "The visit requires a cloudless day,/A resplendent sea in the placid bay,/The dazzling skies of Italy should abate/And the very breezes be calm and still." Inside the grotto, the particularly blue color of the water is caused by the refraction of light, which produces the same effect on the walls of the vault.

NORTH

VESUVIUS AND
THE BURIED CITIES

VESUVIUS AT REST
The oldest image of Vesuvius is a fresco found at Pompeii in the Casa del Centenario ▲ 255. It shows that, prior to the eruption of AD 79, the volcano had a single summit, Monte Somma, and its slopes were wooded and covered with vineyards.

The ascent to the crater of Vesuvius is rather like a pilgrimage to the seat of the lord of Naples. Although the volcano's white plume disappeared in 1944, its gray bulk is no less forbidding, and you can't quite rid yourself of the thought that, even though the volcano is now at rest, this is only a temporary respite. The Neapolitans, faced with this ever-present threat, put their trust in San Gennaro (Saint Januarius), their patron and protector, who is particularly associated with Vesuvius (against which he is traditionally represented).

THE FURY OF VESUVIUS

ERUPTION OF AD 79 ▲ 243. In AD 62 a violent earthquake shook the region of Vesuvius, causing serious damage to the cities of Herculaneum and Pompeii. This warning had long since been forgotten when another earthquake occurred in AD 79. Vesuvius awoke from its slumbers, engulfing Pompeii ▲ 246 and Herculaneum ▲ 272.

THE LONG SLEEP. Although there are very few details relating to the volcanic activity that took place during the thousand years following the disaster of AD 79, violent eruptions occurred in 203, 472, 512, 685, 787, 968 and 1037. After 1139, the volcano lapsed into a period of inactivity; life began to re-assert itself and its slopes were once again covered in vegetation.

THE GREAT ERUPTION OF 1631. In the summer of 1631, when volcanic activity had been forgotten for six hundred years,

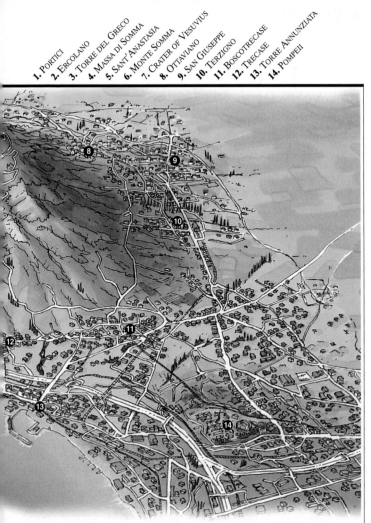

earth tremors began again, becoming increasingly violent as
the days passed. At the beginning of December, the crater
filled with a bubbling liquid and, on the morning of December
16, there was a series of explosions that projected volcanic ash
high into the air. The following day, molten lava poured from
two huge fissures that appeared on the southwest face of the
volcano. This was followed, in the evening, by flows of boiling
mud and more molten lava on the south face. Nearly all the
villages nestling at the foot of the volcano were destroyed and
at least four thousand people perished in the *torrens cineris*
(clouds of burning ash; literally, "torrents of ash") before the
eruption subsided two days later.

TWO CENTURIES OF ACTIVITY. Between 1766 and 1794 nine
major eruptions destroyed many villages (including Torre del
Greco ▲ *219*, in 1794) and claimed hundreds of lives. The
volcano remained active until the 19th century, with the most
memorable eruption occurring in 1872 when lava poured
from an opening on the northwest face of the cone. On May 1
the crater collapsed, forming a caldera, and the volcano
lapsed into silence.

1906. The earth tremors began a week after the first
emissions of lava, during the night of April 8. A "fountain" of
gas and lava was projected from the crater, reaching

**SAN GENNARO
AND VESUVIUS**
"The red hot ashes
were falling in
showers; and the noise
and fire, and smoke,
and sulphur, made me
feel as if I were dead
drunk. To which effect,
the trembling crust of
ground beneath my
feet contributed, no
doubt."

Charles Dickens,
*Letter to Emile de la
Rue, 1845*

The plain was planted with cereals and crops used for textiles, and vines grew in abundance. Poplar trees were introduced to reduce the humidity of the soil, and cypress groves were used to dry out the marshes. The town was surrounded by orchards, and cereals and vast vineyards, dominated by *Aminea gemina* vines, were cultivated on the lower slopes of Vesuvius. At higher altitudes, oak and chestnut woods, the habitat of deer and wild boar, gave way to forests of pure beech on the summit of Monte Somma.

a height of almost 2,000 feet, while ash was projected to more than 42,500 feet. This was followed by explosions of ash which covered Vesuvius in a white, sulfate-rich "powder" subsequently transformed into mud by the rain. The eruption blew the summit off the cone and the width of the crater was increased by around 980 feet.

THE MOST RECENT ACTIVITY. The last eruption of Vesuvius occurred in March 1944. Curzio Malaparte gives a moving description of it in *La Pelle*: "Vesuvius roared in the glowing darkness, and a desperate wailing rose from the town." Once again the villages at the foot of the volcano were affected by the disaster. Since then the crater's blowhole has been blocked, there is no plume of smoke rising from Vesuvius and vines are once more growing among orchards and vegetable gardens. But like Alessandro Malladra, who declared, in 1913, "Vesuvius is asleep, but its heart is awake", modern volcanologists remain cautious. The volcano could become active at any moment, a threat that hangs over the 700,000 people living in the high-risk areas.

ASCENT TO THE CRATER

"PARTITA DELLA MONTAGNE". At the beginning of the 18th century, when the first excavations were being carried out at the foot of Vesuvius, there was a veritable volcano "craze". Many travelers boldly climbed the mountain, described eruptions and brought back gouaches and sketches of the burning volcano, and even samples of lava and ore. The ascent became a social event, a *partita delle montagne* ("mountain outing") along the lines of the traditional "country outing". It also became one of the compulsory stages on the Grand Tour. Informed amateurs such as Sir William Hamilton ▲ *244* began to study the volcano. At the end of the 19th century, the funicular railway ● *6* enabled the less energetic to reach the summit of the crater.

IN THE STEPS OF THE GRAND TOUR. The ascent of Vesuvius has changed somewhat since the days of the Grand Tour: mules are no longer used to accompany travelers to the top of the crater, the funicular railway was destroyed in the eruption of 1944 and the chair-lift that replaced it is no longer running. But the visitors' emotions are much the same: as Alfred Sohn-Rethel wrote, in 1926, "Approaching the cone of the volcano from below is a humbling experience, quite simply because of its size and power, and its spectacular color which gives off an almost magical glow.

This color is in fact nothing but the gray of the ash that covers the entire surface of the mountain. But it is a gray shot with silver, a gray that is in some way alive, that becomes suffused with pink in the moonlight; at least that was the effect created against the darkness of the background."

Today travelers leave Ercolano ▲ *218* or Torre del Greco ▲ *219* by car or coach. The road runs up to the former chair-lift station, passing the Observatory. This was built by Gaetano Fazzini in 1841–5, but it is no longer used as an observation post and only contains ores, samples of volcanic ash, engravings and photographs of Vesuvius. From the chair-lift station you continue on foot to the promontory (3,800 feet), which offers a magnificent view of Naples, and then on to the summit of the crater. Fumaroles (jets of steam) are still emitted from the walls of this huge chasm (1,970 feet in diameter and 656 feet deep), formed after the 1944 eruption. As you follow the path along the edge of the crater, a magnificent panorama of the bay and its islands, from Naples to Sorrento, gradually unfolds.

MONTE SOMMA. It is also possible to approach Vesuvius from the north and climb to Monte Somma and the Punta del Nasone. Monte Summa, a huge, curved rampart, is the original volcano. The cone of Vesuvius developed in the caldera, after a series of eruptions.

Sample of volcanic matter, including a fragment of lava (above, right) "impregnated with salts and sulfur, taken from an extremely hot fissure inside the crater of Vesuvius." (Sir William Hamilton)

VESUVIAN FLORA
Some 610 species of flora grow on the slopes of *Vesuvius*. *Stereocaulon vesuvianum*, a lichen that causes lava to disintegrate, is an endemic colonizing species. It provides the very thin layer of humic subsoil required for the establishment of such species as red valerian and Vesuvian broom. The roots of these two species find their way through the narrowest fissures and then take hold by breaking up the rock. In spring the flowering broom is an extraordinary sight: acres of lava are suddenly covered in a blaze of yellow.

At dawn, on August 24, AD 79, Vesuvius broke its prolonged silence. In two letters to Tacitus, Pliny the Younger, who was staying in Baiae at the time, described the violence of the tragic eruption that engulfed Pompeii ▲ 246, Herculaneum ▲ 272, Stabiae ▲ 221 and Oplontis ▲ 220. He documents the various volcanic phenomena with remarkable accuracy: the earth tremors that preceded the eruption, the huge column of ash and gas that rose in the shape of an umbrella pine, the cascades of volcanic ash and pumice that engulfed the buildings, the total darkness, the toxic sulfurous gases, the continual tremors, the burning ash clouds, the horizontal blasts, the tidal waves provoked by the sudden rises in the land level. . . . The last phase of the catastrophe that destroyed Herculaneum is less well known. It seems that the torrential rain that followed the eruption combined with the pumice and ash accumulated on the edge of the crater, forming a mass of liquid mud which began to slide toward the sea . . .

ERUPTION OF VESUVIUS, COVERED IN SNOW (PLATE V). "Cone of Vesuvius covered in snow, with several streams of lava flowing from the crater."

INTERIOR OF THE CRATER OF VESUVIUS, BEFORE THE ERUPTION OF 1767 (PLATE IX). "While the volcano is active, the shape of the crater is continually changing."

VIEW FROM THE ATRIO DEL CAVALLO, BETWEEN VESUVIUS AND MONTE SOMMA (PLATE XXXIII). "When the volcano is about to erupt . . .. the smoke is often emitted in a circular shape."

From 1764, Sir William Hamilton (1730–1803) was British envoy to the court of Naples. As an informed art lover he was captivated by objects excavated at Herculaneum and Pompeii and built up an extremely valuable collection. But he was soon consumed by a new passion: at the first sign of movement from Vesuvius, this inveterate encyclopedist wanted to learn about the mechanics of volcanos. He began to study the volcano and sent his observations to the Royal Society in London. In 1776, he published his findings, accompanied by fifty-four gouaches by Pietro Fabris, to which he added five new plates after the eruption of 1779.

THE GREAT ERUPTION OF VESUVIUS IN 1767, SEEN FROM THE PIER OF NAPLES (PLATE VI). "It seemed that the mountain was going to explode . . . it split open almost from top to bottom."

INTERIOR OF THE CRATER OF VESUVIUS, IN 1756 (PLATE X). "A smaller peak was formed . . . and lava . . . flowed from the cone of Vesuvius."

THE KING AND QUEEN OF NAPLES VISITING THE SCENE OF THE ERUPTION IN 1771 (PLATE XXXVIII). "[The lava] overflowed into a ravine, where it formed a magnificent fiery waterfall."

Pompeii is undoubtedly the most important and most poignant example of an ancient city. It should be visited in conjunction with the Museo Archeologico Nazionale in Naples ▲ 164, which houses most of the works of art and everyday objects discovered in the Vesuvian cities.

HISTORY

A MARITIME CITY. Pompeii was built on a lava plateau partly bordered, near Porta Marina, by a navigable canal linking the city with the nearby maritime quay, probably situated in the vicinity of Bottaro.

A TRADITIONAL LAYOUT. The city covers an area of some 158 acres. Its enclosure wall is pierced by seven gates, made of Sarno limestone ● 68 and tufa from Nuceria. In the zone of the Foro Triangolare ("Triangular Forum"), there is a nucleus of older housing and irregular streets, dating from the 6th century BC. From the 4th century BC, the city was developed according to a grid layout, with rectangular *insulae* (multistory apartment blocks) defined by the intersections of the *decumani* (streets parallel to the main avenue) and *cardi* (transverse streets) which overlaid the older street network.

AN IMPORTANT COMMERCIAL CENTER. The Roman city, which was larger than neighboring Herculaneum because of the proximity of the estuary of the navigable River Sarno, was an important commercial center, receiving and redistributing merchandise and products from the landlocked towns of the Campanian hinterland. Pompeii was also a flourishing center for traditional crafts, as is evident from the many specialist stores and workshops scattered throughout the excavated part of the city.

REGIONS AND "INSULAE"
The city was divided into regions and *insulae*, and the buildings numbered accordingly. The system, devised by the archeologist Giuseppe Fiorelli, provides valuable landmarks.

EXCAVATIONS

DISCOVERY. In 1748 the excavations at Pompeii superseded those at Herculaneum ▲ 272, which were proving more difficult because of the depth and resistance of the overlying volcanic material. During this period the valuable objects were removed from the houses and taken to the royal museum of Portici, where they were subsequently buried

UNDER THE GUIDANCE OF THE "CICERONE" The discoveries made on the sites of Pompeii and Herculaneum were widely reported throughout Europe. Eighteenth-century travelers, ancient texts in hand, flocked to visit the ruins. They were taken by the *cicerone* (guide) to the most significant places, where macabre tableaux of the type depicted on this engraving were sometimes staged.

once again. In 1763 the discovery of an inscription referring to the *respublica Pompeianorum* enabled the buried city to emerge from the anonymity into which it had hitherto been plunged.

A MORE SCIENTIFIC APPROACH. It was not until the mid-19th century that archeologists began to use more scientific methods. A vast area (corresponding to three-fifths of the ancient city) was excavated under the direction of Amadeo Maiuri, director of excavations between 1924 and 1961, and this gave the city its present appearance. Since then the major problems of maintenance and restoration have meant that the rate of excavation has had to be slowed down.

POMPEII TODAY. The earthquake in 1980 ● 40 caused extensive damage to the buildings of Pompeii. A campaign to heighten public awareness produced additional financing for restoration work, new excavations and the introduction of a system to regulate and improve the standard of visits.

AROUND THE FORUM

Beyond Porta Marina, on the left, are the impressive suburban

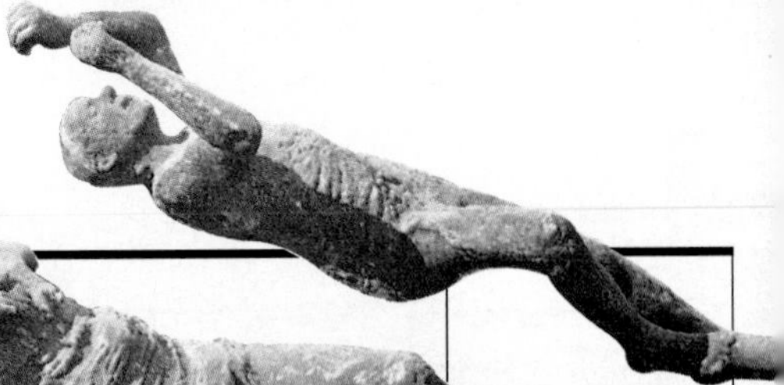

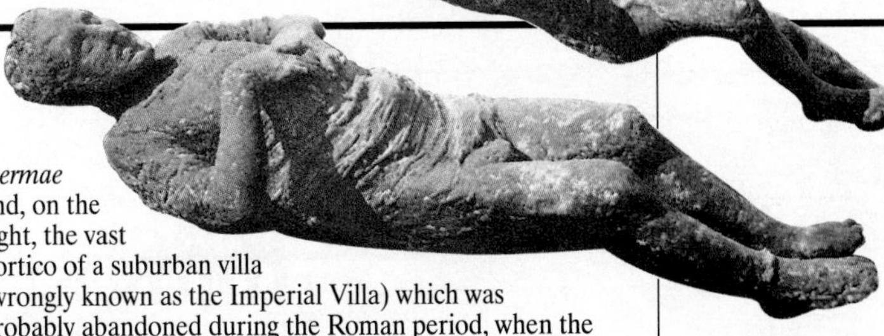

thermae
and, on the
right, the vast
portico of a suburban villa
(wrongly known as the Imperial Villa) which was
probably abandoned during the Roman period, when the
Temple of Venus (above the villa) was extended.
SUBURBAN "THERMAE". The second floor of the edifice, built
against the hill of lava, was used as living accommodation.
On the first floor the rooms of the *thermae* lead onto an open
porticoed area. One of the rooms is vaulted and decorated
with extremely sophisticated stuccowork, incorporating
geometric and floral motifs and tiny cupids. It opens onto a
fountain-nymphaeum in which one of the panels, made of
pâte-de-verre tessera, represents Mars flying beside Cupid.
The *thermae* also housed a small brothel decorated with erotic
panels showing the services offered by the prostitutes. The
building is linked to a quay with stone mooring rings set in
the wall. The quay appears to be part of a port complex built
on the canal that provided a link with the sea and the port
of Pompeii.
TEMPLE OF VENUS. Beyond Porta Marina are the first two
religious buildings in the area of the Forum. Little remains
of the Temple of Venus (on the right) as it was probably
being restored at the time of the eruption and was
subsequently stripped of any re-usable materials. The
cella, facing the sea, was in the center of a vast open area,
extended during the Julio-Claudian period (first half of the
1st century AD) by earthworks that stretched as far as and

**THE FIORELLI
METHOD**
Plaster casts of the
victims of the
catastrophe were
obtained using the
famous method
developed by the
archeologist
Giuseppe Fiorelli in
1863, and still in use
today. It consists of
pouring plaster into
the cavities left by
the bodies.

TEMPLE OF APOLLO
Like the Temple of Venus, to its right, the Temple of Apollo stands in the center of a vast, sacred area surrounded by porticos where copies of the bronze statues of Apollo Sagittarius and Diana Sagittaria (2nd century BC) were placed. Certain elements of this peripteral temple with its Corinthian capitals date from the 2nd century BC.

Statue of Eumachia.

incorporated the so-called Imperial Villa. In 1863 a gold oil lamp was discovered near the temple, unique in both value and origin. It was probably an offering to Venus made by the Emperor Nero and his wife Poppaea when they visited Naples in AD 64.

THE FORUM ● 70. The plinths of many commemorative statues still stand in the square, paved with travertine, that was the center of the city's public life. Vehicles were excluded from the Forum, which was surrounded (except on the north side) by porticos. Part of the 1st-century tufa colonnade is still standing on the south side, but all that remains on the other two sides are the vestiges of travertine columns which were in the process of being restored at the time of the eruption. Many public and religious buildings were situated around the Forum. The BASILICA in the southwest corner was used as a court of law and for the administration of commercial affairs. The triple-naved interior is divided by columns of brick, covered with stucco. The monumental colonnaded avant-corps, opposite the entrance, has been identified as the raised tribunal for the judges. On the south side are three municipal buildings: the first was the local senate-house, the second contained the city archives and the third was the seat of the *decuriones* (the city's most important magistrates). The COMITIUM, where the municipal elections were held, lies beyond Via delle Scuole and is separated from the other monuments on this side of the Forum by Via dell'Abbondanza. Immediately behind the Comitium is the imposing BUILDING OF EUMACHIA ★, the priestess of Venus and heiress to a large commercial enterprise linked to the wool industry. The building includes a vast interior courtyard, probably used for commercial negotiations or as a wool market. Beyond this lies a series of three public buildings: the Temple of Vespasian, whose courtyard has a central marble altar ★ decorated with a sacrificial scene; the Sacrarium of the Lares Publici where

ceremonies in honor of the city's tutelary deities were held, and the MACELLUM (provisions market). The twelve tufa plinths in the center of a courtyard in the Macellum once supported twelve wooden posts, which in turn upheld a conical roof. The covered area thus created was reserved for the sale of fish, as evidenced by the many bones found in a nearby drain. The CAPITOL (below) stands on the north side of the Forum, on a raised podium between two commemorative arches. The temple, dating from the 2nd century BC and subsequently modified, was dedicated to the Capitoline triad (Jupiter, Juno and Minerva). The only remaining piece of statuary found in the temple was a huge marble head of Jupiter. In a niche, on the side of the Forum bordered by the Temple of Apollo, is a MENSA PONDERARIA: a limestone plaque, engraved with the standard weights and measures, designed to prevent fraudulent transactions by merchants. Finally, in the northwest corner of the Forum, is the rectangular FORUM OLITORIUM, with its façade of seven brick pilasters, where cereals and dried vegetables were sold. Today it houses archeological exhibits and plaster casts of the victims of the eruption.

"THERMAE" OF THE FORUM ▲ *258* (VII, 5). The modestly proportioned *thermae* are divided into two sections, the women's baths and the men's baths. The latter section is the only one that can be visited and is reached by Via delle Terme. The walls of the *apodyterium* (undressing room) are lined with stone benches. The *frigidarium* has a circular central pool. The barrel vault of the *tepidarium* has stucco decorations, and the regularly spaced niches in the walls contain elegant telamones. The bronze brazier and three bronze benches were presented by

WOOL WORKSHOPS
About forty of the many different workshops were devoted to wool and the production of clothes. This attests to the fact that Pompeii was an active center for the collection and processing of raw wool from the rich pastures of the hinterland. The high concentration of workshops in the *insulae* of Region VII, to the east of the Forum, can be explained by the proximity of the Building of Eumachia, probably used as a purchasing center and wholesale market for wool.

ACANTHUS LEAVES
A portal in the façade of the Building of Eumachia has a sophisticated marble decoration of birds and insects among acanthus leaves.

251

HOUSES OF THE LARGE FOUNTAIN AND THE LITTLE FOUNTAIN (VI, 8, 22 and 23) These two adjacent houses are named after their elegant mosaic fountains, made of *pâte-de-verre* tessera. Both fountains are in the form of an aedicule with a central niche, and stand at the end of a small peristyle, in line with the *tablinum*, atrium and entrance. In the House of the Large Fountain, two marble tragic masks are set in the uprights of the niche.

MOSAICS IN THE HOUSE OF THE FAUN Although *Darius and Alexander at the Battle of Issus* ▲ 167 is undoubtedly the most remarkable of these mosaics, the other rooms are also decorated with some beautiful scenes: two emblems (a satyr and bacchante, and a cat devouring a partridge) and a frieze depicting tragic masks and festoons of fruit in amazing colors.

M. Nigidius Vaccula, a rich manufacturer from Capua. The *caldarium*, whose vault is striated with stucco ridges, was heated by hot air passed through the wall cavity. The bronze inscription on the edge of the marble ablutions basin indicates that it was presented by the *duumviri* C. Melissaeus Aper and M. Staius Rufus. The marble pool on the north side was used for hot baths.

TEMPLE OF FORTUNE (VII, 4, 1). The temple, dedicated to the imperial cult, was built during the Augustan period on land belonging to the *duumvir* M. Tullius and at his expense, as indicated by an inscription that can be seen inside the temple. The prostyle temple has four façade columns and stands on a raised podium. The altar, in the center of the lower staircase, was used on ceremonial occasions. At the far end of the *cella*, the aedicule, supported by two columns, used to contain a statue of Fortuna.

BETWEEN VIA DI MERCURIO AND VIA STABIANA

INN (VI, 10, 19, 1). In a narrow room, six panels painted on a white background illustrate the daily business of this tiny inn. The customers are depicted with great verve as, wrapped in their hooded cloaks (*cuculli*), they play at dice, eat and drink.

HOUSE OF CASTOR AND POLLUX (VI, 9, 6). The house has an atrium with twelve tufa columns. The vast peristyle (on the right), which was later linked to the living quarters, has paintings in the Fourth style ● 77 and a basin in the garden. Opposite the *oecus* (banqueting hall) there used to be mythological

The discovery of the House of the Faun (1830–2) was a major archeological event, particularly for the wealth of its mosaics.

frescos of Perseus and Andromeda, and Medea in Corinth, above two angle pillars. These are now in the Museo Archeologico Nazionale in Naples ▲ *164*. A second peristyle is aligned with the entrance.

HOUSE OF MELEAGER (VI, 9, 2). The house is characterized by a Corinthian *oecus* with an interior colonnade, which opens onto a vast peristyle with a niched central basin. Next to the *oecus*, the *triclinium* is decorated with mythological paintings in the Third style ● *77* (the *Judgment and Dressing of Paris*), below which are figures of nymphs and satyrs.

HOUSE OF THE FAUN (VI, 12, 2). The house, discovered in 1830, is one of the largest and most sophisticated in Pompeii. The entrance, preceded by the inscription SALVE ("Welcome"), is decorated with paintings in the First style ● *76*. On the upper part of the entrance, the projecting cornice is in the form of a small temple with stucco columns. To the right of the atrium is a second tetrastyle atrium around which the service rooms, including a small bathroom, are arranged. Beyond the *tablinum* are two consecutive peristyles paved with cubes of marble depicting a view. The famous Alexander Mosaic ▲ *167* was found in the room, preceded by two columns, at the far end of the first peristyle.

HOUSE OF THE LABYRINTH (VI, 11, 10). The house has a double atrium followed by a peristyle and, to the left, service rooms. The reception rooms at the end of the peristyle include a Corinthian *oecus* with some valuable frescos in the Second style ● *76* and, to one side, a room containing a mosaic depicting Theseus killing the Minotaur.

HOUSE OF THE VETTII ★ (VI, 15, 1). Two bronze seals found near one of the strong-boxes in the atrium made it possible to attribute this impressive house, characterized by its extremely sophisticated paintings, to Aulus Vettius Restitutus and Aulus Vettius Conviva. To the right of the entrance is a painting of Priapus, whose huge penis is placed on one scale of a balance, while a purse full of coins rests on the other scale. The scene was supposed to protect the house against ill fortune. The slaves' quarters include a small room decorated with three small erotic panels

THE "DANCING FAUN" The bronze copy of the famous *Dancing Faun* (after which the house was named) stands at the center of the *impluvium*, in marble *opus sectile* ● *69*, in the atrium of the House of the Faun.

CASA DEL CENTENARIO (right and bottom) The house has two adjoining atria, followed by a peristyle with a double colonnade at the front end, and a garden with a central basin. At the far end of the peristyle is a monumental *nymphaeum* with an ornamental mosaic niche flanked by paintings of gardens and hunts. To the right are the service rooms. On a wall of the *lararium* was a fresco (now in the Museo Archeologico Nazionale in Naples) ranked among the most original paintings in Pompeii. It shows Bacchus in the form of a bunch of grapes, flanked by a view of Vesuvius whose slopes are covered in vines ▲ 238. The fountain was decorated with a small bronze statuette, dating from the Hellenistic period, of a young satyr squeezing wine from a wine skin.

RESTAVRATION ECHELLE: 0.03 P.M.   POMPEI · MAIS

against a white background. To the right and left of the entrance, two rooms are decorated with panels depicting scenes from mythology: Daedalus and Pasipha, Ixion on the Wheel, Bacchus and Ariadne, Pentheus and the bacchantes, the infant Hercules and the Serpents, Zethus and Amphion.

CASA DEGLI AMORINI DORATI (VI, 16, 7). The house is thought to have belonged to the Poppaei, one of Pompeii's rich and influential families and probably related to the Empress Poppaea, wife of Nero. The *tablinum*, decorated with a painting of Paris and Helen, opens onto the atrium. To one side is the peristyle, raised at one end, and in the left-hand corner is a *sacellum* dedicated to three Egyptian deities: Harpocrates, Isis and Serapis, shown with the god Anubis. The borders of the garden are decorated with numerous *hermae* and marble reliefs representing bacchanalian scenes. To the right of the peristyle, a small *cubiculum* is decorated with a fresco, whose floral motif is also found on fabrics. The walls were decorated with small glass disks inscribed with cupids on gold leaves.

VIA DI NOLA

HOUSE OF L. COECILIUS JUCUNDUS (V, 1, 26). The discovery of a collection of wax tablets made it possible to establish that the owner of this house was a banker. The house is built according to a regular, classic design, with the entrance opening onto the atrium,

ECHELLE: 0.01 P.M.   POMPEI · MAISON · DV · C

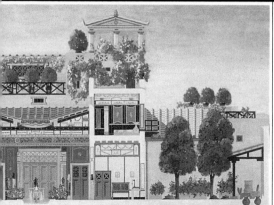

V · CENTENAIRE

CUPIDS IN THE
HOUSE OF THE VETTII
(above and below)
The *oecus* has a
frieze, divided into
thirteen sections,
showing Cupids and
Psyches performing
different crafts and
sporting activities.
The frieze, inspired
by paintings from the
Hellenistic period,
was modified and
adapted for the
Roman world by an
anonymous artist,
with energy, elegance
and restraint.

tablinum and peristyle. In the *sacellum*, to the left
of the atrium, were two famous marble bas-
reliefs representing scenes of the earthquake of
AD 62. To the left of the *tablinum* is a copy of the
bronze portrait-herm of L. Caecilius.

CASA DELLE NOZZE D'ARGENTO (V, 2, 1). The so-
called House of the Silver Wedding (mainly 2nd
century BC) was excavated in 1893, the year of the
silver wedding of King Umberto and Queen
Margherita. It has a rectangular garden with a
central basin and a Rhodian peristyle.

CASA DEL CENTENARIO ▲ *268* (IX, 8, 6). The house was
excavated in 1879, the 1800th anniversary of the eruption of
Vesuvius ▲ *243*.

HOUSE OF MARCUS LUCRETIUS FRONTO (V, 4, A). The house,
which belonged to a family living in Pompeii during the
Augustan period, has a remarkable cycle of paintings.

GLADIATOR BARRACKS (V, 5, 3). Graffiti relating to gladiatorial
combats suggest that the building was used to train gladiators.
The small rooms are arranged around a vast peristyle in which
the intercolumniations are decorated with transennae painted
with hunting and mythological scenes (the Rape of Europa,
Daedalus and Icarus).

HOUSE OF M. OBELLIUS FIRMUS (IX, 14, 4). The house was
being restored at the time of the eruption. Its walls consist of
huge limestone blocks, which make it possible to date its
construction from the Samnite period ● *29*. Its originality
stems from the fact that its many reception and service rooms
are all on the southwest side of the building. The large bronze
strong-box that can still be seen today, to the right of the main
atrium, attests to the wealth of the owners.

**HOUSE OF MARCUS
LUCRETIUS FRONTO**
The *tablinum* is
decorated with still-
lifes and panels (the
Triumph of Bacchus,
the Wedding of Mars
and Venus)
incorporated into a
restrained decorative
and architectural
structure set between
magnificent
candelabra. The lower
frieze represents a
garden, while the
walls on either side
are painted, within a
red framework, with a
scene of animals
hunting behind
statues of satyrs and
nymphs, a theme
frequently found in
Pompeii.

Theatrical
masks.

THE "PISTRINUM" (BAKERY)

This type of
workshop, widely
found in Pompeii
and other
ancient cities,
had an oven
used for making
bread and pastry. The
originality of this
Pompeiian bakery lies
in the fact that every
stage of the process,
from milling
to baking
and selling the bread,
was carried out in this
one workshop.

AROUND VIA STABIANA

"PISTRINUM" OF N. POPIDIUS PRISCUS (VII, 2, 22). The
bakery, linked at the back to the owner's house, has a line
of four lava millstones and, to the right, four low walls used
as work benches. The oven, to the left, has two distinct
openings: one for stoking the fire and the other for baking
the bread.

HOUSE OF THE BEAR (VII, 2, 45). The house is named after
the mosaic in the entrance, depicting a wounded bear. The
rooms surrounding the atrium are decorated with frescos
in the Fourth style ● 77. Behind the *tablinum*, a
small garden has a central mosaic fountain whose
recess is decorated with Venus emerging from a
shell and Neptune armed with his trident.

LUPANAR (VII, 12, 18–20). This is one of the
best-preserved brothels in Pompeii. Five of the
ten small rooms are on the second floor and
can be reached by way of an independent
staircase, which suggests that they were
reserved for special clients. The rooms on the
first floor have stone beds which would have
been covered with mattresses. At the
entrance to each room are small erotic
panels, on which diagrammatic drawings
against a white background advertise the
talents of the prostitutes. Inscriptions on the
walls record the impressions of
their clients.

"THERMAE" STABIANAE ★ ● 73, ▲ 258 (VII, 1, 8). The present
style of the building dates from the 2nd century BC (the
original construction probably dated from the end of the 4th
century BC), the city's most intense period of development.
Particularly worthy of note is the sophisticated decoration of
the stuccoed vault of the

apodyterium (undressing room), which is painted with images of nymphs and cupids inside a geometric motif of circles and octagons.

THEATERS AND THE FORO TRIANGOLARE

FORO TRIANGOLARE (VIII, 7, 30). The Foro Triangolare ("Triangular Forum") was built at the southern end of the lava plateau, overlooking the countryside around Pompeii. It was last modified in the 2nd century BC. Its monumental entrance has a vestibule consisting of six Ionic columns; a portico once ran along the two long sides. In the center of the Forum stood a DORIC TEMPLE, probably dedicated to Hercules and Athena. In front of the Greek temple is the tomb of the mythical founder of the city and a well bordered by Doric columns.

TEATRO GRANDE ● 72 (VIII, 7, 20, 16). This Greek-style theater was built in *opus incertum* ● 68, in the 2nd century BC, using the slope of the terrain, restored many times during subsequent centuries. Basins, which fed fountains, were found in the center, beneath the orchestra pit; this suggests that, from Roman times, it was no longer used as a theater. Behind the orchestra lies the *proskènion*, where the actors performed and, behind that, the monumental *scaenae frons*, built of brick and decorated with marble statues and columns. Near the east entrance of the orchestra is an inscription dedicated to the architect who restored the theater.

ODEUM (VIII, 7, 19). Next to the Teatro Grande, the Odeum or *theatrum tectum* (covered theater), with a capacity of around two thousand, was used for musical performances. The originality of the Odeum, built after 80 BC, lies in the fact that the semicircular *cavea* was truncated at both ends to allow for the construction of a roof with four slopes, which covered the entire structure. Two kneeling telamones are sculpted at either end of the *cavea*.

QUADRIPORTICUS
● 73 (VIII, 7, 16)
The vast porticoed area, behind the *scaenae frons* of the theater, was originally used to receive spectators during the intervals. During the final stage of the urban development of Pompeii, it was transformed into a barracks for gladiators. In fact many gladiatorial weapons, magnificently decorated with scenes from Greek mythology, were found in several of the rooms opening onto the quadriporticus.

In Roman society, thermal establishments were not simply places for taking hot and cold baths, or other physical activities. They were also, and above all, meeting places and places of cultural development. The *thermae* were either administered directly by the urban authorities or placed under the control of a manager who collected the admission charges. *Thermae* with separate men's and women's baths opened at 2pm; the others were reserved for women in the morning and men in the afternoon. They usually closed in the evening.

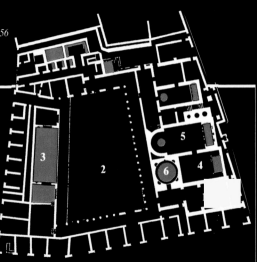

"THERMAE" STABIANAE ▲ *256*
These *thermae* (right), the
best preserved in Pompeii,
had a public area and
private baths.

SENSUALITY
During the second half of
the 19th century, historical
art became increasingly
popular in Europe. Because
of its evocative associations
and state of preservation,
Pompeii provided the
setting for a number of
works inspired by Roman
society. *Thermae* were one
of the favorite themes, and
were often treated with
sensuality, as in this
painting by Théodore
Chassériau.

**ITINERARY OF
A BATHER**
The *apodyterium*
(undressing room) **(1)**
had stone benches and
niches in the walls
where the bathers left
their clothes. They
could then take
exercise in the
courtyard **(2)**,
either take a
refreshing dip in the
adjoining cold pool **(3)**
or go direct to the
thermae proper. Most
bathers went via the
tepidarium **(4)**, an
intermediate room
that was moderately
heated by warm air
passed beneath the
floor and behind the
walls. From there they
went to the most
important room, the
caldarium **(5)**, heated
in the same way as the
tepidarium, for a hot
bath in a large,
rectangular pool. The
labrum, a round
marble basin, enabled
bathers to cool down
by rinsing themselves
with cold water. After
a period in the
tepidarium, they went
to the *frigidarium* **(6)**
for a cold bath in a
circular pool. Finally
they had a massage
and their bodies oiled.

Jupiter or Asclepios.

TEMPLE OF JUPITER MEILICHIOS (VIII, 7, 25). The temple, which dates from the 3rd to 2nd century BC, was attributed with some uncertainty to Jupiter Meilichios ("sweet as honey") on the basis of an inscription on the Porta Stabiana. Two terracotta statues discovered on a raised podium, in the *cella*, were thought to represent Jupiter and Juno, or Asclepius and Hygeia. The statues, of Hellenic inspiration, are probably the work of Campanian artists between the 3rd and 1st centuries BC.

TEMPLE OF ISIS ★ (VIII, 7, 28). The Egyptian cult of Isis was widespread in the region of Vesuvius. The temple, extensively reconstructed after the earthquake of AD 62, originally dated from the 2nd century BC. It is a porticoed edifice, built on a raised podium in the center of a sacred area, with two niches on either side of the entrance. Opposite the entrance is a room open to the sky, the *purgatorium*, whose exterior walls are decorated with Egyptian-style figures and couples (Mars and Venus, Perseus and Andromeda) accompanied by small cupids. Inside, a staircase leads to an underground chamber where the sacred water of the Nile was kept in an earthenware jar.

BETWEEN VIA DELL'ABBONDANZA AND VIA NUCERIA

CASA DEL CITARISTA (I, 4, 25). The House of the Lyre Player, one of the largest residences in Pompeii, in fact consists of two houses. It is characterized by a beautiful series of three peristyles leading to a number of rooms. Among the bronze statues of animals decorating the edge of the basin in the central peristyle was a remarkable group depicting a wild boar being attacked by dogs.

HOUSE OF THE MENANDER (I, 10, 4). To the left of the atrium is a room decorated with three paintings of scenes from the Trojan War: Laocoon and his sons, Cassandra and Ulysses, Cassandra and the entrance of the Trojan Horse. Beyond the *tablinum* lies the peristyle and, to the right, a room decorated with paintings elegantly executed against a green background. A frieze tells the story of the wedding of Hippodameia. On the far wall of the peristyle, in a rectangular niche, is a fresco featuring the poet Menander. Nearby, in another niche, a small altar dedicated to the household gods has a plaster cast of the *Imagines Maiorum*. To the left

FRESCOS OF THE TEMPLE OF ISIS

The frescos of the peristyle and main hall situated behind the temple (possibly a place of initiation to the mysteries of the cult of Isis) are of particular interest for the exactitude of their execution and the themes treated. They are now in the Museo Archeologico Nazionale in Naples ▲ 164.

"FULLONICAE"
This was where new fabrics were finished and clothes were washed and cleaned. The first room on the right in the Fullonica Stephani contained the clothes press. Clothes were

washed in the *impluvium* of the atrium.

of the peristyle is the largest *triclinium* found in Pompeii, where the walls of an earlier house can be seen, as well as an *oecus* containing the bodies of pillagers who perished while trying to steal valuable objects.

HOUSE OF THE CEII (I, 6, 15). The façade, painted with electoral programs, had been stuccoed to create an *opus quadratum* effect. A plaster cast of the door was obtained from the impression left in the lava. In the atrium is an *impluvium* made from fragments of amphorae. A staircase leads to the second floor, which was being built at the time of the eruption. At the end of the house, the far wall of the garden is decorated with paintings, including one of a hunt that makes remarkable use of color. On the side walls are Nile scenes, with Pygmies fighting a crocodile and a hippopotamus, and Egyptian-style figures depicted against sacred buildings that stand on either side of a river.

FULLONICA STEPHANI (I, 6, 7). This fulling-mill was probably owned by a certain Stephanus, whose name appears outside on an electoral sign. It is interesting to note the distribution of the fulling mills (*fullonicae*) which, because they used large quantities of water, tended to be built along Via Stabiana where water was more readily available. This was because of the presence of the water tower, at the Porta Vesuvio, which supplied water via the conduits.

This cantharus was part of a large collection of silver (now in the Museo Archeologico Nazionale in Naples) found in the House of Menander.

HOUSE OF THE SACELLUM ILIACUM (I, 6, 4). The house was in the process of being restored, as is evident from the heaps of plaster found in the garden, which would have been used for making the wall revetments. The rooms opening onto the atrium have unfinished frescos in the Fourth style ● 77. At the far end, on the right, the stucco of the *sacellum iliacum* (Trojan shrine) is decorated with a fresco whose frieze illustrates scenes from the Trojan War, while the central medallion of the vault depicts the Rape of Ganymede. To the left, in the garden, the main reception room has a curious cycle of frescos featuring two elephants *affrontee*. One of the walls is decorated with an alphabet.

HOUSE OF THE CRYPTOPORTICUS (I, 6, 2). This house was also being restored. The cryptoporticus, reached by means of a small staircase, had been transformed into a wine-vault (*cella vinaria*) adjoining the summer *triclinium*, situated above and

VERECUNDUS AT WORK
The façade of the workshop of Verecundus is decorated with a painting of Venus in a chariot drawn by elephants. Beneath this scene is another painting showing three workmen treating wool or a skin and, on the right, Verecundus himself showing a product to customers.

❝The walls of these little cabinets are frequently painted in frescoes, the birds, beasts, and flowers sometimes well executed; the pavement in the better and larger houses is of many-coloured mosaics; but, except in one superior mansion, called the house of Sallust, we did not observe one room long enough to contain an English bed.❞
Lady Morgan (1820)

AN UNUSUAL DISH-STAND
A group of four grotesque bronze statuettes, representing sellers of *placentae* (a kind of girdle cake), was found in the House of Ephebus. The group, used as a dish-stand, is now in the Museo Archeologico Nazionale ▲ *164*.

overlooking the garden. To the left of the cryptoporticus, decorated with frescos in the Second style ● *76* and friezes depicting scenes from the Trojan War, is a small thermal room and, at the far end, a vast room decorated with frescos (*hermae* of satyrs and bacchantes against a yellow background) and a frieze on which bacchanalian scenes alternate with remarkable still-lifes. The walls are covered in graffiti representing gladiators.

VIA DELL'ABBONDANZA. The street, once the busiest in Pompeii, is bordered by many stores and workshops and a thermal establishment. Of particular interest is the WORKSHOP OF VERECUNDUS (IX, 7, 5–7), which specialized in skins and

wool. A similar workshop existed at no. 1 (IX, 7, 1). Painted on the door lintel are the busts of four deities (Diana, Mercury, Jupiter and Apollo) and to the right of the entrance is the famous Procession of Cybele, painted in a simple and spontaneous style well suited to a scene inspired by an actual event. The INN OF ASELLINA (IX, 11, 2) is a tavern with a counter for selling drinks.

HOUSE OF EPHEBUS (I, 7, 11). The house, an agglomeration of smaller dwellings, has two atria. The first, at no. 10, is covered, while the second is in the center of the reception rooms. To the left, between the second atrium and the garden, is a *triclinium* with a rich marble pavement in OPUS SECTILE ● *69* and central tiles in multicolored glass. In the center of the garden a summer *triclinium*, beneath a pergola, has Nile scenes painted on its benches, with a small erotic scene interposed.

THERMOPOLIUM (I, 8, 8). The tavern is one of the best-preserved edifices in Pompeii. One of the terracotta containers, set in the counter used for selling drinks, was full of coins (possibly the day's takings).

HOUSE OF THE FLORAL "CUBICULA" (I, 9, 5). The originality of the layout of the house derives from the fact that its rooms are all on the left-hand side. Of particular note are the paintings in the two *cubicula*, which represent luxuriant gardens and use motifs inspired by Egyptian paintings, and the decoration (in the Third style ● 77) of the *triclinium*, whose walls are decorated with large-scale mythological scenes.

GARDEN OF THE FUGITIVES (I, 21, 5). In 1961 a group of thirteen victims of the eruption was discovered in one of the many zones in Region I planted with vines, olive trees and orchards. They had been suffocated by volcanic gases and ash as they tried to escape.

NECROPOLIS OF PORTA NUCERIA. Part of Via Nuceria was exposed outside the city walls. It was bordered by several monumental sepulchers.

ZONE OF THE AMPHITHEATER

"SCHOLA ARMATURARUM" (III, 3, 6). The weapons found on several wooden stands, set in the walls of this building, support the theory that is was the headquarters of a military organization.

HOUSE OF D. OCTAVIUS QUARTIUS ★. (II, 2, 2). The rooms are all in the front section of the house, originally and erroneously known as the House of Loreius Tibertinus. The rear section (entrance near the Palaestra) is occupied by a garden. The two sections are separated by a basin, covered by a pergola, which leads, on one side of the basin, to a summer *triclinium* and a fountain and, on the other, to a room decorated with elegant paintings against a white background. In the center of the garden, whose original planting has been restored, there is a long *euripus* (transverse basin), decorated with an elegant pyramidal fountain. Around the sides runs a double path beneath an arbor. The pictorial decoration of the house is of an extremely high stylistic standard, especially in the *oecus*, where two friezes recount Hercules' expedition against Laomedon, and several episodes of the Trojan War.

HOUSE OF VENUS AND THE SHELL (II, 3, 3). The house is named after the fresco on the far wall of the garden, depicting the naked goddess supported on a shell.

VILLA OF JULIA FELIX (II, 4)
The villa occupies an entire *insula* and comprises baths, shops and accommodation rented out by the wealthy owner, Julia Felix. To the right of the garden, decorated with a beautiful central basin, is an extremely elegant portico with rectangular marble pilasters.

TRIPOD OF THE VILLA OF JULIA FELIX
In the mid-18th century, this famous bronze tripod, whose central plate is supported by three young ithyphallic satyrs, was found in the garden. It significantly influenced the designers of Empire-style objects.

263

The eruption of AD 79 not only buried the houses, but also the gardens of Pompeii. In the second half of the 19th century there was a move to discover the type of planting used in the gardens, whose flowerbeds and borders were being exposed by stratigraphic excavations. The first step was to identify the plant species represented on the frescos. The spatial distribution of plants was revealed by the root cavities preserved on the site. It was not until the 1970's that new laboratory technology (the most decisive of which was palinology) made it possible to identify the plant species actually cultivated.

"VIRIDARIUM"
The *viridarium* occupied the center of the house. Flowers were grown for their decorative and medicinal value and for making floral crowns.

BAMBOO TRELLIS

The frescos of Pompeii often depict a bamboo trellis surrounding flowerbeds and borders. A recent study of the garden of the House of the Lovers provided information on the composition of a *viridarium*.

The bamboo trellis found in the garden was used to border the geometrically shaped flowerbeds, planted with juniper bushes, roses and cherry trees (revealed by the analysis of wood, pollen and seeds).

PARKS RATHER THAN GARDENS

Wealthy proprietors like Julia Felix and Loreius Tiburtinus, who wanted to own vast gardens, had their villas built in the outlying districts. These villas no longer had a *viridarium* but opened onto veritable parks decorated with fountains and otherwater features, made possible by the construction of the city's aqueduct a few years before the eruption.

EXACTNESS OF FRESCOS
Representations are sometimes so exact that it is possible to identify the species of plant.

GARDEN OF LOREIUS TIBURTINUS
A long marble pool, shaded by vines, runs from one end of the garden to the other.

GREAT PALAESTRA ● *73* (II, 7). The rectangular Palaestra (exercise ground), which dates from the time of Augustus, is delimited by a vast portico, except on the side overlooking the Amphitheater. The exterior walls, in *opus incertum* ● *68*, have paintings in the Third style ● *77*. The columns are covered in graffiti left by the "regulars". The area, whose center is occupied by a pool built on an incline, is surrounded on three sides by a double row of plane trees. The trees were planted recently as part of a program to recreate the green spaces of Pompeii using archeological data.

AMPHITHEATER ● *72* (II, 6). The elliptical amphitheater was built in *opus quasi reticulatum* ● *68*, in c. 80 BC. It is undoubtedly the most ancient structure of its kind to have been preserved in its entirety. The theater was built partly against the walls of the city, while the sides facing the city have several flights of steps supported by arches built against the supporting structure of the *cavea*.

VIA DELLE TERME TO PORTA ERCOLANO

HOUSE OF THE TRAGIC POET (VI, 8, 3). The entrance is decorated with the famous mosaic of a dog accompanied by the inscription "Cave Canem" ("Beware of the Dog"). The entire house is decorated with large mythological panels.

INSULA OCCIDENTALIS (VII, Ins. Occ. 16–19). Several important buildings were constructed in this zone, on the edge of the lava plateau that straddled the enclosure wall. The four-story HOUSE OF M. FABIUS RUFUS, whose extremely elegant pictorial decorations were mostly in the Fourth style ● *77*, enjoyed some magnificent views of the sea. Of equal interest is the HOUSE OF THE GOLDEN BRACELET, with its two rooms decorated with sophisticated garden scenes, combining plants, flowers and a number of birds in flight.

HOUSE OF SALLUST (VI, 2, 4). The house, wrongly attributed to C. Sallust, in fact belonged to A. Cossius Libanus. It dates from the 3rd century BC and is among the oldest in Pompeii. It had only recently been converted into an inn when the city was buried. The entrance is in the center of five stores, two of which open onto the interior of the house. At the far end of the atrium, decorated with frescos in the First style ● *76*, is a small *hortus* with a summer *triclinium* on the left. In the 1st century BC a wing with a small garden was added, to the right of the atrium. On the far wall of the garden is a painting representing Acteon being attacked by his dogs.

VIA DEI SEPOLCRI AND THE SUBURBAN VILLAS

NECROPOLIS OF PORTA ERCOLANO. The most famous and most complete necropolis in Pompeii lies beyond the Porta Ercolano. Excavations carried out between 1763 and 1838 exposed about a quarter of a mile of road (Via dei Sepolcri) bordered by villas and monumental tombs, reminiscent of both Greek and Roman art.

VILLA OF DIOMEDES. The villa was arbitrarily attributed to M. Arrius Diomedes, whose tomb stands opposite the house on Via dei Sepolcri. The extremely beautiful square peristyle on the first floor is bordered by a cryptoporticus. A number of bodies were found in the villa, including that of a young girl whose beauty inspired the French writer Théophile Gautier's novella *Arria Marcella*.

VILLA OF DIOMEDES
"Imagine . . ., first of all, the columns of the portico, decorated with festoons of flowers; the lower part of the columns being painted red, and the walls decorated with various frescos. Behind a curtain, three-quarters open, was the *tablinum*, or sitting room (which could be closed off at will by glass doors, at that moment pushed back against the wall). On the other side of the *tablinum* were some small rooms, one of which was the *cabinet de merveilles*. These rooms and the *tablinum* led into a long gallery, which opened at either end onto terraces. Between the terraces was a large room, adjoining the central part of the gallery, in which the banqueting table stood. All these rooms, although more or less on street level, overlooked the garden from the upper story, while the terraces beyond the gallery continued as raised corridors above the columns which surrounded the garden to right and left."
Edward Bulwer
Lytton,
Last Days of Pompeii
(1842)

▲ VILLA DEI MISTERI

The Villa of the Mysteries, built on the northern edge of Pompeii, has one of the most important decorative and pictorial collections in the Roman world. Although all the paintings in the villa are of remarkable stylistic quality, the room that made it famous is the *triclinium*. Decorated with a cycle of paintings, and probably a copy of an original from the Hellenistic period (4th–3rd century BC), adapted by a Campanian artist.

INTERPRETATION OF A COPY

The fresco depicts twenty-nine life-size figures, painted against a bright red background, and covers all the walls of the room. Although the overall composition lacks narrative fluidity, this is probably because the artist was only familiar with part of the Hellenistic original. In fact, the transposition of works of art from the Greek tradition was achieved by means of cartoons or albums of pictures which were circulated among the studios of Roman artists. The narrative sequences were often sacrificed for the sake of a simplified iconographic typology.

THE DIONYSIAC MYSTERIES

The fresco is read from left to right on entering the room. It comprises ten scenes, which cover the north, east and south walls. The composition starts with the seated figure of a woman, probably the owner of the villa, who is separated from the narrative wall is devoted to a pastoral scene: a Silenus, accompanied by two satyrs, plays the lyre, while a terrified young woman flees.

On the central wall are Dionysus and Ariadne enthroned; to their left are two satyrs and a Silenus and, to their right,

INFLUENCES

The "great painting" (the name given to the room that contains it) is one of the best examples of the fusion of Hellenistic artistic influences and Campanian figurative culture. The composition is Greek, as is the style of the figures and their movements, while the faces, with their large dark eyes, bodies and ample garments, are typically Campanian.

cycle by a door. The narrative begins with the child Dionysus reading the rite, assisted by a seated woman, while another woman approaches. This is followed by a scene of sacrifice: a servant bearing a platter of offerings makes her way toward three women gathered around a table. The far end of the a kneeling bacchante unveiling the basket containing the phallus of fertility, and a winged demon posed to strike. On the south wall a woman is being flogged, while a naked bacchante approaches, dancing. The final image is that of a seated woman; she combs her hair, assisted by a servant and two small cupids.

READING OF THE RITE   SACRIFICE TO DIONYSUS, OR RITES OF PURIFICATION

UNVEILING OF THE "PHALLUS" AND DEMON OR TELLUS, THE "EARTH-MOTHER"

**REPRESENTATION OF
A RITE**
According to
Amadeo Maiuri, the
fresco of the Villa dei
Misteri represents
the rite of initiation
of a bride to the
Dionysiac mysteries,
whose cult was
widespread in
Campania. The first
eight scenes describe
the rites of the
reception of the
bride into the
Dionysian company,
while the last two
evoke the pre-nuptial
preparations.

FLAGELLATION, OR THE INITIATE RESUSCITATED IN ZAGREUS

> **"An unparalleled composition of action and narrative, as in the great frescos of the Italian masters."**
>
> Amadeo Maiuri

Pastoral scene, or birth of Zagreus

Marriage of Dionysus and Ariadne, or Dionysus and Persephone (or Korah)

Dressing of the bride, or the initiation of the initiate

The Orphic mystery
According to some interpretations, the cycle represents the initiation of a woman to the cult of Dionysus-Zagreus, or the Orphic mystery. Zagreus, son of Zeus and Persephone, was delivered by Hera to the Titans, who devoured his body. Athena enclosed his heart in a statue and breathed life into it. Thus the fresco represents the symbolic death of the initiate upon her initiation.

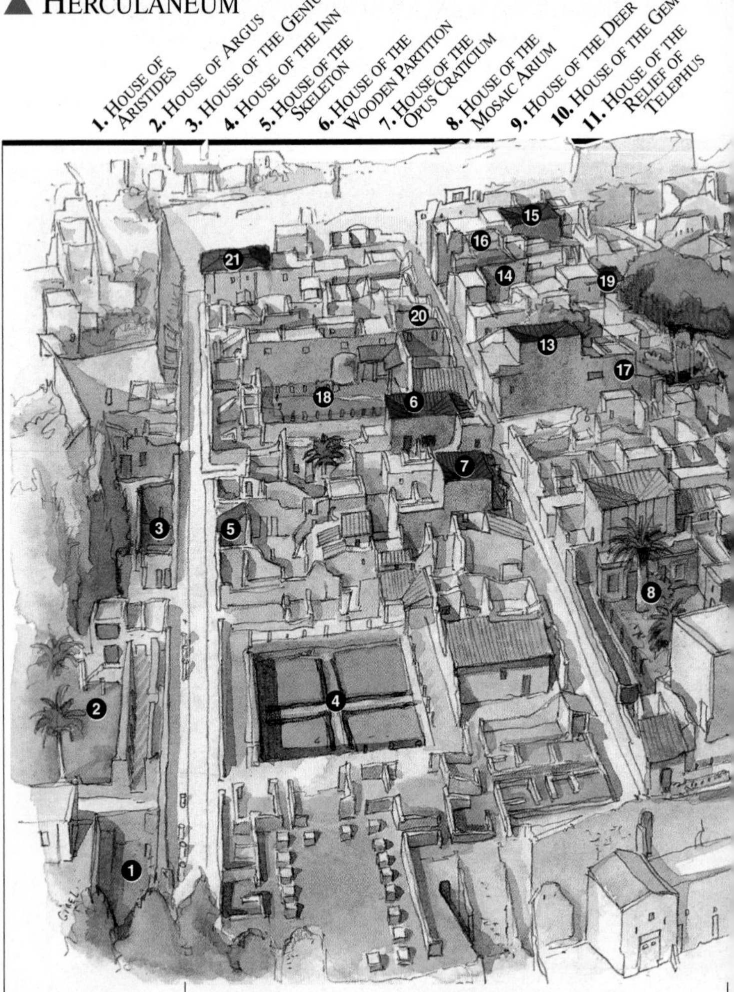

1. HOUSE OF ARISTIDES
2. HOUSE OF ARGUS
3. HOUSE OF THE GENIUS
4. HOUSE OF THE INN
5. HOUSE OF THE SKELETON
6. HOUSE OF THE WOODEN PARTITION
7. HOUSE OF THE OPUS CRATICIUM
8. HOUSE OF THE MOSAIC ATRIUM
9. HOUSE OF THE DEER
10. HOUSE OF THE GEM
11. HOUSE OF THE RELIEF OF TELEPHUS

THE DISCOVERY
In 1711 the Prince d'Elbeuf heard that a peasant had found some rare marbles while digging a well. He bought the land and began to take intensive soundings using a system of vertical shafts and horizontal galleries. In this way the first building was exposed, subsequently identified as the theater ▲ 282. Exploration continued in 1738 thanks to the interest shown by Charles of Bourbon. The piercing of the shafts and galleries, however, caused irreparable damage, and gave rise to bitter criticism.

Herculaneum was a smaller and more elegant town than Pompeii. It was buried during the eruption of AD 79 ▲ 243 by a torrent of liquid mud, lava and ash, which covered the town, slowly at first, to a depth of 65½ feet above the ancient ground level. Although this thick volcanic layer made excavation difficult, it ensured that the buildings remained in a remarkable state of preservation.

HISTORY

ORIGINS. According to legend, the town was founded by Hercules on his return from Iberia. The historian Sisenna (c. 120–67 BC) records that it was built on a small promontory overlooking the sea and was bounded by two rivers. The little historical information that exists concerning its origins states that the town was of Italic origin, passing under Greek and then (in the 5th century BC) Samnite control. At the end of the Samnite Wars (290 BC) the town formed an alliance with Rome, but rebelled in 89 BC with the aim of joining the Italic coalition. The latter proved unsuccessful and the town remained under Roman control.

A RICH RESORT. Since only a modest section of the town has been excavated, it is impossible to establish its exact size or the distribution of its public buildings. It is clear, however,

12. PALAESTRA
13. SAMNITE HOUSE
14. HOUSE OF THE NEPTUNE MOSAIC
15. HOUSE OF THE BICENTENARY
16. HOUSE OF THE BEAUTIFUL COURTYARD
17. HOUSE OF THE GREAT PORTAL
18. "THERMAE"
19. HOUSE OF THE CORINTHIAN ATRIUM
20. HOUSE OF THE BLACK HALL
21. COLLEGE OF THE AUGUSTALI
22. SUBURBAN "THERMAE"

VILLA OF THE PAPYRI
Excavations carried out in the 18th century exposed this grandiose suburban villa, to the northwest of Herculaneum. It was built on several levels, with a frontage of some 820 feet, and lay parallel to the ancient waterfront. A number of papyri (copies of Greek texts, mainly relating to Epicurean philosophy) were found in five different places in the villa, stored on shelves, in chests or simply on the floor. The villa also contained the largest collection of bronze and marble statues found in the Vesuvian cities: busts of Greek dynasts, portraits of Greek philosophers and poets, statues of wrestlers and dancers, a sleeping Mercury and a drunken faun. These statues are now in the Museo Archeologico Nazionale in Naples ▲ 164.

that during the Roman period Herculaneum was a city of some importance. Luxurious residences stood on the edge of the promontory, overlooking the Bay of Naples. Behind these lay more modest dwellings. Unlike Pompeii, there are no ruts on the paved streets to indicate the frequent passage of carts. Together with the elegance of the decorations, this suggests that Herculaneum was a residential town, chosen by the population for its tranquility and healthy environment. This theory is also borne out by its marble *opus sectile* ● 69 paving, the finest in the 1st century AD, created by expert craftsmen who used rare materials from all around the Mediterranean Basin.

INSULAE II AND III

Inside the entrance to the site, a broad pathway enables visitors to appreciate the very specific nature of the city's burial as well as the regularity of its grid layout: rectangular *insulae* defined by the intersections of the *cardi* and *decumani*. Next to the path lies the only original section of the town boundary, where the houses stretched along the waterfront. The ancient shoreline and part of the reef have recently been discovered. The rest of the site is bordered by the modern town of Ercolano ▲ 218.

House of the Opus
Craticium and *sacellum*
of the House of the
Skeleton (below).

**A SENSATIONAL
DISCOVERY**
The discovery of the
House of Argus,
between 1828 and
1830, was of
particular interest
since this was the first
time that the
perfectly preserved
upper floor of a
house had been
exposed. At the time
a balcony overlooked
the sidewalk of *cardo*
III. Wooden shelves
and cupboards still
contained
earthenware crockery
and glassware, and
even food (figs, lentils
and flour).

HOUSE OF ARISTIDES (Ins. II, 1). The lower floor of the
house, which was probably used for storing merchandise, had
been built by extending the edge of the promontory toward
the sea by means of a monumental wall in *opus reticulatum*
● 68. The entrance of the house opened directly onto the
atrium. The use of the other rooms is not clear, because of the
damage caused by the galleries pierced during the Bourbon
period, and the arbitrary restoration work carried out at the
beginning of the 19th century.
HOUSE OF ARGUS (Ins. II, 2). The house was named after a
painting (which has now disappeared) representing the myth
of Io and Argus, found in a reception room opening onto the
vast peristyle.
HOUSE OF THE GENIUS (Ins. II, 3). The house was named
after a small winged statue of a male spirit (*genius*). The only
part that can be visited is the peristyle leading to the service
rooms, with a secondary entrance on *cardo* III.
HOUSE OF THE INN (Ins. III, 1 and 9). The house, which has
two entrances, is one of the wealthiest on the waterfront. The
building, wrongly identified as an inn because of its size, is in
a poor state of repair. To the right of the atrium are the only
private *thermae* to be found in a house in Herculaneum: they
are decorated with frescos in the Second style ● 76. Below the
portico is the garden, now planted with an orchard, where the
carbonized trunk of a pear tree was discovered. The house
also has a large porticoed terrace. The partially excavated
rooms on the first floor are built on the slope of the
promontory.
HOUSE OF THE SKELETON (Ins. III, 3). In 1831 a skeleton lying
next to a bronze vase was discovered in a second-floor room.
The event caused a sensation: this was the first body
to be found inside the town, which had been abandoned by
the population when the eruption began. The house is
probably an agglomeration of three smaller houses, and the
elegance of its marble paving and paintings attests to the
wealth of the owner. The atrium, completely covered by a
roof with exterior gutters, is without the usual *impluvium*
(the basin for collecting rainwater). To the left, at the far
end of the atrium, are two small, elegant *nymphaea*.

The first is formed by two rectangular basins lined with marble, while the decoration of the panels on the far wall uses inlaid limestone. Above the *nymphaeum* is a *pâte-de-verre* frieze and a religious scene, of which only three panels remain, representing a woman making an offering, a man leading a sacrificial ram and a horn of plenty. The second *nymphaeum*, which has an iron grating to prevent thieves entering through the roof, comprises a basin and a recessed niche decorated with mosaics depicting a gorgon, as well as geometric and floral motifs.

STORE WITH A CLOTHES-PRESS (Ins. III, 10). This was probably a store that made and sold woolen sheets. A wooden clothes-press with a central spiral post, used for pressing sheets, was found inside. It is a unique example of ancient technology. The amazing state of preservation of wood in Herculaneum is caused by the high temperature of the volcanic mud that engulfed the town, with the result that the wood was carbonized by the heat.

HOUSE OF THE WOODEN PARTITION (Ins. III, 11–12). The house, overlooking *cardo* IV, was preserved to the level of the third floor. Its façade, which ends in a cornice decorated with ova, is one of the most sophisticated in the Vesuvian region. An elegant wooden partition, in which two of the three panels were hinged and had bronze handles, was found inside the impressive atrium. It was used to close the *tablinum* (reception room).

HOUSE OF THE OPUS CRATICIUM (Ins. III, 13–15). The house, intended to be used by several families, comprises two independent apartments that can be reached via nos. 13 and 14 of *cardo* IV. Both were lit by a small courtyard, and drew their water from the same well. A brightly lit, second-floor room, overlooking the street, has some partially preserved wooden furniture.

Garden of the House of the Wooden Partition.

POPULAR ARCHITECTURE
The House of the Opus Craticium is a fine example of popular architecture. In fact it was almost entirely built in *opus craticium* ● *68*, a type of masonry consisting of a wooden trellis filled with small, irregularly shaped tufa blocks and large quantities of lime. The technique was strongly criticized by Vitruvius because of the potential fire risk.

AN ANCIENT "BAR"
In Insula IV, along the lower *decumanus* and on the corner of *cardi* IV and V, are a series of modest commercial buildings (including stores that sold cereals and wine) and a *thermopolium* (nos. 15 and 16) that sold food and drink. Eight earthenware jars containing cereals and vegetables are set in the counter. A piece of Greek graffiti in the back of the store states: "Diogenes, the philosopher and cynic, seeing a woman being swept away by a river, exclaimed that a scourge was being swept away by a[nother] scourge."

Thermopolium and the House of the Relief of Telephus (below).

INSULA IV

HOUSE OF THE MOSAIC ATRIUM (Ins. IV, 1–2). The house enjoys one of the best views in Herculaneum. The atrium is decorated with a beautiful black-and-white, geometric mosaic which was curiously corrugated by the catastrophe of AD 79 ▲ *243*. The *oecus*, or banqueting hall, is divided into three naves; the central nave is higher than the others and has windows and stuccoed pilasters. The vast garden was surrounded by a portico; during the Roman period the intercolumniations were closed by windows on three sides and, on the fourth, by a glass screen with a wooden armature. This suggests that certain spaces which are now open were once closed (in this case by glass) to provide protection against climatic variations. Four *cubicula* (bedrooms), decorated with elegant frescos, open onto the eastern side of the portico, and a central *exedra* is

painted with two small mythological panels depicting the Punishment of Dirce, and Diana and Acteon, and with architectural motifs on a blue background. The area reserved for receptions, overlooking the sea, is decorated with elegant frescos in the Fourth style ● *77* and a marble pavement in *opus sectile* ● *69*.

HOUSE OF THE DEER (Ins. IV, 21). The Casa dei Cervi was one of the most luxurious waterfront residences discovered in Herculaneum. Its garden had some impressive decorations: two marble groups representing deer being attacked by dogs, a statue of a satyr holding a wine skin and another of a drunken Hercules, an elegant marble vase and a tripod decorated with cats' heads. To the right of the covered atrium, surmounted by a second-floor gallery, a staircase leads to the service rooms (dispensary, kitchen with a hearth, latrines). At the far end of the atrium a door leads into the grand *triclinium* (dining room) which is decorated with frescos in the Third style ● *77* and has the most elegant pavement excavated in Herculaneum: it virtually constitutes a complete sample of all the rare types of marble used in the 1st century AD.

The pediment of the portal opening onto the garden is decorated with a fragmented mosaic of Oceanus and a marine procession of tiny cupids. The garden is surrounded by a portico with four arcades decorated with architectural motifs and more than sixty panels (partly removed in the 18th century) representing scenes with tiny cupids, still-lifes and architectural landscapes (today housed in the Museo Archeologico Nazionale in Naples ▲ 164). Another large *triclinium*, flanked by two smaller rooms, opens onto the side of the quadriporticus that ran along the waterfront. Opposite is a pergola with a small central marble table, with gardens at either side and two siesta rooms that lead to a terrace overlooking the sea.

House of the Deer.

INSULAE ORIENTALIS I AND II

HOUSE OF THE GEM (Ins. Or. I, 1). The house was named

after a stone found there that bore the engraved effigy of Livia, found there. The atrium, with its huge panels of red and black frescos, is characterized by the fact that its walls are reinforced with pilasters. At the far end is a terrace-garden with an opening that lights the basement rooms. To the right of the atrium a narrow passageway leads to the kitchen (which has a chimney) and the latrines, where graffiti on one of the walls records the visit of Apollinaris, physician to the Emperor Titus: "*Apollinaris medicus Titi imp(eratoris) hic cacavit bene.*" Among the rooms opening onto the terrace and situated opposite the *therme suburbane* is a vast chamber whose black-and-white mosaics form a central panel, divided into twenty scenes, surrounding a rosette.

HOUSE OF THE RELIEF OF TELEPHUS (Ins. Or. I, 2–3). The atrium of the house, which is one of the largest and most luxurious in the southern district of Herculaneum, has a colonnade on two sides designed to support the rooms of the upper story (and not the roof around the *compluvium*, as is usually the case). The intercolumniations are decorated with circular marble panels (*oscilla*). The atrium opens onto the peristyle and a garden with a central basin. To the south of the peristyle, a long corridor leads to a terrace overlooking the sea. Magnificent and exceptionally colored marble decoration was discovered in a room opening off the terrace. It not only covers the pavement, but extends to the walls in the form of huge panels separated by demi-columns.

PALAESTRA ● *73* (Ins. Or. II, 4). The partially excavated Palaestra occupies a large part of the Insula Orientalis II and has a frontage of over 260 feet, extending as far as the

THE "RELIEF OF TELEPHUS"
(center)
The "Relief of Telephus" was discovered in one of the rooms overlooking the sea. It recounts the myth of Telephus, the legendary King of Mysia, son of Heracles and Auge. He was suckled by a doe (*elaphos*), and found by a shepherd who gave him to Teuthras, King of Mysia. Having succeeded Teuthras, Telephus was wounded by Achilles, but was healed by the rust on his opponent's spear. The relief is a neo-Attic original from the late 1st century BC. The Pentelican marble plaque depicts two scenes: Achilles consulting the oracle, who tells him that he will not take Troy without Telephus' leadership, and Achilles healing the wound on Telephus' thigh.

"DECUMANUS MAXIMUS"
Unlike the *decumanus maximus* in Pompeii (which was paved), the main street in Herculaneum was made of beaten earth. It was about 40 feet wide, with broad sidewalks, and was closed to vehicles by the installation of small travertine pilasters, while a high step blocked access to *cardo* IV. In the section of the street currently being excavated are two travertine fountains (above) and, on the north side, a portico with stores on the first floor and living accommodation on the second; these contain numerous wooden objects, including a window with shutters and a door. At the far end, in the direction of *cardo* III, is a monumental arch with a stuccoed vault and, on either side, marble plinths for statues.

decumanus maximus. Its walls were built during the post-Augustan period, in *opus reticulatum* ● 68 reinforced by alternate bricks and small tufa blocks. Along *cardo* V a number of stores, built against the monumental edifice, supplied the needs of the public who frequented the Palaestra. They include two bakeries (nos. 1 and 8), which still contain their lava millstones, and a store (no. 9) that sold wine, with a console for the amphorae. The entrance to the Palaestra (no. 4) consists of a rectangular room with a vaulted ceiling, preceded by two columns. At the center of the open area, surrounded by a portico with four arcades, is a cruciform swimming pool where a monumental bronze fountain (a five-headed serpent entwined round a tree trunk) once stood. This has now been replaced by a copy. Above and to one side of the pool is a rectangular basin which may have been used as a fish tank. In the center of the portico, on the wall running parallel to *cardo* V, is a monumental recessed room, originally vaulted, which contained a central marble platform where the winning athletes received their prizes. The north side of the area is closed by a cryptoporticus whose upper story comprises a gallery and a grandiose room linked to the *decumanus maximus*. The entire Palaestra was decorated with sophisticated pictorial and marble decorations, mostly destroyed or removed during the 18th century. The Museo Archeologico Nazionale in Naples ▲ 164 now houses the so-called panel of the Actor King (its exact position in the Palaestra is not known) and another large panel depicting theatrical décor that formed part of the recessed room, where a few fragments of the decoration still exist *in situ*.

INSULA V

HOUSE OF THE NEPTUNE MOSAIC
The house was named after the mosaic panel representing Neptune and Amphitrite. The sides are decorated with a fresco of garden scenes.

SAMNITE HOUSE ★ (Ins. V, 1). The house, which dates from the 2nd century BC, has the typical layout of a pre-Roman house: an entrance leading to the atrium and *tablinum* (terrace). The portal of the entrance has Corinthian capitals and is surmounted by a gallery built as part of the extension of the upper floor, which could only be reached via the staircase at no. 2. The entrance is decorated with frescos in the First style ● *76*, imitating polychrome marble. It leads onto the atrium which has an elegant gallery with Ionic columns and a stuccoed transenna, and is open to the south. To the right of the entrance is one of the few rooms with a green monochrome, extremely elegant fresco. It is decorated with architectural motifs, hangings and in the center, a small panel illustrating the Rape of Europa.

HOUSE OF THE NEPTUNE MOSAIC AND WINE STORE ★

(Ins. V, 6–7). The owner of the house also had a wine store, open to the street, which is the best preserved store in the entire Vesuvian region. Its wooden fittings are intact: shelves for amphorae, the balustrade of the balcony and, behind the counter, a partition with two grilles. Broad beans and chick peas were found in the large vases set in the masonry of the counter. The house proper has a summer *triclinium* decorated with elegant wall mosaics whose *pâte de verre* creates a strikingly colorful effect.

HOUSE OF THE BICENTENARY

(Ins. V, 15–16). The house, discovered by Amadeo Maiuri in 1938, was named after the bicentenary celebrations being held that year to commemorate the beginning of the excavation of Herculaneum. The entrance, situated between stores and modest dwellings, opens onto the *decumanus maximus*. To the right of the vast atrium are several bedrooms, the last of which is closed by an unusual wooden grille. At the far end, the *tablinum* has a superb marble pavement and two large panels, one representing Daedalus and Pasiphae and the other Venus and Mars, surmounted by a frieze of tiny cupids. Beyond the *tablinum* is a porticoed garden with a staircase, on the right, leading to the upper floor. This consisted of several modest dwellings and was probably separate from the rest of the house. A white stucco panel

THE HOUSE OF THE BEAUTIFUL COURTYARD
(Ins. V, 8)
The house, which bears a striking resemblance to 14th- and 15th-century Italian houses, has an atypical layout. The entrance opens directly onto a rectangular room which leads to the service rooms and the "beautiful courtyard". The courtyard is raised and has a mosaic pavement and an elegant staircase leading to the second floor. On the first floor a vast rectangular reception room is decorated with frescos in the Third style ● *77*.

"NYMPHAEUM" OF THE HOUSE OF THE NEPTUNE MOSAIC
The *nymphaeum* is surmounted by a head of Silenus and marble theatrical masks. The sides of the central recessed niche are decorated with geometric and floral motifs and hunting scenes with dogs and deer.

Painted theatrical masks in the House of the Great Portal.

with a cruciform cavity was discovered on the far wall of a small room. According to Maiuri, it was intended to hold a wooden cross, which would make it the oldest-known Christian symbol. Below it was a low, wooden cupboard with a predella, probably used as an altar. A more recent interpretation suggests that the cavity was simply used to support a wooden tablet.

HOUSE OF THE GREAT PORTAL (Ins. V, 35). The building was named after the elegant portal consisting of brick demi-columns (originally stuccoed), surmounted by Corinthian capitals carved with winged Victories. The *triclinium* is decorated with a small panel illustrating a Dionysian theme. Next to the entrance is a small open courtyard designed to make the surrounding rooms lighter and where terracotta conduits channeled the rainwater into a cistern. Two rooms open onto the courtyard: a vestibule, decorated with architectural motifs painted against a black background and a panel depicting birds pecking at cherries, and a room painted with elegant architectural motifs representing hangings.

INSULA VI

"THERMAE" ★, ▲ *258* (Ins. VI, 1–10).
The *thermae*, built at the beginning of the 1st century AD, are divided into men's and women's baths, each with their own respective entrance, on *cardi* III and IV, at nos. 1 and 8. The men's baths, preceded by the latrines, are entered directly from the *apodyterium* (undressing room), which contains a *labrum* (basin), at the far end, and another small basin for the preliminary ablutions performed before entering the other rooms. The circular *frigidarium*, on the left, has a vaulted ceiling decorated with fish and a pool with steps down into the water. To the right are the *tepidarium*, decorated with a mosaic pavement resting on the heating system (*suspensurae*), and the *caldarium* (also with *suspensurae*). The women's baths, preceded by a waiting room, consist of an *apodyterium* decorated with elegant mosaics

The *caldarium* of the men's baths.

THE HOUSE OF THE CORINTHIAN ATRIUM (Ins. V, 30)
The entrance, preceded by a portico, leads to an atrium whose six columns are arranged around a small *impluvium* converted into a garden. In the center is a marble cruciform fountain. To the right of the entrance is a room with a fine mosaic pavement and, to the left, the service rooms which lead to the upper floor. At the far end of the atrium is a vast *triclinium*.

representing Triton, a *tepidarium* decorated with meanders and squares, and a *caldarium*, with a rectangular basin for immersions and a circular *labrum* for ablutions. The vaulted ceiling of the *caldarium* is grooved to collect the condensation. Opposite the baths is a large porticoed garden where customers could exercise or relax. At the back of the building (at no. 10) are the service rooms, a deep well and a *praefurnium* (boiler room) with boilers for heating the water and air.

HOUSE OF THE BLACK HALL (Ins. VI, 11, 13). The many wooden objects found in the house included part of the moldings for the roof and main entrance. The house is characterized by a vast painted hall, decorated with elegant architectural motifs in the Fourth style ● 77 against a black background. In a room near the atrium, twenty wax tablets were discovered which bore the name of L. Venidus Enniychus, probably the owner, as well as a number of texts concerning his eligibility for the office of *sevir Augustalis* and the birth of a daughter by his wife Livia Acte.

COLLEGE OF THE AUGUSTALI (Ins. VI, 21–22). This was the seat of the Augustali, who presided over the imperial cult. It is built according to an almost square layout, with four central columns designed to support the roof. In the center of the far wall is a room with a marble pavement in *opus sectile* ● 69 and frescos in the Fourth style ● 77, including two large panels representing Hercules, Juno, Minerva, and Hercules and Acheloos. The small room to the right was reserved for the porter, whose body was found on the bed.

STORES (Ins. VI, 12, 14, 15, 19) Built against the houses on the side of the *insula* facing the *decumanus maximus* were the store of a lead craftsman (no. 12), what was probably a wine store (no. 14), a store that sold crockery (no. 15; inside was a chest containing glassware which bore the mark of the workshop of Ampliatus) and a *thermopolium*, or tavern (no. 19). On the workbench of the first store was a three-branched candlestick and a celebrated bronze statue of Dionysus, with silver and copper damascening. It was broken in three pieces and was apparently waiting to be restored.

Mosaic of Triton in the women's baths of the *thermae*.

THEATER

The entrance is situated outside the excavation area, about 380 yards from the entrance to the archeological site, on the Corso Resina. Since the theater is still buried, it can only be reached through a section of the Bourbon galleries. Two staircases, at either end of the lower portico, lead to a stuccoed corridor whose walls are covered in graffiti left by visitors at various points in the theater's history. Behind the stage are the remains of the monumental *scaenae frons*, whose decorative marbles and statues were removed during the 18th-century excavations. In a gallery, at the back of the stage, is an impression left in the volcanic mud and lava by the head of a statue.

THE SUBURBAN DISTRICT

This district occupies a large section of the waterfront, which lies below the level of the town. It is reached by two narrow ramps at the end of *cardi* IV and V.

THERME SUBURBANE ▲ *258*. The *impluvium* of the original vestibule is bordered by four columns above which a double series of semicircular arches rises to the centrally pierced vault. An elegant bust of Apollo stands on a pilaster emitting a jet of water into a basin. A corridor leads to the *frigidarium*, with its rectangular ablutions basin, and to an intermediary room whose stuccoed walls are decorated with the figures of warriors. To the left of this room are the *tepidarium*, almost entirely occupied by a basin resting on *suspensurae*, and the *laconicum* (steam bath). To the right is the *caldarium*, with the impressive imprint made by the basin as it was overturned and dragged for almost 6½ feet by the volcanic mud and lava that came in through the window.

THE ANCIENT SHORELINE. On the ancient beach, twelve arcades contain a number of skeletons, a poignant testimony to the final attempts of the inhabitants to escape from the eruption. Among the objects found here were a set of bronze and metal surgical instruments and some sumptuous women's jewelry (rings, earrings, two magnificent bracelets and a splendid gold chain some 5½ feet long that was worn round the shoulders and crossed over the chest). An overturned boat, with most of the hull preserved, was found near the Therme Suburbane.

GULF OF SALERNO

1. BAIA DI IERANTO 2. **POSITANO** 3. LI GALLI 4. VETTICA MAGGIORE 5. PRAIANO 6. VALLONE DEL FURORE 7. GROTTA DELLO SMERALDO

Positano.

The "Costiera Amalfitana", stretching from the Punta della Campanella to Salerno, is one of the most famous panoramic coastal routes in the world. It runs high above the Mediterranean, passing through towns and villages that date from ancient times. This vast coastal balcony can be approached from Sorrento via Sant'Agata dei Due Golfi, which lies between the Bay of Naples and the Gulf of Salerno; via the Colli di Chiunzi, overlooking the ancient plain of the River Sarno; or from Salerno, in the south. Seen from the sea, the coastline is characterized by high peaks and terraces, hewn out of the sheer walls of rock over the centuries for the cultivation of citrus fruit and olives.

POSITANO TO AMALFI

POSITANO ★. The tiny pastel-colored houses of Positano cling to the sun-drenched, rocky slopes of the Amalfi Coast, above arched porticos and vaulted passageways. This ancient coastal town, founded by the inhabitants of Paestum ▲ 296, is today one of the world's most famous resorts. A compact network of narrow streets and flights of steps leads to a beautiful beach facing the two tiny islands of Li Galli, a favorite port of call for pleasure cruisers, and the former home of the great Russian ballet dancer, Rudolf Nureyev. Several hamlets perched between sea and sky high above the town offer some spectacular walks: in particular, the Sentiero degli Dei ("pathway of the gods"), a footpath that crosses the slopes of the Monti Lattari from

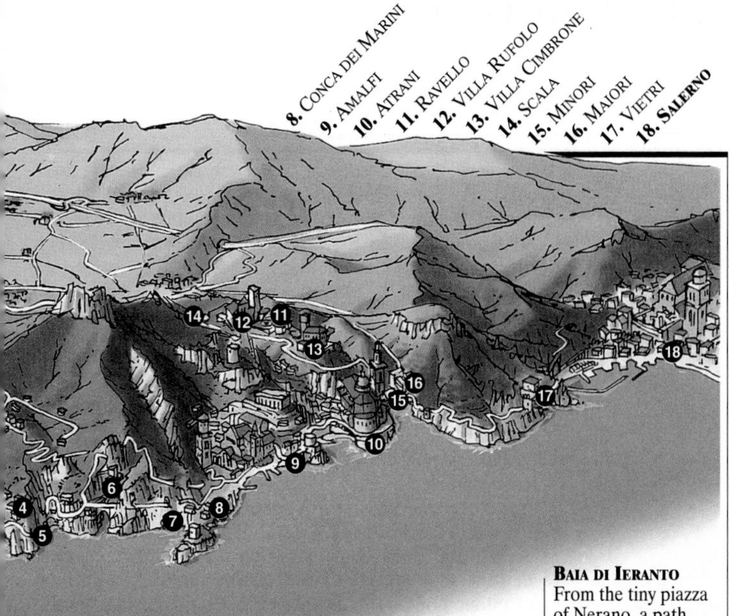

Positano to Agerola, with its magnificent panoramic views of the coast; grottos, natural caves and limestone rocks; old peasant houses, and the village of Nocelle, which has no road and has remained unspoilt over the centuries.

NATURE AND ARCHITECTURE. Vettica Maggiore and Praiano, perched on the rocky hillside above the sea, lie on the road to the Vallone del Furore, where the sea surges between the rocky walls of this formidable gorge. A footpath leads to the recently restored CHURCH OF SANT'ELIA PROFETA, which has capitals dating from the 13th century but is today decorated in elaborate late-Baroque style. Inside, a triptych by Angelo Antonelli of Capua (1479) represents a Virgin and Child flanked by saints Elijah and Bartholomew. Bordering the road is a small esplanade from where a flight of steps and lift lead down to the GROTTA DELLO SMERALDO ★, a magnificent natural cave where the sea is colored emerald by the light that filters through the rock. The grotto can also be reached by boat from Amalfi. About half a mile further on is the old

BAIA DI IERANTO
From the tiny piazza of Nerano, a path winds its way through the olive groves that cling to the narrow terraces perched high above the sea. It passes an isolated Aragonese tower and runs through bushes of rosemary before emerging onto another terrace, also planted with olive trees, overlooking the island of Capri ▲ 226. Then the path forks: one way leads to the Nature Reserve of Ieranto and the other to a peaceful creek. The reserve was founded in 1985 following the donation of an old disused quarry, and has been recolonized with Mediterranean plants.

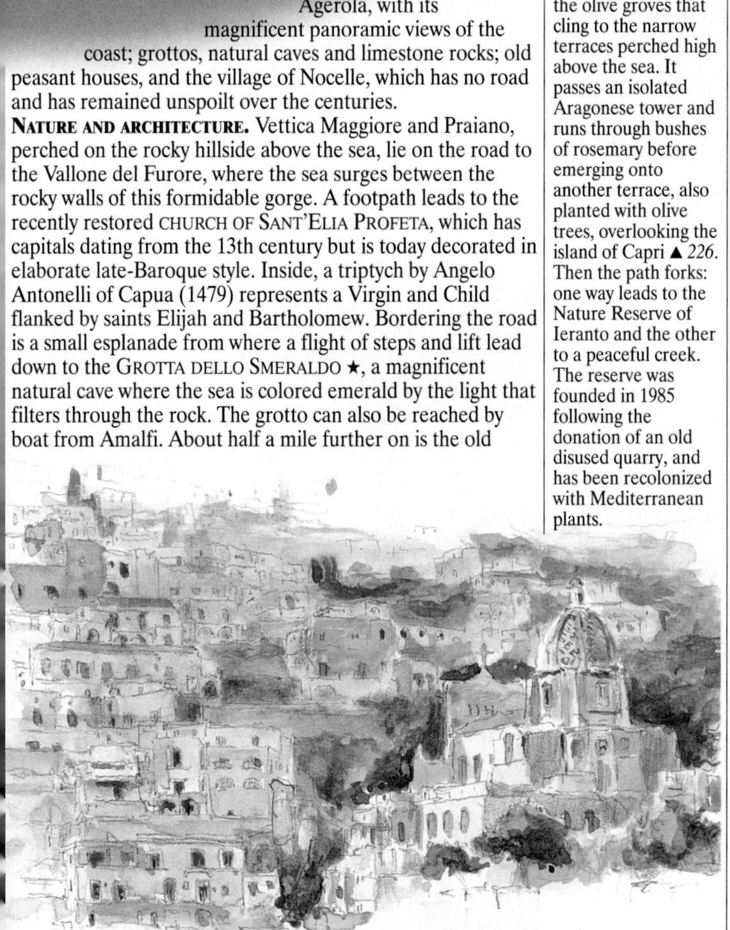

285

VALLONE DEL FURORE
Behind the Piazza del Duomo in Amalfi lies the narrow Valle dei Mulini, once occupied by a series of paper mills (some of which still exist), mills and a forge which harnessed the energy of the many mountain streams. Like the Vallone del Furore, the valley is of great botanical interest. A plentiful supply of running water and a particularly good aspect have preserved the subtropical climate that characterized the entire region before the Ice Age. Thus some very ancient species, such as the fern, *Woodwardia radicans*, are still found in the valley today.

fishing village of CONCA DEI MARINI ★ (below) where the convent of Santa Rosa has been converted into holiday homes. The nuns of the convent used to make *sfogliata Santa Rosa*, delicious flaky pastries filled with cream and ricotta cheese. Neighboring Amalfi is preceded by the Hotel Santa Catarina, one of the most elegant on the coast, and, at the entrance to the town, the Capuchin convent, now also a luxury hotel.

AMALFI

HISTORY. The town, which dates from the time of the Roman Empire, subsequently became part of the Duchy of Naples. It was besieged by the Lombards and then sacked by Sicardo, Prince of Benevento, who deported the inhabitants to Salerno in 836. On the death of the despot, in 839, Amalfiti rebelled, freeing itself from Neapolitan control, and became Italy's first maritime republic. For more than three hundred years it was an autonomous and active power that controlled the markets of the Mediterranean. The republic issued its own laws, including the first nautical code: the *Tabula Amalfitana*. The code was adopted by all the contemporary maritime republics and by the navy of the Kingdom of Naples, which continued to use it until 16th century. It also minted silver and gold *tari*, its own coins engraved on both sides with the symbolic cross of Amalfi.

THE DUOMO. The cathedral, dedicated to Sant' Andrea, was built in the 9th and was partially transformed in the 11th century, since when it has been modified several times. The façade, rebuilt in the 19th century, has a mosaic of Christ enthroned between symbols of the Evangelists and the Earthly Powers.

The main portal of the Duomo has an Assumption painted in the lunette by Domenico Morelli and a magnificent bronze Byzantine door, the oldest of four medieval doors on the Amalfi Coast (the other three are the doors of the Duomo di Salerno ▲ *293*, of San Salvatore di Birecto in Atrani ▲ *288* and of Ravello ▲ *289*). It was the work of Simeon of Syria and was commissioned by the wealthy merchant, Pantaleone di Mauro, in 1065. The Roman campanile (12th and 13th centuries) is decorated with interlaced arches, a distinctly Islamic feature that characterizes the architecture of Salerno and the Amalfi Coast. One of the finest and most sophisticated examples is found in the small Chiostro del Paradiso, beyond the atrium of the cathedral, where slender twin columns support pointed, interlaced arches in a movement of effortless harmony. The same Oriental style with its wealth of polychrome mosaics is found in the cloisters of the Capuchin convent and the monastery of San Francesco (now the Hotel Luna), and in the cloister of the Villa Rufolo, in Ravello.

CHAPEL OF THE CRUCIFIX. The chapel was built against the left-hand wall of the principal nave of the Duomo in the 9th century, incorporating a small 6th-century basilica. It was Amalfi's first cathedral, initially dedicated to Our Lady of the Assumption and then to saints Como and Damian before it was renamed the Chapel of the Crucifix in the 16th century. The two lateral chapels of the left nave contain two beautiful frescos, one 14th and the other 15th–16th century. The Madonna Enthroned, painted on a pillar near the triumphal arch, the Christ in Majesty and the Marriage of Saint Catherine are all examples of 15th-century art. The frescos in the first chapel are of particular interest, especially the figures of the town's patron saints, Como and Damian.

HISTORIC REGATTA AND PROCESSION
Each year, the Italy's ancient maritime republics (Venice,

Pisa, Genoa and Amalfi) take it in turn to organize a regatta in which their appropriately colored vessels (blue for Amalfi) compete. It is preceded by a procession in period costume, evoking the past glories of these cities.

GROTTA DELLO SMERALDO
The grotto, a karstic cave that lies partly below and partly above sea level, is one of the most representative of the Amalfi Coast. It is situated between Conca dei Marini and Praiano and was not discovered until 1932. Light filters through an opening in the rock and gives the water the extraordinary color after which the grotto is named.

VILLAS AND GARDENS

The superb garden architecture of the Amalfi Coast is a fine example of the close relationship between Man and Nature that characterizes this region. The magnificent hillside gardens of the VILLA RUFOLO ★ (opposite page, bottom left) were created in the 13th century. They were much loved by Wagner (works by the great German composer are played here every year) and Boccaccio dedicated one of the stories in his *Decameron* to the villa's wealthy owner, Landolfo Rufolo, who became a pirate to undermine Genoese competition. The VILLA CIMBRONE (opposite page, bottom right), about twenty minutes away, has another idyllic garden. Situated at the end of the promontory of Ravello, it commands an unrivalled view of the coast, from Atrani to Salerno and the Punta Licosa.

ATRANI

This delightful and typically medieval village looks out across the gulf from a sheer clifftop at the end of the valley of the Dragone. It dates from the period of the decline of the Roman Empire and, until the 16th century, shared the fortunes of Amalfi, of which it formed an elegant "suburb".

The doges were elected and buried in the church of San Salvatore di Birecto, built in 940 and extensively modified in the 19th century. Its bronze Byzantine doors, presented (1087) by the aristocrat Pantaleone Viarecta, were divided into panels decorated with reliefs. Today they are preserved in the collegiate church of Santa Maria Maddalena (1274, modified in 1852).

RAVELLO ★

Ravello clings 1,150 feet above the sea to the terraced ramparts which separate the valleys of the Dragone and Reginna.

HISTORY. The wealthy merchant families of Ravello built prestigious residences that reflected the artistic expressions of the town's golden age: from the Romano-Byzantine to the Norman-Saracenic architectural styles. Ravello was one of the jewels in the crown of the Duchy of Amalfi and shared its history. This flourishing medieval

PULPIT OF THE DUOMO OF RAVELLO
The rectangular pulpit stands on six small Solomonic columns, supported by six lions, and is richly decorated with classical-style mosaics and bas-reliefs. The projecting lectern is supported by a colonnette surmounted by an eagle.

town occupied a vast area surrounded by triple fortifications. It had many churches, convents and sumptuous palaces. Its diocese enjoyed the privilege of answering only to the Holy See, and it welcomed such illustrious figures as Boccaccio (who described it in his *Decameron*), Charles II, Robert of Anjou and Pope Hadrian II.
DUOMO ★. The duomo, founded in 1086, was initially dedicated to Our Lady of the Assumption and then to San Pantaleone, the town's patron saint. The façade, which has been entirely rebuilt, has an elegant marble portal with a bronze door by Barisano da Trani (1179). Its eighty panels represent saints, scenes from the Passion and plant motifs. To the right, the 13th-century campanile is crowned with interlaced arches. Inside is the magnificent PULPIT by Niccolò di Bartolomeo da Foggia, commissioned by the aristocrat Nicolò Rufolo (1272). Opposite is the beautiful AMBO, built between 1034 and 1150 by the bishop Constantino Rogadeo and formerly used for reading the Gospel. Its magnificent mosaic decoration includes a representation of Jonah being swallowed and regurgitated by the whale, a symbol of death and resurrection. In the chapel to the left of the apse, a phial containing the blood of San Pantaleone (which liquefies like that of San Gennaro ▲ *158*) stands on a magnificent altar decorated with red, green and yellow marble inlay. The crypt contains a museum of precious objects, including a marble bust of Sigilgaita Rufolo, a fine example of art from the reign of Frederick II of Sicily (13th century).
RELIGIOUS ITINERARY. Among Ravello's many churches, the 13th-century church of SANTA MARIA A GRADILLO, surmounted by a small Sicilian-Saracenic campanile and an original dome, is particularly worthy of note. SAN GIOVANNI DEL TORO (1018) has an extremely beautiful ambo (Alfano da Termoli, 12th century), richly decorated with mosaics and supported by four Egyptian columns with elaborately worked capitals, while the façades of SANTISSIMA ANNUNZIATA (13th century) are entirely covered with gray and white stone inlay. According to tradition, the CHURCH OF SAN FRANCESCO (1222) and the adjoining convent were built at the instigation of Francis of Assisi himself. Although it was renovated in the 18th century, San Francesco still has its 13th-century cloister.

PAPER MILLS
Paper mills once stood along the banks of the River Canneto, which is today partly covered. A descendant of one of the old paper-manufacturing families (Amatruda) still uses traditional methods and materials. A museum dedicated to the history of paper-making in Amalfi has been opened in the Cartiera of Nicola Milano, a former paper mill.

SCALA. The DUOMO, dedicated to San Lorenzo at the end of the 11th century, is one of the region's most important religious edifices. Although it was modified in the 18th century, it still has a fine Romanesque portal with sculpted uprights. The church of Santa Maria Annunziata (11th–12th century), in the hamlet of MINUTA, is one of the finest examples of Romanesque architecture on the Amalfi Coast. The portals are surmounted by Byzantine-style frescos, while the crypt is decorated with a cycle of 12th-century frescos that constitutes an important example of medieval Amalfitan art.

MINORI. The coastal town of Minori, formerly Reginna Minor, has a small beach bordered by a public garden containing an 11th-century fountain decorated with lions. In the Middle Ages Minori shared the fortunes of neighboring Amalfi, to the point of housing the arsenals of the Republic. The plentiful supply of water from the valley favored the establishment of paper-making and pasta industries. Today Minori cultivates and exports citrus fruit. The crypt (restored in the 18th century) of the BASILICA OF SANTA TROFIMENA contains an alabaster urn, sculpted by Gennaro Ragozzino (1722), containing the remains of the saint. In the center of the valley, near the sea, are the remains of a magnificent Roman villa, probably dating from the reign of Augustus. Discovered by chance in 1932, it was buried by the alluvium deposited during the floods of 1954, and later re-excavated. The villa's truly remarkable heating system (a series of conduits and chambers that channeled the hot air from a boiler throughout the house) attests to the Romans' technological achievements.

MAIORI. Maiori, originally named Reginna Maior to distinguish it from neighboring Minori, was founded in the 11th century by Sicardo, Prince of Salerno. It was sacked in the 12th century by the Pisans, the rivals of the Republic of Amalfi, and decreed a royal town by Philip V in the 17th century. Although this small town was significantly changed by the alluvium deposited by the floods that virtually destroyed it in 1954, it still has sections of its old enclosure walls and some of its watchtowers.

CERAMICS MUSEUM OF VIETRI

The history of the ceramics of Vietri is documented by items found and preserved in the Benedictine abbey of Cava, whose museum contains 15th- and 16th-century majolica tiles. Since 1922 Vietri has had its own ceramics museum in the *torretta* of the Villa Guariglia (below), the residence of the Italian king, Vittorio Emanuele during the Salerno Government (1943). It has a comprehensive and elegant collection of ceramics from different periods: from early pottery and tiles, through the so-called German period of the 1950's to modern ceramics. The collection is being continually enriched by donations from private collectors. The concept and location of the museum were the idea of the writer Elena Croce.

The CHURCH OF SANTA MARIA A MARE was built in the 13th century on the site of the ancient fortress of Sant'Angelo and rebuilt during the Baroque period. It is thought to have been named after the wooden statue of the Virgin on the high-altar, said to have been found on the beach of Maiori after a storm. SANTA MARIA DI OLEARIA, which lies, somewhat unexpectedly, between Maiori and Erchie, was probably named after the many olive groves and oil mills that once dominated this part of the hillside. Its first occupant was Pietro, a 10th-century hermit who withdrew to a cave with his nephew Giovanni. The latter founded a small convent whose three chapels are superposed in the vast, natural cavity. The traces of wall paintings suggest that the church must have been entirely decorated with frescos. Several styles co-exist – from figures of obvious Byzantine inspiration to Renaissance images – attesting to the continuation of the cult over the centuries.

VIETRI

Vietri has been renowned since the Middle Ages for its ceramics, which form an integral part of the decoration of its buildings and churches (San Giovanni Battista, Confraternita del Rosario). It was founded by the Etruscans in the small valley of the River Bonea, conquered by the Samnites, and destroyed by the

COASTAL TOWERS
In 1563 the Spanish viceroy Don Parafán de Ribera, Duke of Alcalà, had a system of watchtowers constructed throughout southern Italy. They were built close together to form a kind of

"liaison net" in which it was possible to communicate by signals. The truncated pyramidal towers built on square bases that can be seen on this route (Vettica, Amalfi, Atrani, Maiori, Cetara, Erchie and Vietri) were part of this system.

291

The School of Medicine of Salerno was renowned throughout medieval Europe. In the early Middle Ages Salerno, nourished by Greco-Roman traditions, stood at the commercial and cultural crossroads of the Western and Eastern worlds and Africa, whose influence was felt via Amalfi and Sicily. The great cultural renaissance linked to the Benedictine philosophy, particularly well represented in Salerno by the monks of the convent of San Benedetto, also played an important part in the development of scientific studies and practical medicine. Salerno was a town of convents, several of which functioned as hospitals. Pilgrims and soldiers were given shelter and treated with medicinal herbs grown by the monks in their *herbarium*. Although founded in the 9th century, the School of Medicine's earliest surviving works date from the 11th century. The first document in which the school is mentioned as a fully fledged institution is one of the texts in Frederick II's Constitution of Melfi (1231), in which it was cited as the only school of its kind in the kingdom. A small church in the historic center of Salerno today houses a museum containing facsimiles of the works of the "Four Masters of Salerno"

Vandals in 455. Grimoaldo, Prince of Salerno, captivated by its position on the sun-drenched Gulf of Salerno, chose it for his residence. Today Vietri is a popular resort.

SALERNO

The historic center of Salerno fans out along the waterfront, below the terraces of the Lombard castle.

HISTORY. The Etruscan and Samnite necropolises excavated at San Nicola delle Fratte (half a mile to the north of the town), have made it possible to ascribe the origins of Salerno to the 5th century BC. The Roman colony of Salernum was founded in 194 BC, but it was under the Lombards and especially the Normans, who made the town their capital in 1077, that it really prospered. It began to decline in the 13th century with the accession of the Angevins, who favored Naples.

A CITY OF CONVENTS. This beautiful medieval town still has its enclosure walls and its thirty-six convents, most of which are still standing (although they are now public buildings, barracks or have been abandoned). There were many religious orders in Salerno, attracted by the healthy climate and security of the town, protected by the castle and ramparts. The Benedictines founded the monasteries of San Benedetto, San Lorenzo, Santa Maria Monialium, San Leone and San Nicola della Palma, and the Franciscans founded San Francesco, which was subsequently converted into a prison. The Dominicans and Capuchins were also well represented. The churches in many of the convents are still used for

AN IMPORTANT MARKETPLACE. In 1258 King Manfred of Swabia founded the fair of Salerno, with a view to increasing the town's commercial activity following the construction of its port. The fair became an important Mediterranean trading event and was held twice a year, on September 21 (the festival of San Matteo, the patron saint of Salerno) and on April 4 (the anniversary of the translation of the saint's relics).

worship and contain an important part of the town's artistic heritage.

CHURCH OF SAN GIORGIO. The church, once annexed to the Benedictine convent, was converted into a barracks for the Carabinieri and the Guardia di Finanza. Its magnificent Baroque stuccowork attests to the importance attached to the decoration of their church by these aristocratic nuns.

DUOMO ★. The Duomo was built after the Norman conquest of the town led by Robert Guiscard (1015–85), to celebrate the latter's victory over the Lombards, and dedicated to San Matteo. It was built in Romanesque style, inspired by the basilica of the abbey of Montecassino (Latium), and was modified several times following floods and earthquakes, before being completely rebuilt and covered with Baroque structures in the 18th century. At the top of the great staircase the beautiful PORTA DEI LEONI opens onto a neoclassical façade: the two lions decorating the uprights are a fine example of southern Italian Romanesque sculpture (11th century), as is the magnificent colonnade of the atrium (partially restored) with its Oriental arcatures and inlaid polychrome decoration. The portal has a bronze door cast in Constantinople in 1099. THE INTERIOR of the cathedral reveals the earlier Romanesque structures incorporated into the huge pillars supporting the three naves. The central nave is flanked by two magnificent 12th-century ambos, whose richness of form and color complements the elegance of the stonework and the architectural lines. On the left is the cubic ambo presented by the archbishop, Romuald II Guarna. It has a projecting lectern and is supported by four granite columns surmounted by finely sculpted capitals. Dating from about the same period as the Chiostro di Monreale, it is in fact closer to the classical and early Christian tradition than the beautiful sculptures of the Sicilian abbey. The so-called Ajello ambo, to the right, is rectangular in shape and supported by twelve smooth-shafted columns surmounted by capitals as elaborately decorated as those of its counterpart. Its two projecting lecterns are supported by some remarkable sculptures. The nave also contains an impressive paschal candlestick and has a 12th-century mosaic pavement. The lateral naves and transept house a number of works of art, including the

"LA ROTONDA"
The fair of Salerno, moved to the Portanova district so that it was nearer the sea for the unloading of merchandise, was abolished in 1809. But the district still has a famous market held in the piazza that the Salernitans call "La Rotonda".

293

Atrium of the Duomo.

HEAD OF APOLLO
In 1930 divers recovered a bronze head of Apollo from the depths of the Gulf of Salerno. The sculpture was in the late-Hellenistic style and attributed to the Campanian artist Pasiteles (first half of the 1st century BC). It has become the emblem of the Museo Archeologico.

magnificent marble tomb of Margaret of Anjou, wife of Charles II, by the sculptor Baboccio da Piperno (early 15th century). The CRYPT, like that of the Duomo of Amalfi, was entirely rebuilt in Baroque style. The MUSEO DEL DUOMO contains the magnificent Salernitan cycle, one of the richest collections of medieval Christian (12th century) ivory panels in the world. Since the early Middle Ages the degree ceremonies of the School of Medicine (which has no other known seat) have been held in the adjoining rooms of San Tommaso and San Lazzaro.

MUSEO PROVINCIALE. The archeological museum, housed in the restored buildings of the former abbey of San Benedetto, has a wealth of documentation on the province from prehistoric times to the end of the Roman Empire. The lapidary museum in the entrance contains mainly Roman pieces: statues, inscriptions and cinerary urns. On the first floor are Paleolithic stone tools from Palinuro, objects found in the Grotta di Polla (occupied from the Neolithic to the classical period), and Bronze Age objects found in the Grotta di Pertosa. Items found during the excavations carried out in the valley of the Sarno, at Montecorvino Rovella and Oliveto Citra, have helped to clarify the "grave" burial culture, just as objects found at Sala Consilina and Pontecagnano shed light on the Villanovian "cinerary urn" culture. On the second floor are objects found during the Etruscan-Samnite excavations at Fratte.

CAVA DE' TIRRENI

The flourishing ancient town of Marcina stretched from the sea to the Metelliana valley, between Salerno and what is now the Amalfi Coast. According to Strabo it was founded by the Tyrians, a view that was confirmed by Pliny. Now known as Cava, the town increased in importance under the Lombards, when Prince Gisulf II presented it with the abbey of the Santissima Trinità. The tradition of pigeon-netting, still practiced today on certain occasions, probably originated with the Lombards. But it was Ferdinand I of Aragon who, in 1460, introduced the Disfida dei Trombonieri (Challenge of the Trombonieri), a traditional festival in which hundreds of people dressed in period costume celebrate the defense of the town against the Angevin troops.

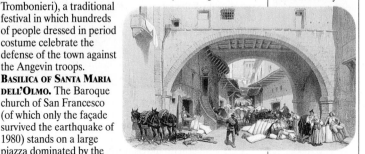

BASILICA OF SANTA MARIA DELL'OLMO. The Baroque church of San Francesco (of which only the façade survived the earthquake of 1980) stands on a large piazza dominated by the basilica of Santa Maria dell'Olmo. According to tradition the basilica was originally a chapel built by the inhabitants of the town of Cava to ward off the constant attacks made by bandits upon travelers on their way to Nuceria.

BORGO DEGLI SCHIACCIAVENTI. The district corresponds to the 15th-century town of Cava: a street bordered by artisans' stores and the small churches of the brotherhoods. In 1396 Cava became a diocese under the jurisdiction of the abbot of the Santissima Trinità.

ABBEY OF THE SANTISSIMA TRINITÀ. The abbey was founded in 1011 by Alferio Pappacarbone (Saint Alferius), a Salernitan noble and Benedictine, who is said to have died there at the age of 120. This religious and cultural center was a veritable economic power since it controlled a congregation of 150 abbeys and 300 churches that lay along the route between Rome and Palermo. The church, consecrated by Urban II in 1095, has a Baroque façade in volcanic stone and is built in the form of a triple-naved Latin cross. From the 11th to the 15th century the monastery (now a school) housed a famous *scriptorium* whose works occupy an important place in the history of Italian miniatures.

MINIATURES OF CAVA
The earliest surviving manuscript is a codex in Beneventine script dating from the mid-11th century.

It contains three works: *De Temporibus* by the Venerable Bede, the *Annales Cavenses*, and a *Florilegium*, decorated with initials in red, black and blue. Its miniaturist art attests to an adherence to the Byzantine style and to links between the monks of Cava, Benevento and Montecassino. The *scriptorium* of Cava experienced its golden age in the 13th century, as can be seen from the remarkable *Exultet* preserved in the Museo del Duomo.

Visiting Paestum constitutes an unforgettable
experience. Paestum is remarkable for the
quality and state of preservation of its
three huge temples, and for the
famous Tomb of the Diver.
It can appear complex as
it covers several
historical periods.

**AT THE MOUTH OF
THE SELE ...**
About 6 miles outside
the city walls, the
inhabitants of
Poseidonia (the City
of Neptune) built a
vast sanctuary
dedicated to Hera,
their principal deity.

It included a huge
temple (c. 500 BC)
and a smaller Archaic
temple (c. 570 BC)
▲ *304*. The metopes
of the first are
decorated with
maidens performing a
dance in honor of the
goddess.

HISTORY

FOUNDATION.
In c. 600 BC Greeks
from Sybaris, a large town on the Gulf of Tarento, founded a
colony (Poseidonia) on the plain that lies on the left bank of
the Sele, and occupied the territory between the mouth of the
Sele, the promontory of Licosa (to the south) and the Monti
Alburni (to the east). The town's regular layout,
huge temples and the vast size of the recently
excavated agora attest to the fact that Poseidonia
was particularly prosperous between 530 and
470 BC.

LUCANIAN OCCUPATION. At the end of the 5th
century BC, the town fell into the hands of Italic
peoples, who became known as Lucanians ● *28*,
▲ *302*.

ROMAN PAESTUM. In 273 BC Poseidonia became a
Roman colony and was officially named
Paestum. The Forum, inscriptions and numerous
other remains attest to a radical transformation
of the town's social structure and its extremely
rapid Romanization. Toward the end of the 3rd
century BC, like many other towns in southern
Italy, Paestum was strongly affected by the repercussions of
the Second Punic War, and was transformed into a small town
that was soon plagued by malaria. It made a modest recovery
during the 1st century AD and became a small center
renowned for its perfume, extracted from the roses extolled
by such poets as Virgil and Ovid. During the late Roman
Empire, although an episcopal see, Paestum was gradually
abandoned by its inhabitants who were driven
out by malaria.

"The truth is more prosaic: Paestum and the surrounding area was rendered unhealthy by malaria and gradually abandoned, and the great temples had the good fortune, exceptional in Magna Grecia, not to be used as a stone quarry."
Georges Vallet

They left the plain for the neighboring mountains and established themselves on the site occupied by modern-day Capaccio, where the cult of the Virgin of the Pomegranate perpetuates the cult of Hera, who is represented in many ex-votos holding a pomegranate.

THE ARCHEOLOGICAL SITE

The most logical starting point for a visit is the north entrance (in front of the "Temple of Ceres").
ATHENAION (TEMPLE "OF CERES"). The temple, initially thought to be dedicated to Ceres, was in fact dedicated to Athena, as can be seen from ex-votos discovered nearby. It is an exquisite example of Doric architecture (only the façade of the *cella* has Ionic columns), built in c. 500 BC. It is the only pagan temple at Paestum to have been used as a church, attended by the town's few remaining inhabitants during the Middle Ages. These last inhabitants gathered on the small hill where the temple stood, the town's highest point.
"AGORA". Further south a vast plateau is occupied by the Greek market place, transformed into a residential district during the Roman period. Excavations have exposed two very important Greek structures: the UNDERGROUND SACELLUM and the EKKLESIASTERION.

INNOVATION
The Athenaion introduced an architectural innovation with the oblique cornices of its pediment (which were coffered on the inside) and the absence of a horizontal cornice.

The Ekklesiasterion, built c. 470 BC, lies opposite the Underground Sacellum, in the direction of the modern road. This was where the citizens assembled to pass laws and elect magistrates. The tiered seats were hewn out of the rock in the form of concentric circles. At the end of the 4th century an altar and a Lucanian stele were placed here and dedicated to Jupiter by a magistrate. When the Roman colony was established, the building was demolished and the vast cavity filled with earth and stone, as well as the remains of large numbers of sacrificial cattle. On the embankment thus created, a sanctuary and a fountain were built, which today overlook the Ekklesiasterion. The *agora*, the center of political life for more than two centuries, also disappeared with the establishment of the Roman colony.

FORUM. The Romans built a new public square, about ten yards further south. The Forum of Paestum (650 feet long x 200 feet wide) is one of the most complete in Italy, even though the eastern edge lies beneath the modern road. Set slightly back on the north side (and bisected by the road) is the Amphitheater, built in the 1st century BC and extended in the 1st century AD by pillars *in latericium* (brick). Opposite the AMPHITHEATER stands the AERARIUM (treasury), built in the form of a large rectangular tower. This is flanked by the COMITIUM, a circular building inscribed in a rectangle, cut by the podium of the GREAT ITALIC TEMPLE (whose metopes are partly preserved on one side). The Forum also has rectangular structures that can be identified as TABERNAE (stores). On the western side, between the stores, is a *lararium* dating from the Imperial period, a temple dedicated to the Lares Publici (tutelary deities). Originally worshiped as household gods, their cult moved into the public domain, and here they protect the town. In the center of the south side of the Forum are two important monuments from the Imperial period: the BASILICA, comprising a covered portico and an open room with a semicircular exedra, and the MACELLUM (market) whose marble courtyard was built above a Greek Archaic temple.

TEMPLE OF FORTUNA VIRILIS. Behind the Italic Temple is a large sanctuary with a swimming pool. The rites of Fortuna Virilis, reserved exclusively for women, included the immersion of a statue of Venus and then of her disciples.

The ritual was supposed to ensure successful births.

TEMPLE "OF NEPTUNE" ● 66. The temple belonged, with the Temple of Hera, to the urban sanctuary of Poseidonia. The latter was delimited by a platform some 160 feet long, dedicated to Asclepius, that lies beyond the Forum. For a long time it was believed that the temple was dedicated to Neptune (the Greek god Poseidon after whom the Greek town was named), but it was more likely to have been used for the worship of Apollo or Zeus. Built just before 450 BC, it is one of the most famous

and most impressive Greek temples in the Western world. Its cella has an anterior and posterior colonnade and is divided into three naves by two interior colonnades.

TEMPLE OF HERA (BASILICA). Built in c. 530 BC, it is the oldest of the great temples of Paestum. It is decorated with characteristically Archaic capitals (flattened and decorated with leaves and palmettes carved in the soft rock). Their profile is very different from the chalice-shaped capitals of the Temple of Neptune, built more than half a century later. The absence of any religious features (especially the pediment) led to the belief, in the 18th century, that the edifice was a civil monument (basilica).

ENCLOSURE WALL. About ten yards further south is the town's south gate, preceded by a ditch spanned by a stone bridge. It is well worth walking round the fortified enclosure wall (about three miles long). It was built between the 4th and 3rd centuries BC and is one of the best preserved in the ancient world.

TRAVELERS' IMPRESSIONS . . . Paestum was usually the last "port of call" for artists and travelers visiting Italy in the 18th century, as part of the Grand Tour.

"CELLA" OF THE TEMPLE OF HERA The *cella* of the Temple of Hera is divided into two naves by a central colonnade, most probably intended to support the beams that in turn upheld the roof. At the far end a closed room (*adyton*) contained the Temple's treasure. Opposite the east façade, facing the mountains, are the great altars that were the focal point of worship and sacrifice. The worshippers never entered the Temple, which was the dwelling of the deity.

299

The Tomb of the Diver was discovered, in 1968, at Tempa del Prete, about one mile south of Paestum. It dates from c. 480 BC and is famous for its frescos, which are the only extant examples of Greek funerary paintings from this period. The deceased was probably an Etruscan merchant living in Poseidonia. A lecythus, a pear-shaped perfume casket and a turtle-shell lyre case had been placed near the body. A banquet intended to accompany the deceased to the hereafter was painted on the walls of the tomb; the decoration on the lid was absolutely unprecedented.

> **"ATHENS HAS PUSHED ITS FRONTIERS AS FAR AS PAESTUM; ITS TEMPLES AND TOMBS FORM A LINE ON THE LAST HORIZON OF AN ENCHANTED SKY."**
>
> FRANÇOIS RENÉ DE CHATEAUBRIAND

THE BANQUET

On the far wall of the tomb, a young man offers a drinking cup to a guest entering the room (preceding wall). In the center two guests are playing the ritual game of *cottabus*, but one is distracted by the couple at the next table. Opposite, the second long wall shows the musicians playing at the banquet. A lyre player holds an egg (an Orphic symbol) in his hand. On the short wall, to the right, a naked young man holds an *oinochoe* (wine-pourer). This bronze vase was used by the cup-bearers to draw wine from the krater (wine vase) on the table and fill the drinking cups. The wall opposite shows a new guest entering the room, dressed in a fine cape, followed by a *paedagogus* holding a knotted staff, and preceded by a young flautist.

THE DIVER

On the lid is the scene after which the tomb is named. The composition is extremely beautiful and the imagery is undoubtedly highly symbolic. The diver is probably the image of the limits of the world, and the action of diving represents the passage into the hereafter.

Frescoed tombs, which were commonly found in Etruria and Campania under the Etruscans, became widespread in the region of Paestum between 400 and 280 BC, when Lucanian populations occupied and then settled in the town. The fusion of this new ethnic group with the existing Greek nucleus gave rise to a new and original type of culture that is well documented in the funerary paintings. Representations of duels, chariot races and gladiatorial combats made it possible to establish that, in Campania, funerary games inspired the creation of the Amphitheater. The paintings also illustrate the practices that accompanied the deceased on their journey into the hereafter.

CROSSING THE RIVER OF HADES
The upper part of this flag represents the deceased boarding the bark of Charon, the awful ferryman of Hades, who will take her to the far bank of the river. Below a herdsman leads a sacrificial ox, followed by two women, one bearing offerings on her head and the other performing a mourning ritual.

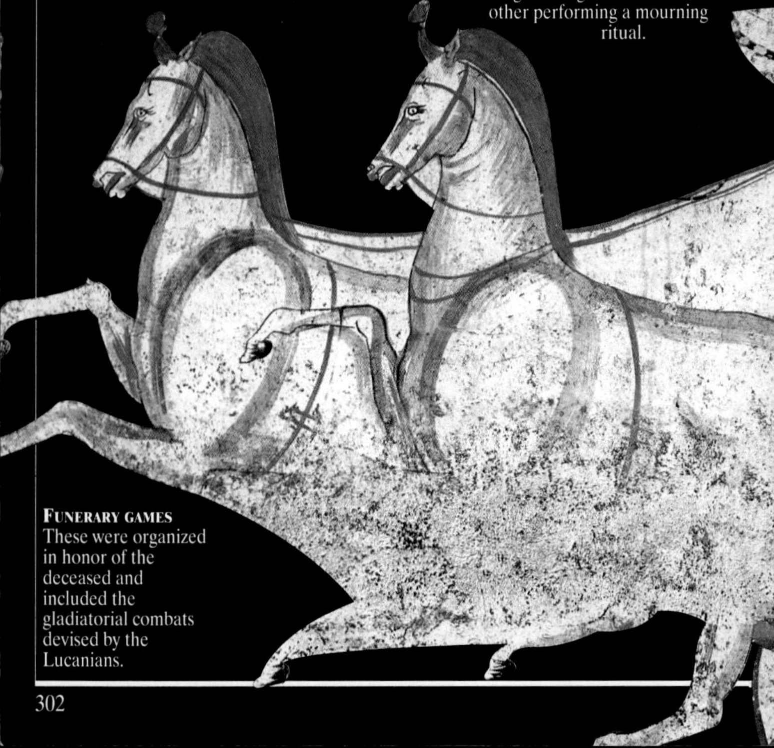

FUNERARY GAMES
These were organized in honor of the deceased and included the gladiatorial combats devised by the Lucanians.

FUNERAL CEREMONY

As the guardians of the house, women are always represented in an enclosed space or, after their death, lying in state (below) and surrounded by mourners and servants bringing water to wash the body. The vase, or hydria, is a female symbol as opposed to the krater, which is associated with male images. Whereas women are represented as the deceased receiving funerary rites, men are always depicted in attitudes that confirm their virility, armed with their finest weapons and often in combat.

HORSEMAN

This armed horseman, mounted on a black horse standing in front of a krater, is undoubtedly a strongly symbolic representation of a warrior, as well as of men in general. Warriors, hunters and horsemen are always shown in heroic attitudes and before a krater, both signifying high social rank.

CHARIOT RACE

A winged Victory drives a *biga* (two-horsed chariot) toward a column probably marking the end of the circuit in the circus, where teams competed in chariot races held in honor of the deceased.

HERCULES AND THE CERCOPES
Among the metopes in the museum at Paestum are these illustrations of the myth of Hercules. The Greek hero is shown punishing the Cercopes, whom he has hung by their feet from a pole. The two brothers had tried to steal the cattle of Geryon as he led them from the west to the east.

HERA
The Museum contains numerous effigies of Hera. Here, as goddess of fecundity, she holds a child in her arms.

The wall is punctuated by four huge gates, corresponding to the four points of the compass, and numerous posterns. The east gate (Porta Sirena) has a semicircular arch decorated with a sphinx; the bastions of the west gate (Porta Marina) are preserved up to the loopholes.

MUSEO NAZIONALE DI PAESTUM

The official excavation of the site of Paestum began in 1907. It was not until after World War One that an *antiquarium* was installed in the bishop's palace. In the mid-1950's the Museo Nazionale di Paestum was founded with a view to presenting, among other objects, the pieces found in the sanctuary of Hera at the mouth of the Sele ▲ *296*. The museum's present layout is the result of the reorganization begun in 1970 following the discovery of the painted Lucanian tombs and the Tomb of the Diver.

METOPES. The metopes of the small temple in the sanctuary of Hera at the mouth of the Sele constitute one of the main attractions of the museum. They also form the most important group of Archaic sculptures discovered in Magna Grecia. Before being installed in the museum, these extraordinary pieces had stood on a 17th-century farm, only a few yards from where they were found. They probably date from c. 570–560 BC and illustrate a number of mythological episodes, including the suicide of Ajax, the labors of Hercules and the myth of Orestes.

PAESTUM THROUGH THE AGES. The archeological pieces from the necropolises and urban sites, including the ex-votos found in the sanctuaries of the town, are presented in chronological order on the first and second floors of the museum.

PRACTICAL INFORMATION

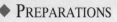 Preparations

Goethe and Wagner, Dumas and Ibsen, Greta Garbo and Liz Taylor, and – a little less sophisticated but no less enthusiastic – Diego Armando Maradona have all visited Naples and fallen under its spell. . . .

Where to find out about Naples

Italian consulates

UK
◆ 38 Eaton Place
London SW1
Tel. 0171 235 9371

◆ 32 Melville Street
Edinburgh E3
Tel. 0131 226 3631

US
◆ 690 Park Avenue
New York
Tel. 212 737 9100

◆ 12400 Wilshire
Blvd
Suite 300
Los Angeles
Tel. 213 820 0622

Consulates in Naples

UK
◆ Via Francesco
Crispi 122
Naples
Tel. (0)81-663511

US
◆ Piazza della
Repubblica
Naples 80122
Tel. (0)81-5838111

Italian Tourist Offices

UK
◆1 Princes Street
London W1
Tel. 0171 408 1254

◆Italian Institute
39 Belgrave Square
London SW1
Tel. 0171 235 1461

US
◆630 Fifth Avenue
Suite 1565
New York, NY 10111
Tel. 212 245 4822

◆401 North Michigan
Suite 3030
Chicago, IL 60611
Tel. 312 644 9448

◆12400 Wilshire
Boulevard
Los Angeles
CA 90025
Tel. 310 820 0098

Formalities and official documents

◆ An identity card or passport for those traveling from EU countries and intending to stay for less than three months.
◆ US citizens just need a passport for stays of under three months.
◆ Unaccompanied minors must have written permission to leave their country of origin.
◆ Drivers must have an international (or European) driving license, a car registration document and a green (international insurance) card.
◆ EU citizens can obtain an "E111" form from their local post office or health authority, which entitles them to free Italian health care. Visitors from outside the EU should take out special insurance or medical insurance before leaving.

Useful information

The offices of the Ente Provinciale per il Turismo (Piazza dei Martiri 58, Tel. (0)81-405311) and the Azienda Autonoma Soggiorno Cura e Turismo (Palazzo Reale, Piazza Plebiscito, Tel. (0)81-418744) provide information (maps, leaflets, calendars of events) and a detailed list of hotels in the region. In Naples the Albergatori Napoletani (Piazza Carità 32, Tel. (0)81-5514902) has a special toll-free number for visitors (167-016221 from within Italy).

When to go

Fall and spring are the best times to visit the region, when you can enjoy clear skies without the summer heat. What is more, the islands and coast are not as crowded with tourists and Neapolitans as in July and August. Some may prefer to visit Naples and walk round the old town during the untypically quiet summer months, but they would be missing one of the city's essential charms: the blend of sounds, voices and colors. Christmas and Easter are ideal if you want to experience the popular traditions, still very much alive in the region. On the coast, temperatures tend to be more moderate than inland, with refreshing sea breezes. Annual rainfall is higher than London or Rome.

SPRING	April to May

Spring brings the first days of sun, sea and outings. It is also the time of such Easter festivals as the "Struscio" and the "Via Crucis" (Way of the Cross), a tradition which is still very much alive.

MAUNDY THURSDAY	SEPOLCRI, in all churches (*Struscio*)
GOOD FRIDAY	VIA CRUCIS, in all towns and villages
	INCAPPUCCIATI (BROTHERHOODS) PROCESSIONS, e.g.: Sorrentine coast, Procida
EASTER SUNDAY	MASS
EASTER MONDAY	*PASQUETTA* outings (picnics)
	FEAST OF THE MADONNA OF THE ARC, Sant'Anastasia
1ST SAT.	PILGRIMAGE OF THE VIRGIN OF CASTELLO, summit of Vesuvius
AFTER EASTER	PROCESSION OF THE VIRGIN OF THE GALLINE, Pagani
APRIL 25	ANNIVERSARY OF THE LIBERATION
APRIL	LOTTERY GRAND PRIX, AGNANO
	Racecourse of Agnano
MAY 1	LABOR DAY
SAT. BEFORE	MIRACLE OF SAN GENNARO,
1ST SUN. IN MAY	the Duomo in Naples
MAY	REGATTA, *Nastro Azzurro* Sailing Cup trophy, Capri
EVERY WEEKEND IN MAY	MONUMENTS OF MAY, cultural and gastronomic itineraries
MAY 14	FESTIVAL OF THE HOLY PATRON, San Costanzo, Capri

SUMMER	June to August

As the heat intensifies, so does the search for cool air: people converge on the beaches during the day and walk on the lungomare in the evening to take advantage of the sea breeze. An ideal time to do your shopping: the sales begin in July.

JUNE, JULY, AUG.	OPEN-AIR CONCERTS AND SHOWS,
	Castel Nuovo (Maschio Angioino), Castel Sant'Elmo, Castel dell'Ovo, Naples
	CONCERTS IN THE *CAPRESE* SEASON, Capri
	CLASSICAL MUSIC AND JAZZ CONCERTS, Ravello
JUNE	FESTIVAL OF MONTE CASTELLO, Cava de' Tirreni
	(Re-enactment of the plague of 1656)
JUNE 6	FESTIVAL OF THE VIRGIN OF THE QUATTRO ALTARI, Torre del Greco
JUNE 13	FESTIVAL OF THE HOLY PATRON, Anacapri
JUNE 21–30	*FESTA DEI GIGLI*, Nola
1ST WEEK IN JULY	WAGNERIAN CONCERTS, Villa Rufolo, Ravello
1ST WEEK IN JULY	*DISFIDA DEI TROMBONIERI*, festival in period costume, Cava de' Tirreni
JULY	FESTIVAL OF THE VESUVIAN VILLAS, theatrical shows
JULY 16	VIRGIN DEL CARMINE FESTIVAL, Naples
	"Burning" of the Campanile of Santa Maria del Carmine
JULY 26	FESTIVAL OF THE HOLY PATRON, procession to the sea, Ischia
AUGUST 5	FESTIVAL OF THE ICON OF THE VIRGIN, religious celebration and
	procession of boats, Torre Annunziata
AUGUST 11–20	FESTIVAL OF THE SEA, Procida
AUGUST 15	ASSUMPTION, RE-ENACTMENT OF THE SARACEN LANDING, Positano

FALL	September to November

The summer heat has passed and Naples is getting back to normal. It is still warm enough for the beach. The theater season is getting underway.

SEP. 1–10	*SETTEMBRE AL BORGO* (theater, music, dance), Caserta
SEP. 1–10	*CITTÀ SPETTACOLO* (theater, music, dance), Benevento
SEP. 1–10	AGRICULTURAL AND CRAFT FAIRS, Colle di Fontanella, Sant'Agnello
SEP. 19	FESTIVAL OF THE HOLY PATRONS, Naples and Pozzuoli (the Miracle of San
	Gennaro in Naples)
SEP.	FESTA DEI GIGLI, Barra
SEP.	INTERNATIONAL MUSIC FESTIVAL, Naples
OCT.	INTERNATIONAL FILM FESTIVAL, Sorrento
22 OCT.	FESTIVAL OF THE HOLY PATRON, Torre Annunziata

WINTER	December to March

Nativity celebrations provide an insight into Neapolitan religious devotion. Local craftsmanship can be seen in the markets, and music pervades the streets and houses, bringing the presepi (cribs) to life.

DEC. TO JUNE	OPERA SEASON, Teatro San Carlo, Naples
DEC. 8	IMMACULATE CONCEPTION
DEC. 24	MIDNIGHT MASS
DEC. 25	CHRISTMAS
DEC.	CHRISTMAS MARKET, San Gregorio Armeno,
	CRIBS AND DEMONSTRATIONS, San Lorenzo and other popular districts
DEC. 31	NEW YEAR CELEBRATIONS, FIRECRACKER DISPLAYS, Naples
JAN. 1st	FOLKLORE PERFORMANCES, Piazza Umberto I, Capri
JAN. 6	EPIPHANY
JAN. 17	FEAST OF SANT'ANTONIO ABATE (burning of Christmas trees), Naples
FEB. 14	FEAST OF SANT'ANTONIO ABATE, Sorrento
FEB.	CARNIVAL, Capua (lasts about 5 days)
MARCH	CONCERTS AND EXHIBITIONS

◆ PREPARATIONS

CLIMATE

Campania, the region of the "Mezzogiorno" (south), is renowned for its mild climate and clear skies.

◆ On the coast and coastal plain, the climate is mild and healthy owing to the influence of the sea. The average annual temperature is 63°F (17°C), 73°F (23°C) in summer and 48°F (9°C) in winter.

◆ Further inland, in the Apennine Mountains, the climate becomes rapidly more continental. The average temperatures in Benevento range from 77°C (25°C) in summer to 45°F (7°C) in winter, while in Avellino they rise to 84°F (29°C) in summer and fall to 41°F (5°C) in winter.

◆ Precipitation, which is fairly high in the mountains, is much less frequent but often more violent on the plain and along the coast.

THE MIRACLE OF SAN GENNARO

The miracle of San Gennaro ▲ *158* is a major tri-annual event for Neapolitans. During the religious ceremony the two phials containing the saint's blood are shown to the congregation. The most devout women then invoke *Faccia Gialla* (the popular name given to the saint) to perform the miracle. The Duomo resounds with incantations, prayers and even insults until the blood liquefies. The event can last for anything between a few minutes and 15 hours. If the miracle does not occur, which has been known to happen, it is a sign that grave misfortune will befall Naples. If you want to go to the ceremony, you should not mind crowds and an atmosphere that is more like that of a football match than one of reflective meditation. It is also advisable to arrive at the Duomo 2 to 3 hours before the start of the ceremony.

WHAT TO PACK

Summer clothing and swimwear are ideally suited to the Mediterranean climate between April and September. And you don't need very warm clothes during the rest of the year. In summer, if you intend to swim, don't forget your snorkel and a pair of sandals (as protection against sea urchins). Don't take valuable jewelry and accessories, which, along with cameras and camcorders, are highly prized by pickpockets.

HOTEL RESERVATIONS

You should try to book your hotel room in Naples in advance, especially during festivals when there is a specific event or exhibition (such as Monuments of May). It is also advisable to reserve well in advance for the peak season (which lasts from mid-July to mid-August) on the islands and along the coast, through a travel agent or by contacting the hotel direct. For these periods, you may be asked for a deposit, which can be paid by credit card or postal order.

TELEPHONING ITALY

◆ FROM THE UK: dial 00 39 + regional code (without the 0) then the number (4–8 digits).

◆ FROM THE US: dial 011 39 + regional code (without the 0) followed by the number (4–8 digits).

REGIONAL CODES
Naples: 081 (Phlegraean Fields, Capri, Procida, Ischia, Sorrento, Pompeii, Ercolano)
Salerno: 089 (Positano, Amalfi, Ravello)
Caserta: 0823

BENEATH THE CITY

Underground Naples is truly fascinating: a network of hundreds of caves and thousands of galleries lies beneath the city and the mysterious silence is a far cry from the hustle and bustle above ground.

ORGANIZATIONS
◆ Napoli Sotterranea Piazza San Gaetano 68
Tel. (0)81-449821
The organization conducts guided tours, Mon. to Fri. from noon to 4pm (Thur. from 5pm to 9pm), Sat. and Sun. 10am to 10pm (cost: 10,000 lire). These tours visit the Roman, Greek and prehistoric remains in old Naples.

◆ Laes (Libera Associazione Escursionisti Sottosuolo)
Via Santa Teresella degli Spagnoli 7
Tel. (0)81-400256
Guided tours on Sat. at 10am and 6pm and Sun. at 10am and 11am. (Thur. open until 9pm). Spanish and surrounding districts. Rendezvous Piazza Trieste e Trento, at the Gambrinus café (cost: 10,000 lire). Access to the underground network via the Vico Sant'Anna di Palazzo. Visits to the cemetery of the Fontanelle and the Catacombe di San Gaudioso on request.

CURRENCY

Italian bank-notes are of 1,000, 2,000, 5,000, 10,000, 50,000 and 100,000 lire, and coins are of 50, 100, 200, 500 and 1,000 lire. Telephone tokens (200 lire) have almost disappeared.

EXCHANGE RATE
About £1=2,800 lire and US$=1,590 lire at the time of the printing.

BANKER'S CARDS
Restaurants, hotels and most stores accept payment by banker's card.

BANKS AND BUREAUX DE CHANGE

BANKS
Banks are usually open from Monday to Friday between 8.30am and 1.30pm and 2.45pm and 3.45pm. Most of them offer foreign exchange facilities.

BUREAUX DE CHANGE
The following bureaux de change may be useful outside regular bank opening hours:

◆ CAMBIO SAN MARCO
Calata San Marco 11
Tel. (0)81-5512761

◆ MODESTINO
Via Toledo 292
Tel. (0)81-414343

AUTO-TELLERS
Although auto-tellers are not found everywhere, there are some in most town centers. All machines accept the internationally recognized Visa and Eurocard.

SOME PRICES

1 ESPRESSO : 1,200 LIRE

1 LIMONATA : 1,500 LIRE

1 PIZZA AND 1 BEER: 15,000 LIRE

1 PIZZA TO GO: 5,000–8,000 LIRE

1 MUSEUM ENTRANCE: 5,000–15,000 LIRE

1-DAY "GIRANAPOLI" TICKET: 4,500 LIRE

1 PLATE OF SEAFOOD SPAGHETTI: 12,000 LIRE

1 DAY'S CAR RENTAL (GROUP B): 140,000 LIRE

Freeway	——
Railway lines	——
Sea routes	----
Air routes	——

BY AIR

AIR FARES TO NAPLES

All of the prices given below are for return flights. The prices quoted are subject to restrictions and/or seasonal variation and are therefore given as guidance only.

◆ ALITALIA

FLIGHTS FROM THE US

Flights from New York to Naples cost between $372 and $970 for a seat in economy class and approximately $5,094 for a seat in business class.

Flights from Los Angeles to Naples cost about $518 to $1,230 in economy class and $6,054 in business class.
Tel. 800 223 5730

FLIGHTS FROM THE UK

ALITALIA
Flights to Naples cost from £279 economy to £659 business class
Tel: 0171 602 7711
Ticket office:
Portman Square
London W1

BRITISH AIRWAYS
Flights to Naples cost from £209 economy to £690 business class.
BA telephone sales (24 hours)
0345 222111
or:
BA Travel Store
Regent St
London W1
Tel. 0171 434 4700

It is also possible to find charter flights to Naples starting at around £150 through travel agents.
Or try:
AIR TRAVEL GROUP
Tel. 0181 533 8888
FINE QUOTE
Tel. 0171 240 4400

FLIGHTS FROM THE US

Most airlines do not fly direct to Naples; they stop in either Rome or Milan.

AMERICAN AIRLINES
Tel. 800 433 7300
Flights from New York to Naples cost from $520 to $1,195 in economy class and about $5,094 in business class.
Flights from Los Angeles to Naples cost from $770 to $1,445 in economy class and $6,354 in business class.

DELTA AIRLINES
Tel. 800 241 4141
Flights from New York to Naples cost $520 to $1,050 in economy class and about $5,094 in business class.
Flights from Los Angeles to Naples cost $678 to $1,230 in economy class $6,354 in business class.

TWA
Tel. 800 892 4141
TWA flies to Rome, from where you can take a connecting flight to Naples on Alitalia.

Casilina 33 8 →

NAPOLI A1 →

FROM THE AIRPORT TO THE CITY CENTER

The airport is 4½ miles from the city center.
BY BUS (CLP SERVICE)
Buses run about every hour, between 6.30am and 11.30pm from the airport and 6am and 11pm from Piazza Municipio. Tickets: 3,000 lire. Bus stops are in the Via Don Bosco, Piazza Carlo III, Corso Garibaldi, Piazza Garibaldi (station), Corso Umberto I and Piazza Municipio.
BY TAXI
The 20-minute trip costs c. 25,000 lire. Tel. 7375140

BY COACH

Eurolines, which is the main coach company operating in Europe today, runs services to Rome. Once you have arrived in Rome, you need to change to local buses or trains in order to get to Naples. Tel. 0171 730 8235 (London)

BY BOAT

There are weekly boats from Tunisia and Malta, plus many Italian coastal cities.

BY CAR

To take a car into Italy, you need a vehicle registration document, a full driving license and insurance papers. Non-EU citizens should ideally have an international driving license with an Italian translation incorporated. All cars should have a nationality plate. In Italy tolls on freeways can be paid using cash (no credit cards) or the Viacard, a magnetic card (50,000, 90,000, 100,000 and 150,000 lire) that can be used on the Italian freeway network. Viacard can be bought from the main toll terminals (in the major towns and

cities) or from automobile clubs. There are also 20,000 lire Viacards, which are very useful for local journeys and which can be purchased in all toll stations. The A2 freeway takes you to the outskirts of Naples, where you should take the ring road (*tangenziale*) for the Phlegraean Fields and the upper districts of the city (Capodimonte, Vomero). Follow the "Napoli Centro" signs for the Piazza Garibaldi. If you want

to get to the coastal towns, you must take the A3 freeway in the direction of Salerno. Once you get to Naples, the main problem is finding somewhere to park ◆ *319*.

DISTANCES (IN MILES) BY ROAD FROM NAPLES TO SOME OF THE MAJOR EUROPEAN CITIES	
Rome	135
Paris	1,020
London	1,245
Berlin	1,095
Madrid	1,385
Amsterdam	1,195
Brussels	1,080
Geneva	1,120

BY TRAIN

There are two routes from London to Naples: via Paris, Turin and Genoa or Lille, Basel, Milan and Florence. Services are daily in summer and you have to change stations in Paris. If you plan to travel around Italy or Europe, the Italian-run travel agency CIT will advise on fares and rail passes that can be purchased before leaving home:
UK
Tel. 0181 686 5533
US
Tel. 212 697 2100
CANADA
Tel. 514 954 8608
Train timetables can be found in most stations for around 4,500 lire.

L'ITALIE par le Sᵗ GOTHARD

Chemins de fer de L'EST

Billets d'excursion en SUISSE et en ITALIE à prix réduits

REDUCTIONS

By air:
Airplane fares are at their cheapest in the low season, which lasts from December to March, excluding the run-up to Christmas.

By train:
Interail or Eurail passes permit unlimited travel around Europe for the under-26's for a period of either one or two months.

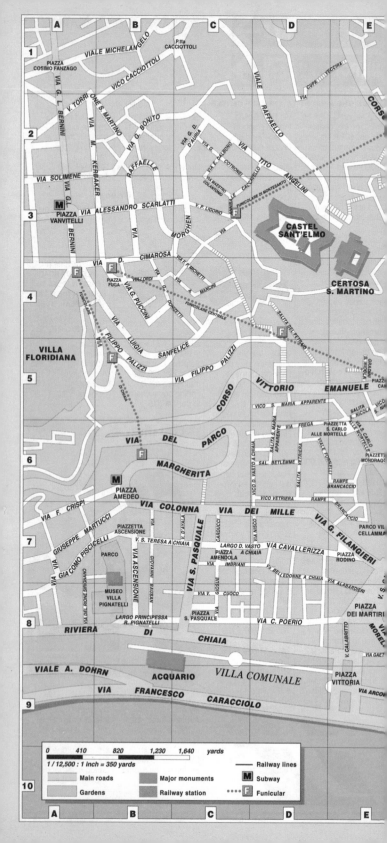

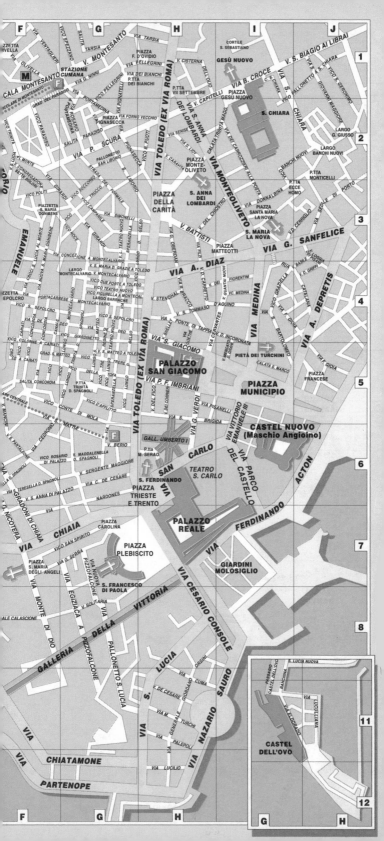

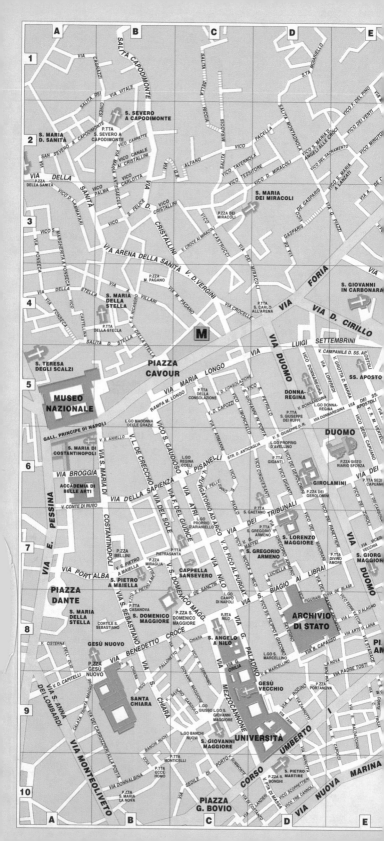

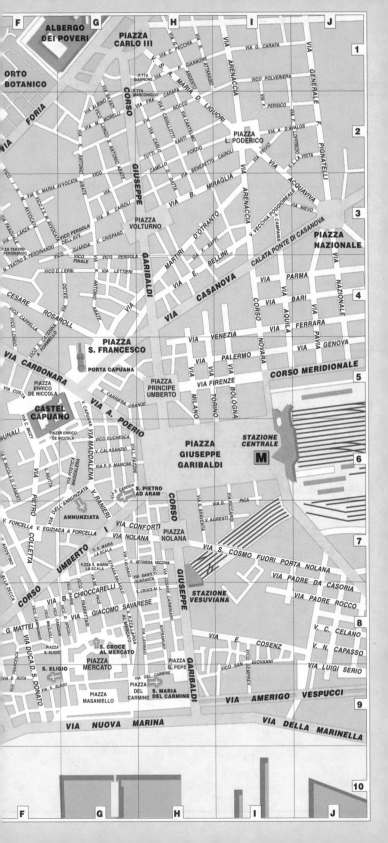

AEROPORTO
DI CAPODICHINO

C66-24   25-33-149

20

12

TANGENZIALE

C55-47   C55-12-26-47

Piazza
CARLO III

C61

C61

C61

Piazza
NAZIONALE

110-127-254

Piazza San
FRACESCO

14-110
127-170-171

STAZIONE
CENTRALE

M   GIANTURCO

PIAZZA
GARIBALDI

C9-CS-C30
C89-16-42
104-150-152-156-172
175-185-192-193-194-195

Piazza NICOLA
AMORE

CORSO UMBERTO I
CD-C55-C88
42-105-116
150-185

STAZIONE
VESUVIANA

172-192-193

OF-25-135

185

C81-1-4-152
157-255

VIA VESPUCCI
4-29-157-194-254-255

C81

4-28-157-194-254-255

STAZIONE
MARITIMA

SORRENTO
CAPRI
REGGIO DI CALABRIA
PALERMO
CAGLIARI
GENOVA
ISCHIA
PROCIDA
POZZUOLI

Railway station (Ferrovie dello Stato)	■
Railway	
Subway	M
Bus	
Bus terminus	●
Ferry links	
Funicular	F

PIAZZA CAVOUR

SUBWAY

METROPOLITANA (FS)
This subway covers a fairly limited route. It is reasonably reliable but rather slow.
◆ Trains run every 12 minutes, from 5.30am to 10.18pm (10.38pm Campi Flegrei).
◆ Route: Napoli Gianturco, Piazza Garibaldi (subway station), Piazza Cavour, Montesanto, Piazza Amedeo, Mergellina (station), Piazza Leopardi (Fuorigrotta), Campi Flegrei (station, Mostra d'Oltremare), Cavalleggeri d'Aosta, Bagnoli, Pozzuoli, Solfatara.

METROPOLITANA COLLINARE
This modern, efficient subway services the Vomero Alto, the hospital district and the popular districts of Chiaiano and Secondigliano. Its proximity to the Vomero station of the Funicolare di Chiaia means that it is completely integrated into the city's urban transport system.
◆ Trains run every 12 minutes, from 6.40am to 10.54pm.
◆ Route: Piazza Vanvitelli, Piazza Medaglie d'Oro, Montedonzelli, Rione Alto, Policlinico, Colli Aminei, Frullone, Chiaiano, Secondigliano.

FUNICULARS

LINES
Three of Naples' four funicular railways are run by the ANM. Permanent service, every 10 minutes, from 7am to 10pm.
◆ Funicolare centrale (Via Toledo, Piazza Fuga) Tel. 7632506
◆ Funicolare di Chiaia (Parco Margherita–Via Cimarosa) Tel. 7632578
◆ Funicolare di Montesanto (Piazza Montesanto–Via Morghen) Tel. 7632514

These three lines provide a rapid link with the hillside district of Vomero.
◆ Funicolare di Mergellina (Via Mergellina–Via Manzoni) Tel. 7145583

BUSES

In Naples the buses are run by the ANM (Azienda Napoletana Mobilità)
◆ INFORMATION Tel. 7631111
Tickets can be bought from newspaper kiosks and tobacconist's. They must be stamped on the bus, but it is advisable to check the date and time indicated by the machines as they don't always work. If this should happen, avoid problems with ticket inspectors by noting the date and time you started your journey in the space provided on the ticket.
◆ Buses run between 5.30am and 10.30pm (Monday to Saturday) every 20 minutes (up to 35 minutes during rush hours). A skeleton service operates on public holidays. Three routes (R1, R2, R3) offer a supposedly more rapid and frequent service. The R1 route links the Vomero and the city center (Piazza Dante, Via Toledo and Piazza Bovio, passing near the Museo Archeologico Nazionale).

In the Via Toledo, the R1 route crosses the R2 route, which services the central station. The R3 route runs from the city center to the Napoli Mergellina station and the waterfront. The R1 terminus is

on the Piazza Medaglie d'Oro (Vomero). The last bus (on weekdays and public holidays) is at 10.00pm and buses should run every 10 minutes. It should be said that the Neapolitan bus service is not renowned for its simplicity, especially by tourists visiting the city for the first time! If you fall into this category, you would be better advised to use alternative means of transport (subways, funiculars and trains).

"GIRANAPOLI"
TICKETS
"Giranapoli" is a system of tickets and season tickets for the Neapolitan urban transport network.
◆ 90 minute ticket (1,500 lire)
◆ day ticket (4,500 lire)
◆ monthly season ticket (45,000 lire)
These three tickets are valid on all types of public transport in the city, except the Circumvesuviana, Circumflegrea and Ferrovia Cumana railway lines.

STOP PRESS
New telephone numbers in Italy
Remember to include the zeros between brackets (0)
when telephoning: they are part of the new area codes

TAXIS

Taxi ranks are indicated by the word "TAXI" on a sign or painted in yellow on the road. Taxis can also be stopped in the street: they are available when their light is on.

BEWARE
When you get into a taxi, the meter should read 4,000 lire (the cost of the municipal tax).

It is advisable to avoid unofficial taxis, usually found near the stations: the vehicles are not always sufficiently safe, they don't have meters and fares are much higher than the official ones.

CALLING A CAB IN NAPLES
You can call the following radio-cab services (an additional charge of 1,500 lire is made for the call):
◆ Cotana
Tel. 5707070
◆ Naples
Tel. 5564444
◆ Partenope
Tel. 5560202

CALLING A CAB IN AND AROUND NAPLES
◆ Amalfi
Piazza F. Gioia
Tel. (0)89-872239
◆ Capri
Piazza Martiri di Ungheria
Tel. 8370543
◆ Anacapri
Piazza Vittoria
Tel. 8371175
◆ Ischia Porto
Via Antica Reggia
Tel. 984998
Piazza degli Eroi
Tel. 982550
◆ Pozzuoli
Piazza della Repubblica
Tel. 5265800
◆ Salerno
Piazza Ferrovia
Tel. (0)89-229947
◆ Sorrento
Piazza Tasso
Tel. 8782204

FARES
There is a rate for Naples and a rate for outside

the city.
In Naples the minimum fare for a journey is 6,000 lire (100 lire per 100 meters, 100 lire per 20 seconds). These rates, which are valid between 7am and 10pm, are doubled outside the city.

ADDITIONAL CHARGES
◆ 2,000 lire on public holidays
◆ 3,000 lire at night
◆ 5,000 lire for a suitcase or an animal

COMPLAINTS
If these rates are not applied, you can complain to the mayor of Naples, Ufficio Corso Pubblico, Galleria Principe di Napoli. Tel. 5642209

CARS

PARKING
Since 1997 parking in Naples has been regulated by the city council. The city's car-parking places are indicated by blue lines on the ground. There is a charge for these spaces between 8am and 8pm; the tarif varies from 2,000 to 3,000 lire an hour, depending on the district. The tickets are distributed by council

employees at the parking zones. You can also purchase 50,000 lire parking cards in kiosks and in tobacconists' shops.

PARKING LOTS
GRILLI
Via G. Ferraris 40
(near the Stazione Centrale)
Tel. 264344
MERGELLINA
Via G. Bruno 112
(near the Napoli Mergellina station)

Tel. 7613470
SANNAZARO
Piazza Sannazaro 142
(near the Napoli Mergellina station)
Tel. 681437
SUPERGARAGE
Via Shelley 11
(near the Piazza del Municipio)
Tel. 5513104
TURISTICO
Via A. de Gasperi
(port district)
Tel. 5525442

ALL-NIGHT GAS STATIONS
◆ City center
Piazza Carlo III
(Q8)
Piazza Municipio
(Q8)
Piazza Mergellina
(AGIP)
◆ Posillipo district
Via Manzoni (ESSO)
◆ Fuorigrotta district
Via Caio Duilio
(AGIP)
◆ Vomero district
Via Falcone (IP)
Viale Michelangelo
(ESSO)

HIGHWAY CODE
Driving in Naples can be an extremely stressful experience for tourists. Traffic is chaotic and the basic rules of the Highway Code are often broken: red lights, priority and one-way streets are usually ignored. Even worse are the daring exploits of the ubiquitous Vespa, moped and motorbike riders, and undisciplined pedestrians who cross the street at the worst possible moment. It is essential to be constantly on your guard, even in situations that are apparently less dangerous.
Don't be lulled into a sense of security simply because a junction has lights: you still have to check that the road is clear before proceeding . . . slowly. Tourist signs (hotels, museums, etc.) are few and far between. In the event of difficulty, ask the traffic police (*polizia municipale*) or a taxi driver for help.

STATIONS

FERROVIE DELLO STATO (FS)
Information
Tel. 5534188
(7am–9.30pm)
It is advisable to buy your ticket in advance from a travel agent displaying the "FS" sign.
Remember to stamp your tickets before getting on the train. Failure to do so can incur a heavy fine.

NAPLES

Naples has four mainline stations:
◆ Napoli Centrale (central station) Piazza Garibaldi
The central station is the main rail junction for the Naples region and the rest of Italy. Most short-, middle- and long-distance trains leave from here.
◆ Napoli Piazza Garibaldi
Subway station for Napoli Centrale (*metrò*).
◆ Napoli Mergellina, near the port.
◆ Campi Flegrei, in the Fuorigrotta district.

AROUND NAPLES

◆ Paestum
FS station:
Via Stazione 1
◆ Pompeii
FS station:
Piazza XXVIII Marzo
◆ Pozzuoli
FS station:
Via Oriani 2
Ferrovia Cumana station:
Via Sacchini
◆ Sorrento
Circumvesuviana station:
Piazza A. de Curtis

◆ Torre Annunziata
FS station:
Torre Centrale
Circumvesuviana station:
Via Plinio
◆ Torre del Greco
Via Ferrovia

CIRCUMVESUVIANA

Information
Tel. 7722444
or 7722144
A high-performance regional network servicing the towns on the coast south of Naples and in the region of Vesuvius. In Naples trains leave from the terminus on the Corso Garibaldi and stop at the subway station on the Piazza Garibaldi.

LINES

There are a total of four lines:
◆ Napoli-Ottaviano-Sarno
◆ Napoli-Pompeii-Sarno
◆ Napoli-Torre Annunziata-Castellamare-Sorrento
◆ Napoli-Nola-Baiano

TYPES OF TRAINS

There are three types of trains:
◆ *accelerato* (ACC) stops at every station
◆ *diretto* (DIR) does not stop at minor stations
◆ *direttissimo* (DD) runs only on the Naples-Torre Annunziata line, apart from Ercolano and Torre del Greco.

FREQUENCY OF SERVICE

Trains run about every 20 minutes. On the Naples-Sorrento line:
◆ there are departures from Naples between 4.51am and 10.48pm
◆ there are departures from Sorrento between 4.13am and 10.41pm
Timetables for other destinations are displayed in all railway stations.

Napoli Mergellina station.

FARES

A Naples-Sorrento train ticket costs 4,300 lire. Fares are based on the distance covered, with a minimum fare of 1,500 lire.

IN SEASON

From March 1 to Nov. 1, the Circumvesuviana also provides a special service – the "Funivia di Monte Faito" – f rom Castellamare and Monte Faito, which runs in conjunction with trains from Naples and Sorrento.

FERROVIA CUMANA

Main station
Piazza Montesanto, Naples
Tel. 5513328
Departures every 10 minutes from 5.21am to 9.21pm (9.41pm for Pozzuoli), stopping at Montesanto, Fuorigrotta, Bagnoli, Pozzuoli, Torregaveta.

CIRCUMFLEGREA

Main station
Piazza Montesanto, Naples
Tel. 5513328
Departures take place every 10 minutes from 5.12am to 9.23pm (9.43pm for Quarto), stopping at Montesanto, Soccavo, Pianura, Quarto, Licola and Torregaveta.
Six trains per day service Cumae, Lido Fusaro and Torregaveta.

COACHES

Several coach companies run services from Naples to the towns of Campania:
◆ ACTP
Via Arenaccia 29
Tel. 7001111
Coaches leave from the Piazza Garibaldi. ACTP mainly services towns around Vesuvius and Caserta.

◆ SEPSA
Via Cisterno dell'Olio 44
Tel. 5429111
Coaches leave from the Piazza Garibaldi.
◆ SITA
Via Campegna 23
Tel. 5522176
Coaches leave from the Via Pisanelli 3-7 SITA mainly services towns on the Amalfi coast (such as Amalfi, Atrani, Maiori, Minori, Positano, Ravello).

FERRIES AND HOVERCRAFT

Traghetti (ferries) and *aliscafi* (hovercraft) move continually between the islands of the bay and the Sorrentine peninsula. In winter you can take your car onto the ferry that goes to the islands. It is advisable to enquire in advance about the availability of ferry and hovercraft places on public holidays.

CIRCUMVESUVIANA
EDIZIONE INVERNALE 1992

HOVERCRAFT

The ferry (*traghetti*) and hovercraft (*aliscafi*) companies (formerly the CAREMAR) now form the LMV (Linee Marittime Veloci) consortium.

◆ From Molo Beverello (opposite the Castel Nuovo)
LMV
Tel. 5527209
Services to Capri (via Sorrento), Ischia Porto, Procida, Sorrento. Summer: services to Amalfi, Positano.
CAREMAR
Tel. 5513882
Services to Capri, Ischia Porto, Procida
◆ From Mergellina
LMV
Tel. 7612348
Services to Capri, Ischia Porto, Ischia Casamicciola, Procida. Summer: services to Ponza, the Aeolian Islands.
◆ From Sorrento
LMV
Tel. 8781430 or 8073024
Services to Capri, Ischia Porto, Procida
◆ From Capri
LMV
Tel. 8376995
Service to Ischia Porto, Sorrento, Castellammare.
◆ From Ischia
LMV
Tel. 991888
Service to Sorrento and Capri.
CAREMAR
Tel. 991953
Service to Procida
◆ From Procida
LMV
Tel. 8969975
Service to Ischia Casamicciola
CAREMAR
Tel. 8957280
Service to Pozzuoli, Ischia.
◆ From Pouzzoles
CAREMAR
Tel. 5262711
Service to Procida

FERRIES

◆ From Molo Beverello, Naples
CAREMAR
Tel. 5513882
Services to Capri, Ischia Porto, Procida
◆ From Sorrento
CAREMAR
Tel. 8073077
Service to Capri
◆ From Pouzzoles
CAREMAR
Tel. 5262711
Service to Ischia, Procida
◆ From Ischia
CAREMAR
Tel. 991953
Services to Procida, Pozzuoli
OTHER SERVICES:
◆ From Naples harbor station:
TIRRENIA
Tel. 7201111
Services to Palermo (Sicily) and Cagliari (Sardinia).
SIREMAR
Tel. 5800340
Services to the Aeolian Islands and Milazzo (Sicily).
INFORMATION: HARBOR MASTERS' OFFICES
◆ Naples:
Molo Pisacane
Tel. 206133
Consorzio Autonomo Porto di Napoli, Molo Angioino
Tel. 5523968
◆ Capri:
Via Marina Grande 6
Tel. 8370226
◆ Amalfi:
Lungomare dei Cavalieri 28
Tel. 871366
◆ Ischia:
Via Lasolino 10
Tel. 991417
◆ Procida:
Via Roma
Tel. 8967381
◆ Pozzuoli:
Largo C. Colombo
Tel. 5261160
◆ Salerno:
Molo Manfredi 1
Tel. (0)89-224544
◆ Sorrento:
Piazza Marinai d'Italia
Tel. 8073071

FUNICOLARE DI CAPRI

In Capri a funicular railway runs from the ferry to the upper part of the city:
◆ Funicolare Marina Grande-Piazzetta
Tel. 8370420 and 8377759

Services:
6.30am to 9.00pm (October–March),
6.30am to 9.30pm (April–May),
6.30am to 12.30am (June–September).
Every 15 minutes
Tickets cost 1,500 lire.

TIMES OF FERRIES AND HOVERCRAFT

Times are published in the "Per chi parte" section of the daily newspaper *Il Mattino*, and the "Per viaggiare" section of *La Repubblica*.

CAR RENTAL

Most car-rental companies have an agency near the station (Piazza Garibaldi), at the Capodichino airport, and on the Via Partenope (on the waterfront opposite the Castel dell'Ovo).
The international car-rental companies have a policy of hiring out their vehicles only to customers with a credit card.
The average rental cost of a Fiat Punto is as follows: 150,000 lire per day, 200,000 lire per weekend (3 days), 500,000 lire per week (5–7 days). These prices include insurance but do not include gas (cars must be returned with full tanks) or optional (especially breakdown) services. Prices are higher if you opt for a deal that gives unlimited mileage, and if you choose to return the car to a different town from your town of departure.
A number of car-rental companies offer special tarifs during holidays and the peak tourist season.

VESPA AND BICYCLE RENTAL

In coastal resorts motorbikes and bicycles are an ideal way to travel, especially in summer. Traffic is more orderly and there are more policemen on duty in the evening. Crash helmets must be worn on motorbikes and Vespas above 125cc and by minors on all types of motorbike.

USEFUL ADDRESSES
◆ Capri
CAPRI NOLEGGIO MOTORINI
Via Marina Grande 280
Tel. 8377941

◆ Ischia
BALESTRIERI
Via dello Stadio 16
Ischia Porto
Tel. 981055
ISLAND CAR DIVISIONE ITALIA
Via Quercia 24
Ischia Porto
Tel. 992276
MOTONOLEGGIO DEL FRANCO
Via A. de Luca 133
Ischia Porto
Tel. 991334
◆ Sorrento
RENT-A-SCOOTER
Via Atilliana 1
Tel. 8771239
SORRENTO RENT-A-CAR
Corso Italia 210/a
Tel. 8781386

alilauro

SHOPPING

In Naples stores are usually open from 9am to 1pm and from 4.30pm to 8pm. In winter they are closed on Sundays and Monday mornings. In summer all stores close on Saturday afternoons and Sundays, except food stores, which usually close on Thursday afternoons and Sundays.

RECEIPTS
Whenever you pay for anything, always ask for a tab or till receipt. You may be asked to produce your receipt(s) by a customs officer as you leave the store and it could be embarrassing if you do not have one.

SERVICE CHARGES AND TIPS
Menu prices in restaurants do not include the service charge (12–15%). There is also a separate cover charge. In bars, a coffee served at a table may cost up to three times more than one served at the counter. Tips are left at the customer's discretion.

SAFETY

THEFT
It is not advisable to carry large amounts of cash about with you. Leave what you don't need in the hotel safe. Don't wear expensive-looking watches and jewelry. If you're traveling by car, don't leave valuable items in view inside the vehicle. Take photocopies of identity papers and documents as these could be useful if you have to report a lost or stolen item. At night it is safer to avoid the streets around the station, the port district and the Spanish districts, but don't give way to paranoia as this could prevent you making the most of your stay.

BLACK-MARKET GOODS
A word of advice to smokers: even if the price of black-market cigarettes is lower than that of the packs sold (with the official seal) in tobacconist's, they could turn out to be a lot more expensive that you had anticipated. Anyone caught in possession of black-market cigarettes by Customs & Excise officers will be fined 100,000 lire. What is more, you will also have to pay for the privilege of having your photograph published in the local paper, alongside a public announcement of your offence.

MARKETS

FOOD MARKETS
Each district has its own food market. Neapolitans prefer these colorful, noisy, busy places to their local food stores.
◆ Typical markets include: the Pignasecca market, behind the Piazza Carità; the Borgo di Sant'Antonio Abate market, behind the Via Foria (always packed and a veritable food bazaar); the Porta Nolana fish market, near the central station (particularly picturesque with the quantity and variety of its stalls; late-night shopping on December 23).
◆ These markets are open every morning during the week.

COLLECTORS' AND ANTIQUES MARKETS
◆ The Naples antiques fair is held in the gardens of the Villa Comunale, up by the Viale Dorhn, usually on the 3rd weekend in the month (from 8am to 2pm) and on certain other occasions (Christmas and Easter holidays). For further information, contact the Naples Antiques Fair association (tel. 7612541). For information on occasional markets, contact the Azienda Autonoma di Soggiorno, Cura e Turismo (tel. 418744)

OTHER MARKETS
For clothes, accessories and items for the home, you should try:

◆ Antignano market, at Vomero (Mon. to Sat. 8am to 1pm)
◆ Casale market (Thur. 8am to 2pm).

FLEA MARKETS
◆ The market on the Via Ponte di Casanova, near the Napoli Centrale station, is open every day except Sundays and public holidays.
◆ The market on the Corso Malta, under the slip-road of the ring road, is only held on Sunday mornings.
◆ Combine a trip to Herculaneum with a visit to the famous Resina flea market (which is open from dawn to 1pm): clothes, shirts, leather jackets, accessories, tablecloths and household linen are offered in good condition and reasonably priced. In order to get to Resina by car, you must take the Naples-Salerno freeway, leave via the Ercolano exit and follow the signs for Pugliano. You can leave your car in the supervised parking lot on the Piazza Santa Maria del Pugliano, which is situated near the market.

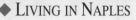

Porta Nolana market.

TELEPHONES

PUBLIC TELEPHONES
◆ You can telephone towns in Italy and other countries using the public telephones (kiosks and public places). They take 100 lire, 200 lire and 500 lire coins (change is given) and phone cards. Dial the operator (170) to make a collect call.
◆ Telephone cards are available from tobacconists', kiosks, Telecom Italia agencies and machines (in stations and post offices). They cost 5,000, 10,000 or 15,000 lire.
◆ Certain public telephones can only be operated by telephone credit cards, which you can obtain by calling free phone 167-156156.

TELEPHONING FROM YOUR HOTEL
There is no restriction on charges made by hotels.

TELEPHONING FROM A PTP
Posti Telefonici Pubblici (PTP) – public telephone centers – have soundproofed booths from which you can make local, national and international calls. You pay after you have made your call. The largest "PTP" in Naples is at Via Depretis 4.

PHONING FROM ITALY
◆ UK:
Dial 00 44 followed by the regional code then the number you require.

◆ US:
Dial 00 1 then the regional code and the number you require.

NEW TELEPHONE NUMBERS IN ITALY

From June 1998, dial 0 and the local code before the number of the person you are calling when telephoning from one area to another and from abroad.

Calls within the same area and to emergency numbers and mobile telephones are not affected by this change.

NEWSPAPERS

◆ *Il Mattino* publishes a daily "Girocittà" of practical information and a calendar of the day's conferences and exhibitions. The "Per chi parte" section gives the times of trains (Naples– Rome), flights from Capodichino airport, ferries and hovercraft. The local edition of the national daily *La Repubblica* devotes 16 pages to Naples. Since June 1997 the 16-page supplement

to the *Corriere del Mezzogiorno*, which is devoted to Naples and the surrounding area, has been available in kiosks. There are two other local daily newspapers: *Il Giornale di Napoli* and *Roma*.
◆ *Qui Napoli* is published by the Naples branch of the Azienda Autonoma di Soggiorno, Cura e Turismo and is distributed free of charge to hotels and tourist offices.

It contains a range of information on the month's events, including the opening times of churches and museums, lists of movie theaters, theaters, hotels, restaurants, bars, and sports clubs.

FOREIGN NEWSPAPERS
Foreign newspapers are available from the kiosks in the central station (Piazza Garibaldi), the Galleria Umberto I, Via Calabritto, and the main tourist areas (Capri, Ischia and Sorrento).

MEDICAL SERVICES
EMERGENCY SERVICE
The service operates between 8pm and 8am and on public holidays. On Sat. and the day before public holidays, it operates between 2pm and 8am the following morning.

●
EMERGENCY SERVICES
CALL 112
●

DRUGSTORES
A list of dispensaries open after hours is published in daily local newspapers and displayed outside pharmacies.

MAIL

◆ A stamp (*francobollo*) for the European Union costs 850 lire (letters) or 700 lire (postcards). You can buy stamps in post offices and tobacconist's.
◆ Letter boxes are red and located near post offices, and usually near tobacconist's.

◆ The main post office (Piazza Matteotti) is open from 8.15am to 7.20pm (8.15am to 2pm on Sundays). Sub-post offices are open daily (except Sundays) from 8.15am to 1.20pm.
◆ Information: Tel. 5511456

HEALTH AND SAFETY
SEAFOOD
It is perfectly safe to eat cooked seafood. However, it is unwise to eat it raw unless you are sure of its origins: cases of hepatitis caused by seafood are quite common in the region.

The Naples region can pride itself on its varied and thriving craft tradition. Visitors who want to take home typical souvenirs are quite literally spoilt for choice: from elegant handmade garments to coral and gold jewelry and ceramics. There are also many well-stocked stores selling ready-to-wear clothing.

HANDMADE GARMENTS

During the Middle Ages Naples – a royal town populated by a powerful local aristocracy – developed a tradition of rich and elegant handmade garments, especially fine-quality shirts, ties, gloves and hats. Until the mid-20th century, the young heirs of the landed nobility who frequented the piazzas and *cafés-concerts* vied with each other in elegance. Today this traditional craft is beginning to disappear: in 1993, 49 glove makers and 18 hat makers closed down, leaving only 54 glove makers and 8 hat makers to carry on the tradition.

HATS

The ancient art of millinery was developed and perpetuated by craftswomen working from home. Neapolitan milliners, who shared some of the characteristics of the Parisian "grisette", were extremely active during the 19th century, passing from the status of "seamstress" to that of "head seamstress" and finally becoming independent craftswomen. The milliner was an artist in her own right, creating personalized hats which combined the very finest fabrics: silk, muslin and velvet. Today milliners are only found among the entourage of eccentric noblewomen. However until World War Two these mistresses of the veiled and velvet-ribboned hat – extremely proud of their expertise – were producing veritable masterpieces in their bedroom-workshops. Men's hatmaking is also a disappearing art. They are today only produced industrially by a few big labels.

LEATHER-WORK

The Naples region still has small craft stores producing small leather objects and made-to-measure shoes. These are the survivors of a traditional craft that experienced its golden age under the Bourbons and inspired the writer Matilda Serao to comment at the turn of the century: "The young smart-set in Naples is the best dressed in Italy . . . the most elegant shoes and gloves are produced in Naples."

TIES

Naples' reputation for handmade ties was established, in particular, by Luigi Marinella who invented the "made-to-measure tie". This son of an early 20th-century Neapolitan shirt-maker made the tie a symbol of male elegance. His designs were unique and cut from beautiful and rare fabrics imported from Manchester. Some of the leading celebrities of the first half of the 20th century frequented his elegant store in the Piazza Vittoria, on the Chiaia riviera: the poet Gabriele d'Annunzio, King Umberto of Savoy, the tenor Caruso, the manufacturer Agnelli and many prominent international figures. Apart from the creations of the "grand master", Naples still has a fairly widespread tradition of made-to-measure ties in silk, wool and knitted fabrics.

GLOVES

Naples has long been renowned for its gloves – once the prerogative of the nobility – but today within the reach of ordinary people. Many of the streets in the old town have been named after this originally medieval tradition, attesting to its importance in times gone by: for example, the Via dei Guantai Nuovi ("street of the new glovers").

Glove-making was a noble tradition, which used mainly lamb and kid skins tanned with alum, chamois and buckskin tanned with oil or used to produce suede, as well as fabrics (linen, wool and cotton). Today, in spite of its very obvious decline, glove-making is one of the most thriving of the Neapolitan traditional crafts.

USEFUL ADDRESSES

◆ TIES:
Luigi Marinella,
Riviera di Chiaia 287
◆ GLOVES:
Pistola,
Via Santa Caterina a Chiaia 12
◆ HATS:
Piscopo,
Via San Pasquale 17
◆ READY-TO-WEAR MENSWEAR:
Marino,
– Via Santa Caterina a Chiaia 73–74
– Via dei Mille 6–8

TRADITIONAL CRAFTS

UNUSUAL ITEMS
The Via San Biagio dei Librai is a busy and lively street lined with stores selling religious art and traditional crafts, antiques, gold and silver. At no. 81 is an *ospedale delle bambole* (dolls' hospital) presided over by the "surgeon" Luigi Grassi. The list of the district's many craft stores is endless: leather-work, metalwork, paper, artificial flowers. Stationer's:
◆ Enrico Gambardella & F., Via Benedetto Croce 28 *Amalfi paper*
◆ Nilo Carta & Cartoni, Via San Biagio dei Librai 1

Window display of a "presepi" craftsman.

CERAMICS
The region's most famous ceramics are made at Vietri ▲ 291, on the Amalfi Coast. Tiles and other objects are decorated with characteristic themes: the grape harvest, Moorish motifs, women and children by a fountain, fishermen, the sun and moon.

MOSAICS
In the Vico Carafocchiole, in Capodimonte, the Sorrentino family has, for three generations, perpetuated an old Neapolitan tradition by producing tables, mosaics and pediments, and reproducing marquetry pictures in marble and hard stone.

"PRESEPI" FIGURES
San Gregorio Armeno is the district of the *presepi* (crib) craftsmen ● 56, ▲ 154, who work throughout the year to create Nativity décors and scenes for the Christmas season which begins at the beginning of November. Crib-making has its fashions: the religious figures have been joined by modern-day celebrities such as Totò, Silvio Berlusconi and the judge Di Pietro.
◆ The most famous *presepi* workshop: Ferrigno, Via San Gregorio Armeno 8

CORAL ● 64, ▲ 220
All the jeweler's in the Naples region offer a wide range of coral items: cameos, earrings, necklaces . . .

The most renowned coral craftsmen are found in Torre del Greco, a small town on the slopes of Vesuvius, where the art of engraving has been carried on for generations and claims to predate Asiatic techniques.

FASHION
The fashionable and elegant Italian designer boutiques are found in the Chiaia district: Via Chiaia, Via dei Mille, Via Filangieri, Via Carlo Poerio.

The Vomero (especially Via Scarlatti, Via Luca Giordano, Piazza Vanvitelli) also offers a wide range of luxury fashion boutiques.

SALES
Winter: early January to early March.
Summer: early July to early September.
Reductions may be as much as 50%, especially in fashion boutiques.

DON'T JUDGE A STORE BY ITS SIGN

Don't be surprised if you find more than just cigarettes in the famous tobacconist's store of Don Peppino (left), on the corner of the Via San Gregorio and the Via San Biagio dei Librai, or washing powder in the pork butcher's. In Naples store signs are relative.

MUSIC
Music enthusiasts will find many stores selling musical scores and instruments on the Via San Sebastiano, near the Conservatory of San Pietro a Maiella.

"Pizza Margherita was born here 100 years ago."   There are many fishmonger's in Naples.

Neapolitan food is characterized by a number of specialties: fish, pasta dishes and some very elaborate cakes – a cocktail of flavors to enjoy with locally produced wine. And what better to end your meal than a *limoncello* liqueur from the Sorrentine peninsula.

TRADITIONAL CUISINE

PIZZA ● 60
The pizza is the Neapolitan dish *par excellence*. With a wood-fired oven and an infinite range of simple ingredients, the pizza – the first example of fast food – has become an international favorite. Neapolitans prefer the Margherita which, according to tradition, was created in 1889 in the pizzeria Brandi (in the Chiaia district) by Raffaele Esposito for Queen Margherita. Its basic ingredients – tomatoes, mozzarella cheese and basil – represent the Italian national colors. Over the years, and aided by the creative imagination of the *pizzaioli*, the range of toppings has been extended to include a number of – very simple or very unusual – new ingredients.

OTHER SPECIALTIES
Neapolitan food is rich and varied, often delightful to behold and even more delightful to eat. Some of the better-known dishes include: *spagetti* with seafood, *gnocchi à la*
sorrentine, *pizzaiola* (slices of beef in tomato sauce flavored with garlic and oregano), *minestra maritata* (a soup made with chicory, chicken and pork eaten the day after public holidays, especially December 26), *soffritto* (a very spicy offal stew) and *pasta e fagioli* (pasta and beans, sometimes mixed with mussels). Neapolitan *ragù* is a tomato sauce garnished with pork, beef and *braciola* (a thin slice of meat, rolled and stuffed with parsley and garlic). *Ragù* still forms the basis of Sunday lunch for many families, even though it sometimes has to compete with *genovese* (beef cooked in an onion purée).

FISH AND SEAFOOD
There is a vast choice of seafood in Naples, but it is advisable to ensure that it is fresh. *Vongole* (clams), *cozze* (mussels) and *fasulare* (large, smooth shellfish) are served as an appetizer or to flavor main courses.
Fish includes *baccalà* (dried salt cod), *alici* (anchovies), *polipi* (octopus), *triglie* and *cefali* (mullet), *calamari* (squid), *gamberetti* (shrimps) and every kind of Mediterranean fish, including swordfish grilled *à l'acquapazza* (steamed with tomatoes and garlic). Fish is prepared according to a strict culinary code to ensure maximum flavor. According to a Neapolitan proverb – "every fish has its own death" – there is a recipe for every type of fish.

CHEESE
True mozzarella ● 60, made with buffalo milk, is produced in Caserta and Battipaglia. When it is fresh, mozzarella made with cows' milk *(fioredilatte)* is also delicious.

FRUIT
The region produces a vast range of fruit that can be found in the local markets: sun-soaked lemons, mandarins and oranges, bursting with scent and flavor, fresh figs, dessert grapes and delicious-looking tomatoes.

PATISSERIE
On special occasions, meals often end with such traditional patisserie as *pastiera* ● 62, which is served at Easter, and *rococò* (almond biscuits), *mustaccioli* (cake iced with chocolate) and *struffoli* (small honey cakes), served at Christmas. And not forgetting *sfogliatelle* ● 64, ▲ 155 and *babà* (with or without confectioner's cream).

RECIPE
Braciolone alla Neopolitana
Prepare a mixture of breadcrumbs, *provolone* (cheese), ham, garlic and chopped parsley. Add some pine nuts, raisins and a pinch of pepper and mix together with a beaten egg. Spread the mixture on a thin, tenderized slice of beef and then roll and tie in a "sausage". Brown the *braciolone* over a high heat before cooking in the oven (350°F/180°C) for 30 minutes.

In summer you can quench your thirst at one of the city's many "acquaiuoli".

Neapolitan patisserie is an art form. One of the city's many tripe stalls. The Gambrinus.

MEALS AND COFFEE BREAKS

The day begins with *'na tazzulella 'e café* (a cup of coffee), as sung by Pino Daniele, served at the counter. Large cafés and small bars are the Neapolitan meeting place *par excellence*, according to a time-honored ritual. There are no fixed meal times and in most of the city's districts you can eat throughout the day, in the street or sitting comfortably at a table overlooking the sea. A pizza can be bought on the street at any time of day and only costs 2,000 lire. In the evening, in one of the many pizzerias on the Piazza Sannazaro, you can try a *caponata* (a sort of breakfast biscuit topped with tomatoes, aubergines, artichokes in oil and anchovies . . .).

A TRADITIONAL MEAL

The courses are usually as follows:
– *antipasto* (starter)
– *primo piatto* (first course, usually pasta)
– *secondo piatto con contorno* (second course, meat or fish with an accompaniment)
– *frutta* (fruit, always on the table)
– *dolce* (patisserie)
– *caffè*
– *amaro*, *nocino* or *nocillo* (a liqueur made from unripe nuts).

WHERE TO EAT

Restaurants, pizzerias, patisseries, bars, rotisseries . . . the choice can be rather confusing for visitors. Restaurants (*ristorante*, *trattoria*) and pizzerias are a generic term: restaurants often have a wood-fired pizza oven, while pizzerias often serve pasta and meat and fish dishes. The bar-rotisseries (*rosticcerie*) serve the famous Neapolitan sandwich (*panino*) – bread dough stuffed with hard-boiled egg, salami and bacon – which is highly recommended.

"CAFFÈ"

In Naples coffee is more than just a drink. The coffee break has become a custom and an art of living. Coffee is drunk – black and piping hot, with a topping of tobacco-colored froth – at breakfast and after meals, but also throughout the day, and even late into the evening (in the "chalets" of Mergellina, for instance). Most of Naples' historic cafés have disappeared. The Gambrinus ▲ 134 (Piazza Trieste e Trento) and Caflish (Via Chiaia, recently restructured) are the sole survivors of a tradition, established in the 18th and reaching its peak in the 19th century. In spite of successive managements, the Gambrinus – the oldest of these cafés – has preserved some beautiful paintings by Scoppetta, Migliaro, Caprile and other local artists.

OTHER BEVERAGES

FRESH FRUIT JUICE
There is nothing like a *limonata* (freshly squeezed lemon juice) to quench your thirst on a hot summer's day. There are still a few drink kiosks – *acquaiuoli* – in the historic center and near the Lungomare. Some have a traditional décor of oranges and lemons. Mint cordial and barley water are also very refreshing. These "refreshment sellers" are perpetuating one of the city's oldest traditions ● 64.

WINE ● 64
Wines include the famous *Lacrima-Christi* and *falanghina*, ideal accompaniments for fish dishes. The slightly sparkling red *gragnano*, from the vines of Vesuvius, is usually served with meat. White and red *solopaca*, and red *asprino* and *taurasi* are ideal with cheese and the noble meats. The wines of Ischia and Capri are also well worth tasting, as are the *ravello* and *furore* wines of the Amalfi Coast, which are excellent with fish.

A SPECIALTY
Brodo di polipo (octopus stock) is a very individual "hot drink" that can be found at the Porta Capuana, near the Piazza Garibaldi. Why not give it a try?

◆ ACCOMMODATION

The Vesuvio and the Excelsior, on the Lungomare, have retained their 19th-century charm.

The "Grand Tour" – the formative journey that brought so many young aristocrats to Italy during the 18th century – made the city and region of Naples one of the favorite destinations of travelers from all over Europe. And in more than one instance, the beauty of the surroundings, the warmth of the inhabitants and the scent of the lemon trees turned a chance encounter into an indissoluble bond. Although the Neapolitan landscape has undergone significant changes, an off-peak holiday in an historic hotel will enable you to recapture the atmosphere of days gone by.

HOTEL INFRASTRUCTURE

On the islands and along the Amalfi Coast, where there has always been a constant flow of tourists, accommodation ranges from luxury hotels to simple family boarding houses. Naples is making every effort to meet the demands of its vocation as a tourist destination by providing a wide and varied range of hotel accommodation. However, there is still a degree of imbalance in the middle-top range, with the quality-price ratio occasionally leaving something to be desired. There is also a limited choice for visitors on a fairly restricted budget.

CLASSIFICATION
Hotels are classified (* to *****) by the provincial authorities and the Ente Provinciale del Turismo, according to the services provided. In the coastal resorts, even middle-range hotels often have their own swimming pool and private access to the sea.

PRICES
Official prices always include taxes and are displayed on the door of rooms. In Naples there is no distinction between the high and low season. However it is worth asking for special rates as it is possible to obtain reductions of up to 20% or 25% for weekends or off-peak periods. Hotels in coastal resorts do have seasonal rates (sometimes even distinguishing between low, middle, high and peak season). Half-board is often compulsory, especially during the first two weeks of August.

YOUTH HOSTELS
In Naples the Ostello Mergellina (23, salita della Grotta, tel. 7612346) is an excellent solution for those on a very limited budget. The hostel is near the Napoli Mergellina and subway stations, and has 65 rooms (some with a panoramic view of the city) with 2, 4 or 6 beds, most with their own bathroom. The price per night, including breakfast, ranges from 22,000 lire for rooms with 4 or 6 beds, to 25,000 lire for double rooms. Ask at the Ostello Mergellina for information on youth hostels in Agerola, Paestum, Salerno and Sorrento.

CAMP SITES
There are no camp sites in Naples and campers have to stay in the surrounding area. The most convenient site for visiting the city is the Vulcano Solfatara (Tel. 5267413) in Pozzuoli, in the park of the same name. It is about half a mile from the subway, from where it takes about 20 minutes to the city center (Montesanto station). There are other good-quality camp sites in Ischia, the Sorrentine peninsula and in the Salernitano, especially along the coast between Paestum and the Marina de Camerota.

WHERE TO STAY
- The luxury hotels tend to be in the vicinity of the Lungomare.
  - Hotels in the commercial and administrative districts are less "atmospheric" but comfortable.
  - The historic center has small, family-run hotels.
- There are a lot of hotels near the station, but the district is not very salubrious, especially at night.

Useful information

The following hotels have been chosen for their quality, friendly service and pleasant surroundings, but they are also located near places of interest. Some are well-known themselves, and they all enable visitors to find out more about the region via their food, décor, setting and, in many cases, their own history and that of their famous guests or customers.

A HOTEL ON THE WATERFRONT

QUISISANA & GRAND
HOTEL*****
Capri ◆ 332
400,000–800,000 lire
LA CERTOSELLA***
Capri ◆ 332
250,000–400,000 lire
VILLA KRUPP** ★
Capri ◆ 332
170,000–230,000 lire
CAESAR AUGUSTUS***
Anacapri ◆ 333
130,000–380,000 lire
SAN MICHELE***
Anacapri ◆ 334
200,000–240,000 lire
MEZZATORRE*****
Forio ◆ 334
300,000–420,000 lire
HOTEL DELLA BAIA***
Fori ◆ 334
180,000–220,000 lire
HOTEL MIRAMARE
E CASTELLO*****
Ischia Porto ◆ 334
260,000–540,000 lire
IL MORESCO
GRAND HOTEL
E TERME****
Ischia Porto ◆ 335
380,000–520,000 lire

HOTEL REGINA
ISABELLA*****
(LUXURY)
Lacco Ameno ◆ 335
400,000–800,000 lire
SANTA CATERINA*****
Amalfi ◆ 336
390,000–560,000 lire
HOTEL CAPPUCCINI
CONVENTO**** ★
Amalfi ◆ 336
200,000–240,000 lire
LUNA CONVENTO****
Amalfi ◆ 336
210,000 lire
per person,
half-board
BRITANNIQUE****
Naples ◆ 337
210,000–270,000 lire
EXCELSIOR ****
Naples ◆ 337
470,000 lire

MIRAMARE****
Naples ◆ 338
250,000–390,000 lire
PARADISO****
Naples ◆ 338
290,000 lire
PARKER'S****
Naples ◆ 338
310,000–365,000 lire
SANTA LUCIA****
Naples ◆ 338
380,000–440,000 lire
VESUVIO**** ★
Naples ◆ 338
470,000 lire
SAN PIETRO*****
Positano
◆ 341
640,000–720,000 lire
LE SIRENUSE*****
Positano
◆ 341
396,000–748,000 lire

PALAZZO MURAT**** ★
Positano ◆ 342
290,000–390,000 lire
POSEIDON****
Positano ◆ 342
310,000–390,000 lire
CASA ALBERTINA***
Positano ◆ 342
160,000–220,000 lire
VILLA
CIMBRONE**** ★
Ravello ◆ 343
350,000–400,000 lire
VILLA MARIA***
Ravello ◆ 343
120,000–260,000 lire
JOLLY ****
Salerno ◆ 344
245,000 lire
COCUMELLA*****
Sant'Aniello – Sorrento
◆ 344
440,000–490,000 lire
EXCELSIOR
VITTORIA**** ★
Sorrento ◆ 345
282,000–563,000 lire
IMPERIAL
TRAMONTANO****
Sorrento ◆ 345
360,000 lire

WITH POOL OR PRIVATE BEACH

QUISISANA & GRAND
HOTEL*****
Capri ◆ 332
400,000–800,000 lire
LA CERTOSELLA***
Capri ◆ 332
250,000–400,000 lire
SAN MICHELE***
Anacapri ◆ 334
200,000–240,000 lire
MEZZATORRE*****
Forio ◆ 334
300,000–420,000 lire
HOTEL MIRAMARE
E CASTELLO*****
Ischia Porto ◆ 334
260,000–540,000 lire
HOTEL REGINA
ISABELLA***** (LUXURY)
Lacco Ameno ◆ 335
400,000–800,000 lire
LA VILLAROSA**** ★
Ischia Porto ◆ 335
120,000–150,000 lire
per person half-board
SAN MICHELE***
Sant'Angelo ◆ 335

330,000–380,000 lire
SAN PIETRO*****
Positano ◆ 341
640,000–720,000 lire
POSEIDON****
Positano
◆ 342
310,000–390,000 lire
VILLA MARIA***
Ravello ◆ 343
120,000–260,000 lire
COCUMELLA*****
Sant'Aniello –
Sorrento
◆ 344
440,000–490,000 lire
LLOYD'S BAIA
HOTEL****
Vietri ◆ 345
250,000–280,000 lire

IN AN UNUSUAL SETTING

QUISISANA & GRAND
HOTEL*****
Capri ◆ 332
400,000–800,000 lire
CAESAR
AUGUSTUS***
Anacapri ◆ 333
130,000–380,000 lire
LA VILLAROSA**** ★
Ischia Porto ◆ 335
120,000–150,000 lire
per pers. half-board
SANTA CATERINA*****
Amalfi ◆ 336
390,000–560,000 lire
HOTEL CAPPUCCINI
CONVENTO**** ★
Amalfi ◆ 336
200,000–240,000 lire
LUNA CONVENTO****
Amalfi ◆ 336
210,000
lire per
person,
half-board

PARKER'S****
Naples ◆ 338
310,000–365,000 lire
SANTA LUCIA****
Naples ◆ 338
380,000–440,000 lire
SAN PIETRO*****
Positano ◆ 341
640,000–720,000 lire
PALUMBO*****
Ravello ◆ 343
410,000–610,000 lire
VILLA CIMBRONE**** ★
Ravello ◆ 343
350,000–400,000 lire
COCUMELLA*****
Sant'Aniello – Sorrento
◆ 344
440,000–490,000 lire
EXCELSIOR
VITTORIA**** ★
Sorrento ◆ 345
282,000–563,000 lire
BELLEVUE
SYRENE****
Sorrento ◆ 345
280,000–400,000 lire

FISH RESTAURANTS

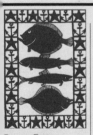

BAGNI DI TIBERIO
Capri ♦ *332*
40,000–70,000 lire

DA PAOLINO
Capri ♦ *333*
60,000–80,000 lire

TORRE SARACENA
Capri ♦ *333*
50,000–80,000 lire

ADD'O RICCIO
Anacapri ♦ *334*
50,000–75,000 lire

DAI TU
Ischia Porto ♦ *335*
40,000–60,000 lire

'O PORTICCIULL
Ischia Porto ♦ *335*
50,000–90,000 lire

LA BRICIOLA
Fango 14
Lacco Ameno
♦ *335*
40,000–50,000 lire

LA MISENETTA
Bacoli ♦ *336*
60,000–100,000 lire

TAVERNA DEL CAPITANO
Nerano
(Massa Lubrense)
♦ *337*
50,000–70,000 lire

LA BERSAGLIERA
Naples ♦ *339*
50,000–80,000 lire

CIRO A SANTA BRIGIDA
Naples ♦ *340*
40,000–90,000 lire

DA DORA
Naples ♦ *340*
60,000–100,000 lire

LA SACRESTIA
Naples ♦ *341*
70,000–120,000 lire

LA BUCA DI BACCO
Positano ♦ *342*
50,000–80,000 lire

LO GUARRACINO ★
Positano ♦ *343*
30,000–60,000 lire

ALLA BRACE
Salerno ♦ *344*
45,000–60,000 lire

DON ALFONSO
1890 ★
Sant'Agata dei Due
Golfi ♦ *344*
95,000–160,000 lire

RESTAURANTS WELL WORTH A DETOUR

LA FONTELINA
Capri
♦ *333*
35,000–80,000 lire

TORRE SARACENA
Capri ♦ *333*
50,000–80,000 lire

DA PEPPINA DI RENATO
Forio ♦ *334*
40,000–60,000 lire

MARIA GRAZIA
Nerano
(Massa Lubrense)
♦ *337*
40,000–70,000 lire

LA CANTINA DI TRIUNFO
Naples ♦ *339*
45,000–60,000 lire

LA CANTINELLA
Naples ♦ *339*
60,000–100,000 lire

CIRO A MERGELLINA
Naples ♦ *339*
55,000–85,000 lire

CIRO A SANTA BRIGIDA
Naples ♦ *340*
40,000–90,000 lire

DON SALVATORE
Naples ♦ *340*
50,000–70,000 lire

EUROPEO
Naples ♦ *340*
40,000–60,000 lire

LA SACRESTIA
Naples ♦ *341*
70,000–120,000 lire

LA TAVERNA DELL'ARTE
Naples ♦ *341*
35,000–50,000 lire

VADINCHENIA
Naples ♦ *341*
40,000–60,000 lire

LA CAMBUSA
Positano ♦ *342*
50,000–80,000 lire

CUMPÀ COSIMO
Ravello ♦ *344*
35,000–60,000 lire

ALLA BRACE
Salerno ♦ *344*
45,000–60,000 lire

DON ALFONSO 1890 ★
Sant'Agata dei Due
Golfi ♦ *344*
95,000–160,000 lire

CARUSO
Sorrento ♦ *345*
40,000–80,000 lire

'O PARRUCCHIANO
Sorrento ♦ *345*
40,000–60,000 lire

THE VERY BEST IN PIZZAS

AURORA
Capri ♦ *332*
45,000–75,000 lire

DA GEMMA
Capri ♦ *333*
30,000–60,000 lire

BRANDI
Naples ♦ *339*
30,000–60,000 lire

CIRO A MERGELLINA
Naples ♦ *339*
55,000–85,000 lire

CIRO A SANTA BRIGIDA
Naples ♦ *340*
40,000–90,000 lire

DI MATTEO
Naples ♦ *340*
7,000–20,000 lire

EUROPEO
Naples ♦ *340*
40,000–60,000 lire

DA MICHELE
Naples ♦ *340*
5,000–10,000 lire

PULCINELLA A SANTA BRIGIDA
Naples ♦ *341*
30,000–70,000 lire

TRIANON
Naples ♦ *341*
10,000–20,000 lire

ALLA BRACE
Salerno
♦ *344*
45,000–60,000 lire

AND IN MUSIC . . .
'O PORTICCIULL
Ischia Porto
♦ *335*
50,000–90,000 lire

PULCINELLA A SANTA BRIGIDA
Naples
♦ *341*
30,000–70,000 lire

THE VERY BEST IN WINES

LA CAPANNINA
Capri ♦ *333*
50,000–80,000 lire

ADD'O RICCIO
Anacapri ♦ *334*
50,000–75,000 lire

'O PORTICCIULL
Ischia Porto ♦ *335*
50,000–90,000 lire

LA MISENETTA
Bacoli ♦ *336*
60,000–100,000 lire

LA CANTINA DI TRIUNFO
Naples ♦ *339*

LA CANTINELLA
Naples ♦ *339*
60,000–100,000 lire

DON SALVATORE
Naples ♦ *340*
50,000–70,000 lire

AL POETA
Naples ♦ *341*
50,000–70,000 lire

LA SACRESTIA
Naples ♦ *341*
70,000–120,000 lire

VADINCHENIA
Naples ♦ *341*
40,000–60,000 lire

LA BUCA DI BACCO
Positano ♦ *342*
50,000–80,000 lire

DON ALFONSO 1890 ★
Sant'Agata ♦ *344*
95,000–160,000 lire

CARUSO
Sorrento ♦ *345*
40,000–80,000 lire

'O PARRUCCHIANO
Sorrento ♦ *345*
40,000–60,000 lire

331

◆ USEFUL ADDRESSES

The hotel prices given below are for a double room including breakfast (except for the *College Europeo* and the *Soggiorno Sansevero*, which do not serve breakfast).
The two prices given for each hotel are the minimum price in the low season and the maximum price in the high season, except for hotels in Naples, where there is no high and low season. Instead, the two prices quoted for double rooms in Naples relate to levels of comfort.

ISLAND OF CAPRI

CAPRI

POSTAL CODE
80073

HOTELS

QUISISANA & GRAND HOTEL***
Via Camerelle 2
Tel. (0)81-8370788
Fax (0)81-8376080
Closed Nov.–one or two weeks before Easter
149 rooms,
400,000–800,000 lire
(suite 900,000–1,000,000 lire)
The "sanatorium", founded by British physician George Sidney Clark in 1845, is now an ultra-luxury hotel and the rendezvous par excellence for royalty and other celebrities staying on the island. It is considered one of the world's most beautiful hotels, a reputation that has not altered over the years, as it has, among other things, appreciated

the need to adapt to the requirements of its modern clientele. It has two restaurants (one of which – the Quisi – is recommended by the famous Italian chef Gualtiero Marchesi), two swimming pools and a fitness center.

LA PALMA**
Via Vittorio Emanuele 39
Tel. (0)81-8370133
Fax (0)81-8376966
74 rooms,
210,000–430,000 lire
In 1820 the lawyer Don Giuseppe Pagano converted his house, which overlooked a very tall palm tree, into the island's first inn. At the time there were few visitors to the island, which could only be reached after a long and often dangerous crossing. The name of the establishment has remained unchanged over the years. Today La Palma is a large

hotel in the center of Capri. This typically Mediterranean, white-painted building, with its arches and arcades, has perpetuated the tradition of hospitality that was established by its founder.

LA CERTOSELLA*
Via Tragara 13–15
Tel. (0)81-8370713
Fax (0)81-8376113
18 rooms,
250,000–400,000 lire

A small and unassumingly charming hotel, with a garden and restaurant overlooking the pool and a panoramic view from all rooms. It is on the road leading to the "enchanted" belvedere of Tragara ▲ 233, where legend has it that if you lean over the parapet holding someone's hand,

with your fingers crossed, you will fall madly in love.

RESTAURANTS

AURORA
Via Fuorlovado 18–22
Tel. (0)81-8370181
Closed Tue. in Oct.
45,000–75,000 lire
No breathtaking views here, but a charming setting of narrow, whitewashed streets and arched passageways.
For many years the restaurant has served the best pizzas on the island, as well as offering a vast range of hors d'oeuvre, cooked vegetables and omelettes to suit every taste.

BAGNI DI TIBERIO
Via Palazzo a Mare
Tel. (0)81-8377688
Closed evenings from Oct. 15 to May 15
40,000–70,000 lire
The villa ▲ 228 that once stood on the creek of the ancient Roman port was the summer residence of the

★ **VILLA KRUPP****
Via G. Matteotti 12
Tel. (0)81-8370362
Fax (0)81-8376489
12 rooms,
170,000–230,000 lire
The Villa Krupp offers an opportunity to enjoy the peace and tranquility of a simpler side of Capri that manages to co-exist with the fashionably elegant island of the jet-set. It overlooks the flowering vegetation of the Gardens of Augustus ▲ 231, whose terraces descend to the sea and the Marina Piccola. The hotel was named after Friedrich Alfred Krupp ▲ 231, the strangely tormented 19th-century steel magnate. He was devoted to the island, to which he bequeathed the vertiginously steep

Via Krupp – hewn out of the rock – that winds down to the sea. Before becoming a hotel about thirty years ago, the villa was a residence

frequented by such illustrious figures as Maxim Gorky, who received Lenin there. Half of the simply furnished rooms overlook the sea and

the Faraglioni ▲ 232–233. This family-run hotel offers very basic comfort and a pleasant atmosphere. There is no restaurant.

STOP PRESS
New telephone numbers in Italy
Remember to include the zeros between brackets (0)
when telephoning: they are part of the new area codes

emperors Tiberius and Augustus, chosen because it was cool and near to the sea. A thermal establishment with a reasonably priced restaurant was opened near these romantic ruins that rise from the waters of the bay. Why not take time out to enjoy its shade, if only long enough to sample a plate of pickled anchovies and a glass of the island's clear, sharp and low-alcohol white wine ● 64.

LA CAPANNINA
Via delle Botteghe 12–14
Tel. (0)81-8370732
Closed from mid-Nov. to Easter (except during the Christmas holidays) and on Wed. until the end of July
50,000–80,000 lire
For fifty years this has been the best restaurant with incontestably the best cellar on the island, serving French and Italian wines, good-quality Campanian wines and the island's own appellation contrôlée wines: the white punta vivara and bordo and the red solaro. The wines, liqueurs and typical food products served in the restaurant are on sale in the Capannina Più along the street.

LA FONTELINA
Località Faraglioni
Tel. (0)81-8370845
Closed Oct. to Easter
40,000–80,000 lire
A beautiful downhill walk or a short boat trip from the Scoglio delle Sirene at the Marina Piccola brings you to the baths of La Fontelina, on the sun-drenched rocks opposite the Faraglioni ▲ 232–233. The natural beauty of the setting remains untouched and is enhanced by the fact that it lies off the beaten track. Regular clientele of Italians and other

nationalities. The terrace restaurant serves some delicious aubergine croquettes with "caciotta" (cheese). See you at sundown.

DA GEMMA
Via Madre Serafina 6
Tel. (0)81-8370461
Closed Jan. and Mon. from Feb. to Mar.
30,000–60,000 lire
This restaurant near the Piazzetta is an indissociable part of the island's history. One of the old ovens is still in use and old copper saucepans and utensils decorate the walls. The amiable Silvio is a true master of the art of pizza and patisserie. The verandah opposite is decorated with hundreds of signed photographs of both major and minor celebrities, all delighted with their visit to Da Gemma.

LE GROTTELLE
Via Arco Naturale 13
Tel. (0)81-8375719
Closed from beginning Nov. to Palm Sunday, and Thur. from May to mid-July.
40,000–60,000 lire
A small, rustic trattoria, 5 minutes from the road to the Arco Naturale ▲ 232, on the bay of the Grotta di Matromania. It stands in an enchanting and untouched natural setting that changes with the seasons: sinister in winter, restful in spring, resplendent in summer. The terrace is shaded from the sun by a cane awning. The kitchen and wood-fired oven, used to prepare a delicious "focaccia bianca" (without tomatoes) flavored with garlic and rosemary, are hewn out of the rock.

DA PAOLINO
Via Palazzo a Mare 11
Tel. (0)81-8376102
Closed from Nov. to Easter and lunchtime from June to Sep.
60,000–80,000 lire
A truly delightful setting. As soon as the weather is warm enough, the tables are set out in the shade of a lemon grove at the Marina Grande. The restaurant offers a wide choice of hors d'oeuvre and a superb range of fresh fish: sea bream, bass, mullet, scampi and prawns. In cooler weather, try a dish of pasta with "cicerchie" (the tasty local chick peas) followed by the restaurant's own delicious lemon tart.

★ LA SAVARDINA
Via Lo Capo 8
Tel. (0)81-8376300
Closed from Jan. 7 to beginning Mar., and Tue. (except in summer)
35,000–45,000 lire
Since walking is one of the island's great pleasures, the 20–25-minute walk, in the direction of the Villa Jovis ▲ 232, to the path leading to La Savardina is ideal for sharpening the appetite. The restaurant garden is planted with lemon and orange trees, vines and aromatic plants (the island prides itself on having over five hundred varieties). The owner, Eduardo, is a very singular figure – a host-poet passionately devoted to his native island – who uses home-grown produce to prepare dishes that he describes as "ecological and rustic". His greatest successes echo local tradition: Capri ravioli, filled with fresh "caciotta", devilled chicken and rabbit chasseur, baked aubergines and a superb chocolate tart. Fish is not on the

menu, but you can place a special order 24 hours in advance.

TORRE SARACENA
Via Krupp
Tel. (0)81-8370646
Closed Oct.–Easter
50,000–80,000 lire
Open-air trattoria with a thermal establishment at the Marina Piccola, both opened in 1902 following one of the first land concessions. The menu offers original interpretations of traditional dishes and improvised dishes: rigatoni with pumpkin and shrimps, rotelle with courgettes, linguine with limpets and mantis shrimps (a house specialty), baked fish with olives and capers, almond and carrot tart and stewed fruit tart.

ANACAPRI

POSTAL CODE
80071

HOTELS

CAESAR AUGUSTUS★★★
Via G. Orlandi 4
Tel. (0)81-8371421
Fax (0)81-8371444
Closed Nov. to Mar.
58 rooms,
130,000–380,000 lire
(suite 450,000 lire)
Caesar Augustus, the first Roman emperor, was also one of the island's first devotees ▲ 226. An impressive statue of Augustus, at the end of the large terrace, looks out over the Bay of

Naples toward Vesuvius and Sorrento. The hotel's luxury wing has several small suites, which are hewn out of the rock, and perched like eagles' eyries high above the sea. There is no restaurant.

SAN MICHELE***
Via G. Orlandi 5
Tel. (0)81-8371442
Fax (0)81-8371420
Closed Nov. to Mar.
60 rooms,
200,000–240,000 lire
The San Michele, built in 1880, is another symbol of Anacapri's hospitality. It is rather old-fashioned and popular with those tourists not seeking to join the island's "social whirl". Queen Maria-Christina of Sweden stayed here when she visited her friend and physician, Axel Munthe ▲ 234. It has a magnificent view of the sea and Monte Solaro ▲ 235 and a semi-olympic pool in a natural setting.

RESTAURANTS

ADD'O RICCIO
Via Grotta Azzurra 11
Tel. (0)81-8371380
Closed Nov. to Mar. Open Thurs. eve. to Sunday from June to Sep.
50,000–75,000 lire
Restful pergola high above the sea on the road to Anacapri. About 100 yards further down is the famous Grotta Azzurra (Blue Grotto) ▲ 236. An exclusively seafood menu, ideal for fish enthusiasts, cooked a variety of ways and washed down with a wide choice of good-quality white wines. Remarkable "linguine alla Fra'Diavolo" with lobster and seafood.

MAMMA GIOVANNA
Via Boffe 3–5
Tel. (0)81-8372057

Closed Jan. and Feb. and on Wed., except between June 21 and Sep. 21
35,000–60,000 lire
This small restaurant is located in the historic center of Anacapri. Its owner-chef laments: "Even our simplest recipes are immediately copied, with the result that – in order to maintain our individuality – we are constantly obliged to change the menu." This means that you will be able to taste a wide range of specialties, including "pennete al cartoccio" (en papillote) with seafood, olives and mushrooms, and a delicious lemon tiramisù.

ISLAND OF ISCHIA

CASAMICCIOLA TERME

POSTAL CODE
80074

RESTAURANT

IL FOCOLARE
Via Cretaio 68
Tel. (0)81-980604
Closed Wed. (except in summer) and lunchtime Mon., Tue. and Thur.
45,000–60,000 lire
This pleasant, hillside trattoria, run by Riccardo and Loretta d'Ambra (formerly of the wine-making company of the same name) and their many children, serves traditional rustic dishes which vary with the seasons. An absolute "must" in the fall is polenta with ceps, and snails

flavored with herbs; in summer try the delicious fruit risotto. Most of the "primi" are based on fresh pasta: the broccoli "gnocchi" and "bucatini" with rabbit sauce are excellent. The wine tradition dates from the late 19th century.

FORIO

POSTAL CODE
80075

HOTELS

MEZZATORRE*****
Località San Montano
Tel. (0)81-986111
Fax. (0)81-986015
Closed Nov. to April
58 rooms, 300,000–420,000 lire (suite 450,000–570,000 lire)
The road to the Mezzatorre passes through a dense forest stretching down to the sea. The growing impression that this is going to be a pleasant experience is confirmed when you catch a glimpse, through the dense vegetation, of the 16th-century dungeon, clinging to a rocky spur, that once defended the coast against Saracen attacks. Today it is a magnificent luxury hotel, with delightful, elegantly furnished rooms, tennis courts, thermal baths, a pool and a private beach.

HOTEL DELLA BAIA***
Via San Montano 18–22
Tel. (0)81-986398
Fax (0)81-986342
Closed Oct. to April
20 rooms,
180,000–220,000 lire
This small and truly delightful Mediterranean-style hotel is only a few yards from the beach of San Montano ▲ 212. The rooms in the main body of the building are light and brightly furnished. Visitors who want to relax will appreciate the offer reserved for guests

who have chosen the half-board option: free admission (except in August) to the "Negombo", the island's most elegant thermal establishment.

RESTAURANT

DA PEPPINA DI RENATO
Via Bocca 42
Tel. (0)81-998312
Closed Wed. (except in summer) and from mid-Nov. to mid-Mar.
40,000–60,000 lire
Open evenings only. This delightful "trattoria" is perched on the hill overlooking the beach of Citara. Its menu is based on the flavors of the kitchen garden and is more akin to the countryside than the sea: soups, vegetable pasta, rabbit "à la mode d'Ischia", sweet pepper stew and excellent patisserie and fruit tarts. All made on the premises, of course.

ISCHIA PORTO

POSTAL CODE
80077

HOTELS

HOTEL MIRAMARE E CASTELLO*****
Via Pontano 9
Tel. (0)81-991333
Fax (0)81-9984572
Closed Oct. 15.–Apr.
40 rooms,
260,000–540,000 lire (suite 340,000–540,000 lire)
Four years' restoration work were well worth the effort: the Miramare is the only five-star hotel in Ischia Porto. This 16th-century manor stands on the edge of a beach and is linked to terra firma by a narrow causeway, directly opposite the Aragonese castle ▲ 213. Noted for its high-quality service, it has a private beach and landing stage, thermal pool and beauty salon: an oasis of luxury.

★ LA VILLAROSA ★★¹
Via G. Gigante 5
Ischia Porto
Tel. (0)81-991316
Fax (0)81-992425
Closed Nov. to
Easter
37 rooms,
120,000–150,000 lire
*Set in a garden
of eucalyptus, pines,
banana, olive and
palm trees, where
Mediterranean
scrub co-exists
happily with exotic
plants, this quiet and
discreetly elegant
residence
is in fact virtually
in the center of Ischia.
The beautiful late
19th-century
farmhouse, which
was converted into
a hotel in the early
1950's, has lost
none of its very
individual atmosphere:
large lounges that are*

*decorated with
furniture by the
Neapolitan and
Sicilian schools, a
small library, brass
and wrought-iron
bedsteads in the
individually decorated
bedrooms, a shady
terrace where you*

*can sit and have
breakfast while
contemplating
the sea . . .
And not forgetting
the thermal pool
with hydromassage,
which is concealed
among the abundant
vegetation.*

IL MORESCO GRAND HOTEL E TERME ★★★★
Via E. Gianturco 16
Tel. (0)81-981355
Fax (0)81-992338
Closed Oct. to March
76 rooms,
380,000–520,000 lire
*A truly remarkable
location: set in a
pine grove, bordered
by a beach and only
a few minutes' walk
from the shopping
streets. Sophisticated
and elegant, with a
large Moorish-style
lounge opening onto
the garden, a well-
equipped beauty
salon and thermal
establishment.
Most of the extremely
comfortable bedrooms
have a terrace
overlooking the sea.*

RESTAURANTS

DAI TU
Lungomare C. Colombo
Tel. (0)81-983093
Closed Nov. to March
40,000–60,000 lire
*This waterfront
restaurant, with its
superb view of
Procida and Vivara
▲ 215, is lovingly*

*run by Aniello and
his large family,
including daughters-
in-law and
grandchildren.
Good fishermen's
fare served in a
pleasant, friendly
atmosphere to the
sound of waves
washing onto the
shore: from simple to
more elaborate dishes
including some
remarkably light
fried fish.*

'O PORTICCIULL
Via Porto 42
Tel. (0)81-993222
Closed Mon. (except
in summer)
50,000–90,000 lire
*The busy right bank
of the port is teeming
with fashionable inns
and tavernas.
Nothing but extremely
fresh fish on the
menu: seafood,
fish soup, spaghetti
with clams, fish à
l'acquapazza, all
washed down with
excellent local
wines and often
accompanied by
music, especially
the guitar.*

LACCO AMENO

POSTAL CODE
80076

HOTEL

HOTEL REGINA ISABELLA ★★★★★ (LUXURY)
Piazza Santa Restituta
Tel. (0)81-994322
Fax (0)81-900190
Closed mid-Jan. to
end Mar. 133 rooms,
400,000– 800,000 lire
(suite 1,400,000 lire)
*This hotel, which was
built in the 1950's when
the "green island" was
competing with Saint
Tropez for the attention
of successful movie-
makers, movie stars and
playboys, became the
rendezvous par
excellence of the
international jet set. Gina
Lollobrigida, Truman
Capote, Liz Taylor and
Richard Burton were just
a few of its many famous
guests. This pleasant
and elegant venue has
everything you need for
a relaxing holiday:
private beach, tennis
courts, thermal pools
and saunas.*

RESTAURANT

LA BRICIOLA
Via Provinciale
Fango 14
Tel. (0)81-996060
Closed at noon and
on Tue. (except
in summer)
40,000–50,000 lire
*Intimacy and
atmosphere in this
small restaurant
skillfully dedicated to
the sea. Excellent fish
hors d'oeuvre, shellfish
and crustaceans,
delicious lemon
tagliolini and linguine
alla briciola (shellfish,
scampi, squid and other
fish of the day). For
dessert, the restaurant's
own profiteroles, with
whipped cream and
chocolate, are
irresistible. In summer
(reservations essential),
you can dine in a
beautiful garden of
exotic plants.*

SANT'ANGELO

POSTAL CODE
80070

HOTEL

SAN MICHELE ★★★★
Tel. (0)81-999276
Fax (0)81-999149
Closed Nov. to mid-April
52 rooms,
330,000–380,000 lire
*Sant'Angelo ▲ 213 is
indisputably the island's
most charming village: it
has a handful of
multicolored houses,
a labyrinth of narrow
streets (pedestrians
only) and the sleepy
atmosphere of a
peaceful fishing village.
The San Michele stands
in a quiet corner, a few
minutes from the center,
surrounded by a garden
of palm trees and
mimosa. It has a
swimming pool and
thermal facilities.*

NAPLES AND THE BAY

AMALFI

POSTAL CODE
84011

HOTELS

SANTA CATERINA
*****

SS Amalfitana 9
Tel. (0)89-871012
Fax (0)89-871351
70 rooms,
390,000–560,000 lire
(suite 680,000–
1,100,000) lire
This magnificent hotel, perched high above the sea about ½ mile outside Amalfi, has retained all the charm of an early 20th-century aristocratic residence. Visitors will be delighted by the light, airy lounges decorated with antique furniture, the impeccably designed restaurant and the beautiful, citrus-scented paths leading down to the sea. The extremely luxurious suites have their own jacuzzi and terrace garden.

★ HOTEL CAPPUCCINI CONVENTO ****

Via Annunziatella 46
Tel. (0)89-871877
Fax (0)89-871886
54 rooms,
200,000–240,000 lire
(suite 360,000–
400,000 lire)
Half-board only
throughout August:
170,000 lire per person
in a double room
This 13th-century
monastery, set in
the rock, was
converted into a
hotel in the mid-
18th century.
Although it may
have lost a little of
its former splendor,
it is nonetheless
delightful. It is reached
by means of an
exterior elevator,
which runs up to a
partly decorative and
partly kitchen garden
where the monks
used to pray. The

LUNA CONVENTO ****

Via P. Comite 33
Tel. (0)89-871002
Fax (0)89-871333
40 rooms,
210,000 lire per person,
half-board
The hotel has been
run by the same
family for two hundred
years. The French
writer Simone de
Beauvoir was
captivated by the
former convent,
perched high above
the sea. She stayed
there for two nights
and, as she later wrote
to Jean-Paul Sartre,
would never have
left had the porter not
so insistently offered
to alleviate her
solitude! The "convent"
had already
fascinated playwright
Henrik Ibsen before
her, and one of its
cells had provided
the inspiration for his
play "A Doll's House".
You can breakfast
in a Byzantine
cloister where
Saint Francis of
Assisi once walked,
but for sleeping

purposes, the rooms
in the annex are
more comfortable
and spacious.

RESTAURANT

DA GEMMA

Via Fra' Gerardo
Sasso 9
Tel. (0)89-871345
Closed Wed. (except
in summer), at noon
in Aug., and from
mid-Jan. to mid-Feb.
50,000–100,000 lire
The trattoria, run
with the same
devotion by the
Cavaliere family for
over one hundred
years, is an
institution in Amalfi.
It serves regional
fish dishes made with
ultra-fresh ingredients,
and it is worth eating
there merely to taste
the excellent soup.
In summer, you can
dine on the terrace
overlooking the
roof tops. The
cozy interior is
decorated with old
photographs and
autographs of
famous customers.

BACOLI

POSTAL CODE
80070

RESTAURANT

LA MISENETTA

Via Lungolago 2
Tel. (0)81-5234169
Closed Mon. from Dec.
23 to Jan. 2 and from
June 25 to Sep. 25
60,000–100,000 lire
The reputation of this
restaurant, set in the
Phlegraean Fields
▲ 198, is closely linked
to that of its owner,
Salvatore di Meo, an
inventive chef who gives
an original interpretation
to traditional
Mediterranean dishes.
Fish occupies pride of
place and the dishes,
under the influence of
the French school, are
meticulously presented:
from oyster risotto to
aubergine pastry, and
from sea bream with
saffron to desserts and
sorbets. A visual and
gastronomic feast,
accompanied by an
excellent choice of
Italian and foreign wines.

side overlooking
the sea is bordered
by the famous
colonnade
(immortalized in
a number of
19th-century
photographs),
from where visitors
can enjoy blazing
sunsets and
impressive views
likely to inspire
thoughts of
eternity. Of the
many famous
guests who have
meditated here,
Wagner was so
entranced by
such beauty
that he remained
beneath the
colonnade all
night. The monks'
cells have been
converted into
pleasant rooms
opening onto long,
silent corridors.
The restaurant

prepares the convent's
traditional dishes to
order, including the
Santa Rosa, a cake in

the form of a priest's
hat, filled with dried
fruit and flavored with
orange liqueur.

MASSA LUBRENSE

POSTAL CODE
80061

RESTAURANT

ANTICO FRANCESCHIELLO (DA PEPPINO)
Via Partenope 27
Tel. (0)81-5339780
Closed Wed. (except in summer)
60,000–100,000 lire
A romantic garden overlooking the bay, ancient ceramics, copper utensils hanging on the walls, old sideboards spread with all kinds of hors d'oeuvre: it is immediately obvious that the restaurant has a long-standing tradition to its credit. Flavors are typical of the peninsula and tend to be traditional, with a few notable exceptions, such as the excellent crab-meat or bass ravioli, and the fresh pasta with ceps and fresh tomatoes. The lemon dessert (almond sponge cake and whipped cream), invented about forty years ago, has aged well.

NERANO (MASSA LUBRENSE)

POSTAL CODE
80061

RESTAURANTS

MARIA GRAZIA
Spiaggia di Marina del Cantone
Tel. (0)81-8081011
Closed Wed. (except in summer) and from Dec. 1 to Jan. 20.
40,000–70,000 lire
This waterfront "trattoria" is renowned for its spaghetti and sautéed courgettes. According to tradition, the dish was created when a prince of the nobility arrived at this modest

restaurant, where Maria Grazia cooked in the inter-war period for the fishermen of the bay. The kitchen was closed and Maria had to improvise, producing a simple meal of spaghetti flavored with the only vegetables to hand. The dish proved a great success and made the restaurant's reputation.

TAVERNA DEL CAPITANO
Piazza delle Sirene 10
Marina del Cantone
Tel. (0)81-8081028
Closed Mon. (except in summer) and from Jan. 10 to Feb. 27
50,000–70,000 lire
Chicory and prawn soup, tagliatelle with "pesce azzurro" (anchovies, sardines) and wild fennel, prawn "canelloni" with a vegetable garnish, fish ravioli, cod "paupiettes" with artichokes: the captain and his family blend the flavors of land and sea to excellent effect. For dessert, try the aubergines in chocolate, a dish based on an ancient Arab recipe.

NAPLES

POSTAL CODE
80100

HOTELS

BRITANNIQUE ★★★★
Corso Vittorio Emanuele 133
Tel. (0)81-7614145
Fax (0)81-660457
86 rooms,
210,000–270,000 lire
Those who find the rather kitsch appearance of some of the big hotels oppressive will like the pleasantly restrained and traditional style of the Britannique. Its light, pleasant rooms look out over the bay. Across the

street a private garden full of exotic plants is reserved for hotel guests.

EXCELSIOR ★★★★
Via Partenope 48
Tel. (0)81-7640111
Fax (0)81-7649743
120 rooms,
470,000 lire
(suite 700,000–1,100,000 lire)
The Excelsior, overlooking the Castel dell'Ovo ▲ 190 and Capri ▲ 226, is the epitome of the grand hotel. It is soon to be restored to its former glory, but guests can still enjoy the somewhat decaying charm of its Empire-style public rooms, with their profusion of marble and stuccowork. The private rooms enjoy spectacular views and have welcomed a host of famous visitors. Sample traditional Mediterranean cuisine in the Casanova Grill or dietetic dishes in the bar, which also serves kosher food on request.

JOLLY ★★★★
Via Medina 70
Tel. (0)81-416000
Fax (0)81-55518010
252 rooms,
250,000–300,000 lire
Located in the city center, in a skyscraper built in the 1950's. The huge bay windows of the restaurant offer a panoramic view of the city. You can clearly see the secluded

cloisters of the historic center, the narrow streets of the Spanish district ▲ 149, the ultra-modern silhouette of the Centro Direzionale, the hill of Posillipo ▲ 192 and the waterfront. Rooms with a view are from the 17th floor upward.

MEDITERRANEO ★★★★
Via Nuova Ponte di Tappia 25
Tel. (0)81-5512240
Fax (0)81-5525868
253 rooms,
280,000 lire
The Mediterraneo, which is situated right in the city center and only a stone's throw from the Piazza del Municipio, is one of the major stop-overs for business men and women. It has large, functional rooms that are decorated in authentic 1950's style. The roof terrace offers a magnificent view of the city with the Castel Nuovo ▲ 134 and the iron and glass dome of the Galleria Umberto ▲ 134 in the foreground.

MERCURE ANGIOINO ★★★★
Via A. Depretis 123
Tel. (0)81-5529500
Fax (0)81-5529509
85 rooms,
280,000 lire
The hotel, opened in January 1993, is located between the University district and the Piazza del Municipio. It is also near the Molo Beverello, which makes it an ideal venue for visitors who want to combine a stay in Naples with excursions along the coast and to the islands. All rooms are soundproofed and some are reserved for non-smokers. A young and relaxed atmosphere in the Angioino bar.

337

MIRAMARE ★★★★
Via Nazario Sauro 24
Tel. (0)81-7647589
Fax (0)81-7640775
30 rooms,
250,000–390,000 lire
A small hotel in an early 20th-century aristocratic villa. Do not be put off by the austerity of the entrance hall. The hotel's pastel-colored rooms offer a level of comfort that is not often found in the big hotels (for instance, tea- and coffee-making facilities). In summer you can have breakfast on a delightful flower-filled terrace, complete with hammocks and loungers, which offers a spectacular view of Vesuvius.

PARADISO ★★★★
Via Catullo 11
Tel. (0)81-7614161
Fax (0)81-7613449
75 rooms,
290,000 lire
The Paradiso stands on the quiet hillside of Posillipo ▲ 192, which is located far from the city crowds and overlooks the bay. The hotel's rooms face east and look toward the Castel dell'Ovo ▲ 190 in the distance, dominated by the impressive bulk of Vesuvius. Although it is a long way from the noise and bustle of the city, the Paradiso is situated only a few minutes from the funicular railway near the busy little port of Mergellina ▲ 192. Breakfast and candlelit dinners are served on the hotel's panoramic terrace.

PARKER'S ★★★★
Corso Vittorio
Emanuele 135
Tel. (0)81-7612474
Fax (0)81-663527
80 rooms,
310,000–365,000 lire
(suite 750,000–
1,500,000 lire)
Parker's, first opened in 1870, still retains all the sophistication of a long-standing tradition in its elegant lounges, decorated with antique furniture and works of art, and the library, adjoining the Napoleon bar, containing valuable and rare editions. Its comfortable bedrooms face south toward Capri and each floor is decorated in a different style. The Bellevue restaurant, overlooking the bay, provides a perfect setting for the hotel's high-quality cuisine.

SANTA LUCIA ★★★★
Via Partenope 46
Tel. (0)81-7640666
Fax (0)81-7648580
102 rooms,
380,000–440,000 lire
(suite 540,000–
700,000 lire)
Opposite the Castel dell'Ovo ▲ 190 and the Borgo Marinaro ▲ 190. An atmosphere of cocooned elegance, created by a neoclassical décor of stuccowork, columns and rich hangings, attracts a regular clientele. The delicately and discreetly decorated rooms are comfortable and spacious, and the Bar del Pavone, on the first floor, is an ideal place in which to relax.

TERMINUS ★★★★
Piazza Garibaldi 91
Tel. (0)81-286011
Fax (0)81-206689
168 rooms,
250,000–340,000 lire
(suite 340,000–
460,000 lire)
A veritable oasis of calm amid the chaos of the piazza, the Terminus has always been one of the leading hotels in the district. Its extremely comfortable rooms all have a balcony, and the hotel also has a number of "business suites", which are equipped with a fax and computer and are available on request. The top floor of the Terminus boasts a modern seminar and conference facility, which is surrounded by a beautiful panoramic terrace.

EXECUTIVE ★★★
Via del Cerriglio 10
Tel. (0)81-5520611
Fax (0)81-5520611
19 rooms,
220,000–270,000 lire
The Executive backs onto the 13th-century convent of Santa Maria la Nova ▲ 147 and is close to the historic center. The rooms are light and comfortable (single rooms are particularly spacious and have three-quarter beds). A small but well-equipped gym, complete with sauna, and a flower-filled terrace where you can breakfast overlooking the rooftops, add to the enjoyment of your stay.

★ VESUVIO ★★★★
Via Partenope 45
Tel. (0)81-7640044
Fax (0)81-7644483
165 rooms,
470,000 lire
(suite 700,000–
1,400,000 lire)
The charm of Naples' oldest waterfront hotel (a fashionable rendezvous for so many famous travelers since the late 19th century) is inescapable. Sophia of Sweden was the first to stay here, in a gesture of public support, after a cholera epidemic. She was followed shortly afterward by Guy de Maupassant, who wrote some of his travel sketches during his stay, and by Oscar Wilde and Alfred Douglas, who were involved in a "scandalous" liaison. During the 1950's, Hollywood stars came to play out their scenes of love and betrayal, from Errol Flynn to Clark Gable. But the hotel's most poignant memory is that of the great tenor, Enrico Caruso, who died here. The most luxurious suite (which still contains his piano) is named after him, as is the romantic top-floor, terrace restaurant, where you can dine on summer evenings overlooking the sea.

PINTO STOREY ***
Via G. Martucci 72
Tel. (0)81-681260
Fax (0)81-667536
25 rooms,
185,000 lire
Since 1878 the boarding house has occupied the upper floors of a modern-style building in this elegant part of Naples. It has a beautiful wood staircase and elevator, clean, quiet rooms (some with a panoramic view) and a tiny lounge, decorated with period furniture and an unbelievable number of plants, creating the cozy atmosphere of a private house. Guests tend to be visitors who prefer places of charm and character to the cold efficiency of modern hotels, but one reader has informed us of a few technical problems that need to be resolved.

COLLEGE EUROPEO *
Via Mezzocannone 109
Tel. (0)81-5517254
Fax (0)81-5522262
17 rooms,
140,000 lire
The hotel occupies the 4th floor of an anonymous, modern building (with no elevator), opposite the University and behind the Astra cinema. But it is well placed and its small, pleasant rooms have been recently renovated. Unfortunately it has no bar and therefore does not serve breakfast. The Europeo is ideal for those on a tight budget and is popular with young tourists who like the district's many night clubs, where they can listen to live music.

SOCCIORNO SANSEVERO *
Via San Domenico Maggiore 9
Tel. (0)81-5515949
6 rooms,
70,000–120,000 lire
This recently opened, family boarding house enjoys a remarkable situation, which makes up for the very ordinary and rather depressing furnishings of its few rooms. Housed in the former palace of the Prince of Sansevero ▲ 142, a fascinating and mysterious figure of 18th-century Naples, it overlooks an elegant and busy piazza in the historic center, dominated by the Baroque spire and church of San Domenico ▲ 142.

RESTAURANTS

53
Piazza Dante 53
Tel. (0)81-5499372
Closed Wed.
35,000–55,000 lire
Situated right in the historic center, this is a traditional restaurant with an established reputation. The menu changes with the seasons: substantial dishes, such as the rich "minestra maritata" soup, in winter, and lighter but equally delicious dishes in summer. The hors d'oeuvre (more than ten) are an absolute must and are virtually a meal in themselves. In summer you can dine outside, but the few tables have to be reserved well in advance.

LA BERSAGLIERA
Borgo Marinaro
Tel. (0)81-7646016
Closed Tue. and for the Aug. 15 holiday
50,000–80,000 lire
This old restaurant, almost on the water's edge, is steeped in the magical atmosphere of the Borgo Marinaro ▲ 190. The irresistible charm of the surroundings makes up for the fact that the food is sometimes disappointing. To avoid unpleasant surprises, choose simple dishes: spaghetti with fresh tomatoes, baked fish and, for dessert, "pastiera" ● 62 or baba.

BRANDI
Salita Sant'Anna di Palazzo 1
Tel (0)81-416928
Closed for 3 days around Aug. 15
30,000–60,000 lire
The Brandi, over one hundred years old, is renowned for the invention of the famous pizza Margherita ● 60 (garnished with tomatoes and mozzarella), in honor of Queen Margherita of Italy. The walls are decorated with souvenirs of its long history: signed photographs of famous customers, newspaper cuttings, awards and diplomas. Fast, friendly service and excellent pizzas (around 14,000 lire for a pizza and beer).

LA CANTINA DI TRIUNFO
Riviera di Chiaia 64
Tel. (0)81-668101
Closed at noon, Sun. and Aug.
45,000–60,000 lire
This former bar has for a long time been a small (only a few tables, so reservations are essential) rustic restaurant renowned for its delicious cuisine. The menu, which changes each evening,

is recited passionately and with precision by the mistress of the house: a choice of two primi and two main courses, prepared as you watch, in the huge, open kitchen. High-quality, light dishes, skillfully chosen wines, house "rossolis" (liqueur) and patisserie that comes straight from the oven make this an exceptional gastronomic experience.

LA CANTINELLA
Via Cuma 42
Tel. (0)81-7648838
Closed Sun. evenings all year round, and noon Aug. 20–30.
Closed Aug. 8–19.
60,000–100,000 lire
This elegant and sophisticated restaurant, near the big waterfront hotels, is popular with business men and women who want to combine business with gastronomic pleasure. Friendly atmosphere, efficient service and such excellent dishes as the "linguine alla Santa Lucia" (flat spaghetti with clams and prawns) and "papardelle al cielo di Napoli" (broad tagliatelle with courgettes and scampi). A wide range of wines from Italy and other countries.

CIRO A MERGELLINA
Via Mergellina 18
Tel. (0)81-681780
Closed Mon. (Fri. in summer)
55,000–85,000 lire
One of the temples of Neapolitan cuisine where you can also enjoy excellent pizzas. A fairly banal décor (in

summer, it is much more pleasant to eat outside), but always full owing to a superbly varied cuisine: unforgettable fried fish "à l'italienne", with tender pieces of octopus in tomato sauce, huge buffalo-milk "mozzarelle" with seafood spaghetti, rich fruit salads with smooth ice-cream that is among the best in the city.

CIRO A SANTA BRIGIDA
Via Santa Brigida 71
Tel. (0)81-5524072
Closed Sun.
40,000–90,000 lire
The restaurant, opened in the 1930's and run ever since by the same family, is ideal for pure traditionalists. It serves "sartù di riso", an elaborate rice cake with meat and mushrooms and usually only found in family cooking, "o pignatiello 'e vavella", a fish soup made with shellfish, octopus and squid, cooked in a terracotta pot and served with croutons, as well as a range of remarkable pizzas.

DI MATTEO
Via dei Tribunali 94
Tel. (0)81-455262
Closed Sun. and for 2 weeks in Aug.
7,000–20,000 lire
Set in the heart of Greco-Roman Naples ▲ 151, this pizza restaurant scored a hit with Bill Clinton during the G7 Summit. Newspaper cuttings show the American president holding a Margherita folded "a libretto" (in two), like a true Neapolitan. At noon customers queue at the take-out stand for "arancini di riso" (rice croquettes), potato croquettes and fried pizza.

DON SALVATORE
Via Mergellina 5
Tel. (0)81-681897
Closed Tue.
50,000–70,000 lire
An absolute must for lovers of traditional cuisine re-interpreted with sophistication and imagination. Apart from the hors d'oeuvre (the small fried clams and prawns with rocket salad are delicious) the "primi", a successful blend of seafood and vegetables, are highly recommended. The cellar is the restaurant's pride and joy: the best local and national wines and a collection of "rare" bottles over twenty-five years old. In summer it is advisable to reserve in advance if you would like to eat outside.

DA DORA
Via F. Palasciano 28
Tel. (0)81-680519
Closed Sun. from Dec. 22 to Jan. 2 and for 2 weeks in Aug.
60,000–100,000 lire
Fish enthusiasts will not be disappointed by this informal trattoria, which is located in a narrow street on the Riviera di Chiaia. Here you can sample the very freshest pickled anchovies, sautéed clams and cuttlefish, grilled squid, fish "à l'acquapazza" and baked bass. The "linguine alla Dora", with shellfish, scampi and lobster, are truly memorable. The Da Dora is a family-run restaurant with the atmosphere of a fishermen's bar.

EUROPEO
Via Marchese Campodisola 4
Tel. (0)81-5521323
Closed Sun. and evenings (except Fri. and Sat.) and 2 weeks in Aug.
40,000–60,000 lire
This small restaurant, near the University, has a pleasant décor, friendly service and a family atmosphere. Checked tablecloths set off a good-quality local cuisine: very good pizzas and classic dishes washed down with wines from Campania.

MASANIELLO
Via Donnalbina 28
Tel. (0)81-5528863
Closed Sun. (except in Dec)
35,000–50,000 lire
This small restaurant, which occupies the stables of a former nobiliary residence, is one of the best in the city's historic center. The rooms have been skillfully

restored to reveal Bohemian vaults and trachyte pillars. The menu includes such traditional dishes as pasta soup and potato soup with "provola" (a strongly flavored cheese) and "bucatini con il soffritto" (pasta flavored with aromatic herbs and bacon). Excellent desserts and a well-stocked cellar with more than sixty regional labels.

DA MICHELE
Via C. Sersale 1/3
Tel. (0)81-5539204
Closed Sun. and for 3 weeks in Aug.
5,000–10,000 lire
Opened in the late 19th century, this is one of Naples' oldest pizzerias. The décor is extremely basic: long marble tables and a large wood-fired oven. Apart from the pizza marinara (the restaurant's own invention, with garlic, oil, oregano and tomatoes) and the classic Margherita, the "calzone" stuffed with fresh cheese is highly recommended.

MIMI ALLA FERROVIA
Via A. d'Aragona 21
Tel. (0)81-5538525
Closed Sun. and 2 weeks in Aug.
50,000–75,000 lire
Only a stone's throw from the station and law courts, this restaurant is popular with the city's lawyers, who are well acquainted with its quality. There is a good range of hors d'oeuvre, but the traditional main courses, such as "pasta e ceci" (pasta and garbanza bean soup) and "maccheroncelli lardiati" (with bacon), are even better. Although renovations have spoilt the distinctive style of the interior, the restaurant has retained its family atmosphere.

AL POETA
Piazza Salvatore di
Giacomo 133
Tel. (0)81-5756936
Closed Mon. and 2
weeks in Aug.
50,000–70,000 lire
*The restaurant, which
is at the top of the
hill of Posillipo ▲ 192,
is very popular with
the local inhabitants.
In summer they queue
to eat at the few
outside tables
overlooking the
shady piazza.
The restaurant
serves good seafood
cuisine, which is
accompanied by a
vast choice of mainly
regional wines.*

**PULCINELLA A
SANTA BRIGIDA**
Via Santa Brigida 49
Tel. (0)81-5517117
Closed for one week
around Aug. 15
30,000–70,000 lire
*Punchinello ('Pulcinella'),
without doubt the most
famous Commedia
dell'Arte ● 52 character,
is honored in this
recently-opened
restaurant-pizzeria.
The artist Lello
Esposito has filled the
place with sculptures
representing the
part lazy, part wise
Neapolitan character.
Besides 40 different
types of pizza
(including a Nutella
pizza!), the menu offers
simple and tasty
traditional grilled meat
and fish dishes.
Try the "tagliere di
pulcinella", which the
chef re-invents every
day according to his
mood and inspiration.
There is a good
wine list, with a
choice of more
than 100 Italian
and foreign wines.*

LA SACRESTIA
Via Orazio 116
Tel. (0)81-7611051
Closed Sun. evening
and Mon. lunchtime
70,000–120,000 lire
*You will not be
disappointed in Naples'
most famous restaurant,
with its elegant décor,
well-stocked cellar,
excellent cuisine
and a panoramic
view worthy of a
postcard. Although
inspired by tradition,
its chefs give free rein
to their creativity and
have produced such
memorable dishes
as "fagottini" filled
with chives and
ricotta, aubergine
ravioli, timbales
and meat sauces.
Extremely fresh fish
and elaborate
desserts. In summer
you can dine on a
flower-filled terrace
overlooking the bay.*

**LA TAVERNA
DELL'ARTE**
Rampa San Giovanni
Maggiore 1/a
Tel. (0)81-5527558
Open evenings only.
Closed Sun. and
in Aug.
35,000–50,000 lire
*This tastefully and
lovingly decorated
taverna stands on a
piazza where the
chefs' corporation
used to meet in the
17th century. It
serves delicately
flavored dishes that
are based on ancient
recipes: vegetable
quiche, endive pizza
or pasta omelette are
followed by soups and
various types of meat.
The excellent desserts
are accompanied by
house liqueurs.
In summer you can dine
beneath a romantic
pergola opposite the
basilica of San Giovanni
Maggiore
▲ 146.*

TRIANON
Via P. Colletta 46
Tel. (0)81-5539426
Closed Sun. and at
noon
10,000–20,000 lire
*The most popular
pizzeria in Naples
(it is always packed),
the Trianon has
retained its original
1930's décor: the
only "cutlery" on
the big marble
tables are the paper
serviettes. Enjoy
huge, delicious pizzas
in the restaurant's
chaotic and friendly*

*atmosphere, and
admire the skill of
the "pizzaioli" who work,
as you watch, at an
unbelievable speed.*

VADINCHENIA
Via Pontano 21
Tel. (0)81-660265
Closed at noon, on Sun.
and in Aug.
40,000–60,000 lire
*The gray and white
of the décor by
Philippe Stark
constitute the
"non-colors" of this
restaurant, opened
by two committed
professionals. The
Mediterranean
cuisine, dominated
by seafood, changes
every month. The
delicate vegetable*
*mousses and the
swordfish "taglierini"
are excellent. An
interesting wine-list
with more than
200 labels.*

POSITANO

POSTAL CODE
84017

HOTELS

SAN PIETRO ★★★★★
Via Laurito 2
Tel. (0)89-875455
Fax (0)89-811449
Closed Nov. to
Palm Sun.
59 rooms,
640,000–720,000 lire
(suite 850,000–
1,150,000 lire)
*About 1¼ miles
outside Positano, a
small 17th-century
chapel acts as a
landmark for the
San Pietro. The
hotel's spectacular
situation (the plant-
and flower-covered
building is partly
hewn out of the
rock and perched
high above the sea)
and exceptional
comfort (pool, tennis
court and private
beach) make it one
of the jewels of the
Amalfi Coast. The
visitors' book is full
of famous names.*

LE SIRENUSE ★★★★★
Via C. Colombo 30
Tel. (0)89-875001
Fax (0)89-811798
60 rooms,
396,000–748,000 lire
(junior suite
649,000–902,000 lire)
*The hotel enjoys
a magnificent view
of the bay of
Positano ▲ 284
and the islands of
Li Galli, the home
of the sirens who
tormented Ulysses.
In this former
residence of the
marquises of
Sersale, the family's
valuable antiques
and furniture are
skillfully combined
with the latest in
modern comfort.*

STOP PRESS
New telephone numbers in Italy
Remember to include the zeros between brackets (0)
when telephoning: they are part of the new area codes

★ PALAZZO MURAT ★★★★

Via dei Mullini 23
Tel. (0)89-875177
Fax (0)89-811419
Closed Nov. to Mar.
30 rooms,
290,000–390,000 lire
This peaceful hotel, only few minutes from the Marina Grande, is reached via a steep, pergola-covered track leading down to the sea. The magnificent 18th-century residence is said to have been built for Joachim Murat, King of Naples, in Neapolitan Baroque style. In summer, the copious breakfast buffet (there is no restaurant) is served in a courtyard filled with muticolored flowers and succulent, tropical plants, and pervaded by the intense perfume of orange and lemon trees. In the evening, the bougainvillea-clad walls form the backdrop for concerts of chamber music. The most pleasant rooms are in the old wing: no. 5 on the 3rd floor offers a panoramic view of the sea from its two balconies and has an ecru-dominated (late-18th to early-19th century) décor.

The menus, consisting entirely of "primi" (pasta and risottos) and patisserie, served in the hotel's restaurant, are highly recommended.

CASA ALBERTINA ★★★

Via della Tavolozza 3
Tel. (0)89-875143
Fax (0)89-811540
20 rooms,
160,000–220,000 lire
Simplicity, comfort and a panoramic view are on offer at this hotel, which clings to a rocky ridge – like one of the little houses in a Neapolitan crib – with a flight of some three hundred steps leading down to the sea. The casa has been run by the Cinque family for generations. In winter, when the town goes into "hibernation", there is a wonderfully relaxing atmosphere which further enhances the flavor of grandmother Albertina's cooking.

POSEIDON ★★★★

Via Pasitea 148
Tel. (0)89-811111
Fax (0)89-875833
Closed Nov. to Palm Sun.
52 rooms,
310,000–390,000 lire
Rooms overlooking the sea, a terrace-garden and swimming pool, a bar and restaurant, a fitness center, a reception and seminar rooms, a garage . . .
This hotel combines efficiency with attention to detail, such as the strategically placed floral displays and the beautiful Vietri ceramic dinner service, each piece a different design and color.

RESTAURANTS

DA ADOLFO

Spiaggia di Laurito
Tel. (0)89-875022
Closed Oct. to the end of May

30,000–35,000 lire
There is a relaxed and somewhat "baba cool" atmosphere on this wooden, reed-roofed terrace, where the customers eat in their bathing costumes. The Laurito beach restaurant is open until sundown and is reached easily by sea (there is a free boat service) but less easily by land (there is a long descent). On the menu: fresh cheese grilled between lemon leaves, aubergine "parmigiana" (en gratin with tomatoes and mozzarella), fish "a l'acquapazza".

LA BUCA DI BACCO

Rampa Teglia 8
Tel. (0)89-875699
Closed Nov. to Mar.
50,000–80,000
"See you in the bar at La Buca for a granità"; "We're eating at La Buca"; "I ordered rice croquettes, meatballs and chilled wine at La Buca to take on the boat". . . snatches of conversation that form the leitmotif of Positano. It seems impossible not to visit the famous beach restaurant with its bar and rented studio apartments, a symbol of the town's hospitality.

LA CAMBUSA

Piazza Amerigo Vespucci 4
Tel. (0)89-875432
Closed Wed. (except in summer)
50,000–80,000 lire
Particularly romantic in winter (when the Marina is half-deserted and boats of all sizes have been pulled up onto the beach), and busy and fashionable in summer. For twenty-five years Luigi and Baldo have maintained the quality and variety of their cuisine. The "linguine" with mussels and limpets, and the baked fish with new potatoes are highly recommended.

DONA ROSA

Via Montepertuso 97–99
Tel. (0)89-811806
Closed Mon. (except in summer) and in Feb.
35,000–60,000 lire
Not far from Positano, at Montepertuso, and set apart from the social whirl of the coast. Offers family cooking that you can eat on the veranda overlooking the village of Nocelle. Among the specialties are "house" pâtés and excellent seafood tagliatelle, aubergine ravioli and grilled meat and fish. The delicious desserts include fruit tarts, bavarois and strawberries with mascarpone. There is live music once a week.

★ **LO GUARRACINO**
Via Positanesi
d'America 12
Tel. (0)89-875794
Closed Nov. to Palm
Sun. (but open
Dec. 26–Jan. 14) and
Tue. from mid-Dec to
end of June.
30,000–60,000 lire
*A short walk along the
coast from the Marina
Grande to the tower
and beach of Fornillo
brings you to this
pleasant waterfront
terrace opposite the
headland of Praiano
and the islands of
Li Galli. The
"guarracino" or
"costagnola" is a small
sea bream found
throughout the
Mediterranean and
featured in a
famous*

*18th-century
Neapolitan song that
lists all the species of
local fish. This list is
repeated, almost
exactly, on a menu
whose traditional
dishes are seasoned
with ultra-fresh
ingredients and
culinary imagination.
Ideal for summer
evenings and
traditional romantic
dinners: spaghetti
with clams, bass in
aromatic stock,
salad "di rinforzo"
(cauliflower and
anchovies) and
"struffoli" (Christmas
cake with honey and
citrus fruit).*

★ **VILLA
CIMBRONE ★★★★**
Via Santa Chiara 26
Tel. (0)89-857459
Fax (0)89-857777
12 rooms,
350,000–400,000 lire
(junior suite
450,000–550,000 lire)
*A magnificent long
avenue leads to the
Villa Cimbrone, the
perfect choice for
those seeking peace
and tranquility. The
original building dates
from the 12th century
and was in a very poor
state of repair when an
English lord fell in love
with it and decided to
renovate it in neo-
Gothic style. The
English staying on the*

*coast became
regular visitors to this
romantic villa, with
its lancet windows,
frescoed ceilings,
pleasant lounges, huge
fireplaces and library,
and guests included
such famous names
as E.M. Forster,
D.H. Lawrence,
Lytton Strachey,
J.M. Keynes,
Winston Churchill
and the Dukes of Kent.
The villa gardens,
overflowing with
flowers and exotic
plants, are open
to the public until
dusk when they are
reserved exclusively
for hotel guests.
André Gide remarked
of the belvedere (a
magnificent natural
balcony decorated with
statues) that
it made you feel
"very close to
the heavens".*

POSTAL CODE
84010

HOTELS

PALUMBO ★★★★★
Via San Giovanni del
Toro 16
Tel. (0)89-857244
Fax (0)89-857133
21 rooms, 410,000–
610,000 lire (suite
660,000–860,000 lire)
*The Palumbo, a
favorite with Paul
Valéry and Richard
Wagner, occupies the
12th-century palazzo
Confalone. The former
residence, which is a
fine example of the
distinctive Moorish-
style architecture of
the "divine coast", is
now a five-story, luxury
hotel, characterized
by vaults, niches and*

*some spectacularly
panoramic viewpoints.
The rooms have
antique furnishings
and overlook a
citrus grove whose
terraces lead down to
the sea.*

**CARUSO
BELVEDERE ★★★★**
Piazza San Giovanni del
Toro 2
Tel. (0)89-857111
Fax (0)89-857372
24 rooms,
180,000–340,000 lire
*Greta Garbo and
Leopold Stokowski
enjoyed an amorous
interlude in this very
special setting: a
romantic and
somewhat decadent
atmosphere, with
frescoed vaults and
terraces overlooking
vineyards tumbling
down to the sea. The*

*hotel is certainly
not as luxurious as
it was then, but its
remarkable location
and family atmosphere
continue to exert an
undeniable charm.*

VILLA MARIA ★★★
Via Santa Chiara 2
Tel. (0)89-857255
Fax (0)89-857071
17 rooms,
120,000–260,000 lire
(suite 450,000–
490,000 lire)
Half-board only
July–Sep: 170,000 lire
per person in a
double room
*Situated only a stone's
throw from the main*

*piazza, this early
20th-century villa
has retained all the
characteristics of a
private residence.
The rooms are
peaceful, cool and
simply furnished
and enjoy views of
the sea or the garden.
The pool of the
neighboring Giordano
hotel, which is
also owned by the
Palumbo family,
may be used by
guests of the
Villa Maria.*

RESTAURANT

CUMPÀ COSIMO
Via Roma 42–44
Tel. (0)89-857156
Closed Mon. (except
from Mar. to Oct.)
35,000–60,000 lire
*This small family
restaurant has, in its*

time, welcomed a long list of famous customers from Humphrey Bogart to Jackie Kennedy, who have enjoyed the simple and authentic cuisine of the Bottone family. Most of the pasta is home-made, by hand, and seasoned with "pesto" (basil, pine nuts and olive oil) or vegetables. Meat occupies pride of place on the rest of the menu: the lamb and grilled sausage are particularly good. Local wines.

Restaurant

Alla Brace
Lungomare Trieste 13
Tel. (0)89-225159
Closed Sun. and Dec. 20 to Jan. 2
45,000–60,000 lire
Local cuisine based on fresh, authentic products which vary with the seasons. In winter dishes are substantial and include "zuppa di soffritto" (soup with bacon) and the delicious "pasta e fagiole" (pasta and white kidney-bean soup) with mussels and "tagliatelle lardiate" (with bacon). In summer seafood occupies pride of place on the menu: grilled fish, fried "cicinielli" (small local fish) and pizzas cooked on a wood fire.

Sant'Aniello-Sorrento

Postal code
80067

Hotel

Cocumella *****
Via Cocumella 7
Tel. (0)81-8782933
Fax (0)81-8783712
Closed from Nov.–Mar.
60 rooms,
440,000–490,000 lire (junior suite 550,000–615,000; suite 700,000–870,000 lire)
In 1597 a Sorrentine nobleman gave his residence to the Jesuits in order to save his soul. Two centuries later a certain Gargiulo came across this particularly unmonastic convent and transformed it into an inn. Today the Cocumella has every modern comfort, including a beauty salon, while still retaining the "historic" charm that so delighted Goethe, Andersen and Murat, as well as many other visitors. The hotel has a swimming pool, tennis courts among the olive trees, a private beach and a vast park full of rare species, suspended between sea and sky.

Salerno

Postal code
84100

Hotel

Jolly ****
Lungomare Trieste 1
Tel. (0)89-225222
Fax (0)89-237571
104 rooms,
245,000 lire
This waterfront hotel is only a few minutes away from the Amalfi and Capri ferries. It belongs to the Jolly chain (the largest four-star hotel chain in Italy), which guarantees a standard level of luxury. This particular establishment lacks the character of some of the coast's more "historic" hotels, but the Jolly is modern, efficient and extremely comfortable.

Sant'Agata dei Due Golfi

Postal code
80064

Restaurant

★ Don Alfonso 1890
Piazza Sant'Agata 11
Tel. (0)81-8780026
Closed Mon. and Tue. (Mon. only in summer)
95,000–160,000 lire
The Don Alfonso 1890, with its linen tablecloths, silverware and elegant décor, is the only gastronomic inn in the "Relais & Châteaux" guide to Southern Italy. Alfonso and Livia Laccarino are pleased to welcome customers to their pink restaurant in its beautiful garden setting, where they demonstrate their long-standing passion for true and authentic flavor. Most of the dishes are carefully prepared with produce from their farm, opposite the island of Capri: delicious ricotta soufflé, oyster and asparagus risotto, and a fish and seafood casserole which is alone worth a visit. For dessert, the cedar sorbet and the fresh warm donuts with cream and Morello cherries are particularly recommended, while the well-stocked cellar contains an amazing range of different labels. After a delicious evening meal, guests can spend the night in one of the three apartments (280,000 lire for two people).

SORRENTO

POSTAL CODE
80067

HOTELS

**IMPERIAL
TRAMONTANO ★★★★**
Via Veneto 1
Tel. (0)81-8781940
Fax (0)81-8072344
116 rooms,
360,000 lire (suite
450,000–570,000)
*Romantic poets such as
Byron, Musset, Keats,
Leopardi and Lamartine
came here in search
of hospitality and
inspiration. This historic
inn, perched high
above the sea, was
the birthplace of
Tasso, the author of
"Gerusalemme
liberata" ▲ 222. It
became a kind of
secondary residence for
a number of crowned
heads impressed by its
literary associations.
Today the elegant
lounges, the park with
its age-old plants and
the old-fashioned
atmosphere of the
rooms make for an
extremely pleasant stay.*

**★ EXCELSIOR
VITTORIA ★★★★**
Piazza Tasso 34
Tel. (0)81-8071044
Fax (0)81-8771206
105 rooms
282,000–563,000 lire
(suite 574,000–
1,191,000 lire)
*The Excelsior Vittoria
clings to a ridge of
volcanic rock,
high above the
Mediterranean,
ensconced between
the sea and an orange
orchard. It has retained
all the atmosphere of
the days when Goethe,
Byron, Alexandre
Dumas and Oscar
Wilde – following in the
footsteps of the Italian
aristocracy and royal
family – came to spend
the winter in the
shadow of Vesuvius.
The different styles of
the hotel's four
buildings merely add to*

**BELLEVUE
SYRENE ★★★★**
Piazza della Vittoria 5
Tel. (0)81-8781024
Fax (0)81-8783963
73 rooms, 280,000–
400,000 lire (suite
450,000–500,000 lire)
*The Empress Eugénie,
wife of Napoleon III,
loved this residence,
built in c. 1820 on*

*the ruins of a
Roman villa. She
stayed here several
times, always in
Room 308. Romantic
and elegant, the
Bellevue has
retained all the
atmosphere of an
aristocratic residence:
frescoed ceilings,
a monumental
marble staircase,
neoclassical
decorations and
crystal chandeliers.
The hotel's beautiful
suites all have
a fireplace and a
terrace overlooking
Vesuvius.*

*the overall charm,
which inspires dreams
of wandering forever
between the huge
frescoed lounges,
winter garden, peaceful
reading rooms and
terrace, suspended
between sea and sky,*

RESTAURANTS

CARUSO
Via Sant'Antonio 12
Tel. (0)81-8073156
Closed Mon. (except
in summer)
40,000–80,000 lire
*This centrally located
restaurant is
undoubtedly the most
elegant in Sorrento.
The walls are
decorated with
photographs and
posters of the famous
tenor after whom it is
named. Traditional
cuisine is given
an imaginative
interpretation:
lobster ravioli in
broccoli sauce,
"taglioni" pie with
seafood and ceps,
squid fried with
almonds... The "fresh"
cheeses are ultra
fresh and the desserts
are delicious.*

'O PARRUCCHIANO
Corso Italia 71
Tel. (0)81-8781321
Closed Wed. (from Nov.
15 to Mar. 15)
40,000–60,000 lire
*This atmospheric
restaurant is a veritable*

*high above the bay.
The most popular suite
is that of the tenor
Enrico Caruso ● 51,
decorated with all kinds
of memorabilia. But
there are also rooms
with a view and a
balcony where you can
enjoy a romantic
breakfast.*

*institution. Its
several levels are
centered around a
beautiful garden
and citrus orchard.
The cuisine is not
wildly imaginative, but
the great classics of
the Sorrentine
peninsula are given
pride of place:
"gnocchi" and
"cannelloni sorrentino",
"poor man's" dishes
such as white kidney-
bean or rice soup
and potatoes, fresh
cheeses cooked in
lemon leaves and, to
finish, lemon, orange
and chocolate tarts
and profiteroles.*

VIETRI

POSTAL CODE
84019

HOTEL

**LLOYD'S BAIA
HOTEL ★★★★**
Via de Marinis 2
Tel. (0)89-210145
Fax (0)89-210186
120 rooms,
250,000–280,000 lire
(suite 350,000–
380,000 lire)
*Vietri is a picturesque
village that is
renowned for its
ceramics ▲ 291.
It is also the most
southerly resort on
the Amalfi Coast.
Today Vietri is
seen as an extension
of Salerno, and the
Baia has the dual
advantage of being
situated in a peaceful
village and only
1¼ miles from the
center of Salerno.
The hotel has every
modern convenience:
rooms with a view,
two pools and a
private beach.*

◆ Addresses and opening times of places of interest

The times given below are subject to changes. Museums and archeological sites extend their opening hours during the tourist season.
Church opening times vary according to services.
Appropriate dress is advised during visits to churches.

NAPLES

ALBERGO DEI POVERI Via Foria	*No visits permitted*	▲ 171
BASILICA SAN PAOLO MAGGIORE Piazza San Gaetano	*Open daily: 9am–2pm and public holidays 11am–noon* *(☎ (0)81-454048)*	▲ 152
BOTANICAL GARDENS Via Foria 233	*By arrangement Mon–Fri 9am–2pm. Free entry Wed.* *and Thur. Mar. 15 to June 15 (☎ (0)81-299101)*	▲ 171
CASTEL CAPUANO Via C. Muzy and Piazza E. de Niccola	*This castle now houses the law courts*	▲ 157
CASTEL DELL'OVO Borgo Marinaro	*Open only for cultural events* *(☎ (0)81-5524888)*	▲ 190
CASTEL NUOVO AND MUSEO CIVICO Via Vittorio Emanuele III	*Open Mon.–Sat.: 9am–7pm* *(☎ (0)81-7952003)*	▲ 134 ● 80
CASTEL SANT'ELMO Via T. Angelini	*Open Tue.–Sun.: 9am–2pm* *(☎ (0)81-5560203)*	▲ 185
CATACOMBE DI SAN GENNARO Via Capodimonte 13	*Guided tours daily: 9.30am, 10.15am, 11am, 11.45am* *(☎ (0)81-7411071)*	▲ 178
CAPELLA PAPPACODA Largo San Giovanni Maggiore	*Located opposite the Institute of Oriental Studies.* *Visits by arrangement (☎ (0)81-5526948)*	▲ 147
CAPELLA PONTANO Via Tribunali (opposite no. 376)	*Open daily: 8am–noon and 4.30–7pm. Closed public* *holidays*	▲ 151
CAPELLA SAN GENNARO Via Duomo 147	*Open Mon.–Sat.: 8am–noon, 4.30–7pm; Sun. and* *public holidays 8am–noon. (☎ (0)81-294764)*	▲ 147
CAPELLA SAN SEVERO Via F. de Sanctis 19	*Open daily 10am–7pm;* *(☎ (0)81-5518470)*	▲ 144
CERTOSA SAN MARTINO Largo San Martino 5	*Open Tue.–Sun.: 9am–2pm* *(☎ (0)81-5781769)*	▲ 184
CEMETERY OF THE FONTANELLE Via Fontanelle 77	*Closed to the public*	▲ 170
CHURCH OF THE ANNUNZIATA Via dell'Annunziata 35	*Open daily: 8am–noon and 4.30–7pm, public* *holidays 8am–1pm (☎ (0)81-207455)*	▲ 182
CHURCH OF THE GIROLAMINI Piazza Girolamini 107	*Church and cloister open daily: 9.30am–1pm. Church* *closed Sun. and public holidays.*	▲ 155
CHURCH OF GESÙ NUOVO Piazza del Gesù Nuovo	*Open daily: 7am–1pm and 4–7.30pm,* *(☎ (0)81-5519613)*	▲ 140 ● 84
CHURCH OF GESÙ VECCHIO Via G. Paladino 38	*Open Mon.–Sat.: 8am–noon and 4–6pm;* *Sun. morning 8am–noon (☎ (0)81-5526639)*	▲ 146
CHURCH OF SANTA CHIARA **AND CHIOSTRO DELLE CLARISSE** Via B. Croce and Via Santa Chiara 49/c	*Church and cloister, open daily:* *8.30am–12.30pm* *and 3–6pm* *(☎ (0)81-5526280)*	▲ 140
CHURCH AND CONVENT OF **SAN DOMENICO MAGGIORE** Piazza San Domenico Maggiore 8/a	*Open daily: 7.30am–noon and 4.30–7pm ,* *public holidays 9am–1pm* *(☎ (0)81-5573204)* *No visits permitted to the convent.*	▲ 143
CHURCH AND CONVENT OF **SAN GREGORIO ARMENO** Via San Gregorio Armeno 44 Piazzetta San Gregorio Armeno 1	*Church: open daily 9am–noon, public holidays* *9.30am–1pm. Cloister: open daily 9.30am–noon,* *public holidays and Sat. 9.30am–1pm* *(☎ (0)81-5520186)*	▲ 154
CHURCH OF THE NUNZIATELLA Via Generale Parisi 16	*Open Oct–May: Sun 10–11am* *(☎ (0)81-7641520)*	▲ 188
CHURCH OF SAN FERDINANDO Piazza Trieste and Trento	*Open daily: 8am–noon and 5–7pm* *public holidays 9.30am–1pm (☎ (0)81-400543)*	▲ 134
CHURCH OF S. FRANCESCO DI PAOLA Piazza del Plebiscito	*Open daily: 7.30am–11.30am and 3.30–6pm* *public holidays 7.30am–1pm (☎ (0)81-7645133)*	▲ 132
CHURCH OF SAN GIOVANNI **A CARBONARA** Via Carbonara 5	*Open Mon–Sat 9am–1pm* *Closed Sun. and public holidays* *(☎ (0)81-295873)*	▲ 160
CHURCH OF S. LORENZO MAGGIORE **AND ARCHEOLOGICAL EXCAVATIONS** Via dei Tribunali 316	*Church, open daily: 8am–noon and 5–7.30pm* *Excavations, open Mon., Wed.–Sun.: 9am–1pm* *and 3–5.30pm (☎ (0)81-454948)*	▲ 152 ● 78
CHURCH OF SAN PIETRO A MAIELLA Via San Pietro a Maiella 4	*Open daily: 7am–noon and 5–7.30pm* *public holidays 8.30am–1pm (☎ (0)81-459008)*	▲ 151
CHURCH OF SAN SEVERO **A CAPODIMONTE** Via Porta San Severo 91	*Open daily: 9.30am–noon and 5–8.30pm* *public holidays 9.30am–1.30pm (☎ (0)81-454684)* *Catacombe di San Severo: same opening times*	▲ 170

CHURCH OF SANT'ANNA DEI LOMBARDI Piazza Monteoliveto 3	Open Tue., Wed., Thur. and Sat.: 8.30am–12.30pm (☎ (0)81-5513333)	▲ 148
CHURCH OF S. MARIA DEL CARMINE Piazza del Carmine	Open daily: 6.30am–12.30pm and 5–7.30pm public holidays 6.30am–1.30pm (☎ (0)81-201196)	▲ 181
CHURCH OF SANTA MARIA DELLA SANITÀ Via Sanità 124	Open daily: 8am–noon and 5–7pm, public holidays 8am–2pm. Guided tours of the Capella San Gaudioso Sun.10am and noon (☎ (0)81 5441305)	▲ 170
CHURCH OF SANTA MARIA DELLE ANIME DEL PURGATORIO Via Tribunali 39	Open daily: 9am–2pm Hypogeum, open daily: 11.30am–12.30pm Closed public holidays	▲ 152
CHURCH OF SANTA MARIA DI PIEDIGROTTA Piazza Piedigrotta 24	Open daily: 7am–noon and 5–8pm (☎ (0)81-669761)	▲ 191
CHURCH OF SANTA MARIA DONNAREGINA NUOVA Largo Donnaregina 7	Open 9am–1pm Closed Sun. and public holidays	▲ 162
CHURCH OF SANTA MARIA DONNAREGINA VECCHIA Vico Donnaregina 7	Open Sat. 9.30am–12.30pm Group visits by appointment. (☎ (0)81-299101)	▲ 161
CHURCH OF SANTA MARIA LA NOVA Largo Santa Maria la Nova 44	Open daily: 7.30am–12.30pm and 4.30–6pm public holidays 8.30am–1pm (☎ (0)81-5523298)	▲ 147
CHURCH OF SANTA MARIA MAGGIORE Via dei Tribunali	Open daily: 9am–2pm Closed public holidays	▲ 151
CHURCH OF THE SANTI APOSTOLI Largo Santi Apostoli 9	Open daily: 9am–noon and 4.30–8pm public holidays 8.30am–1.30pm (☎ (0)81-299375)	▲ 161
DUOMO Via Duomo 147	Open daily: 7.30am–12.30pm and 4.30–7.30pm, (☎ (0)81-449097)	▲ 155
FILANGIERI MUSEUM Via Duomo 288	Open daily: 9am–7pm and public holidays 9am–2pm (☎ (0)81-203175)	▲ 145
MUSEO ARCHEOLOGICO NAZIONALE Piazza Museo 35	Open daily: 9am–2pm and public holidays 9am–1pm Closed Tue. (☎ (0)81-440166)	▲ 164
MUSEO NAZIONALE DELLA CERAMICA Villa Floridiana Via D. Cimarosa 77	Open Tue.–Sun.: 9am–2pm (☎ (0)81-5788418)	▲ 187
MUSEUM AND PARK OF CAPODIMONTE Via Miano 2	Open Tue.–Sat.: 10am–7pm; Sun. 10am–2pm (☎ (0)81-7441307). Park open 9am until one hour before sundown	▲ 173
PIGNATELLI MUSEUM Riviera di Chiaia 200	Open Tue.–Sun.: 9am–2pm (☎ (0)81-669675)	▲ 191
OBSERVATORY Salita Moiariello 16	Visits by appointment Mon.–Sun. (☎ (0)81-293266)	▲ 171
PALAZZO DI DONN'ANNA Largo Donn'Anna 9	No visits permitted	▲ 192
PALAZZO REALE AND BIBLIOTECA NAZIONALE Piazza del Plebiscito 1	Open Mon., Tue. and Sun. 9am–1pm and Thur., Fri. and Sat. 9am–6pm (☎ (0)81-413888) Library, open Mon.–Fri. : 9am–7pm and Sat. 9am–1pm	▲ 131 ● 86
PALAZZO SANFELICE Via Sanità 2/6	No visits, except public holidays 8am–7pm, when access is permitted to view the staircase	▲ 165 ● 88
PARCO VIRGILIANO Salita della Grotta 20	Open daily: 9am–1.30pm and public holidays 9am–12.30pm (☎ (0)81-669390)	▲ 191
PHARMACY OF S. MARIA DEL POPOLI DEGLI INCURABILI Via M. Longo and Via L. Armani	No visits permitted.	▲ 163
VILLA FLORIDIANA Via D. Cimarosa 77	Open 9am until one hour before sundown	▲ 186
ZOOLOGICAL STATION (VILLA COMUNALE) Piazza Vittoria, Piazza Repubblica	Open Tue.–Sun. 9am–5pm (☎ (0)81-5833263)	▲ 190 ● 87

CAPRI

CERTOSA DI SAN GIACOMO Viale della Certosa	Open Tue.–Sun.: 9am–2pm and public holidays 9am–1pm (☎ (0)81-8376218)	▲ 230
CHURCH OF SANTO STEFANO Piazza Umberto I	Open daily: 6.30am–6pm and public holidays 6.30am–2pm (☎ (0)81-8370072)	▲ 229
GARDENS OF AUGUSTUS Via Matteoti	Open daily	▲ 231

GROTTA DI MATROMANIA	Take Via Sopramonte, then Via Matromania toward the natural arch. Fairly steep steps to the grotto.	▲ 232
MUSEO ARCHEOLOGICO Palais Cerio Piazzetta Cerio 8/a	Open Mon.–Fri.: 10am–noon (☎ (0)81-8370858)	▲ 230
PALAZZO A MARE **AND BAGNI DI TIBERIO**	By sea: excursions from the port. Contact "Bagni di Tiberio" on the waterfront (☎ (0)81-8370703). Journey time: 15 minutes By foot: from the port, take Via C. Colombo, and just before a sharp bend, turn right into Via Palazzo a Mare. Journey time: 15 minutes.	▲ 228
VILLA MALAPARTE Via Pizzolungo	No visits permitted.	▲ 233
VILLA FERSEN Via Lo Capo	No visits permitted.	▲ 232
VILLA JOVIS Via A. Maiuri	Open 9am until one hour before sundown	▲ 232

ANACAPRI

CASA ROSSA Piazza G. Orlandi	No visits permitted.	▲ 234
CHURCH OF SAN MICHELE Piazza San Nicola	Open Apr.–Oct. : 9am–7pm, Nov.–Mar.: 10am–3pm (☎ (0)81-8372396)	▲ 234
GROTTA AZZURRA Length of visit: 2 minutes (Journey: 25 minutes)	By boat: motor boats leave from the port. On foot: take Via Provinciale Grotta Azzurra right to the end, then go down to the pier.	▲ 236
MONTE SOLARO Cable car: via Caposcuro 10	Open Mar.–Oct.: 9.30am until an hour before sundown; Nov.–Apr.: 10.30am–3pm. Closed Tue. Nov–Apr. and in poor weather conditions (☎ (0)81-8371428)	▲ 235
VILLA SAN MICHELE Viale A. Munthe 34	Open Nov.–Mar. 10.30am–3.30pm, April–Oct 9am–6pm (☎ (0)81-8371401)	▲ 234

ISCHIA

ISCHIA PONTE

ARAGONESE CASTLE Piazzale Aragonese	Open daily: 9am until one hour before sundown. Closed Dec. 1–6 and Jan. 8.–end Feb. (☎ (0)81-992834)	▲ 213
CATHEDRAL OF SANTA MARIA ASSUNTA Via L. Mazzela	Open daily: 8am–noon and 4–7pm public holidays 8am–1pm	▲ 211

LACCO AMENO

MUSEO ARCHEOLOGICO OF THE VILLA ARBUSTO Corso Rizzoli	Museum currently undergoing restoration work.	▲ 212

PROCIDA

ABBEY OF SAN MICHELE Via Terra Murata	Open daily: 9am–12.30pm and 3.30–7pm (☎ (0)81-8967612)	▲ 215
VIVARA NATURE RESERVE Opposite Chiaioiella	The park is under the care of the Protection Civile de Procida, contact them for authorization to visit (☎ (0)81-8967400).	▲ 215

OTHERS

AMALFI

DUOMO Piazza Duomo	Open daily: 9am–1pm and 3–8pm	▲ 286
GROTTA DELLO SMERALDO	By car: take the national route 163 Sorrento–Positano, Grotto is 2½ miles from Amalfi	▲ 286
PAPER MUSEUM Valle dei Mulini	Open all year: 9am–1pm. Closed Mon. and Fri. (☎ (0)89-872615)	▲ 289

BACOLI

CENTO CAMERELLE Via Cento Camerelle 165	To arrange visits contact the caretaker, Scotto di Vetta (☎ (0)81-5233690).	▲ 206
LAGO DI FUSARO (PARK) Via Fusaro 162	Open daily: 8am–8pm (☎ (0)81-8687080)	▲ 208

Piscina Mirabilis Via A. Greco 16	*To arrange visits contact the caretaker, Ida Basile* *(☎ (0)81-5232819 or 5233199).*	▲ 207
Tomb of Agrippina Via Agrippina	*To arrange visits contact Giovanni Castiglia* *(☎ (0)81-5234368).*	▲ 207
BAIA		
Archeological Museum of the Phlegraean Fields Castello di Baia. Via Castello	*Open daily 8am–4pm; public holidays 8.30am–2pm* *(☎ (0)81-5233797)*	▲ 206
Parco Archeologico Via Acropoli	*Open 9am until one hour before sundown* *(☎ (0)81-8687592)*	▲ 206
CASERTA		
Cathedral Piazza del Duomo-Caserta Vecchia	*Open daily: 9am–1pm and 3–7.30pm*	▲ 196
Church of the Annunziata Via Torre-Caserta Vecchia	*To arrange visits contact the curator* *(☎ (0)823-371318).*	▲ 196
Palazzo Reale Piazza Carlo III	*Open daily: 9am–2pm (☎ (0)823-277111)*	▲ 194
CASTELLAMARE DI STABIA		
***Thermae* of ancient Stabiae** Piazza Amendola	*Open Jun.–Oct.: 7am–1pm* *(☎ (0)81-8714422)*	▲ 221
Villa di Arianna Via Passeggiata Archeologica	*Open 9am until one hour before sundown* *(☎ (0)81-8714541)*	▲ 221
CAVA DE' TIRRENI		
Abbey of the Santissima Trinità Località Badia di Cava	*Open daily: 9am–12.45pm* *(☎ (0)89-463922)*	▲ 295
CUMAE		
Parco Archeologico Via Acropoli	*Open 9am until one hour before sundown* *(☎ (0)81-8543060)*	▲ 208
ERCOLANO-HERCULANEUM		
Archeological excavations of Herculaneum Piazza Museo 1	*Open 9am until one hour before sundown* *(☎ (0)81-7390963)*	▲ 272
Villa Campolieto Corso Resina 283	*Open Tue.–Sun.: 10am–1pm* *(☎ (0)81-7322134)*	▲ 219
Villa Favorita Corso Resina 291	*No visits permitted.*	▲ 219
FURORE		
Church of Sant'Elia Profeta Via Sant'Elia	*Open Apr.–Oct.: Sat. 6–7pm and Nov.–Mar.:* *Sat. 5–6pm (☎ (0)89-830301)*	▲ 285
MAIORI		
Church of Santa Maria de Olearia On the national route between Maiori and Salerno	*To arrange visits contact Anna Maria Bove* *(☎ (0)89-851354).*	▲ 291
MINORI		
Roman Villa Via Capo di Piazza 28	*Open daily: 9am until one hour before sundown* *(☎ (0)89-852893)*	▲ 290
MINUTA		
Church of Santa Maria Annunziata Piazza di Minuta	*Open Sun. 9am–10.30am. For opening times* *throughout the week contact Angelina Cuomo* *(☎ (0)89-858230).*	▲ 290
PAESTUM		
Museum and archeological excavations Via Magna Graecia ☎ (0)828-811023	*Open daily: 9am–6.30pm except the 1st and 3rd* *Mon. of the month.* *The archeological excavations are open* *daily from 9am until one hour before sundown*	▲ 304 ▲ 297
POMPEII		
Archeological excavations Porta Marina, Piazza Esedra Porta Anfiteatro, Piazza Immacolata ☎ (0)81-8610744	*Open daily: 9am until one hour before sundown*	▲ 246

PORTICI

CHURCH OF SAN CIRO Piazza San Ciro	*Open daily: 7am–12.30pm and 4.30–8pm* *(☎ (0)81-475291)*	▲ 217
PALAZZO REALE Via Università 100	*Visits by previous arrangement* *(☎ (0)81-7751251)*	▲ 218
VILLA D'ELBEUF Porto del Granatello	*No visits permitted.*	▲ 217

POZZUOLI

AMPHITHEATER OF POZZUOLI Via Terracciano 75	*Open daily: 9am until one hour before sundown* *(☎ (0)81-5262341)*	▲ 200
THE SOLFATARA Via Solfatara 161	*Open 8.30am until one hour before sundown* *(☎ (0)81-5262341)*	▲ 201
SERAPEUM (TEMPLE OF SERAPIS) Piazza Serapide	*Guided tours by appointment (☎ (0)81-440166)* *The temple is visible from the piazza.*	▲ 200

RAVELLO

DUOMO Piazza Duomo	*Open Apr.–Oct.: 8am–8pm, Nov.–Mar. 8am– 7pm.* *Museum open 9am–1pm, 3–7pm (☎ (0)89-858311)*	▲ 289
VILLA CIMBRONE Via Santa Chiara 26	*Open 9am until one hour before sundown* *(☎ (0)89-857138)*	▲ 288
VILLA RUFOLO Piazza Duomo	*Open Apr.–Oct.: 9am–8pm and Nov.–Mar.: 9am–5pm* *(☎ (0)89-857657)*	▲ 288

SALERNO

DUOMO Piazza Alfano I	*Open daily: 7.30am–noon and 4–8pm* *(☎ (0)89-231387)*	▲ 293
MUSEO PROVINCIALE Via San Benedetto 28	*Open daily 9am–7.30pm;* *public holidays 9am–2pm (☎ (0)89-231135)*	▲ 294

SCALA

DUOMO Piazza Municipio	*Open daily: 8am–8pm*	▲ 290

SORRENTO

BASILICA OF SANT'ANTONIO Piazza Sant'Antonio	*Open daily: 7am–11.30am, afternoon opening times* *vary*	▲ 225
DUOMO Via Santa Maria della Pietà 44	*Open daily: 8am–noon and 3–10pm* *(☎ (0)81-8782248)*	▲ 224
CHURCH OF SAN FELICE BACOLO Via Tasso	*Open daily: 8am–noon. Afternoon opening times* *vary*	▲ 224
CHURCH OF SAN FRANCESCO D'ASSISI Via San Francesco	*Open daily: 7am–12.30pm and 4–7.30pm* *(☎ (0)81-8781269)*	▲ 225
CHURCH OF SAN PAOLO Via San Paolo	*Closed*	▲ 224
MUSEO CORREALE DI TERRANOVA Via Correale 50	*Open Apr.–Sep.: 9am–12.30pm and 5–7pm,* *Oct. and Mar.: 9am–12.30pm and 3–5pm, Nov.–Feb* *9am–1.30pm, public holidays 9am–12.30pm.* *Closed Tue. (☎ (0)81-8781846)*	▲ 225

TORRE ANNUNZIATA

EXCAVATIONS OF OPLONTIS Via Sepolcri	*Open 9am until one hour before sundown* *(☎ (0)81-8621755)*	▲ 220

TORRE DEL GRECO

VILLA PROTA Via Nazionale 1009	*No visits permitted.*	▲ 219

VESUVIUS

	Easiest route: from Naples, take the freeway toward *Salerno and exit at Ercolano. After the toll booth,* *turn left along Via Cozzolino to the Vesuvius* *observatory. Turn right at the crossroads, past a* *small square, from here climb the rest of the way to* *the crater.*	▲ 238

VIETRI

CERAMICS MUSEUM Torretta di Villa Guariglia	*Open Tue.–Sat. morning: 9am–1pm and 3–7pm* *(☎ (0)89-211835)*	▲ 290

APPENDICES

◆ LIST OF ILLUSTRATIONS

Front cover (UK):
Bay of Naples, illustration by Bruno Lenormand.
Initiation to the Dionysiac mysteries, fresco, Villa dei Misteri © Pedicini.
Chamaerops humilis.
Seafood vendor by Dominique Mansion.
Santa Lucia, M. de Vito, 1830, all rights reserved. Horn, coll. Gallimard.
Spine (UK): Blue vase, Museo Arch. Naz. Stamp, *Republiche marinare*, all rights reserved.
Back cover (UK):
Theater masks, all rights reserved.
Pulcinella, Duclère and Fusaro, all rights reserved. *Dancing Faun*, House of the Faun, Museo Archeo. Naz.
© Pedicini. Baroque decoration, drawing by Claude Quiec.
Gladiator's helmet, Museo Archeo. Naz. © Pedicini. Aleppo pine, drawing by François Desbordes.
Cat and partridge, mosaic detail, House of the Faun, Museo Archeo. Naz.

Prelims
1 Street in Basso Porto, all rights reserved.
2–3 Macaroni makers, Portici, all rights reserved.
4–5 Musicians, Piedigrotta, all rights reserved.
6–7 Funicular, Vesuvius, 1895, all rights reserved.
9 *Eruption of Vesuvius*, Wright of Derby, Museum & Art Gallery, Derby © Giraudon.

Nature
18–19 Map of the region © Franck Stéphan.
Computer graphics © Jean-Claude Bousquet.
18 Island of Capri © Gotin/Scope.
19 Naples and Vesuvius © Krafft/Hoa Qui.
Lava flow, Etna © Krafft/Hoa Qui.
Effects of the earth tremors, Jean-Claude Bousquet.
20–1 Cross-section of Vesuvius © Franck Stéphan.
20 Vesuvius © Krafft/Hoa Qui.
21 Cone of Vesuvius © Krafft/Hoa Qui.

Vesuvius smoking, all rights reserved.
22–3 Cross-sections of the Phlegraean Fields © Franck Stéphan.
22 Monte Nuovo © Krafft/Hoa Qui.
Solfatara, coll. Gallimard.
Solfatara © Krafft/Hoa Qui.
23 Phlegraean Fields, in *Campi Phlegraei*, Pietro Fabris, 18th century, all rights reserved.
Temple of Serapis at Pozzuoli, coll. Jean-Claude Bousquet.
24–5 Cliff, drawing by Denis Clavreul.
24 Aleppo pine, drawing by François Desbordes.
Euphorbia acanthothamnos Chamaerops humilis, drawings by Dominique Mansion.
Sea fennel, drawing by Claire Felloni.
25 Alpine swift and herring gull, drawings by Jean Chevallier.
Swift, drawing by François Desbordes.
26 Lichen, all rights reserved.
Spanish broom and red valerian, drawings by Claire Felloni.
Etna broom and *Pteris vittata*, drawings by Dominique Mansion.
General view, drawing by Denis Clavreul.

History and language
27 *Ferdinand IV as King David*, Art Deco cameo, Bordeaux © Lauros-Giraudon.
28 Cumae panatheonic amphorus, Museo Archeo. Naz. © Pedicini.
Gorgon's head, Santa Maria Capua Vetere, Museo Archeo. Naz. © Pedicini.
29 *Punic wars, Hannibal in Italy*, J. Ripanda, Museo di Capitole, Rome © Dagli Orti. Casa dei Fontani, A.-D. Denuelle © ENSBA.
30 *Romulus Augustule*, coin, BN. *Roger of Anjou*, Palazzo Reale, coll. Gallimard.
31 *Conquest of Naples by Charles de Durazzo*, casket, detail from left panel, *Charles entering Naples, victorious*, anon. Italian, early 15th century, tempera on wood © 1993 by the Metropolitan Museum of Art,

Rogers Fund 1906 (07.120.1).
View of Naples and the return of the Aragonese fleet, anon., late 15th century, Museo San Martino © Pedicini.
32 *Charles V*, Pantoja de la Cruz, Monastery of the Escurial, Madrid © Oronoz/Artephot.
The plague, Naples, 1656, Carlo Coppola, Museo di San Martino © Giraudon.
33 *Largo dello Spirito Santo e via Toledo*, F. Wenzel, Museo di San Martino © Pedicini.
Plan of the center of Naples, late 19th century, all rights reserved.
34 Departure of the troops in the port of Naples, 1935, priv. coll.
34–5 Emigrants in 1910 © Touring Club Italiano.
35 Arrestat, coll. N. Pascarel. Beach and Bagnoli, coll. N. Pascarel.
36 *Frederick II*, Palazzo Reale, coll. Gallimard.
36–7 *Coronation of Roger II*, 12th-century mosaic, Chiesa Martorana, Palermo © Scala.
37 *Charles of Anjou invested with the kingdom of Sicily*, fresco, Pernes-les-Fontaines © Giraudon.
Alfonso the Magnanimous, Pisanello, medal © BN. *Charles VII*, anon., Museo Naz., Bogot © Giraudon.
38 *Duke of Arcos*, manuscript Molini, Sopraintendenza Beni Architettonici e Storici.
Cardinal Ascanio Filomarino, Massimo Stanzione, coll. Corsini, Florence © Scala.
Burial of Masaniello, Gatti and Dura in *Album Masaniello*, Museo di San Martino © Massimo Velo.
38–9 *Revolt of Masaniello*, D. Gargiulio, Museo di San Martino © Scala.
39 *Masaniello*, Onofrio Palumbo, coll. Martino Oberto, Gênes.
Funeral of Masaniello, Gatti and Dura in *Album Masaniello*, Museo di San Martino © Massimo Velo.
40 Cholera in a busy residential district in *l'Illustrazione Popolare*,

1884, all rights reserved.
Effects of the tremors 1980, Palazzo Spagnolo © M. Jodice/TCI.
41 *Plague in Naples, 1656*, Carlo Coppola, Museo di San Martino © Giraudon.
Eruption of Vesuvius in *Le Petit Parisien*, April 29, 1906, all rights reserved.
42 *Public writer*, all rights reserved.
42–3 *On board the Santa Lucia*, all rights reserved. Naples costumes, Gatti Dura, all rights reserved.
43 Salvatora di Giacomo, G. Tabet, all rights reserved.
44 *Neapolitan*, all rights reserved.
45 Actors © N. Pascarel. Ex-voto, coll. Gallimard.
Neapolitans, priv. coll.
46 *Bronze bust of Epicurus*, Museo Archeo. Naz. © Pedicini.
Tomb of Virgil, engraving, all rights reserved. Benedetto Croce © Roger Viollet.

Arts and traditions
47 *Pulcinella*, all rights reserved.
48 *Il Tronaro*, T. Duclère in *Usi e Costumi di Napoli*, De Bourcard, 1866, all rights reserved.
48–9 Return of the feast of the Madonna dell'Arco, L. Robert, Musée du Louvre © RMN.
49 Procession of the dead Christ, Procida, coll. G. Roli.
Festival of Piedigrotta in *La Tribuna Illustrata*, 1907 © Pedicini.
50 La 'Ndrezzata, coll. G. Roli.
50–1 Tarantella, Museo NATP, Rome.
51 Sheet music *O Sole Mio*, all rights reserved.
Mandolin, Musical Instrument Museum of the Conservatoire of Music © Giraudon.
52 *La Gatta Cenerentola*, Roberto de Simone, coll. F. Donato. *Zingari*, Raffaele Viviani, coll. F. Donato. *Pulcinella*, Duclère and Fusaro, all rights reserved.
52–3 Peppe Barra as Pulcinella and his mother Concetta in *Il Marchese di Sansevero*, coll. F. Donato.

352

◆ LIST OF ILLUSTRATIONS

We would like to thank:

Dottoressa Rosa Romano/Elio de Rosa Editore, Naples.
M. Golvin, director of research CNRS, Paris.
Architetto Viola, Naples. Nicoletta Ricciardelli, Sopraintendenza ai Beni Architettonici, Naples.

◆ ESSENTIAL READING ◆

◆ DOUGLAS (N.): *Late Harvest*, Lindsay Drummond, 1948
◆ GUNN (P.): *Naples, a palimpsest*, London, Chapman & Hill, 1961
◆ EVELYN (J.): *Diary*, ed. De Beer (E.S.): Macmillan, London, 1906
◆ MONTAIGNE (M. de.): *Journal du Voyage en Italie, 1580–81*, trans. Lautrey (L.): Hachette, Paris, 1906
◆ GELL (Sir W.): *Reminiscences of Sir Walter Scott's residence in Italy, 1832*, ed. Corson (J.C.): Nelson, London, 1957

◆ GENERAL ◆

◆ ANDREWS (I.): *Pompeii*, Cambridge University Press, Cambridge, 1978
◆ BARONE (G.): *Naples, present, past and future . . .*, Alfredo Guida, Naples
◆ BARZINI (L.): *From Caesar to the Mafia – Sketches of Italian life*, Hamish Hamilton, London, 1971
◆ BISEL (S.C.) with BISEL (J.) et al, *The secrets of Vesuvius*, Hodder & Stoughton, Sevenoaks, c. 1990
◆ BLUNT (Rev. J.J.): *Vestiges of Ancient Manners and Customs Discoverable in Modern Italy and Sicily*, London, 1823
◆ DAVID (E.): *Italian Food*, Macdonald, London, 1954
◆ DELLE DONNE (V.): *Naples*, trans. McMaster (I.) & Shaw (R.), Insight Guides, London, c. 1992
◆ DOUGLAS (N.): *Footnote on Capri*, Sidgwick and Jackson Limited, London, 1952
◆ DOUGLAS (N.): *Siren Land*, E.P. Dutton & Co., New York/J.M. Dent & Sons, London, 1911
◆ ETIENNE (R.): *Pompeii, the day a city died*, Thames & Hudson, London, 1992
◆ FACAROS (D.) & PAULS (M.): *The Bay of Naples and the Amalfi Coast*, Cadogan, London, c. 1994
◆ FREDERIKSEN (M.): *Campania*, British School at Rome, Rome 1984
◆ GRANT (M.): *Cities of Vesuvius, Pompeii and Herculaneum*, Penguin Books, Harmondsworth, 1979
◆ *Guida Gastronomica d'Italia*, Touring Club Italiano, Milano, 1951
◆ HUTTON (E.): *Naples and Campania Revisited*, London, 1958
◆ JASHEMSKI (W.) & JASHEMSKI (S.A.): *The gardens of Pompeii, Herculaneum and the villas destroyed by Vesuvius*, Caratzas, New Rochelle, 1979
◆ KELLY (M.): *Reminiscences*, Oxford University Press, London, 1975
◆ LABANDE (Y. and E.R.): *Naples and its Surroundings*, trans. Shaw (J.H.), Nicholas Kaye, London, 1955
◆ LEE (V.): *Studies of the Eighteenth Century in Italy*, London, 1881
◆ LEWIS (N.): *Naples '44*, Collins, London, 1978
◆ MULFORD (W.): *The Bay of Naples*, Reality Studios, London, c. 1992
◆ MUNTHE (A.): *The Story of San Michele*, John Murray, London, 1930
◆ PEACHMENT (B.): *The tiger of Naples, the story of Father Borelli and the street boys*, Religious Education Press, Exeter, 1978

◆ PEREIRA (A.): *Pompeii, Naples and Southern Italy*, Batsford, London, 1977
◆ PICHEY (M.): *Naples and Campania*, A. and C. Black, London, 1994
◆ POLOVTSOFF (A.): *The Call of the Siren*, Selwyn & Blount, London, 1939
◆ *Pompeii, the vanished city*, Time Life Books, Alexandria, Va., c. 1992
◆ SEAFORD (R.): *Pompeii*, Constable, London, 1978
◆ SEWARD (D.): *Naples, a traveller's companion*, Constable, London, 1984
◆ SITWELL (O.): *Winters of Content and other discursions on Mediterranean Art and Travel*, Gerald Duckworth & Co. Ltd., London, 1950
◆ STEFANILE (M.) & Stefanile (F.): *The Gulf of Naples*, Sagep, Genova, 1993
◆ TREVELYAN (R.): *The shadow of Vesuvius, Pompeii AD 79*, Joseph, London, 1976
◆ TROWER (H.E.): *The book of Capri*, Detken and Rocholl, Naples, 1924

◆ HISTORY ◆

◆ ACTON (H.): *The Bourbons of Naples (1734–1825)*, Methuen, London, 1957
◆ ACTON (H.): *The last Bourbons of Naples (1825–1861)*, Methuen, London, 1961
◆ ASFARITA (T.): *The continuity of feudal power, the Caracciolo di Bienza in Spanish Naples*, Cambridge University Press, Cambridge, 1992
◆ BENTLEY (J.H.): *Politics and Culture in Renaissance Naples*, Princeton University Press, Princeton, N.J., 1987
◆ BULWER-LYTTON (E.): *The last days of Pompeii*, Tauschnitz, Leipzig, 1842
◆ BURCKHARDT (J.): *The Civilisation of the Renaissance in Italy*, trans. Middlemore, Phaidon Press, Oxford, 1945
◆ CALABRIA (A.): *The cost of empire – finances of the Kingdom of Naples in the time of Spanish rule*, Cambridge University Press, Cambridge, 1991
◆ GIRAFFI (A.): *An Exact Historie of the late Revolutions in Naples*, trans. Howell (J.), London, 1652
◆ HENSTOCK (M.E.): *Fernando de Lucia, son of Naples, 1860–1925*, Duckworth, London, 1990
◆ HILL (C.A.R.): *The destruction of Pompeii and Herculaneum*, Dryad, London, 1987
◆ JONGMAN (W.): *The economy and society of Pompeii*, J.C. Gieben, Amsterdam, 1988
◆ JONES (F.M.): *Alphonsus de Liguori, the saint of Bourbon Naples, 1696–1787*, Gill and Macmillan, Dublin, 1992
◆ KOGAN (N.): *A political history of post-war Italy*, Pall Mall Press, London, 1966
◆ KOGAN (N.): *The Government of Italy*, Thomas Y. Crowell, New York , 1982
◆ KREUTZ (B.M.): *Before the Normans – Southern Italy in the ninth and tenth centuries*, University of Pennsylvania Press, Philadelphia, 1991
◆ LAURENCE (R.): *Roman Pompeii, space and society*, Routledge, London, 1994

◆ McKAY (K.): *A remarkable relationship, the story of Emma Hamilton and her impact on the lives of Charles Francis Greville, Sir William Hamilton and Horatio Nelson*, Ken McKay, Milford Haven, 1992
◆ MARINO (J.A.): *Pastoral economics in the Kingdom of Naples*, Johns Hopkins University Press, Baltimore, 1988
◆ SNOWDEN (F.M.): *Naples in the time of cholera, 1884–1911*, Cambridge University Press, Cambridge, 1995
◆ SWINBURNE (H.): *The Courts of Europe at the close of the last century*, London, 1841
◆ RYDER (D.): *Alfonso the Magnanimous, King of Aragon, Naples, and Sicily, 1442–1458*, Clarendon Press, Oxford, 1990
◆ RYDER (A.): *The Kingdom of Naples and Alfonso the Magnanimous, the making of a modern state*, Clarendon Press, Oxford, 1976
◆ TREASE (G.): *The Condottieri – Soldiers of Fortune*, Thames & Hudson, London, 1990
◆ TREVELYAN (J.P.): *A short history of the Italian people*, G.P. Putnam's Sons, New York and London, 1920
◆ VILLARI (R.): *The Revolt of Naples*, trans. Newell (J.) & Marino (J.A.), Polity Press, Cambridge, 1993

ARCHITECTURE AND ◆ ARCHEOLOGY ◆

◆ BLUNT (A.): *Neapolitan baroque and rococo architecture*, Zwemmer, London, 1975
◆ HOGG (J.): *The Charterhouses of Naples and Capri*, Institut für Englische Sprache und Literatur, Universität Salzburg, Salzburg, 1978
◆ D'ONOFRIO (M.) and PAVE (V.): *Campanie romane*, Zodiaque, La Pierre-qui-Vire, 1981
◆ PARSLOW (C.C.): *Rediscovering antiquity, Karl Weber and the excavation of Herculaneum, Pompeii and Stabiae*, Cambridge University Press, Cambridge, 1994
◆ RICHARDSON JNR (L.): *Pompeii, an architectural history*, Johns Hopkins University Press, Baltimore, 1988

◆ MUSIC ◆

◆ ATLAS (A.W.): *Music at the Aragonese court of Naples*, Cambridge University Press, Cambridge, 1985

PAINTING AND ◆ SCULPTURE ◆

◆ DWYER (E.J.): *Pompeian domestic sculpture, a study of five Pompeian houses and their contents*, G. Bretschneider, Rome, 1982
◆ GRANT (M.): *Erotic art at Pompeii, the secret collection of the National Museum of Naples*, Octopus Books, London, 1975
◆ LAIDLAW (A.): *The first style in Pompeii, painting and architecture*, Bretschneider, Rome, 1985
◆ LEAR (E.): *Edward Lear in Southern Italy – Journals of a Landscape Painter in Southern Calabria and the Kingdom of Naples*, William Kimber, London, 1964

◆ NAPIER (Lord): *Notes on modern painting at Naples*, London, 1855
◆ *Pompeii AD79*, treasures from the National Archeological Museum, Naples, and the Pompeii Antiquarium, Museum of Fine Arts, Boston, 1978
◆ POWELL (C.): *Turner in the South: Rome, Naples, Florence*, Yale University Press, New Haven, Conn., 1987
◆ WHITEFIELD (C.) & MORTIMER (J.): *Painting in Naples 1606–1705, from Caravaggio to Giordano*, Catalogue, Royal Academy of Arts, London, 1982

◆ LITERATURE ◆

◆ CROCE (B.): *Croce, the King and the Allies – extracts from a diary by Benedetto Croce, July 1943–June 1944*, trans. Sprigge (S.), George Allen & Unwin Ltd., London, 1950
◆ DICKENS (C.): *Pictures from Italy*, Chapman & Hall, London, 1845
◆ FENIMORE COOPER (J.): *Excursions in Italy*, 2 vols., London, 1838
◆ GOETHE (J.W.): *Italian Journey*, trans. Auden (W.H.) and James (F.) and Collected Travel Writings: The Continent, the Library of America, New York, 1993
◆ GONCOURT (E. and J.): *L'Italie d'Hier. Notes de Voyages 1855–1856*, Paris, 1894
◆ KEATS (J.): *The Letters of John Keats*, ed. Forman (M.B.), Oxford University Press, London, 1931
◆ MILTON (J.): *The Works of John Milton*, vol. viii, Columbia University Press, New York, 1933
◆ MELVILLE (H.): *At the hostelry and Naples in the time of Bomba*, ed. Poole (G.) Instituto Universario Orientale, Naples, 1989
◆ STENDHAL: *Rome, Naples and Florence*, trans. Coe (R.C.), London, 1959

◆ TRAVELERS' TALES ◆

◆ CLAY (E.): *The idler in Italy, Selections*, Lady Blessington at Naples, Hamish Hamilton, London, 1979
◆ CRAVEN (R.K.): *A Tour through the Southern Provinces of the Kingdom of Naples*, London, 1821
◆ LABAT (J.-B.): *Voyages du Père Labat de l'Ordre des F.F. Presceurs en Espagne et en Italie*, Paris, 1730
◆ LASSELS (R.): *An Italian Voyage, or, A Compleat Journey Through Italy. In two parts. The Second Edition with large Additions, by a Modern hand*, Richard Wellington, London, 1698
◆ MORTON (H.V.): *A Traveller in Southern Italy*, Methuen & Co. Ltd., London, 1969
◆ MORYSON (F.): *Ten Yeares Travell through the twelve dominions of Germany, Böhmerland, Switzerland, Netherlands, Poland, Italy, Turkey, France, England, Scotland and Ireland*, 1710
◆ PIOZZI (H.): *Glimpses of Italian Society in the Eighteenth Century*, Seeley & Co. Ltd., London, 1892
◆ RAY (The Rev. J.): *Travels through the Low Countries, Germany, Italy and France*, London, 1738
◆ SANDYS (G.): *A Relation of a Journey Begun AD 1610*, Alfred Knopf, New York, 1986

◆ INDEX

Page numbers in bold refer to the
Practical information section.